Security of Cloud-based Systems

Security of Cloud-based Systems

Edited by:

Jovan Pehcevski

ARCLER
PRESS

www.arclerpress.com

Security of Cloud-based Systems

Jovan Pehcevski

Arcler Press
224 Shoreacres Road
Burlington, ON L7L 2H2
Canada
www.arclerpress.com
Email: orders@arclereducation.com

ISBN: 978-1-77407-777-1 (Hardcover)

DECLARATION

ABOUT THE EDITOR

Jovan obtained his PhD in Computer Science from RMIT University in Melbourne, Australia in 2007. His research interests include big data, business intelligence and predictive analytics, data and information science, information retrieval, XML, web services and service-oriented architectures, and relational and NoSQL database systems. He has published over 30 journal and conference papers and he also serves as a journal and conference reviewer. He is currently working as a Dean and Associate Professor at European University in Skopje, Macedonia.

TABLE OF CONTENTS

LIST OF CONTRIBUTORS

Ahmad Fayez S. Althobaiti
Department of Computer and Information Sciences, Al-Imam Muhammad Ibn Saudi Islamic University, Riyadh, Saudi Arabia

Arif Sari
Department of Management Information Systems, European University of Lefke, Lefke, Cyprus

Sabah Alzahrani
Department of Electrical & Computer Engineering, Tennessee State University, Nashville, TN, USA

Liang Hong
Department of Electrical & Computer Engineering, Tennessee State University, Nashville, TN, USA

Sai Kiran Mukkavilli
Department of Electrical & Computer Engineering, Tennessee State University, Nashville, TN, USA

Sachin Shetty
Department of Electrical & Computer Engineering, Tennessee State University, Nashville, TN, USA

Liang Hong
Department of Electrical & Computer Engineering, Tennessee State University, Nashville, TN, USA

Amir Mohamed Talib
Faculty of Computer Science & IT, University Putra Malaysia UPM, Serdang, Malaysia

Rodziah Atan
Faculty of Computer Science & IT, University Putra Malaysia UPM, Serdang, Malaysia

Rusli Abdullah
Faculty of Computer Science & IT, University Putra Malaysia UPM, Serdang, Malaysia

Masrah Azrifah Azmi Murad
Faculty of Computer Science & IT, University Putra Malaysia UPM, Serdang, Malaysia

Harshit Srivastava
Information Technology, Maharaja Agrasen Institute of Technology, New Delhi, India

Sathish Alampalayam Kumar
Computer Science and Information Systems, Coastal Carolina University, Conway, USA

Jassim R. Mlgheit
Faculty of Computers and Informatics, Benha University, Benha, Egypt

Essam H. Houssein
Faculty of Computers and Information, Minia University, Minia, Egypt

Hala H. Zayed
Faculty of Computers and Informatics, Benha University, Benha, Egypt

Guoqiang Hu
Network and Education Technology Center, Northwest A&F University, Yangling, China

Yanrong Yang
Network and Education Technology Center, Northwest A&F University, Yangling, China

Li Li
Network and Education Technology Center, Northwest A&F University, Yangling, China

Mohammad Anwar Hossain
Department of Computer Science and Engineering, World University of Bangladesh, Dhaka, Bangladesh

Ahsan Ullah
Department of Computer Science and Engineering, World University of Bangladesh, Dhaka, Bangladesh

Newaz Ibrahim Khan
Department of Computer Science and Engineering, World University of Bangladesh, Dhaka, Bangladesh

Md Feroz Alam
Department of Computer Science and Engineering, World University of Bangladesh, Dhaka, Bangladesh

Hassan Reza
School of Aerospace Sciences, Department of Computer Science, University of North Dakota, Grand Forks, ND, USA

Madhuri Sonawane
School of Aerospace Sciences, Department of Computer Science, University of North Dakota, Grand Forks, ND, USA

Mohammad Waseem
Department of Computer Science and Engineering, Southeast University, Nanjing, China

Abdullah Lakhan
Department of Computer Science and Engineering, Southeast University, Nanjing, China

Irfan Ali Jamali
Department of Computer Science and Engineering, Southeast University, Nanjing, China

Fawaz S. Al-Anzi
Compute Engineering Department, Kuwait University, Kuwait City, Kuwait

Ayed A. Salman
Compute Engineering Department, Kuwait University, Kuwait City, Kuwait

Noby K. Jacob
Compute Engineering Department, Kuwait University, Kuwait City, Kuwait

J. Athena
Department of ECE, Government College of Technology, Coimbatore, India

V. Sumathy
Department of ECE, Government College of Technology, Coimbatore, India

Patrick Mosca
Department of Computer Science, Gonzaga University, Spokane, USA

Yanping Zhang
Department of Computer Science, Gonzaga University, Spokane, USA

Zhifeng Xiao
Department of Computer Science & Software Engineering, Penn State Erie, Erie, USA

Yun Wang
Department of Computer Science and Information Systems, Bradley University, Peoria, USA

Michael Perez
Department of Electrical and Computer Engineering, University of Texas-RGV, Edinburg, TX, USA

Sanjeev Kumar
Department of Electrical and Computer Engineering, University of Texas-RGV, Edinburg, TX, USA

P. Premkumar
Department of Computer Science and Engineering, K.L.N. College of Engineering, Pottapalayam, India

D. Shanthi
Department of Computer Science and Engineering, PSNA College of Engineering & Technology, Dindigul, India

Gabriela Cajamarca-Palomo
Facultad de Ciencias Administrativas, Universidad Técnica de Ambato, Ambato, Ecuador.

Mauricio Quisimalin-Santamaría
Facultad de Ciencias Administrativas, Universidad Técnica de Ambato, Ambato, Ecuador.

Patricio Medina-Chicaiza
Facultad de Ciencias Administrativas, Universidad Técnica de Ambato, Pontificia Universidad Católica del Ecuador, Ambato, Ecuador.

LIST OF ABBREVIATIONS

ACAS	Access Control Aware Search
ACMs	Access Control Mechanisms
AAD	Adaptive Anomaly Detection Systems
AES	Advanced Encryption Standard
ADS	Anomaly Detection System
API	Application programming interface
BDH	Bilinear Diffie-Hellman
BGP	Border Gateway Protocol
CPU	Central Processing Unit
CDAA	Cloud Data Availability Agent
CDSs	Cloud Data Storages
CSP	Cloud Service Provider
CSQD	Cloud service queuing defender
COTS	Commercial off-the-shelf systems
CaaS	Communication as a Service
CLA	Compliance Level Agreements
CRM	Customer Relationship management
DES	Data Encryption Standard
DAC	Discretionary Access Control
DDoS	Distributed Denial of Service Attack
DNS	Domain Name System
ECC	Elliptical curve cryptography
EKM	Encryption and Key Management
EM	Expectation Maximization
FSKTM	Faculty of Computer Science and Information Technology
FBC	Flow based classifier
GMM	Gaussian Mixture Model
HDFS	Hadoop Distributed File System

HDE	Hybrid Detection Engine
HECC	Hyper Elliptic Curve Cryptography
ISG	Information Security Group
IaaS	Infrastructure-as-a-service
IAT	Inter-arrival time
IDMEF	Intrusion Detection Message Exchange Format
IDS	Intrusion Detection Systems
LSA	Latent Semantic Analysis
LSB	Least Significant Bit
LATE	Longest Approximate Time to End
MAC	Mandatory Access Control
MCC	Mobile cloud computing
MAS	Multi-agent system
MLP	Multi-Layer Perceptron
MCA	Multivariate Correlation Analysis
NIST	National Institute of Standards and Technology
PIDM	Person-Item Differential Map
PCA	Principal Component Analysis
PEKS	Public Key Encryption with keyword Search
ROC	Receive-operation
RAID	Redundant Array of Inexpensive Disks
RCM	Risk and Compliance Management
RSSNS	Robust, Scalable and Secure Network Storage
SSL	Secure Sockets Layer
SOM	Self-organization map
SLAs	Service Level Agreements
SMEs	Small and medium enterprises
SaaS	Software-as-a-Service
SRK	Storage Root Key
SML	Stored Message Logs
TPA	Third Party Auditor
TDES	Tripple Data Encryption Standard
TPR	True Positive rate
TPM	Trusted platform module

TVDs	Trusted Virtual Domains
VCCI	Virtualized Cloud Computing Infrastructure
VMI	Virtual Machine Image
VMM	Virtual Machine Monitor
VPC	Virtual private cloud
WRT	Web response time

PREFACE

Cloud computing is becoming the dominant way of using information and communication technologies in the business. Along with traditionally well-known challenges of ICT business applications, the cloud computing environment requires the business user to answer new and numerous specific questions from an economic, organizational, legal, fiscal, technological, and especially security point of view. Cloud-based storage and processing resources are shared and used by many unknown tenants (users). It is important for users to become familiar with the specifics of cloud computing in order to be ready, effective and efficient in addressing the security challenges in manipulating business data in a multi-tenant dispersed environment. The main topics of this book include the specifics of the cloud computing environment, especially regarding the security and protection of business assets and customer interests.

Regulations in the USA, the European Union and many other countries should be considered in defining the frameworks for planning and coordinating action at the microeconomic unit level. The differences in perceptions of customers and professionals in the field of information security are another topic whose elaboration certainly contributes to the successful understanding and implementation of security measures. Isolation of tenant data, tenant workspace, tenant performance and availability, and tenant specific occasions and extensions of business logic – all important information security issues – are inherent in the cloud computing environment. A structured approach to the security areas of cloud computing, the need to standardize and meet existing certification standards, go beyond the cloud model and the level of implementation of security measures. As the cloud computing environment matures, the security challenges bring the need for ongoing personal development and training for information security professionals.

This edition covers different topics from security of cloud-based systems, including: threats detection in cloud environments, frameworks for cloud security, enhancing the security in the cloud systems, as well as relevant security-related case studies.

Section 1 focuses on threats detection in cloud environments, describing analysis of security threats to virtual machines in cloud computing environment; a review of anomaly detection systems in cloud networks and survey of cloud security measures in cloud storage applications; a survey of cloud computing detection techniques against DDoS attacks; and generation of labelled datasets to quantify the impact of security threats to cloud data centers.

Section 2 focuses on frameworks for cloud security, describing a comprehensive security framework of cloud data storage based on multi agent system architecture; control framework for secure cloud computing; security model for preserving privacy over encrypted cloud computing; trusted heartbeat framework for cloud computing; and education technology cloud platform framework establishment and security.

Section 3 focuses on enhancing the security in the cloud systems, describing design and development of a novel symmetric algorithm for enhancing data security in cloud computing; enhancing mobile cloud computing security using steganography; data security of mobile cloud computing on cloud server; a newly proposed robust, scalable and secure network cloud computing storage architecture; and a survey on public key cryptography scheme for securing data in cloud computing.

Section 4 focuses on case studies specifically related to cloud security: services, risks, and a case study on Amazon cloud services; quick survey on cloud computing and associated security, mobility and IoT issues; block-level data integrity assurance using matrix dialing method towards high performance data security on cloud storage; and a current status of the use of cloud computing in SME-s in the city of Latacunga, Ecuador.

SECTION 1
THREATS DETECTION IN CLOUD ENVIRONMENTS

CHAPTER

1

Analyzing Security Threats to Virtual Machines Monitor in Cloud Computing Environment

Ahmad Fayez S. Althobaiti

Department of Computer and Information Sciences, Al-Imam Muhammad Ibn Saudi Islamic University, Riyadh, Saudi Arabia

ABSTRACT

The data and applications in cloud computing reside in cyberspace, that allowing to users access data through any connection device, when you need to transfer information over the cloud, you will lose control of it. There are multi types of security challenge must be understood and countermeasures. One of the major security challenges is resources of the cloud computing

Citation: Althobaiti, A. (2017), "Analyzing Security Threats to Virtual Machines Monitor in Cloud Computing Environment". *Journal of Information Security*, **8**, 1-7. doi: 10.4236/jis.2017.81001.

infrastructures are provided as services over the Internet, and entire data in the cloud computing are reside over network resources, that enables the data to be access through VMs. In this work, we describe security techniques for securing a VCCI, VMMs such as Encryption and Key Management (EKM), Access Control Mechanisms (ACMs), Virtual Trusted Platform Module (vTPM), Virtual Firewall (VF), and Trusted Virtual Domains (TVDs). In this paper we focus on security of virtual resources in Virtualized Cloud Computing Infrastructure (VCCI), Virtual Machine Monitor (VMM) by describing types of attacks on VCCI, and vulnerabilities of VMMs and we describe the techniques for securing a VCCI.

Keywords: Cloud Computing, Security Threats, Virtual Machine Monitors, Cloud Security

INTRODUCTION

Deploying cloud computing in an enterprise infrastructure brings significant security concerns. Monitoring of the virtual machines with high security and minimal overhead is always very important, especially in those environments where hundreds of Virtual Machines VMs are running on dozens of physicals servers. In this paper we focus on security of virtual resources in Virtualized Cloud Computing Infrastructure (VCCI), Virtual Machine Monitor (VMM) by describing types of attacks on VCCI, and vulnerabilities of VMMs and we describe the techniques for securing a VCCI. Also it is identified that either monitoring hypervisor only will be enough to collect detailed resources consumptions or VMMs will also be required. To complete the experiment of resource monitoring, techniques for securing a VCCI, VMMs such as Encryption and Key Management (EKM), Access Control Mechanisms (ACMs), Virtual Trusted Platform Module (vTPM), Virtual Firewall (VF), and Trusted Virtual Domains (TVDs) is required [1] [2] [3] .

FIVESAAS SECURITY CHALLENGES

Top security concerns in cloud computing: Insecure Application Program Interface (APIs) or programming interfaces, Data protection, Access management inside employee threats, and Share technology issues:

1. Hypervisor security.
2. Cross-side channel attacks between VMs.

In this paper we discuss attacks between Virtual Machines, and how we protected and isolation from attackers. In his case, Virtual Machines share the physical memory, Central Processing Unit (CPU) cycles, network buffers, DRAM of the physical Machines. So Attacks takes place in two steps:

1) Placement of attacker virtual machine on the same physical machine.
2) Exploiting the shared resources.

CPU cache leakage attack:

Measure load of the other virtual web server.

Extract AES and RSA keys.

Keystrokes timing analysis.

Extract user passwords from SSH terminal.

SECURITY ISSUES IN CLOUD ENVIRONMENT

Infrastructure-as-a-service (IaaS) security issues:

The resources such as servers, storage, networks, and other computing resources are provided by IaaS in the form of virtualized systems, which are accessed through the Internet. Access to cloud resources over the network takes essentially three distinct forms: Admin command to the cloud provider, admin command to Virtual Machine, and user interaction with the virtual machine using network services [4] .

SECURITY THREATS TO CLOUD COMPUTING INFRASTRUCTURES

Application of clients running on Virtual Machine residing on Virtual Cloud Computing Infrastructure (VCCI), VMs aren't deal directly with physical hardware, VMs are manage by Virtual Machine Monitor, which is running in physical infrastructure. The VMM or hypervisor is software layer that allows several Virtual Machines to run on a physical machine. We have two types of hypervisors: type1 run directly upon HW. Type 2 run together with host OS. Type 2 includes Xen, and Kernel Virtual Machine (KVM), as shown in Figure 1.

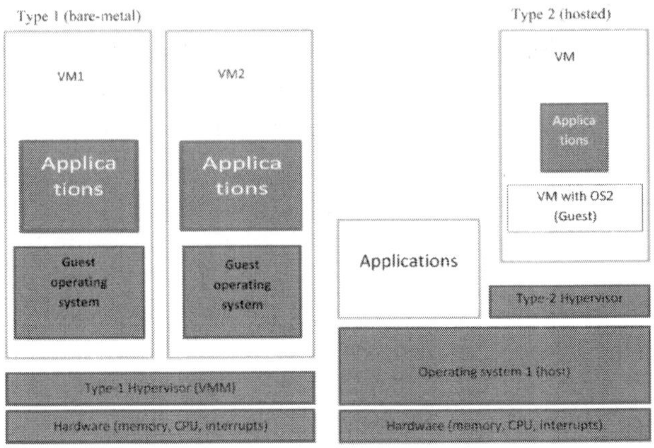

VMware ESX, Microsoft hyper-v, XenVMware workstation, Microsoft Virtual PC, KVM

Figure 1.Types of hypervisors [5].

Cross VM Side Channel Attacks

Attackers can use security gaps to attack on any component of VCCI that may effect on the others. In this paper we describe technique to overcome attackers on VCCI, and vulnerabilities of VMMs, the infrastructure needs to be secured by implementing security techniques that isolates the VMM, guest/host OS and physical hardware from the side effects of each other [2] . Identified two major attacks on VCCI (VM to VM and VM to Hypervisor) as shown in the Figure 2.

From above figure, attacks can take place through the major vulnerabilities (VM hopping, VM escape and VM mobility) identified in hypervisors.VM hopping: this attack can effect on denial of service, which make resources unavailable to user.VM Escape: this vulnerability allows a guest-level VM to attack its host.VM Mobility: under a VCCI, VMs can move from one physical host to another is called as VM mobility [5] [6] .

SOME OF THE SECURITY TECHNIQUES FOR SECURING THE VCCI

In this work we identified and analyzed some major approaches for securing a VCCI; these include EKM, ACMs, vTPM, VFs, and TVDs.

Describe Security Threats to Virtualized Cloud Computing Infrastructures A multi-tenant Cloud Computing Infrastructure(CCI) consists of several Virtual Machines (VMs) running on same physical platform by using virtualization techniques. The VMs are monitored and managed by kernel based software i.e. Virtual Machine Monitor (VMM) or hypervisor which is main component of Virtualized Cloud Computing Infrastructure (VCCI). Due to software based vulnerabilities, VMMs are compromised to security attacks that may take place from inside or outside attackers. In order to formulate a secure VCCI, VMM must be protected by implementing strong security techniques such as Encryption

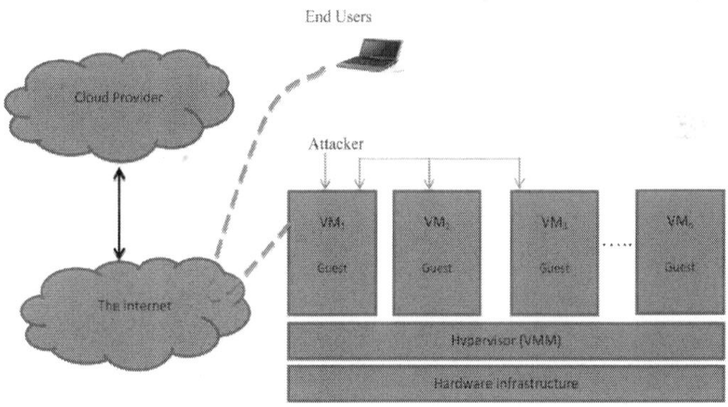

Figure 2. Attack on Virtual Cloud Computing Infrastructure (VCCI).

and Key Management (EKM), Access Control Mechanisms (ACMs), Intrusion Detection Tools (IDTs), Virtual Trusted Platform Module (vTPM), Virtual Firewalls (VFs) and Trusted Virtual Domains (TVDs). In this work we describe the techniques of virtualizing a CCI, types of attacks on VCCI, vulnerabilities of VMMs and we describe the significance of security techniques for securing a VCCI.

Encryption and Key Management (EKM)

Encryption and Key Management (EKM) is the common encryption methods that can be used on VCCI include symmetric and asymmetric algorithms. In this method, we protected data against the loss and theft is a shared responsibility of cloud customer and CSP. The common strongly encryption technique is Service Level Agreements (SLAs) [6] . Three different stages for protect confidential data for consumer:

a) Encryption of data-at-rest (encrypting the data on desk storage that protects data from illegal used and malicious CSP).

b) Encryption of data-at-transit (encrypting the confidential information such as credit cards while transmitting over the internet).

c) Encryption of data on backup media (external or internal storages), this protect from misuse of lost or stolen media.

Access Control Mechanisms (ACMs)

ACMs are responsible of protecting of a VCCI by restricting access, denying, limiting or to a system or an entity such as processes, VM and VMMs according to the well-defined security policies. Most common ACMs used in VCCI include Mandatory Access Control (MAC), Discretionary Access Control (DAC) and Role Based Access Control (RBAC). All these techniques are known as identity based ACMs as user subjects and resources objects are identified by unique names. Identification may be done directly or through roles assigned to the subjects [7] . ACMs guarantees integrity and confidentiality of the resources.

Virtual Trusted Platform Module (vTPM)

It's proposed by IBM researchers, is based on certificate chain linking vTPMs to the physical TPM in order to provide its capabilities and make it available to all VMs running on a platform. vTPMs can be located in a specific layer over the hypervisor. A vTPM instance is created for each VM by vTPM Manager which is built in a specific VM and may invoke its own vTPM through the hypervisor [8] . Each VM has its associated vTPM instance that emulates the TPM functionality to extend the chain of trust from the physical TPM to each vTPM via careful management of signing keys and certificates. A vTPM has its own virtual Endorsement Key (EK) and virtual Storage Root Key (SRK) beside some software on the host. In multi-tenant VCCI the system of vTPM virtualizes a physical TPM to be used by a number of VM on a single hardware platform.

Virtual Firewall (VF)

It is a firewall service running in a virtualized environment which provides usual packet filtering and monitoring services that a physical firewall provides [9] . VFs can execute in hypervisor-mode (hypervisor resident) and bride-mode. In order to protect the VMs and VMM, hypervisor-resident VFs must be implemented on the VMM where it is responsible to capture malicious VM activities including packet injections. These VFs require a modification to the physical host hypervisor kernel to install process hooks or modules allowing the VF system access to VM information and direct access to the virtual networks witches as well as virtualized network interfaces moving packet traffic between VMs. The hypervisor-resident

VF can use the same hooks to then perform all firewall functions like packet inspection, dropping, and forwarding but without actually touching the virtual network at any point. Hypervisor resident VFs can be faster as compared to bridge-mode VFs because they are not performing packet inspection in VFs, but rather from within the kernel at native hardware speeds.

Trusted Virtual Domains (TVDs)

It is security technique formed at VCCI by grouping the related VMs running on separate physical machine into a single network domain with a unified security policy. The multiple instances of TVDs co-exist on a single platform under a shared resource policy. The use of TVD provides strong isolation among un-related VMs as the communication among TVDs takes places only according to the security policies defamed by administrator configured in the VMM. A malicious VM cannot join any TVD because in order to join TVD, a VM should fulfill the requirements of the policy so no malicious VM can affect the VMs of trusted users on cloud [10] . Normally the VMs residing in a TVD are labeled with a unique identifier. For instance the VMs of one customer will be labeled differently from the other customer. The labeling is used to identify the assigned VMs to a particular customer and to allow the same labeled VMs to run on inside the same TVD that must be designed by following a proper security guidelines and policies that doesn't exhibit any loop holes [11] .

CONCLUSION AND FUTURE WORK

Many security challenges are facing the cloud computing, and it will be difficult to achieve end to end security. According to the above analysis, we can see that, each client assigned with one or multiple Virtual Machines, VMM is major target of the attack on VCCI. However, to achieve secure VMM, we describe several techniques applied by various researchers to secure VCCI. However, the security must be applied at different layers of resources such as storage, network, and applications by considering to resource management issues such as SLAs (Service Level Agreements) are concerned in delivering software for a million users to use as a service via a data center, which is a lot more complex, as compared to distributing software for a million users to run on their individual personal computers. Our future work would investigate new models and techniques for securing VMM, VCCI depending on resources efficiency and cost of cloud computing providers.

REFERENCES

1. Kulkarni, G., et al. (2012) Cloud Security Challenges. 7th International Conference on Telecommunication Systems, Services, and Applications (TSSA), India, October 2012, 88-91.
2. Zhang, L.J., et al. (2009) CCOA: Cloud Computing Open Architecture. IEEE International Conference on Web Services, IBM T.J. Watson Research Center, New York, 6-10 July 2009, 607-616.
3. Mehra, P., Katsaros, D., Vakali, A., Pallis, G. and Dikaiakos, M.D. (2009) Cloud Computing: Distributed Internet Computing for IT and Scientific Research. IEEE Internet Computing, 13, 10-13.
4. Shengmei, L., et al. (2011) Virtualization Security for Cloud Computing Service. International Conference on Cloud and Service Computing, China, 174-179.
5. Fu, W. and Li, X. (2011) The Study on Data Security in Cloud Computing Based on Virtualization. International Symposium on IT in Medicine and Education (ITME), Chongqing College of Electronic Engineering, 9-11 December 2011, 257-261.
6. Buyya, R., Garg, S.K. and Calheiros, R.N. (2011) SLA-Oriented Resource Provisioning for Cloud Computing: Challenges, Architecture, and Solutions. International Conference on Cloud and Service Computing, IEEE Computer Society, Washington DC, 1-10.
7. Liang, C., Zhang, Y. and Han, Z.H. (2013) Quantitatively Measure Access Control Mechanisms across Different Operating Systems. 7th International Conference on Software Security and Reliability, Beijing, 18-20 June 2013, 50-59. https://doi.org/10.1109/sere.2013.12
8. Berger, S., et al. (2006) vTPM: Virtualizing the Trusted Platform Module. Security'06: 15th USENIX Security Symposium, Vancouver, BC, 31 July-4 August 2006, 305-320.
9. Brohi, S.N., Bamiah, M., Brohi, M.N. and Kamran, R. (2012) Identifying and Analyzing Security Threats to Virtualized Cloud Computing Infrastructures. Proceedings of International of Cloud Computing, Technologies, Applications & Management, 151-155.
10. Griffin, J.L., Jaeger, T., Perez, R., Sailer, R., van Doorn, L. and Cáceres, R. (2005) Trusted Virtual Domains: Toward Secure Distributed Services. The 1st Workshop on Hot Topics in System Dependability, Yokohama, 30 June 2005, 1-6.
11. Iqbal, A., Pattinson, C. and Kor, A.-L. (2015) Performance Monitoring

of Virtual Machines (VMs) of Type I and II hypervisors with SNMPv3. World Congress on Sustainable Technologies (WCST), Leeds, 14-16 December 2015, 98-99.

CHAPTER

2

A Review of Anomaly Detection Systems in Cloud Networks and Survey of Cloud Security Measures in Cloud Storage Applications

Arif Sari

Department of Management Information Systems, European University of Lefke, Lefke, Cyprus

ABSTRACT

Cloud computing has become one of the most projecting words in the IT world due to its design for providing computing service as a utility. The typical use of cloud computing as a resource has changed the scenery of computing. Due to the increased flexibility, better reliability, great scalability, and decreased costs have captivated businesses and individuals

Citation: Sari, A. (2015), "A Review of Anomaly Detection Systems in Cloud Networks and Survey of Cloud Security Measures in Cloud Storage Applications". *Journal of Information Security*, **6**, 142-154. doi: 10.4236/jis.2015.62015..

alike because of the pay- per-use form of the cloud environment. Cloud computing is a completely internet dependent technology where client data are stored and maintained in the data center of a cloud provider like Google, Amazon, Apple Inc., Microsoft etc. The Anomaly Detection System is one of the Intrusion Detection techniques. It's an area in the cloud environment that is been developed in the detection of unusual activities in the cloud networks. Although, there are a variety of Intrusion Detection techniques available in the cloud environment, this review paper exposes and focuses on different IDS in cloud networks through different categorizations and conducts comparative study on the security measures of Dropbox, Google Drive and iCloud, to illuminate their strength and weakness in terms of security.

Keywords: Anomaly Detection Systems, Cloud Computing, Cloud Environment, Intrustion Detection Systems, Cloud Security

INTRODUCTION

Cloud computing is not a promise but a fulfillment in the IT world. The benefits of cloud computing have no infinite end as to what can't be done using the cloud environment due to a variety of deployment model such as Software as a Service, Platform as a Service, and Infrastructure as a Service. The cloud computing technology allows for much more efficient computing by centralizing storage, memory, processing and bandwidth. This allows flexibility in accessing of data over the cloud network.

Network traffic analysis in cloud environments is one of the most important tasks in cloud management to guarantee the quality of services, validate performance of new applications and services, build accurate network models and detect anomalies in the cloud. The flow of network that is been created by cloud computing systems shows users' behavior in service operation or use. Traffic analysis and the recognition of all significant application flows are important tools for modeling service usage, building up patterns for identifying normal system operations [1] .

The cloud computing environment has faced numbers of security challenges. Most of them have been fixed up to an extent, other security aspects spring up and it's vital to know before organizations switch fully. Intrusion detection system in cloud networks plays a very important role as the active security defense against intruders. IDS needs to be employed properly in the cloud networks, because it requires scalability, efficiency and virtualized-based approach in implementation. Sabastian Roschke et al.

proposed that the users of cloud computing have a limited control over its data and resources that have been hosted on a cloud service provider remote servers [2] . Due to this proposed theory, it automatically becomes the responsibility of the cloud service provider to oversee the IDS in the cloud environment. Additionally, network communication between cloud provider and its customers affects significantly the performance of most cloud-based applications [3] . Analyzing the flow of network traffic provides insights on how applications behave and also their performance in cloud environment. Therefore, it is necessary to develop network traffic measurement and analysis techniques to improve availability, performance and security in cloud computing environments.

On the other hand, managing and analyzing network traffic of large scale cloud systems is a challenging task. The techniques used to monitor and analyze traffic in conventional distributed systems differ from cloud computing systems. In conventional approaches, assumptions are made that network flows follow some patterns, which is acceptable for corporate applications, but cloud applications may have significant changes in traffic patterns [4] .

In the first section of this paper the concept of anomaly detection is described and taxonomies of anomalies are discussed broadly. Additionally, separate sections discuss security measures and comparison among basic cloud storage applications such as Google Drive, ICloud and Dropbox to highlight their security preferences and mechanisms.

CONCEPT OF ANOMALY DETECTION SYSTEMS

Anomaly Detection System (ADS) is a technique of the Intrusion Detection System which identifies activities that are not normal among the normality of a system behavior as it is illustrated on Figure 1 as N represents malicious nodes, R represents routers, G represents anomaly guard modules and "n" represents nodes.

Whenever such anomaly occurs an alert is generated to the administrators that shows the occurrence of an anomaly in the system, this makes a suitable supposition that the anomaly or changes are caused by either malicious or disrupting activities, and the IDS is also capable of suspending or blocking the connection where the anomaly is originating from. The ADS identifies intrusions by classifying activities as either anomalous or normal, and also a training phase needs to be done for the ADS to recognize "new" attacks. The ADS generates more false alarms than the Misuse based IDS systems. The

Intrusion Detection System technique is split into two forms or categories which are the Misuse Detection System and the Anomaly Detection System [5] .

Misuse Detection System

Most IDS that are well known make use of the Misuse Detection System approach in the IDS algorithm. The misuse detection system has a pre-defined rules because it works based on the previous or known attacks, that's how intrusion is been detected in the system. It's like the database of an antivirus signature, if it's not up to date it cannot detect new attack signature because such virus signature it's not in its database. The effectiveness of the Misuse Detection System is in detecting only "Know Attacks", because the rules or pattern of the Misuse Detection System are stored in the database of the system. The main downside in the Misuse Detection System is that it doesn't detect new attacks because it's not in its pre-defined rules.

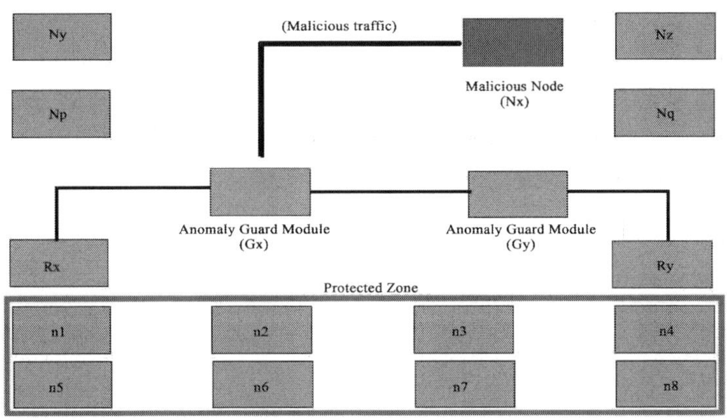

Figure 1. Illustration of anomaly detection.

Anomaly Detection Systems

There have been studies or research in the Anomaly Detection System in different problem domain, but in the cloud environment it has not been widely researched on. The Anomaly Detection technique in cloud based computing is still in view and evolving because it provides challenges that's still in the cooking pot. Anomaly Detection Systems in cloud based networks detects unwanted traffic in the network and this can be caused by loss of packets, unwanted behavior of application etc.

In a traditional network, IDS monitor detects, and alert the administrative user by deploying IDS on important points on the user site. But in the cloud network IDS has to be managed by the service providers [6] . The data that the intrusion communicates through is passed through the cloud service provider, this makes it only possible for the service provider to be the administrator and the user just has to depend on the service provider. Most times the user is not aware of such activities so as to keep the reputation and image of the cloud service provider.

A solution was proposed by Roschke and et al. [2] that combines and integrates various IDS sensor output reports on a single interface. The communication between different IDS has been with the Intrusion Detection Message

Exchange Format (IDMEF) standards. The positioning of IDS sensors on various layers of the cloud environment like the application layer, system layer, and platform layer can create better communication between the IDS sensors and also increases the detection process within the cloud environment. Generated pro- mpts or alerts are sent to the "Event Gatherer" program. The Event Gatherer program acts as a collector of alerts that spring up as a result of intrusion in the cloud based network. The alert received by the Event Gatherer is converted in the IDMEF standard and is stored in the Event Gatherer database with the help of a plug-in known as the Sender and Receiver Handler plug-in [7] .

TAXONOMY OF ANOMALIES

Anomaly detection aspires at finding the presence of anomalous patterns in network traffic and usual detection of such outline can provide network administrator with extra information source to identify network behavior or tracing and locating the root cause of faults in a network [8] . Anomalies can be classified into three categories: as Point Anomalies, Contextual Anomalies and Collective Anomalies [9] [10] .

Point Anomalies

This is when an individual data instance deviates from its normal activity or form it is said to be anomalous, because other data are normal. This shows that the anomalous activity lies outside the boundaries of the normal region. This is the easiest type of anomaly amongst the 3 types or categories and it is the strength or importance of anomaly detection. Figure 2 illustrates the point anomalies.

From Figure 2, N_1 and N_2 are regions of normal behavior, Points O_1 and O_2 are anomalies and Points in region O_3 are anomalies.

Contextual Anomalies

The contextual anomalies occur when the occurrence of information is or shows traces of anomalous character in an exact or precise context, which is the unwanted behavior of activities that surrounds an individual data instance. Figure 3 illustrates the Contextual Anomaly.

As it is shown on Figure 3, when this occurs it is characterized as a related anomaly. This requires an idea or notion of context in the data instance. It is also referred to as conditional anomalies.

Collective Anomaly

This is when related data instances collected acts as anomalous or show unwanted activities related to the entire data set. In collective anomaly, the individual data instance with collective anomaly are not otherwise said to be anomalous on their own because the collective anomaly requires a relationship between or among data instances; Sequential, Spatial, and Graph data to cause a collective anomaly. But their occurrence as a whole or collection is or can be anomalous. Figure 4 illustrates the Collective anomaly.

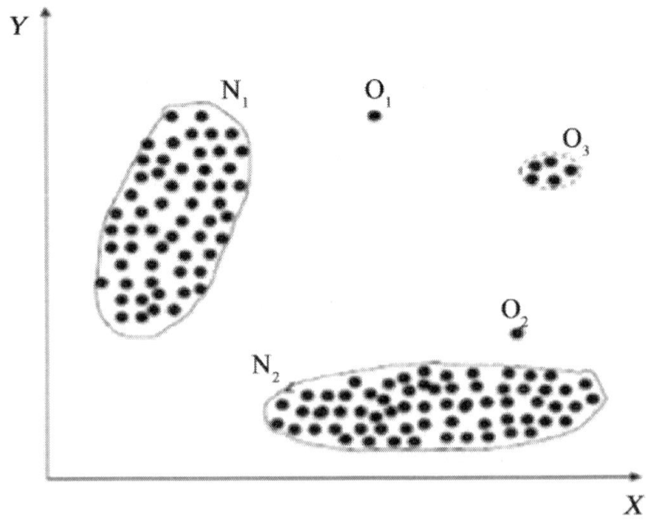

Figure 2. Illustration of point anomaly.

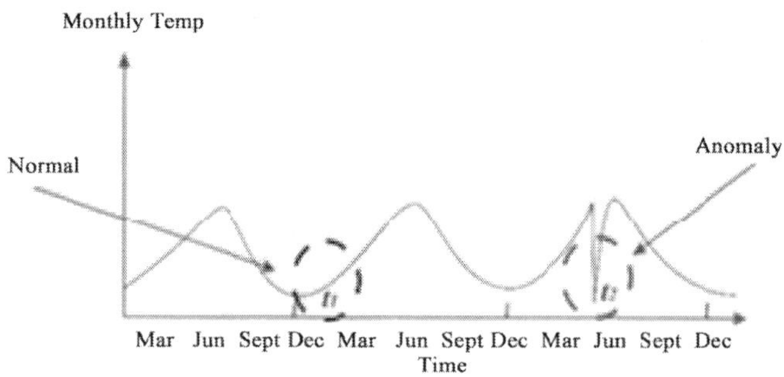

Figure 3. Illustration of contextual anomaly.

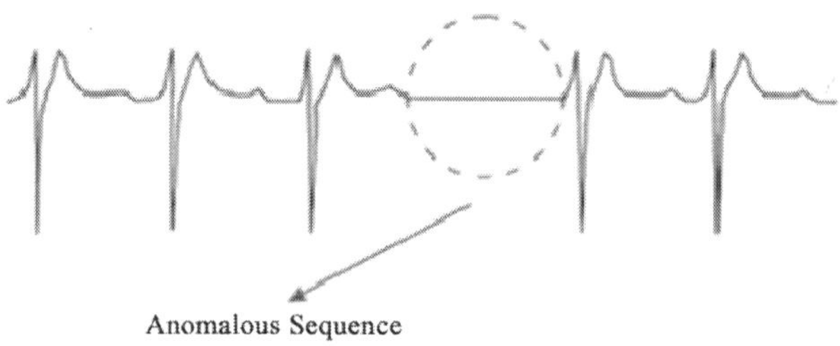

Figure 4. Collective anomaly.

ANOMALY DETECTION IN CLOUD NETWORKS

In cloud networks, traffic or flow of packets comes from more than one domain. There's a rapid change that occurs in the cloud environment due to the patterns or behavior of clients/tenants using the cloud infrastructure and the state of the unprotected services. In cloud environment, various challenges of identifying anomaly detection such as misconfiguration or high volumes of legitimate traffic in the network. The importance of the anomaly detection in cloud networks is the unwanted activities in data that brings the importance of reason for such anomaly in the information. Generally, the commercial off-the-shelf systems (COTS) for detecting intrusions are based on signatures or rules [11] [12] .

Signature based IDS can be used to detect known attacks in the cloud network, although the point of deploy can be before the cloud to detect external or incoming attacks or at the back end of the cloud to detect both external and internal attacks.

Methods and Techniques of Anomaly Detection in Cloud Based Networks

In the cloud networks, there are different techniques or methods that have been used in the detection of anomalous activities; these include Threshold detection, statistical analysis, Rule-based measures, neural networks, genetic algorithms, data mining and machine learning [13] . This section exposes a comparative view of the different method of anomaly detection in cloud networks. A comparison between the three main methods or techniques and others would be researched on namely; Statistical, data mining and machine learning.

Statistical Anomaly Detection Systems

This method of anomaly detection in cloud base network detects anomaly by observing computations in the network and creates a profile which keeps or stores the generated value in resenting their behavior. In identification of anomaly using this technique, there are two profiles created; the first one stores the normal or anomaly rules or signatures while the second one updates at regular intervals. During the update anomaly scores are calculated. If the threshold value is lower than the current anomaly profile generated, then it is known to be anomalous and detected. There's high probability of occurrence of normal data instances in dense regions of the model, while irregularities is seen in the low possibility regions [14] . Some proposed model of Statistical Anomaly Detection Systems are: Cloud Diag [15] , EbAT (Entropy based Anomaly Testing) [16] etc.

The benefits of using this technique are that there is no previous or prior knowledge or training of security risks or knowledge domain required. Additionally, it has the capability of detecting even recent anomaly generated in the network or data and there's accurate notification of anomalies that have occur over extended time frame.

Data Mining Based Anomaly Detection Systems

The analyzing or extracting knowledge of large data set to fine patterns that are useful to the data owner is known as Data Mining [17] [18] . This technique uses the classification, clustering and association rule mining methods in the detection of anomalies in cloud environment. An analyst mechanism is in the data mining technique that detects anomaly by differentiating between normal and abnormal activities within the cloud. This is accomplished by stating or delineating some boundaries for valid and normal activities in the cloud network. There's also an added level of focus in this technique for anomaly detection. Data mining techniques are more flexible and easily to deploy at any point. Putting data mining into effect in the cloud network makes available the opportunity to extract meaningful information from data warehouse that are integrated into the cloud, this reduces the infrastructure storage costs. Customers or users of a cloud service only have to pay for the data mining tool that's been used [19] .Data mining is typically used by Cloud Service Providers to provide a much better service for their users or clients using their cloud service [19] . The downside in this is that if the clients are not informed of the information that's been collected and used for mining, there's a violation of their privacy and it's illegal. There are varieties of issues available in data mining detection in cloud based networks which are the priority replacement of preserving privacy and setting the wrong parameters of these privacy settings while using different rules and strategy to enhance cloud network security.

Machine Learning Based Anomaly Detection Systems

The ability for programs or software to improve performance of their task over time by learning is an important technique in the detection of anomaly. Verified values or normal behavior of data are stored, when anomaly occurs or is being detected the machine learns its behavior, stores the new sequence or rule. This technique creates a system that can improve on performance of the program by leaning from the previous results. The interesting part in this technique is that upon improving of performance from previous results, new information are extracted and if it requires a change in the strategy of execution to improve performance it is done on the basis of the new information from the previous results. There are various categories of Machine leaning based anomaly detection such as; Bayesian Network, Genetic Algorithm, Neural Network etc.Bayesian Network has the ability to include in its process both the old knowledge or signature and the data in detecting of anomalies. This technique is combining with the statistical mechanism which is highly advantageous in anomaly detection [20] .

Neural Networks has the capability to improve on data that is not complete to create a potential to detect and understand patterns that are not visible. The Neural network does not only detect previous attacks but also unseen behavior or patterns [21] . Genetic Algorithms employs the evolutionary algorithm techniques such as mutation, selection etc. their different process is based on collected rules from the information on the network analysis carried out by the IDS.

Adaptive Anomaly Detection Systems

The Adaptive Anomaly Detection Systems (AAD) employs data description using hyper-sphere for adaptive failure detection. In cloud networks, possible failures or anomaly which are detected by cloud operators are detected by the AAD using the performance data of the cloud service. The AAD detection systems utilize or capitalize on the log of the detected failure records that have been sent in by the cloud operators to identify new types of failures subsequently. The AAD detection algorithm changes its behavior by repeatedly learning from the new certified results or detection from the cloud provider so as to be prepared for future detections. According to Husanbir S. Pannu et al. [22] a prototype of AAD system was built and experiment was conducted in it testing the prototype in a 362-node cloud computing environment.

It was noted that the prototype was lightweight, and it took couple of seconds to startup the detector and couple of seconds more for the set adaptation and the failure detection to be up and running. 518 metrics were profiled every minute, the profiling covered or circled through the entire statistics of a typical cloud server, its Central Processing Unit usage, task switching processes, memory and swap space utilization, paging and page faults, input and output data transfer, interrupts, and more. Failure detector such as subspace regularization was used in comparing the ADD algorithm. The failure detector in [23] achieves 67.8% sensitivity in the experiments. The Bayesian sub-models and decision tree classifiers that were proposed only have 72.5% detection sensitivity. In the AAD the failure detector could get up to 92.1% and 83.8% detection sensitivity and detection specificity [22] .

As shown on Figure 5, to make failure detection it takes 7.26 seconds on an average control node in the cloud network, to extract the performance metrics, create the hyper sphere and make failure detections. It is even more lightweight in updating of the hyper sphere and identifies failures in about 2.17 seconds.

COMPARATIVE SURVEY OF CLOUD SECURITY MEASURES IN CLOUD STORAGE APPLICATIONS

Cloud storage is a useful way of storing data and also sharing of information online. The important question asked is "is it safe to store sensitive information on the cloud?" well that's a question we are trying to evaluate and answer if possible.

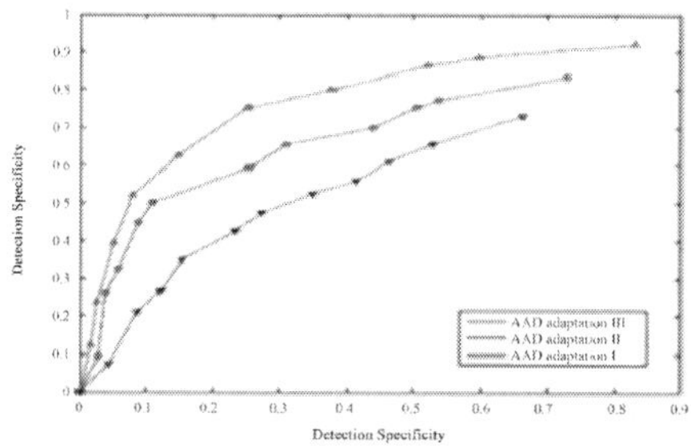

Figure 5. Illustration of failure detection with AAD.

Security in the cloud is not all that 100% guarantee. Files maybe encrypted in transmission, and at the final destination, the CSP might decrypt the file to gain access because the encryption algorithm used is provided by them. Access to your account can be gotten by anyone and your sensitive files can be compromised. In this case encryption on the client or the cloud user side is important and also using of a strong encryption key is advised.

In cloud computing, the usability of the computing capabilities have been moved from the users side to that of the CSP end; meaning users can access their files from anywhere at any time even using of multiple devices such as laptops, tablets, smart phones etc. this gives the user a sense of data mobility than just storing the data in a computer at home only [20] .

Dropbox

Dropbox is a public cloud storage, which was developed by 2 graduate of MIT who always forget or misplace their USB devices holding information that they need to use momentarily. Due to this Dropbox was brought to light in the IT world. In 2007 Dropbox Inc. was founded, it provides cloud storage, client software and file synchronization [21] . Dropbox allows it users to upload their files or folders into the Dropbox folder where it can be viewed or shared on any device at any time as long as the device has Dropbox installed along with a username and password and also internet connection for synchronization.

Dropbox was developed for personal use that was the intention of the two MIT graduate, but as of 2011 the cloud application have housed over 50 million users worldwide storing over 20 billion files and occupying petabyte of storage. Dropbox gives a 2 GB cloud storage space for free, but additional space can be purchased. Dropbox application is available for windows, Apple OS X, Android, and Linux [21] .

Figure 6 illustrates the example of working mechanism of Dropbox protocol. The basic mechanism is working based on so called hand-shaking process of basic networking standards.

Dropbox Security Measures

The cloud computing environment has many security issues affecting its usability. Dropbox being a cloud application or storage has several security measures put in place to ensure the data integrity and data security is in check. Dropbox saves all deleted and earlier versions of files for thirty days; this feature is supported by both the free and the premium (that's the paid account) account. In the free account the "save earlier version of files" feature only apply for 30 days, while in the paid or premium account the features saves the files indefinitely.

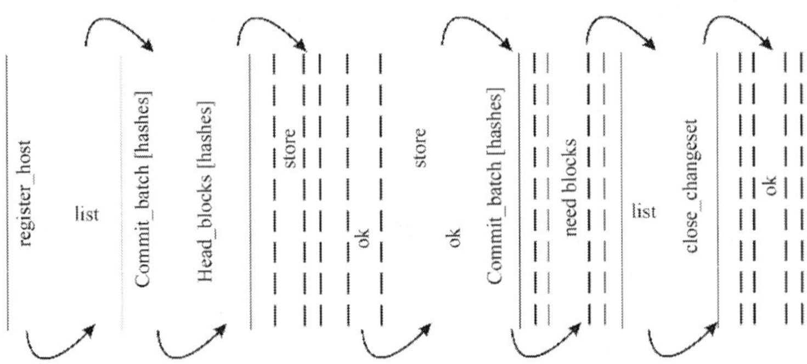

Figure 6. Illustration of Dropbox protocol.

The Amazon S3 (Simple Storage Service) is used in the Dropbox cloud computing environment for their file storage. This is done for high integrity and data availability, and multiple data center replication is also used [14] .

An AES-256 encryption is used for ensuring privacy of data in the Dropbox cloud environment. In Dropbox, encryption is machine-protected that is the encryption key is stored in the machine not in the cloud storage [14] . Additionally the Dropbox encryption algorithm uses a TEA symmetric encryption [15] .

The SSL secure tunnel protocol is utilized for data in transit, and it's also an AES-256 encryption standard. Two-step verification process is used for or to increase security measures and it is recommended [15] [16] . Availability of third-party applications in the Dropbox cloud environment also adds another form of security in data encryption [15] [16] . Additionally

Dropbox uses SQLite 3 database for ensuring data integrity and no data redundancy when users communicate with the database. The network traffic is fully transported over HTTPS, Proper certificate checking is done during the authentication process and OpenSSL is used to tackle with security issues in Dropbox services [17] .

The usage of OpenSSL increase security for authentication and authorization of Dropbox users. NCrypt wrapper is used by the Dropbox. The NCrypt wrapper creates security where there's none. The NCrypt is a file encyptor/decryptor and uses AES as its encryption algorithm [17] [18] .

It minimizes the exposure of plaintext password in memory and converts the plaintext to a SHA-1 hash before erasing the plaintext from hard drive immediately, and once the SHA-1 is used to make a key for encryption it is wiped form the memory too [17] -[19] . RSYNC (Remote Synchronization) Protocol is used, which allows a user to synchronize files between two or more computer device making sure that the same file is available in all connected device. Remote device unlinking is another technology used in Dropbox [24] .

Google Drive

The "Google Drive" is the Google version of cloud storage, and it is one of the popular cloud services. It supports photos, videos, documents and other files. There's a 15 GB free storage given that can be increased at any time by the user. Google drive provides generic applications for viewing of more than 30 file types without having to install the corresponding application into your computer system for viewing the corresponding file type. The Google drive provides unlimited file size upload quotation for uploading files into corresponding user drive.

Google Drive Security Measures

The Google Drive is integrated into Gmail services and once user owns a Gmail account can automatically have a Google drive account setup. Since Google drive uses a 2 step verification feature, the data security becomes one of the important obstacles for the corresponding technology users since 3-tier security architectures are more important and enhance data security for users [25] -[27] .Additionally, "Cloud lock" feature is used to improve personal security of information and this also ensures PCI compliance. Files in Google drive are encrypted using AES-256 and RSA-4096 standards and in addition to his, there is an automatic data encryption on Google drive and server-side encryption mechanisms are used [28] [29] .

iCloud

iCloud is cloud storage from Apple Inc. It was launched on October 12, 2011 [30] . iCloud offers its users with the means to store data such as; documents, images, videos, etc. users can also backup their iOS devices directly to the iCloud wirelessly. As of July 2013, the iCloud service had 320 million users [31] [32] . The iCloud was first branded as iTools in 2000, Mac in 2002, and MobileMe in 2008 [32] .

iCloud Security Measures

iCloud keeps data of its users secure by encrypting it when it is sent over the Internet or in transition which also contains 2 step verification processes [33] . Secure tokens are used for authentication, this creates a secure and unauthorized access both in transit and while it is stored in the iCloud. For the messages transferred over the network, iCloud introduced iCloud Keychain, which uses a 256-bit AES encryption to store password and also to store credit card information. It uses elliptic curve asymmetric cryptography and key wrapping. The iCloud Keychain encryption keys are created and stored on the user's device not on the iCloud server [34] [35] . iCloud sessions are encrypted with SSL protocol to enhance security for login information and a minimum of 128-bit AES encryption is used for encrypting documents in iCloud. The files that will be transferred are encrypted in transition using 128-bit AES encryption algorithm [36] .

Comparison of Cloud Services: iCloud, Dropbox and Google Drive

The various cloud services that this paper is characterized on, having their various service requirements to their clients as well as their cost. In Table 1, a detailed comparison was carried out to determine which among the three cloud services has a better security feature. We'd find out that the Dropbox cloud service incorporate more security measure compared to the Google Drive and iCloud.

Dropbox cloud storage service accounts for about 100 GB of traffic daily in one of their networks that was monitored [37] . A deduplication mechanism was developed to help avoid the duplication of data [38] [39] . Dropbox has the sharing of content ability and the percentage of files or folder shared amongst home users is about 70%, while linked devices is about 30%. Amongst students in campus about 40% of them share 5 folders or more. Dropbox uses delta encoding mechanism when transferring or transmitting chunks, “a chunk is a split large file”. In Dropbox, a file larger than 4 MB is split into chunks which are identified by a SHA256 hash value, which is included in the meta-data description of files [40] .

The two major components in the Dropbox architecture that can be identified are the control and data storage [37] . In Dropbox cloud service, each linked device has a unique identifier (host_int), these unique identifier are also used for each shared folder in Dropbox. The various devices that belong to a single user are deduced by relating namespace lists [40] .

Table 1. Secuirty comparison between Dropbox, Google drive, and iCloud.

Security Measures	Google Drive	Dropbox	iCloud
Secure Connection	YES	YES	YES
Files Stored Encryption	YES	YES	YES
SSL Protocol	YES	YES	YES
Open SSL	NO	YES	NO
128-bit AES encryption Algorithm	NO	NO	YES
2-step Authentication process	YES	YES	YES
HTTPS protocol	YES	YES	YES
Remote Device Unlinking	NO	YES	NO
AES-256 Encryption	NO	YES	YES
RSYNC (Remote Synchronization)	YES	YES	YES
NCrypt Wrapper	NO	YES	NO

Contents that are stored in Dropbox can be viewed and accessed using a web interface like a browser. Different set of domain names are used to identify public and private operations; URLs that contain dl-web.dropbox.com are associated with the private contents, while the dl.dropbox.com is associated with the public shared files [37] .

Google Drive is best for creating of documents and sharing of files. You can create spreadsheets, presentations, drawing, a new document etc. and stored files can be accessed anywhere with smartphones having Google Drive apps installed and desktop applications are available for PCs and Mac. Synchronization of files between PC and Google Drive is done automatically [37] .

As it is shown on Figure 7, Google Drive supports Microsoft Word documents, PowerPoint presentations, Adobe InDesign, Adobe Illustrator,

Microsoft Excel, Adobe Photoshop, Wave Audio files, Adobe Reader, etc. with these applications installed in the Google Drive by the cloud service provider, it makes it may easy for users to edit, create and view respective documents without having to install corresponding application on every device.In Table 1 shown, the various security measures of the Dropbox, Google Drive, and iCloud shows that the security infrastructure of various cloud services differs in the perspective of data security, availability, and control.In Table 2, Dropbox gives 2 GB of free storage to a subscribed user of its cloud services; additional storage space can be added by buying a premium package. Google Drive gives 15 GB free storage space to its users, also additional storage can be purchased to increase the storage capacity, finally iCloud gives 5 GB free storage to its users and additional storage is available to users for a price. For users going for a free large storage capacity Google Drive has a better offer. Dropbox, Google Drive and iCloud allow any file type to be stored in their cloud server by their clients. Offline feature is also available so users can download a file to view later even when there's no internet connection.

Dropbox, Google Drive and iCloud allow any file type to be stored in their cloud server by their clients. Offline feature is also available so users can download a file to view later even when there's no internet connection.

As it is shown in Table 3, the cloud services differ also in terms of price, storage and performance. Table 3 shows the price difference in services of Dropbox, Google Drive, and iCloud. However, it depends on the user and its choice of product.

Table 4 indicates the overall capability of Cloud storage applications. As it can be seen from the table, the Dropbox is the only cloud storage application that allows all features while iCloud and Google Drive does not.

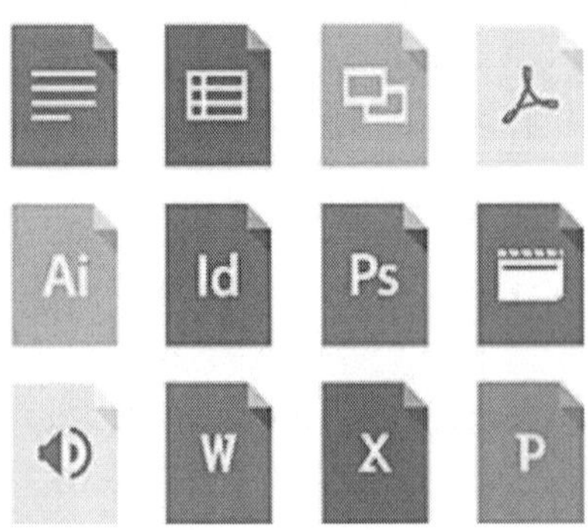

Figure 7. Generic applications of Google drive.

Table 2. Storage comparison between Dropbox, Google drive, and iCloud.

	Dropbox	Google Drive	iCloud
Storage Space	2 GB	15 GB	5 GB
Maximum File Space	N/A	250 MB	N/A
File Type	Anything	Anything	Anything
Offline Services	YES	YES	YES

Table 3. Service cost of Dropbox, Google drive, and iCloud.

Storage	Dropbox	Google Drive	iCloud
100 GB	$99	$60	N/A
200 - 250 GB	N/A	$120 (200 GB)	$3.99 (200 GB)/month
400 - 500 GB	$499 (500 GB)	$240 (400 GB)	$9.99 (500 GB)/month
1 TB	$119.99	$600	$19.99/month
2 - 16 TB	N/A	$1200 - 7600	N/A

Table 4. Capability measures of Dropbox, Google drive, and iCloud.

Capability	Dropbox	Google Drive	iCloud
Chunking	YES (4 MB)	YES (8 MB)	NO
Bundling	YES	NO	NO
Client-Side Deduplication	YES	NO	NO
Data Encoding	YES	NO	YES
Data Compression	YES	YES	NO

CONCLUSION

Arif Sari Anomaly detection in could networks is a wide area of research, and it holds a good number of developments and proposing of detection systems. Anomalous activities occur always in our networks cloud based or non- cloud based. With the different types of methods or techniques in anomaly detection in cloud based network, detection of unwanted behavior can be traced, detected, stopped. These techniques have their limitations that create a gap between their performance metrics. In cloud based network hybrid anomaly detection system or method should be used so as to have a more efficient and high performance system. In this paper, we have discussed the importance of anomaly detection system in cloud environment, its types, methods, and the limitations that each method is faced with such as, false alarm being created; detection accuracy is hinged on the basis of previous collected information on anomalous behavior; more time is needed in the identification of attacks etc. These limitations can create inaccuracy in anomaly detection. A wide study should be conducted to develop a more reliable and efficient model that would encompass and try to improve on the limitations that are associated to the anomaly detection systems. Security in the cloud computing environment is very important as individuals and companies utilize their services. In this paper we have compared the security measures of Dropbox, Google Drive, and iCloud; we have found that most of the cloud service providers have similar security measures while few are different. Some of their similarities are the use of AES encryption algorithm, the communication over HTTPS, the use of SSL protocol, and the 2-step authentication process. This helps to secure data both in transit and in the cloud storage. Dropbox security measures tend to be intense in protecting the information of its cloud users; it incorporates Ncrypt wrapper and the Remote Device Unlinking mechanism. From the security measures, I'd say that for a more secured cloud service the Dropbox is a best choice although you can increase the storage by going for the premium offer which is costly, but for storage and application variety the Google Drive is a take.

REFERENCES

1. Oliveira, A.C., Chagas, H., Spohn, M., Gomes, R. and Duarte, B.J. (2014) Efficient Network Service Level Agreement Monitoring for Cloud Computing Systems. 2014 IEEE Symposium on Computers and Communications (ISCC), Funchal, 23-26 June 2014, 1-6.
2. Roschke, S., Cheng, F. and Meinel, C. (2009) Intrusion Detection in Cloud. Eight IEEE International Conference on Dependable Automatic and Secure Computing, Liverpool, 729-734.
3. Zhang, Q., Cheng, L. and Boutaba, R. (2010) Cloud Computing: State-of-the-Art and Research Challenges. Journal of Internet Services and Applications, 1, 7-18. http://www.springerlink.com/index/10.1007/s13174-010-0007-6
4. Wang, C. (2009) Ebat: Online Methods for Detecting Utility Cloud Anomalies. Proceedings of the 6th Middleware Doctoral Symposium, ser. MDS '09. New York, ACM, 4:1-4:6. http://doi.acm.org/10.1145/1659753.1659757
5. Hussain, M. (2011) Distributed Cloud Intrusion Detection Model. International Journal of Advanced Science and Technology, 34, 71-82.
6. Gul, I. and Hussain, M. (2011) Distributed Cloud Intrusion Detection Model. International Journal of Advanced Science and Technology, 34, 71-81.
7. Shelke, P.K., Sontakke, S. and Gawande, A.D. (2012) Intrusion Detection System for Cloud Computing. International Journal of Scientific & Technology Research, 1, 67-71.
8. Denning, D.E. (1987) An Intrusion Detection Model. IEEE Transactions on Software Engineering, Vol. SE-13, 222- 232.
9. Marhas, M.K., Bhange, A. and Ajankar, P. (2012) Anomaly Detection in Network Traffic: A Statistical Approach. International Journal of IT, Engineering and Applied Sciences Research (IJIEASR), 1, 16-20.
10. Gu, Y., McCallum, A. and Towsley, D. (2005) Detecting Anomalies in Network Traffic Using Maximum Entropy Estimation. Proceedings of Internet Measurement Conference, October 2005.
11. IBM Security Network Intrusion Prevention System. Technical Report. http://www-01.ibm.com/software/tivoli/products/security-network-intrusion-prevention/
12. Cisco Intrusion Prevention System. Technical Report, Cisco.

13. Cisco Network Solutions, 2015. http://www.cisco.com/go/ips
14. Hand, D.J., Mannila, H. and Smyth, P. (2001) Principles of Data Mining. The MIT Press, Cambridge.
15. Wu, X., Kumar, V., Ross Quinlan, J., Ghosh, J., Yang, Q., Motoda, H., et al. (2008) Top 10 Algorithms in Data Mining. Knowledge and Information Systems, 14, 1-37. http://dx.doi.org/10.1007/s10115-007-0114-2
16. Pannu, H.S., Liu, J.G. and Fu, S. AAD: Adaptive Anomaly Detection System for Cloud Computing Infrastructures.
17. Garcia Teodora, P., Diaz Verdejo, J., Macia Farnandez, G. and Vazquez, E. (2009) Anomaly-Based Network Intrusion Detection: Techniques, Systems and Challenges. Computers & Security, 28, 18-28. http://dx.doi.org/10.1016/j.cose.2008.08.003
18. Zhang, Y.M., Hou, X., Xiang, S. and Liu, C.L. (2009) Subspace Regularization: A New Semi-Supervised Learning Method. Proceedings of European Conference on Machine Learning and Knowledge Discovery in Databases (PKDD), Bled, 7-11 September 2009, 586-601. http://dx.doi.org/10.1007/978-3-642-04174-7_38
19. Alsafi, H.M., Abduallah, W.M. and Khan Pathan, A. (2012) IDPS: An Integrated Intrusion Handling Model for Cloud Computing Environment. International Journal of Computing and Information Technology (IJCIT).
20. Mi, H.B., Wang, H.M., Zhou, Y.F., Lyu, M.R.T. and Cai, H. (2013) Toward Fine-Grained, Unsupervised, Scalable Performance Diagnosis for Production Cloud Computing Systems. IEEE Transactions on Parallel and Distributed Systems, 24, 1245-1255. http://dx.doi.org/10.1109/TPDS.2013.21
21. Wang, C.W., Talwar, V., Schwan, K. and Ranganathan, P. (2010) Online Detection of Utility Cloud Anomalies Using Metric Distributions. IEEE Network Operations and Management Symposium (NOMS), Osaka, 19-23 April 2010, 96- 103.
22. Chandola, V., Banerjee, A. and Kumar, V. (2009) Anomaly Detection: A Survey. ACM Computing Surveys, 41, 1-58.
23. Han, S.J. and Cho, S.B. (2006) Evolutionary Neural Networks for Anomaly Detection Based on the Behavior of a Program. IEEE Transaction on Systems, Man, and Cybernetics, Part B: Cybernetics, 36, 559-570.

24. Buyya, R., Yeo, C.S., Venugopal, S., Broberg, J. and Brandic, I. (2009) Cloud Computing and Emerging IT Platforms: Vision, Hype, and Reality for Delivering Computing as the 5th Utility. Future Generation Computer Systems, 25, 599- 616. http://dx.doi.org/10.1016/j.future.2008.12.001
25. Sara, T., Vance, C., Fenger, T., Brunty, J. and Price, J. (2013) Forensic Analysis of Dropbox Application File Artifacts Recovered on Android and iOS Mobile Devices.
26. Bermudez, I., Mellia, M., Munafo, M.M., Keralapura, R. and Nucci, A. (2012) DNS to the Rescue: Discerning Content and Services in a Tangled Web. Proceedings of the 12th ACM SIGCOMM Conference on Internet Measurement, IMC'12, Boston, 14-16 November 2012, 413-426. http://dx.doi.org/10.1145/2398776.2398819
27. Ruff, N. and Ledoux, F. A Critical Analysis of Dropbox Software Security.
28. Wallen, J. (2014) Easy Steps for Better Google Drive Security. www.techrepublic.com/article/easy-steps-for-better-google-drive-security
29. www.hongkiat.com/blog/dropbox-gdrive-skydrive/
30. Singh, J. and Jha, A. (2014) Cloud Storage Issues and Solutions. International Journal of Engineering and Computer Science, 3, 5499-5506.
31. Barth, D. (2013) Google Cloud Storage now Provides Server-Side Encryption. www.googlecloudplatform.blogspot.com/2013/08/google-cloud-storage-now-provides.html
32. GBacom News. http://GBaom.com/apple/apple-may-have-snapped-up-icloud-com
33. CNET News. http://news.cnet.com/8301-13579_3-20068165-37.html
34. Computerworld Report Articles, on iCloud. http://www.computerworld.com/s/article/9216301/Reports_Apple_acquires_icloud.com_domain
35. Voo, B. (2014) Cloud Storage Face-Off: Dropbox vs Google Drive vs SkyDrive. http://www.hongkiat.com/blog/dropbox-gdrive-skydrive/
36. http://www.whois.net/whois/icloud.de
37. Marshall, G. (2014) Best Cloud Services Compared: Google Drive vs OneDrive vs Amazon vs iCloud vs Dropbox. http://www.techradar.com/news/internet/cloud-services/best-cloud-storage-dropbox-vs-skydrive-vs-google-drive-vs-icl oud-1120024/2#articleContent

38. Drago, I., Mellia, M., Munafo, M.M., Sperotto, A., Sadre, R. and Pras, A. (2012) Inside Dropbox: Understanding Personal Cloud Storage Services. Proceedings of the 12th ACM Internet Measurement Conference, IMC'12, Boston, 14-16 November 2012, 481-494. http://dx.doi.org/10.1145/2398776.2398827
39. Halevi, S., Harnik, D., Pinkas, B. and Shulman-Peleg, A. (2011) Proofs of Ownership in Remote Storage Systems. Proceedings of the 18th ACM Conference on Computer and Communications Security, CCS'11, Chicago, 17-21 October 2011, 491-500. http://dx.doi.org/10.1145/2046707.2046765
40. Harnik, D., Pinkas, B. and Shulman-Peleg, A. (2010) Side Channels in Cloud Services: Deduplication in Cloud Storage. IEEE Security and Privacy, 8, 40-47. http://dx.doi.org/10.1109/MSP.2010.187.

CHAPTER 3

A Survey of Cloud Computing Detection Techniques Against DDoS Attacks

Sabah Alzahrani, Liang Hong

Department of Electrical & Computer Engineering, Tennessee State University, Nashville, TN, USA

ABSTRACT

A Distributed Denial of Service Attack (DDoS) is an attack in which multiple systems compromised by a Trojan are maliciously used to target a single system. The attack leads to the denial of a certain service on the target system. In a DDoS attack, both the target system and the systems used to perform the attack are all victims of the attack. The compromised

Citation: Alzahrani, S. and Hong, L. (2018), "A Survey of Cloud Computing Detection Techniques against DDoS Attacks". *Journal of Information Security*, **9**, 45-69. doi: 10.4236/jis.2018.91005.

systems are also called Botnets. These attacks occur on networked systems, among them the cloud computing facet. Scholars have tried coming up with separate mechanisms for detecting and preventing such attacks long before they occur. However, as technology progresses in advancement so do the attack mechanisms. In cloud computing, security issues affect various stakeholders who plan on cloud adoption. DDoS attacks are such serious concerns that require mitigation in the cloud. This paper presents a survey of the various mechanisms, both traditional and modern, that are applied in detecting cloud-based DDoS attacks.

Keywords: DDoS, IDS, Signature, Anomaly, Hybrid, SVM, Neural Network, Cloud, Machine Learning, Big Data

INTRODUCTION

Internet has led to cloud computing which constitutes three major services namely platform as a service, infrastructure as a service, and software as a service [1] . This increase in data and information storage within the cloud environment has raised cloud security concerns on the safety of data and information. It has also led to distributed attacks such as ICMP flood, the Ping of Death, the slowloris, the SYN flood attack, the UDP flood attack, malformed packet attacks, protocol vulnerability exploitation, and the HTTP flood molest [2] [3] . The choice on any attack type depends on the ease of such exploitation or its mastery by the attacker.

Previous researchers have expounded on how Distributed attacks in the cloud can be detected, prevented and mitigated. These techniques greatly apply two major detection mechanisms of signature or anomalies. They can use one, both, or be intelligent enough to learn new attacks based on set rules. The next section offers a review of various traditional based intrusion detection techniques. Further, it reviews the various classes of cloud computing based detection methods and offers examples. The underlying purpose being to compare the various detection methods and point out the strengths and limitations they pose. Beyond the review, the paper will show how specific techniques by specific scholars were successful or failed in the detection process against DDoS attacks in the cloud. In the analysis, the performance evaluation metrics used in a given technique will be shown. Additionally, the analysis will point out the various data sets and tools used by these techniques. As such, it will be possible to decide which of the techniques is efficient or has potential for future enhancement.

LITERATURE REVIEW

Existing techniques utilize different forms of algorithms to detect and determine attack levels within the cloud. HTTP-DoS and XML-Dos attacks are known to lead to exhaustion of resources [4]. Cloud-based intrusion detection techniques are an improved version of traditional intrusion detection system. The first section of this paper discusses various traditional intrusion detection techniques that are as well applied in the cloud. The second section will show cloud-specific intrusion detection techniques.

Traditional Intrusion Detection Techniques

Signature Based Detection Technique

This detection, also known as misuse technique, compares known information to already captured signatures stored in the database. The technique is only suitable for the detection of known attacks. A common tool used in signature detection technique is the SNORT tool [5] . SNORT is greatly used as it allows its users to set their rules and use those rules in regulating attacks on either the training set or real data set of attack.

In the study conducted by Mazzariello, Canonico, and Bifulco, the authors deployed the network based IDS at separate cloud positions. By considering two scenarios in calculating the performance of the IDS, two results were depicted. First, they inferred that the load on the controller increased, and the IDS detected the likelihood of the attack. Secondly, deploying an IDS close to the virtual machine resulted in the increase of the CPU load [6] .

Anomaly Based Detection Technique

These techniques observe the behavior of an event and determine existing anomalies. Shannon-Wiener's index theory analyzes random data with an aim to unravel existing uncertainty. Reference [7] defines an entropy as the measure of abnormal behavior or randomness. In the separate study, data from a single class proved to contain a lesser entropy unlike statistics from multiple ones.

Headers present in the sampled data are analyzed to determine the IP and ports before computing their entropy. A certain threshold is then constituted to detect a DDoS attack where incase the observed abnormality surpasses a set threshold, the IDS raises alarm alerts [8] [9] . An approach for detecting

HTTP based DDoS attacks is proposed by [10] . It entails a five step filter tree approach of cloud defense. These steps include filtering of sensors and Hop Counts, diverging IP frequencies, Double signatures, and puzzle solving [10] . The approach helped in determining anomalies with the various Hop Counts and treating the sources of such anomaly as attack source.

Artificial Neural Network Intrusion Detection Technique

Techniques utilizing ANN to detect intrusions aim at generalizing incomplete data and classifying it as either intrusive or normal. An ANN IDS can either utilize a Multi-Layer Perceptron (MLP), Back propagation (BP), or a Multi-Layer Feed-Forward (MLFF) technique. An approach by Gradiega Ibarra, Ledesma, and Garcia compared the use of self-organization map (SOM) to MLP in determining intrusion rates and found that SOM provides high accuracy rates of detection compared to ANN [11] .

Cannady utilized a signature-based detection mechanism in a three layer neural network as a means to detect any intrusions. He used a nine network feature vector consisting of the Source port, protocol id, Raw data, destination port, Data Length, source IP address, ICMP code, the type of ICMP, and the destination IP address to determine the intrusions [11] .

Genetic Algorithm Intrusion Detection Systems

The use of genetic algorithms in the development of IDS helps in incorporating various network features towards determining best possible parameters for accuracy improvement and result optimization. Gong, Zulkernine, and Abolmaesumi implemented seven network features namely Duration, Protocol, Source IP, Destination IP, Source port, destination port, and attack name in analyzing packets. By using fitness function frameworks that support confidence, the authors were able to detect and determine network intrusions with high accuracy levels.

Reference [11] proposed a solution that combined both genetic algorithms and fuzzy to detect signature and anomaly attacks. Fuzzy logic helps in accounting for quantitative parameters while genetic algorithm determines the best fit parameters that are introduced by the fuzzy logic. This approach proved to solve the best fit problem in Cloud environment. It also showed that since selecting optimal network features as the parameters for intrusion detection increases an IDS accuracy level, the use of Genetic algorithm in developing IDS is effective for Cloud use [11] .

Fuzzy Logic Intrusion Detection System

Fuzzy logic provides high flexibility levels to intrusion detection problems. It helps deal with imprecise intrusions. A Fuzzy IDS was proposed by Tillapart, Thumthawatworn, and Santiprabhob to deal with network intrusions such as the Ping of Death, SYN, UDP floods, E-mail Bomb, port scanning, and FTP password guessing. Chavan, Shah, Dave, and Mukherjee implemented both Fuzzy logic and ANN to develop Evolving fuzzy neural network (EFuNN) that applied both unsupervised and supervised learning. Their experiment concluded that the used of EFuNN with fewer inputs produces high accuracy levels than the use of ANN alone [11] .

Support Vector Machine (SVM) Intrusion Detection Systems

Techniques utilizing SVM detect intrusions using limited samples of data whose dimensions do not affect the accuracy of the outcome. Comparing SVM to ANN, Chen, Su and Shen determined that rates of false positive were more accurate with SVM since the parameters set with SVM are minimum. A limitation for SVM is that it is only usable to test binary data. Li and Liu proposed and alternate intelligent network intrusion and prevention system that utilized a configurable firewall and a SNORT tool to reduce the rates of alarm and raise the accuracy levels of the intrusion detection system [12] .

Hybrid Intrusion Detection Systems

Hybrid IDS combine the advantages of two or more techniques discussed above. A new DDoS detection mechanism was introduced by Krishna and Quadir who implemented an architecture based on the Hidden Markov Model and the double TCP mechanism. Five packets apply the 3-way handshake procedure twice, and a SYN is used to maintain a log [13] . The purpose of the double TCP technique is to ensure that there is an identity match before a connection is completed.

Reference [14] notes that the Markov's model when applied to wireless sensor networks helps in detecting any unusual activity. No connection is left half open as the client cannot reciprocate a matching pattern, and an attack is traceable back to its originator [15] . Vissers proposed the Cloud Trace Back (CTB) approach as a defense mechanism for web services through detection at the edge routers. In a reverse manner, SOA is applied to trace back the exact source of a distributed denial of service attack. A Cloud Traceback Mark (CTM) is placed within the header of a web message. All requests are then passed through the CTB thereby preventing any direct attack. To detect it, the victim client requests for message reconstruction in order to pull out the CTM which helps in retracing the source of the attacking request [16] [17] .Ismail presented the covariance matrix approach to detect flood based denial of service attacks. A statistical method scrutinizes the correlativity aspects of network traffic and evaluates the resulting covariance matrix to the already preset one as exhibited by normal traffic. The covariance approach proved to be very effective and accurate in the Neptune and Smurf attack simulation experiments [16] . A separate variation that utilizes both the covariance approach and entropy based system is proposed by [18] that offers in-depth detection at the host and network levels.A table illustrating the discussed traditional intrusion detection techniques and as presented in the works of [8] [10] and [11] alongside their advantages and limitations is depicted in Table 1.

Intrusion Detection Systems (IDS) Used in the Cloud

There exist four main IDS types that are applicable to cloud computing. They are the Host based IDS (HIDS), Network-based IDS (NIDS), Hypervisor based IDS, and Distributed IDS (DIDS). A pictorial representation of the various categories of IDS used in the cloud as illustrated by [6] is shown in the Figure 1.

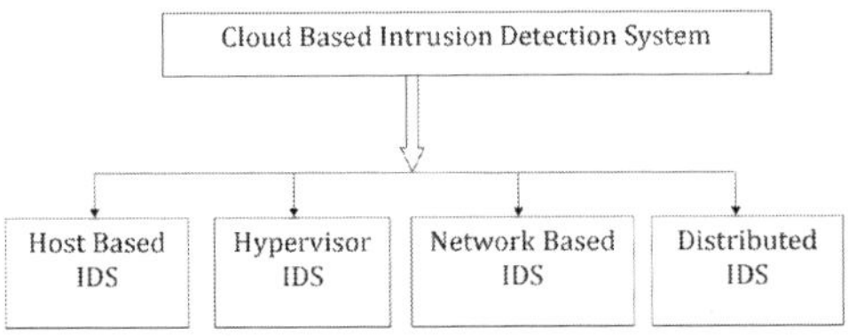

Figure 1. Cloud-based intrusion detection systems.

Table 1. Summary of traditional IDS techniques.

IDS Technique	Advantages	Limitations
Signature-based IDS	1) High accuracies in detecting known attacks 2) Offers low computational costs 3) Easy to track and stop an attack since log files are exhaustive	1) Cannot track down intelligent intrusions. 2) New attacks have to be updated in the database 3) Huge traffic limits the inspection of every packet causing unattended packets to pass through

Anomaly-based IDS	1) Higher the false alarm rate for unknown attacks 2) New threats are easily detectable without updating the database 3) System is self learning. It gradually learns the network and builds profile 4) The more it is used the higher the accuracy level	1) While building profile, a network is left in an unmanaged state hence prone to attack 2) When malicious activities assume the features of normal traffic it is untraceable. 3) Collected behavior and features determine the accuracy of detection
Fuzzy logic IDS	1) Increased flexibility in addressing uncertain problems	1) Offers low accuracy levels compared to ANN
SVM based IDS	1) Correctly classifies intrusions even with limited sample data 2) Ability to handle huge number of features	1) Classifies only distinct features hence the features have to be preprocessed before their application
Genetic algorithm IDS	1) Offers best detection features 2) Has better efficiency	1) Very complex 2) Its usage is of specific pattern as opposed to a general pattern
ANN based IDS	1) Effectively classifies unstructured network packets 2) Classification efficiency achieved by introducing multiple hidden layers	1) Requires a lot of time at the training phase 2) Has lesser flexibility 3) Effective training requires larger data samples
Hybrid Techniques	1) Efficient as it combines multiple techniques to accurately classify rules	1) Its computational costs are high

Network Based Intrusion Detection Systems (NIDS)

These are IDS that detect malicious network activities by monitoring the network traffic. Collected information is the compared to already known attacks before an intrusion is confirmed. This approach is utilizes signature and anomaly techniques to determine both known and unknown network attacks. However, the approach is ineffective as it offers very limited visibility in the host machines and cannot be used to detect intrusion for encrypted network traffic.

Reference [19] proposed a network-based Intrusion Detection System by conducting a turning test for all the IP addresses in the network. It identifies faulty IPs and labels them as blacklist addresses. When an IP requests for the resource, it is checked against the blacklist list. If it exists in the survey, the IP request is dropped. In case the IP address is not faulty, the system checks if the requested resources are available and do not surpass the set threshold. Reference [20] recommended a trilateral trust mechanism for detection and protection against traffic injection attacks. A client always requests for a service through the specified data center hosted by the cloud service provider. Further, the request is routed via a traffic injection rate detector which is preset with the maximum threshold.

A survey by [21] on what security can help detect ARP spoof attacks concluded that by combining XArp 2 tool with an ARP request storm and ARP scanner, ARP spoofing can be greatly managed. Another study analyzed DDoS detection in the multilevel environment whereby a new user freely connects via a router, and the detection algorithm is used to verify the individual as genuine. A register status is stored in CDAP logs [22] During the subsequent access via the router, an entropy is calculated based on data packet size and then compared to already stored range to determine its legitimacy or raise the alarm [23] [24] .

Reference [25] recommended a network-based intrusion detection mechanism by combining the rough set theory with the K-nearest neighbor classification technique. Their approach aimed at performing mathematical analysis on connections within a network to determine their categories as either normal, probing, DOS, R2L, or U2R. The analysis further gives the rates of imperfect data that helps in determining the connection.

Host Based Intrusion Detection System (HIDS)

HIDS are deployed at the host machine to monitor and analyze the information collected by the host. They first learn the host's file system, network events, system calls and then observes any modification that may occur at the kernel or file system of the host before raising an alert.

In a cloud environment, HIDS are placed on all VMs, host machines, and hypervisors to monitor and analyze log files, policies of security access, user login information in the bid to detect intrusions. Vieira and Schulter proposed a grid architecture where each node in the cloud has an IDS that interacts with the service offered such as IaaS, storage and IDS services. The IDS service consists of an analyzer and an alert system. Data is captured from and event auditor and the IDS uses either behavior techniques to detect unknown attacks or knowledge techniques to detect known attacks. When one host detects an attack, the IDS raises an alert and informs other IDS in other hosts. However this approach cannot detect any insider intrusion occurring within the hosts themselves [11] .

Reference [15] implemented a network-based IDS against known and unknown attacks. In their model, they used a snort tool and Bayesian classifier. The tool helps in detecting known attacks by comparing them to stored signatures while the classifier tracks any anomalies within the network. When the component of the model determines a possible intrusion, it sends an alert into a common knowledge base to be accessed by the other thereby increasing the rates of intrusion detection [6] [26] .

In another approach, a host-based IDS (HIDS) incorporates the external software agent at each cloud server with an aim to increase the resiliency of attacking the VMs without disrupting normal services in the cloud. The agents securely connected to the center of control using virtual LAN. An attack analyzer then decides whether to block or accept the user's request [27] . Reference [28] proposed two way detection techniques that apply the bother tree in packet transmission and augment attack to enforce bottom up detection.

Distributed Intrusion Detection System

Multiple IDS can be combined to save a large network. All IDS collect information and transmit to the central analyzer where centralized analysis takes place. Reference [29] proposed a flexible, scalable and cost effective mechanism for intrusion detection in cloud applications using mobile agents. The mechanisms were meant to help monitor and protect VMs that were outside an organization. The approach was not as effective as it introduced large network loads with increase VMs attached to the mobile agent.

Reference [30] proposed DIDS with various agents for intrusion detection namely the collector agent, the misuse detection agent, the anomaly detection agent, the classifier agent, and the alert agent. Their approach used mobile agent to detect known and unknown attacks and centrally place them in a classifier before raising an alert via the alert agent.

Reference [31] proposed a Cloud service queuing defender (CSQD) technique that aims at protecting the cloud from HTTP and XML forms of DDoS attacks. Using this approach, a server has to be up before a request is processed which is uniquely prefixed with an ID. Reference [32] proposed a VM profiling model aimed at detecting virtual networks attacks by ensuring resilience in the explorations of zombies.

A team led by Lonea proposed a DDoS attack detection technique that uses the Dempster-Shafer theory [33] . In their proposition, the authors set a private cloud consisting of the front-end server and set of three virtual machines (nodes) each with a snort. The IDS set within nodes generate and store alerts in the Mysql database located within the CFU. These alerts are further analyzed and converted into basic probability assignments (bpa) of either true, false, or (true, false). By using the Dempster-Shafer's combination rule to analyze the computed bpa's, the system increases true positive rates and greatly reduces false positive alarm rates [33] . Reference [34] ascertains the Dempster-Shafer Theory by arguing that the use of the centralized database reduces data loss risk and improves the capacity for result analysis and reduces any conflicts.

Hypervisor Based Intrusion Detection System

These are intrusion detection systems running at the hypervisor level. A hypervisor is a platform for running VMs. IDS at hypervisor levels work on virtual networks and allows a user to monitor and analyze all communications occurring within the hypervisor, between the various VMs, and between the VM and the hypervisor. The VM introspection based IDS is an example of a hypervisor intrusion detection system. Research by IBM gives hope to virtual machine introspection approach that creates layered security service levels within a protected VM running on the same machine consisting of guest VMs running in the cloud [11] .

Reference [35] proposed a VM introspection based approach that directly observes the hardware state, events, and software states of host machine and offers a robust view of the system. A VM monitor virtualizes the hardware and offers isolation and interposition. This approach helped in lie detection and row socket detection. A table summarizing the strengths and weaknesses of the above cloud based intrusion detection systems is depicted in the Table 2.

ANALYZING SPECIFIC DDOS DETECTION TECHNIQUES

Different scholars have presented specific techniques for detecting distributed denial of service attacks in the cloud. Each technique depicts the metrics used for performance evaluation alongside the datasets and tools.

Big Data Testbed for Detecting Network Attacks

The detection method presented by [35] simulated network traffic and relied heavily on packet per second passing via a certain route. The technique only captures HTTP based traffic and avoids other possible network attacks like the UDP and SMTP attacks that may lead to DDOS.

Table 2. Summary of cloud based IDS techniques.

IDS Technique	Strengths	Limitations
Network based IDS	1) Ability to monitor multiple systems at once 2) Their placement is only done on the underlying network	1) Cannot detect intrusions from encrypted network traffic 2) Difficult to detect intrusion in virtual networks 3) Only detects external intrusions
Host based IDS	1) No external hardware required	1) Only monitors attacks on the host it is deployed and set 2) Costly as it is installed on every network host machine
Distributed IDS	1) Has benefits of both NIDS and HIDS as it combines the features of both	1) Central server may become too overloaded and hard to manage 2) High costs of computation and communication
Hypervisor based IDS	1) User is able to examine and explore communication between separate VMs, hypervisors, or between VM and hypervisor	1) Its new and difficult to comprehend

This method is meant to detect HTTP GET flood attacks. This application layer attacks never use malformed packets and less consumers of bandwidth compared to other attacks like spoofing. Additionally, they do not generate significant traffic hence they are hard to detect [35] . The approach involved two phases of analyzing a training set of certain normal traffic and then using the parameters as inputs for detecting DDoS attacks using Snort tool

However, there is need to adjust the system in order to allow for detection of dynamic threats. There is need for a self-correction mechanism on already compromised data and a way for detecting already exploitable weaknesses. Introducing aspects of Fuzzy logic or SYSSTAT can help in leveraging the dynamism of the technique in offering proactive defense. Security for big data is an important aspect that needs integration into existing and upcoming cloud based intrusion detection system [35]. In the event that system component such as the memory are compromised, there is need to develop detective mechanisms using reactive defense strategies. This is possible if the system incorporates neural networks and machine learning techniques [36] .

Change-Point Detection Framework in the Cloud

Reference [37] proposed a conceptual cloud DDOS change-point detection mechanism as a means to detecting and preventing DDOS attacks. The technique consists of a change point detection, a packet inter-arrival time (IAT), and a flow based classifier (FBC). The technique is still in its conceptual stage and not practically tested but claims that by reading a packet header to determine its source and destination addresses, it will be possible to determine the packet inter-arrival time of packets from the same source and hence easy to detect any anomalies in packet transmission. A probable demerit with the approach is the possibility of high rates of false negatives and false positives [37] .

Hybrid Intrusion Detection System (H-IDS) for DDoS Attacks

Reference [38] presented a technique combining signature based and anomaly based mechanisms for attack detection. They used two different types of datasets; real data from previous penetration tests done on a commercial bank; and DARPA 2000 dataset. A time analysis was conducted on the DARPA 2000 dataset to offer a priori idea of the detection issue and results presented graphically in Figure 2. The performance metrics used included the packet inter-arrival time, the packet size, and the protocol frequencies.

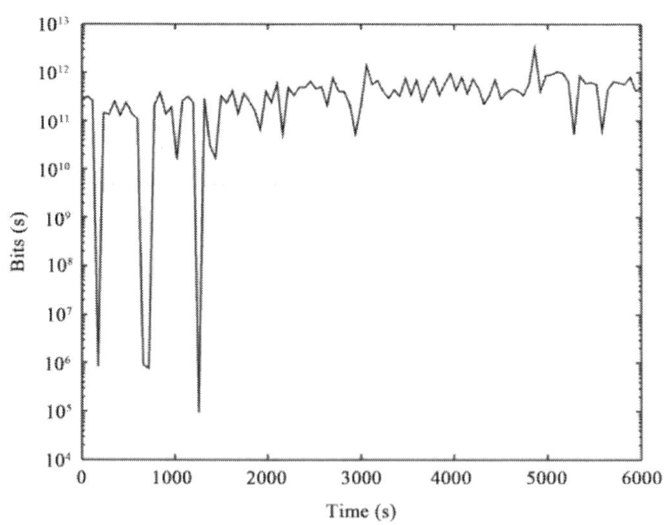

Figure 2. DARPA Analysis of time domain by evaluating density in bits per second (bps) against time in logarithmic scale.[1]

Anomaly detection is provided for by use of the Gaussian Mixture Model (GMM). The detector distinguishes normal traffic from abnormal traffic using data from the extraction phase. The parameters for GMM are estimated using the Expectation Maximization (EM) algorithm and the informatics distance metric method. The EM algorithm helps in determining the probability density function denoted by p(x). Distance between the parameters is computed and detection determined on that comparison. Using $X=\{x_1,x_2,\cdots,x_n\}$ as a dataset and x_i as a measure of M-dimensional vector, then it a probability density function, p(x) having a finite K component is calculated as below.

$$p(x\mid\theta)=\sum_{k}(\omega_k p_k)(x\mid\theta_k)$$

On the other hand, the information distance metric helps in determining the alarm level or mechanism of an attack [38] . The second part of the H-IDS system is the signature-based detective mechanism that uses the SNORT tool to set and modify rules as per the required performance results. A Hybrid Detection Engine (HDE) sets the rules granularity and the SNORT output is denoted as isAlarm_r which is calculated based on the number of alerts within a given time frame as is noted with the formula below.

$$\text{isAlarm}_r=\begin{cases}0, & \mathcal{A}(k)=0\\ 1, & \mathcal{A}(k)\geq 0\end{cases}$$

Using the HDE, the authors were able to calculate the attack probability by combining both the anomaly and signature-based detectors. Using the penetration test data, 99% accuracy on True Positive rate (TPR) was attained while DARPA dataset produced a 92.1% accuracy level on TPR [38] .

Hadoop as a Tool for Live DDoS Detection

Reference [39] proposed a live DDoS detection with Hadoop that comprises four stages of Network capturing and Log generation, Log transfer, DDoS detection, and Result notification.

This technique utilizes a web interface with parameterized parameters before capturing the network traffic. A strength with the approach is its ability to detect and analyze live network traffic.

The technique proved efficient while analyzing large data sizes unlike in the analysis of small data logs. The approach is as well non-intelligent to handle internal attacks resulting from compromised systems within itself. Introducing fuzzy and machine-learning approaches within the technique can help in tracking dynamic DDoS attacks.

A similar technique is proposed by [40] in which hadoop is used to analyze incoming HTTP, ICMP, UDP, and or TCP packets. The process will involve capturing the packets and generating logs, transferring the logs to HDFS, determining the DDoS attack, and keeping the result. A diagrammatic illustration of the above phases is depicted in Figure 3. Packet capturing is done by Wireshark as it proves to capture huge traffic amounts. Each packet consists of source IP, the packet protocol, some header data, and destination IP. A Traffic Handler is used in the generation of log files. The handler suspends the capturing process of Wireshark upon generating a log. It then transmits the file to the detecting server using a flume as illustrated in Figure 4.

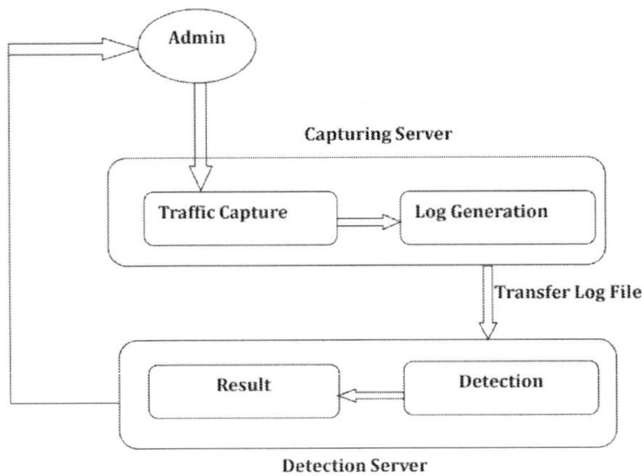

Figure 3. Phases of Hadoop DDoS detection framework.[2]

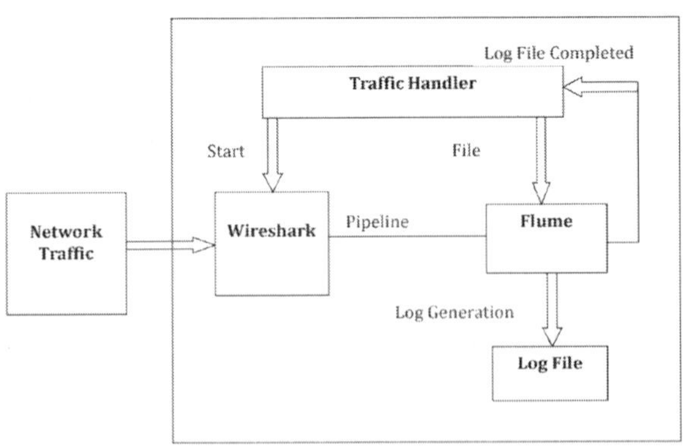

Figure 4. Component for network traffic monitoring and log generation.[3]

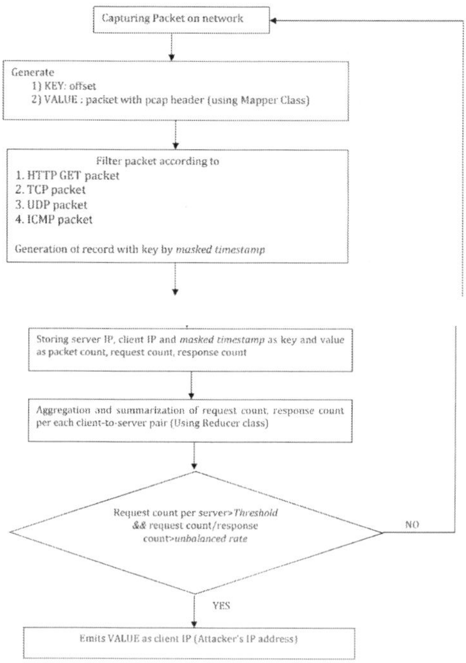

Figure 5. Counter-based DDoS detection algorithm using mapreduce.[4]

The DDoS detection phase utilized a counter-based algorithm presented in Figure 5. The algorithm uses time interval, threshold and unbalanced ratio as the inputs for the detection. Time acts as a limiting feature to monitor page requests while threshold determines the page request frequency to the server in comparison to normal network status. An unbalanced ratio is calculated as the ratio of page request response for a client and its server. An alarm is raised when requests by a client exceeds a threshold [40] . Even though the technique proves to be fast in detection of DDOS attacks and has low complexity of computation, mechanisms for internal attack detection need be introduced. Additionally, the success of its implementation lies in the capability to having beforehand determinacy of threshold value.

Real-Time Intrusion Detection Using Hadoop and Naive Bayes

Reference [41] proposed an approach for detecting intrusions in real-time by using Hadoop and Naive Bayes classifier. In their approach, the two created a heterogeneous and homogenous clusters for performing the training job. The Snort tool is used to capture packets from the NIC of a firewall and convert them into a binary file. Using Tshark, the system converts the binary data into CSV file which is then converted into UDP stream by a streamgen. A Naive Bayes Classifier present through MapReduce job writes records into an output file which is then read by a java program into disk. The results are graphically presented on a web interface using a D3 render. An architecture of this system is presented in Figure 6. Their approach proved a proof-of-concept technique with 90% success in detecting intrusions through the use of Hadoop and Naives classifier. But then, their results were based on comparison with another technique which is a small percentage of all available techniques and parameters for analyzing and detecting attacks.

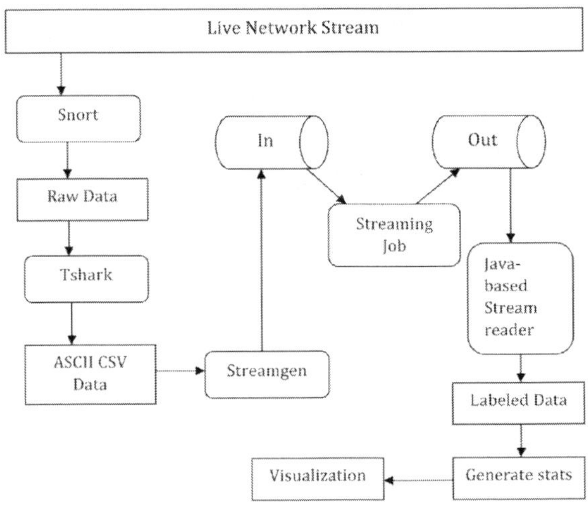

Figure 6. Proposed real-time intrusion through Hadoop and naives bayes.[5]

Botnet Detection Using Big Data Analytics

The work of [42] presented an important approach to combating botnet attacks in a peer-to-peer network. Their approach included three components; a traffic sniffer that captures and preprocesses packets, a feature extraction mechanism for engendering feature sets, and a machine learning techniques provided by Mahout that offers parallel processing in building a random forest based decision tree model. The technique uses dumpcap to sniff into network packets while Tshark extracts fields and sends them to Hadoop based

Distributed File System. At feature extraction, an Apache Hive program extract, transforms, and loads the datasets. Using hadoop's HQL language, selection of packet features is extracted using a group by clause based on an algorithm present in MapReduce. Mapping generated key-value pairs that are transmitted to a reducer that groups all values based on given key. This implies that Hadoop's MapReduce framework is dependent on pair [42] . Both the input and output are pairs as presented in the formula below.

(input) <k1; v1> → map → <k2; v2> → combine → <k2; v2> → reduce → <k3; v3> (output)

The key and value pair is basically the source IP and port and the destination IP and port. This approach utilized the key and value pair mechanism as the great interest was determining problems based on raw data packet flow. By using the Ranker algorithm, the authors were able to determine from the entire feature set for the most influential features. The method measures Information Gain as described in the equation below.

Information Gain (Class, Attribute)= H(Class)− H(Class/Attribute)

Capture files from existing Bot attacks such as those of Keliho-Hlux, Conficker, Storm, Zeus, and Waledac were used to train the system's classification module. The datasets were PCAP captures. 90% of the dataset was used as training set while 10% formed the testing set. The classifier validity was tested by comparing results of the predicted against those of the experiments using the Pearson product-moment coefficient derived by the formula below [42] .

$$r = \frac{\sum_{i=1}^{n}\left(X_i - \bar{X}\right)\left(Y_i - \bar{Y}\right)}{\sqrt{\sum_{i=1}^{n}\left(X_i - \bar{X}\right)^2}\sqrt{\sum_{i=1}^{n}\left(Y_i - \bar{Y}\right)^2}}$$

A 99.7% accuracy level using Random Forest Algorithm with 10 trees was attained by the classifier as is presented in Table 3. A receive-operation (ROC) curve of various classifiers is presented in Figure 7. The Random Forest is seen to outperform all other machine learning algorithms like Naïve Bayes and SVM. The presented architecture ensures fault tolerance and dynamically adapts to various network situations [42] . The model can be applied in peer-to-peer security modules of threat detection.

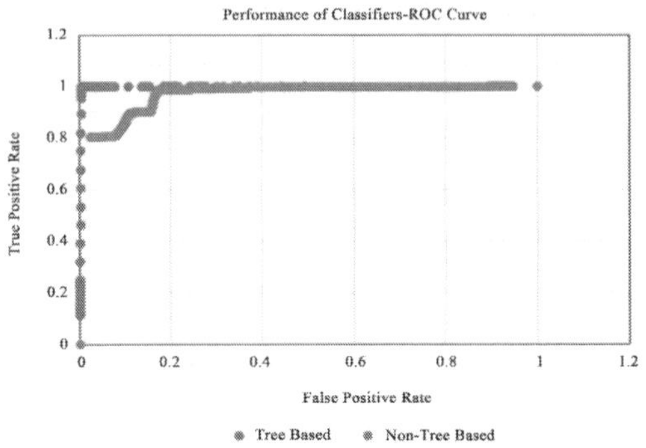

Figure 7. Classifiers' performance comparison.[6]

Table 3. Accuracy Measures of the proposed classifier.

True Positive Rate	False Positive Rate	Precision	Recall	Class
0.998	0.003	0.999	0.998	Malicious
0.997	0.002	0.996	0.997	Non-malicious

MDRA-BASED DDOS DETECTION TECHNIQUE

Reference [43] proposes an almost perfect technique for detecting DDoS attacks using Multivariate Dimensionality Reduction Analysis (MDRA). This technique combines the features of Multivariate Correlation Analysis (MCA) and Principal Component Analysis (PCA) with aim to increase detection efficiency, reduce resource consumption and computing complexity, as well as handle large network traffic in Big Data. Even though the technique is still theoretical, its practicality will result in better detection mechanisms and reduced resource consumption. A KDD Cup 1999 dataset is used for verification against the novel algorithm. A flowchart for the novel method is illustrated in Figure 8.

The PCA method helps in obtaining P principal components. Linear combination for the maximum variance forms the first principal component. In the event that the first principal component does not satisfy the total reflection of the original variable, a second linear combination is formed. In their analogy, a sample set X of network traffic having n samples each with a dimension d then the principal components can be illustrated as below.

$X = \{X_1, X_2, \cdots, X_n\}$ and $X_i = (x_{i1}, x_{i2}, \cdots, x_{id}) R^d, i = 1, 2, \cdots, n$. A DDoS attack detection algorithm based on MDRA is shown in Figure 9. Using Precision, FPR, TNR, and DR formulae, this approach helps in DDoS attack detection using MDRA and MCA [43] .

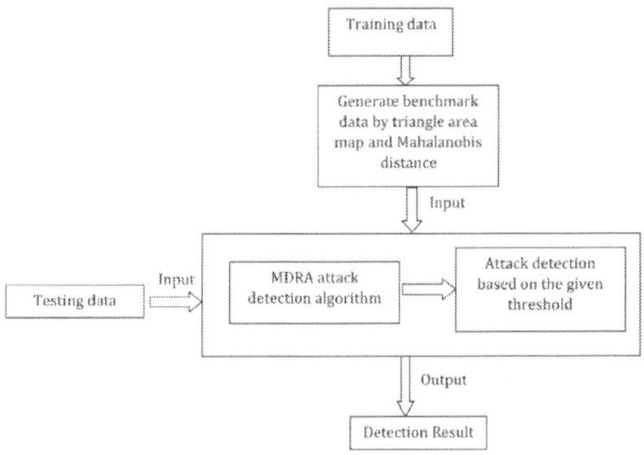

Figure 8. Attack detection flowchart.[7]

1) Input a set of training data of normal network traffic records $X^{nor} = \{x_1^{nor}, x_2^{nor}, \ldots, x_t^{nor}\}$ where $x_i^{nor} = [f_1^i, f_2^i, \ldots, f_m^i]$, $1 \le i \le n$.
2) Extract the principal components of X^{nor} to reach *70%* for the accumulative contribution rate based on PCA, and obtain the principal component dataset X^{Pnor}
3) Calculate TAM_{lower}^{Pnori} and $\overline{TAM}_{lower}^{Pnori}$ of X^{Pnor}
4) Calculate the covariance matrices between the areas of every two triangles T^{Pnor} in X^{Pnor}
5) **for** $i = 1$ to t **do**
6) Input TAM_{lower}^{Pnori} and $\overline{TAM}_{lower}^{Pnori}$
7) Calculate MD^{Pnori} between TAM_{lower}^{Pnori} and $\overline{TAM}_{lower}^{Pnori}$
8) Output MD^{Pnori}
9) **end for**

10) Calculate μ by MD^{Pnori}
11) Calculate σ by MD^{Pnori} and μ
12) Input a fresh incoming traffic record x^{fresh}
13) Reduce the dimensions of the features for x^{fresh} based on PCA, then get the records which include the principal components x^{Pfresh}
14) Calculate TAM_{lower}^{Pfresh} of x^{Pfresh}
15) Calculate MD^{Pfresh} between TAM_{lower}^{Pfresh} and $\overline{TAM}_{lower}^{Pnor}$
16) Input the threshold value α
17) **If** $(\mu - \sigma * \alpha) \le \mu + \sigma * \alpha$ **then**
18) **return** Normal
19) **else**
20) **return** Attack
21) **end if**

Figure 9. MDRA-based DDoS detection algorithm.[8]

Precision=TP/(TP+FP)

TNR=TN/(FP+TN)

FPR=FP/(FP+TN)

DR=TP/(TP+FN)

where:

1) TP is True Positive and represents attack numbers correctly classified as attacks,
2) FP is False Positive and represents normal record numbers in correctly classified as attacks,
3) TN is True Negative and represents normal record numbers correctly classified as normal records,
4) FN is False Negative and represents attack numbers incorrectly classified normal records.

Using a set between 1 and 3 with an increment of 0.2, Table 4 shows the resulting detection results of TP, TN, FN, and FP. Figure 10 and Figure 11 illustrates the tabulated detection results graphically for precision and TNR respectively. The approach led to high precision rate of almost 100% in True Negative Rate (TNR) with reduced computing time which equated to an eighth of the previous CPU time by MCA method. And even though the process was theoretical in nature, its practicability could alter how DDoS attacks are detected in Big Data environment. It would lead to greater efficacy even with heavy network traffic.

The strengths and limitations of the various specific cloud computing DDoS detection techniques as stipulated in this section are illustrated in Table 5.

Table 4. TP, FP, TN, and FN Results using MDRA and MCA.

α	Indicator on MDRA basis				Indicators on MCA basis			
	TP	FP	TN	FN	TP	FP	TN	TN
α = 1	166,299	278	60,315	63,554	223,587	1743	58,850	6266
α = 1.2	166,299	249	60,344	63,554	221,873	1469	59,124	7980
α = 1.4	166,292	227	60,366	63,561	206,504	1313	59,280	23,349
α = 1.6	166,289	217	60,376	63,564	191,190	1214	59,379	38,663
α = 1.8	166,289	204	60,389	63,564	190,394	1159	59,434	39,459
α = 2	166,289	194	60,399	63,564	190,342	1115	59,478	39,511
α = 2.2	166,289	191	60,402	63,564	190,311	1065	59,528	39,542
α = 2.4	166,289	188	60,405	63,564	190,277	1027	59,566	39,576
α = 2.6	166,282	180	60,413	63,571	190,254	988	59,605	39,599
α = 2.8	166,282	176	60,417	63,571	190,230	953	59,640	39,623
α = 3	166,282	172	60,421	63,571	190,199	927	59,666	39,654

Table 5. Specific DDoS detection techniques based on author.

Author/ Date	Detection Technique	Performance Evaluation metrics	Datasets	Tools used	Advantages	Disadvantages	Limitations
Csubak, Szucs, Voros, and Kiss, 2016	Big data Testbed for Network Attack detection	Packets per second rate	Simulated network traffic using NS3, Normal traffic data ranging from MBs to GBs	1) Snort 2) NS3 3) Wireshark, 4) Python-dpkt package	1) Using Snort, a user defines their own rules for which network traffic is analyzed against 2) Snort can analyze and log network packets in real time. 3) Big data testbed is capable of handling hundreds of GB network traffic	1) Since the technique checks the already set packet rates threshold, attacks occurring below the set threshold are undetectable	1) The technique has not been applied on large scale rather only tested via simulation
Chen Xu, Mahalingam Ge, Nguyen, Yu, and Lu, 2016	Cloud computing based network monitoring and threat detection system for critical infrastructures	Traffic volume per minute to detect abnormal behavior	Uses real Large traffic data from logs	1) Hadoop 2) Spark 3) Mysql database 4) PHP with AJAX	1) Three-fold solution of network monitoring, threat detection, and system performance 2) Fast data processing by concurrently running Hadoop and Spark 3) Easy for network administrators to detect any abnormal network behaviors	1) Accuracy level relies on collected data samples. 2) Cannot detect dynamic attacks 3) New components require extra monitoring agents	1) Accuracy of the detection greatly relies on collected traffic information 2) The technique is only suitable for analyzing static data

Osanaiye, Choo, and Dlodlo, 2016	Conceptual Cloud DDoS change-point detection framework	Packet inter-arrival time (IAT)	Conceptual network traffic data. No simulation or real data tests done.	1) CUSUM algorithm	1) Easily detects abnormal packet pattern by comparing with normal packet behavior 2) Able to detect DDoS attacks using statistical anomaly 3) IAT feature helps determine the probability of a DDOS attack long before it occurs	1) Abnormally based attacks cannot learn new attack types 2) Leads to a lot of false positives and false negatives and no optimal threshold is set	1) There is no standard mechanism to determine the optimal threshold for determining abnormal traffic	
Borisenko, Smirnov, Novikova, and Shorov, 2016	DDOS attack detection in cloud computing using Data Mining Techniques	Incoming network traffic data vectors	Uses Hping to simulate SYN, NTP, and HTTP-based traffic data, source IP and port, destination IP and ports, packets, data bytes length	1) Real Service in Virtual Network Framework (RSVNet) 2) Ansible 3) Siege 3.1.0 4) Hping	1) The technique performs test on real and virtual nodes 2) RSVNet is used to implement and create new protection mechanisms, and attack scenarios 3) Fast data processing and prediction of less than one second 4) This technique can be tailored to independently detect TCP, UDP, and ICMP flood attacks	1) For attack detection, powers have to be set to act as threshold and hence the process is not dynamic in nature 2) Separate attacks require separate classification models	1) The technique has no capacity for complex attacks	
Hameed, Ali, and IT Security Labs, June 2015	Live DDOS Detection with Hadoop	File size, number of files before detection, path to save captured file	Real-time Live network traffic	1) HADEC 2) Apache Hadoop	1) Ability to analyze huge volume of DDOS flood attacks in less time	1) Hadoop does not offer parallelism for small log files 2) Capturing consumes over half of the overall detection	1) Using small log files implies reduced number of attackers	

eetil and Gao, 2013	Real-time Intrusion Detection System by using Hadoop and Naive Bayes Classification	Packets per second, packets per minute	10% KDD intrusion detection dataset, Live network stream packets as training data	1) Snort 2) Tshark 3) D3	1) Increased parallelism due to the Naive Bayes algorithm 2) Using Hadoop-based Naive Bayes algorithm training speed increases implying faster detection rates 3) High detection rate of over 434 network packets per minute	1) This approach compared its performance to a previous approach rather than testing new attacks	1) The technique may not perform well in a distributed environment since its ineffective in a heterogenous cluster
Cepheli, Buyukcorak, and Kurt, 2016	Hybrid Intrusion Detection System (H-IDS) for DDOS attacks	Protocol frequencies, packet sizes, packet inter-arrival times	DARPA 2000 dataset, Real training data from a past penetration test of commercial bank in Turkey	1) Gaussian Mixture Model 2) SNORT	1) Combines the power of anomaly and signature based techniques for a more accurate detection 2) Combining anomaly and rule-based detection reduces detection delays 3) Easily integrates as a module with other IDS	1) Cannot detect complex DDoS attacks 2) Cannot detect attacks internally generated attacks	1) Training data does not reflect real network data implying reduced performance

Singh, Guntuku, Thakur, and Hota, 2014	Using Random Forests for Big Data Analytics in Peer-to-Peer Botnet detection	Packet buffer sizes	CAIDA datasets. 84,030 instances of mixed traffic	1) Hadoop 2) Mahout 3) MapReduce 4) Tshark using Libpcap library	1) Usable for predictive data modeling as Mahout ensures high data accuracy and time efficacy 2) Ease of detecting peer-to-peer attacks due to ability to process high bandwidths in real-time with 30 seconds delay	1) High computational costs due to the use of MapReduce jobs 2) Cannot run with non-distributed classifiers due to the large space required by data and JVM	1) Inability to block traffic from botnets or isolate compromised machines

Korad, Kadam, Deore, Jadhav, and Patil, 2016	Using Hadoop on Live Network to detect DDOS	Packet file sizes and packet pairs	Simulation of Live HTTP GET packet, UDP, TCP, and ICMP packet. Masked timestamp	1) Hadoop 2) Wireshark	1) Ability to handle and analyze petabytes of data with ease 2) Hadoop clustering help in harnessing the processing power of many computer as one 3) Ease of management and paremeter setting through a web interface	1) Cannot be used to detect internal attacks such as from memory corruption 2) High computational costs from combining multiple nodes	1) Ineffective with few nodes due to the high computational costs
Jia, Ma, Huang, Lin, and Sun, 2016	Novel Real-Time DDoS Attack Detection Mechanism Based on MDRA Algorithm in Big Data	Precision rate, TNR, memory resource, computing complexity, and time cost		Knowledge Discovery and Data Mining (KDD) Cup 1999 data set for training and testing. The data set is real	1) High precision rates of almost 100% for True Negative Rates (TNR) 2) Reduced CPU computation cost 3) Reduced memory consumption compared to MCA based techniques 4) Network DDoS attacks in real-time	1) The technique only depicts abnormal network traffic after it has been predefined	1) Since the approach is theoretical, it may not be possible to ascertain its effectiveness

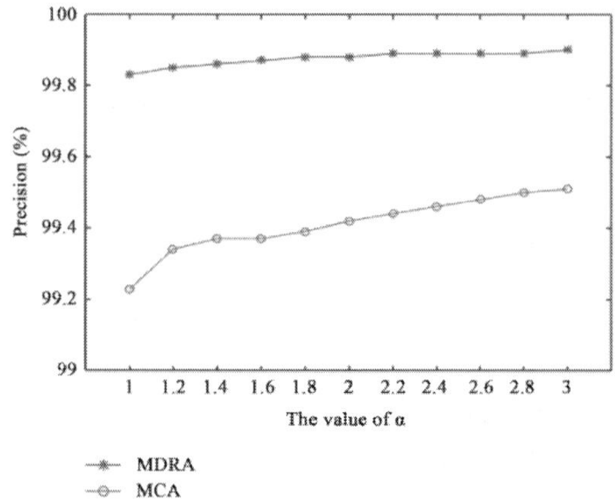

Figure 10. Using precision to compare detection based on MDRA and MCA.[9]

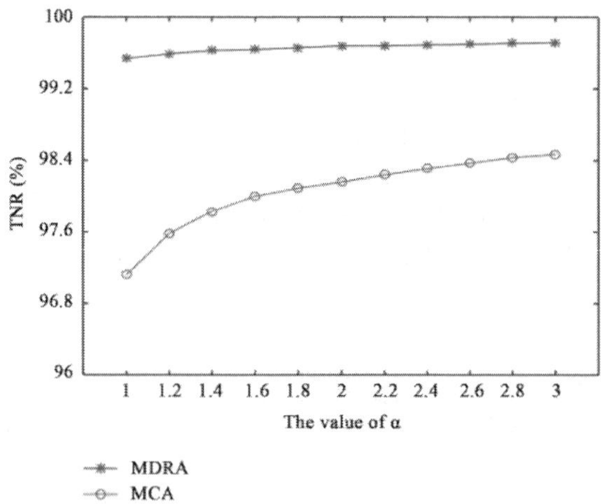

Figure 11. Using TNR to compare detection based on MDRA and MCA.[10]

CONTRASTIVE ANALYSIS

Each discussed technique possesses its strengths and limitations. Their strengths are based on the need to fill a certain limitation offered by a previous technique. Before a scholar assumes the feasibility of their technique they make comparisons of their methods to those of their predecessors. To study an ideology, a researcher has to consider all the variants and objects making it up and their interrelation [44] . Further, they need to apply objective research to analyze and contrast their findings.

With DDoS attacks, contrastive analysis is greatly applied when using training data set to prepare the detection mechanism. For instance, datasets from previously known attacks are used to first test the new method before applying it into real-time situation. For instance, [10] used a DARPA 2000 dataset with already known anomalies so as to test if their technique could detect anomalies compared to other techniques that utilized the same set. Similarly, the same technique used data set from a previous penetration test done on a Turkish commercial bank. The tests results are already known and using the dataset as input is only meant to compare the technique's output to that of the penetration test. Other than mere detection, the use of datasets helps in determining the accuracy levels of the current technique in comparison to previous techniques.

In most instances, the use of contrastive research is successful since it is possible to adjust parameters to fit the required outcome or to alter the expected outcome to a given level. In the technique presented by [42] to combat botnets attack in a peer-to-peer network, training data was pulled from previous Bot attacks. These were the Conficker, Storm Zeus, Waledac, and Keliho-Hlux Bot attacks that then helped in creating a classification mechanism for this technique. The experimental results compared to the already predicted results helped to gauge the efficacy of the technique. The researchers would then alter their parameters to determine the attack outcome on those features.

In other scenarios, attacks are directly launched on hosts and the detection mechanisms deployed to try and detect. This is enabled through the use of rules that define attack behaviors. SNORT is one such tool that has rules defined to detect an attack based on those rules and threshold. Additionally, setting a threshold level helps in detecting traffic anomalies by raising an alarm if traffic goes beyond such level. However, threshold may not be as effective. Attacks such as HTTP GET consume little bandwidth resulting in insignificant network traffic. Using threshold as a measure to such attacks would lead to a lot of false negatives.

CONCLUSIONS AND FUTURE WORK

There is need to ensure that data in the cloud is safe from any form of attack. Securing the cloud is hard but inevitable. One among the many feared attacks in the cloud is the Distributed Denial of Service attack. As this paper has expounded, the techniques against DDoS attacks borrow greatly from the already tested traditional techniques. However, no technique has proven to be perfect towards the full detection and prevention of DDoS attacks. In determining the detection or prevention mechanism for a DDoS attack, the motivation behind the attack has to be determined. Reference [45] stipulates seven motivations for DDoS attacks namely; financial and economic gain, slow network performance, ideological belief, revenge, intellectual challenge, cyberwarfare, and service unavailability.

One or multiple motivations can lead to an attack. Future researchers need to develop techniques that not only detect an attack but also intelligently identify the attacker's methods and the traffic rates. As well, the mechanisms should be capable of determining the legitimacy of the source of the attack.

Most of the previously proposed and implemented approaches can further be advanced to ensure an increase in the IDS performance. For instance, instead of concentration on one point for detecting an attack, the approach can work towards having distributed points of attack detection and correction. To increase the detection and inference speed, the approaches can further provide distributed points of attack analysis separate from the attack points but relaying attacks descriptions to a central point. This would ensure that all facets of an attack are determined without negatively affecting performance.

NOTES

[1]Cepheli, O., Buyukcorak, S. and Kurt, K., G. (2016) Hybrid Intrusion Detection System for DDoS Attacks. Journal of Electrical and Computer Engineering, 2016. Article ID 1075648, 8 pages, Figure 3.

[2]Korad, S., Kadam, S., Deore, P., Jadhav, M., and Patil, R. (2016) Detection of Distributed Denial of Service Attack with Hadoop on Live Network. International Journal of Innovative Research in Computer and Communication Engineering, 4, 93, Figure 2.

[3]Korad, S., Kadam, S., Deore, P., Jadhav, M., and Patil, R. (2016) Detection of Distributed Denial of Service Attack with Hadoop on Live Network, 95, Figure 3.

[4]Korad, S., Kadam, S., Deore, P., Jadhav, M., and Patil, R. (2016) Detection of Distributed Denial of Service Attack with Hadoop on Live Network, 95, Figure 6.

[5]Veetil, S., and Gao, Q. (2014) Real-time Network Intrusion Detection Using Hadoop-Based Bayesian Classifier. Emerging Trends in ICT Security, 288, Figure 1.

[6]Singh, K., Guntuku, S. C., Thakur, A., and Hota, C. (2014) Big Data Analytics framework for Peer-to-Peer Botnet detection using Random Forests. Information Sciences, 278, 492, Figure 4.

[7]Jia, B., Ma, Y., Huang, X., Lin, Z., and Sun, Y. (2016) A Novel Real-Time DDoS Attack Detection Mechanism Based on MDRA Algorithm in Big Data. Mathematical Problems in Engineering, 2016, 3, Figure 3.

[8]Jia, Ma, Huang, Lin, and Sun, A Novel Real-Time DDoS Attack Detection Mechanism Based on MDRA Algorithm in Big Data , 4, Algorithm 1.

[9]Jia, Ma, Huang, Lin, and Sun, A Novel Real-Time DDoS Attack Detection Mechanism Based on MDRA Algorithm in Big Data, 4, Figure 4.

[10]Jia, Ma, Huang, Lin, and Sun, A Novel Real-Time DDoS Attack Detection Mechanism Based on MDRA Algorithm in Big Data , 4, Figure 5.

REFERENCES

1. Subramaniam, T. and Bethany, D. (2016) Preventing Distributed Denial of Service Attacks in Cloud Environments. International Journal of Information Technology, Control and Automation, 6, 23-32. https://doi.org/10.5121/ijitca.2016.6203
2. Sivamohan, S., Veeramani, R., Liza, K., Krishnaveni, S. and Jothi, B. (2016) Data Mining Technique for DDoS Attack in Cloud Computing. International Journal of Computer Technology and Applications, 9, 149-156.
3. Masdari, M. and Marzie, J. (2016) A Survey and Taxonomy of DoS Attacks in Cloud Computing. Security and Communication Networks, 2, 3274-3751. https://doi.org/10.1002/sec.1539
4. Bonquet, A. and Martine, B. (2017) A Survey of Denial-of-Service and Distributed Denial of Service Attacks and Defense in Cloud Computing. Future Internet, 9, 1-9. https://doi.org/10.3390/fi9030043
5. Kaur, A. and Anupama, K. (2015) A Review on Various Attack Detection Techniques in Cloud Architecture. International Journal of Advanced Research in Computer Engineering & Technology, 4, 3861-3867.
6. Kene, S.G. and Deepti, P.T. (2015) A Review on Intrusion Detection Techniques for Cloud Computing and Security Challenges. 2nd International Conference on Electronics and Communication Systems, Coimbatore, 26-27 Februaty 2015, Vol. 2, 227-231. https://doi.org/10.1109/ECS.2015.7124898
7. Deshmukh, R.V. and Kailas, K.D. (2015) Understanding DDoS Attack & Its Effect in Cloud Environment. Procedia Computer Science, 49, 202-210. https://doi.org/10.1016/j.procs.2015.04.245
8. Sattar, I., et al. (2015) A Review of Techniques to Detect and Prevent Distributed Denial of Service (DDoS) Attack in Cloud Computing Environment. International Journal of Computer Applications, 115, 23-27. https://doi.org/10.5120/20173-2370
9. Navaz, S., et al. (2013) Entropy Based Anomaly Detection System to Prevent DDoS Attacks in Cloud. International Journal of Computer Applications, 15, 42-47.
10. Ankita, P. and Fenil, K. (2015) Survey on DDoS Attack Detection and Prevention in Cloud. International Journal of Engineering Technology, Management, and Applied Sciences, 3, 43-47.

11. Modi, C., Dhiren, P., Bhavesh, B., Avi, P. and Muttukrishnan, R. (2013) A Survey on Security Issues and Solutions at Different Layers of Cloud Computing. The Journal of Supercomputing, 63, 561-592. https://doi.org/10.1007/s11227-012-0831-5
12. Kacha, C.C., et al. (2013) Improved Snort Intrusion Detection System using Modified Pattern Matching Technique. International Journal of Emerging Technology and Advanced Engineering, 3, 81-88.
13. Parwani, D., et al. (2015) Various Techniques of DDoS Attacks Detection and Prevention at Cloud: A Survey. Oriental Journal of Computer Science & Technology, 8, 110-120.
14. Dewal, P., et al. (2016) A Survey of Intrusion Detection Systems and Secure Routing Protocols in Wireless Sensor Networks. International Journal for Research in Emerging Science and Technology, 3, 16-20.
15. Modi, K. and Abdul, Q. (2014) Detection and Prevention of DDoS Attacks on the Cloud using Double-TCP Mechanism and HMM-Based Architecture. International Journal of Cloud Computing and Services Science, 3, 113-120.
16. Chawla, I., et al. (2015) DDoS Attacks in Cloud and Mitigation Techniques. International Journal of Innovative Science, Engineering & Technology, 2, 596-600.
17. Reddy, S.V., et al. (2012) Efficient Detection of Ddos Attacks by Entropy Variation. IOSR Journal of Computer Engineering, 7, 45-67. https://doi.org/10.9790/0661-0711318
18. Girma, A., et al. (2015) Analysis of DDoS Attacks and an Introduction of a Hybrid Statistical Model to Detect DDoS Attacks on Cloud Computing Environment. 12th International Conference on Information Technology—New Generations, Las Vegas, 13-15 April 2015, 212-217. https://doi.org/10.1109/ITNG.2015.40
19. Nitesh, B., et al. (2017) Mitigating Distributed Denial of Service Attack in Cloud Computing Environment using Threshold based Technique. Indian Journal of Science and Technology, 3, 1-7.
20. Iyengar, N. and Gopinath, G. (2015) Trilateral Trust Based Defense Mechanism against DDoS Attacks in Cloud Computing Environment. Cybernetics and Information Technologies, 15, 122. https://doi.org/10.1515/cait-2015-0033
21. Al-Hemairy, M., et al. (2009) Towards More Sophisticated ARP Spoofing Detection/Prevention Systems in LAN Networks.

International Conference on the Current Trends in Information Technology, Dubai, 15-16 December 2009, 1-6. https://doi.org/10.1109/CTIT.2009.5423112

22. Jeyanthi, N. and Chris, M. (2014) A Virtual Firewall Mechanism using Army Nodes to Protect Cloud Infrastructure from DDoS Attacks. Cybernetics and Information Technologies, 14, 71-85. https://doi.org/10.2478/cait-2014-0034
23. David, J. and Ciza, T. (2015) DDoS Attack Detection using Fast Entropy Approach on Flow-Based Network Traffic. Procedia Computer Science, 50, 30-36. https://doi.org/10.1016/j.procs.2015.04.007
24. Singh, N., et al. (2015) Comprehensive Study of Various Techniques for Detecting DDoS Attacks in Cloud Environment. International Journal of Grid and Distributed Computing, 8, 119-126. https://doi.org/10.14257/ijgdc.2015.8.3.12
25. Adetunmbi, A.O., et al. (2008) Network Intrusion Detection Based on Rough Set and K-Nearest Neighbor. International Journal of Computing and ICT Research, 2, 60-66.
26. Gourkhede, M.H. and Peter, T. (2014) Preserving Privacy and Illegal Content Distribution for Cloud Environment. International Journal of Computing and Technology, 1, 124-148.
27. Gayatri, P., et al. (2015) Comprehensive Comparative Study on Intrusion Detection System in Cloud Computing. International Journal for Research in Applied Science & Engineering Technology, 3, 926-930.
28. Parwani, D. and Amit, D. (2017) Prevention Mechanisms of DDoS Attacks: A Critical Review. International Journal of Science, Engineering and Technology, 5, 99-112.
29. Dastjerdi, A.V., et al. (2009) Distributed Intrusion Detection in Clouds using Mobile Agents. 3rd International Conference on Advanced Engineering Computing and Applications in Sciences, Sliema, 11-16 October 2009, 175-180. https://doi.org/10.1109/ADVCOMP.2009.34
30. Karthi, M.M., et al. (2013) Intrusion Detection System for Cloud System using Intelligent Agents. International Journal Of Engineering And Computer Science, 2, 1868-1873.
31. Sahardi, R.M. and Vahid, G. (2013) New Approach to Mitigate XML-DOS and HTTP-DOS Attacks for Cloud Computing. International Journal of Computer Applications, 72, 27-31. https://doi.

org/10.5120/12579-9201

32. Subapriya, S. and Nathan, R. (2014) DNIDPS: Distributed Network Intrusion Detection and Prevention System. International Journal of Innovative Science, Engineering & Technology, 6, 56-67.
33. Lonea, A.M., et al. (2012) Detecting DDoS Attacks in Cloud Computing Environment. International Journal of Computers Communications & Control, 8, 70. https://doi.org/10.15837/ijccc.2013.1.170
34. Patel, S. and Fenil, K. (2016) A Review Paper of an Encryption Scheme using Network Coding for Energy Optimization in MANET. International Conference on Wireless Communications, Signal Processing and Networking, Chennai, 23-25 March 2016, Vol. 34, 45-67. https://doi.org/10.1109/WiSPNET.2016.7566298
35. Csubak, D., Szucs, K., Voros, P. and Kiss, A. (2016) Big Data Testbed for Network Attack Detection. Acta Polytechnica Hungarica, 13, 47-57.
36. Chen, Z., Xu, G., Mahalingam, V., Ge, L., Nguyen, J., Yu, W. and Lu, C. (2016) A Cloud Computing Based Network Monitoring and Threat Detection System for Critical Infrastructures. Big Data Research, 3, 10-23. https://doi.org/10.1016/j.bdr.2015.11.002
37. Osanaiye, O., Choo, K.R. and Dlodlo, M. (2016) Distributed Denial of Service (DDoS) Resilience in Cloud: Review and Conceptual Cloud DDoS Mitigation Framework. Journal of Network and Computer Applications, 67, 147-165. https://doi.org/10.1016/j.jnca.2016.01.001
38. Cepheli, O., Buyukcorak, S. and Kurt, K.G. (2016) Hybrid Intrusion Detection System for DDoS Attacks. Journal of Electrical and Computer Engineering, 2016, Article ID: 1075648. https://doi.org/10.1155/2016/1075648
39. Hameed, S. and Ali, U. (2016) Efficacy of Live DDoS Detection with Hadoop. IEEE/IFIP Network Operations and Management Symposium, Istanbul, 25-29 April 2016. https://arxiv.org/pdf/1506.08953.pdf
40. Korad, S., Kadam, S., Deore, P., Jadhav, M. and Patil, R. (2016) Detection of Distributed Denial of Service Attack with Hadoop on Live Network. International Journal of Innovative Research in Computer and Communication Engineering, 4, 92-98.
41. Veetil, S. and Gao, Q. (2014) Real-Time Network Intrusion Detection using Hadoop-Based Bayesian Classifier. In: Akhgar, B. and Arabnia, H.R., Eds., Emerging Trends in ICT Security, Elsevier Inc., 281-299.

https://doi.org/10.1016/B978-0-12-411474-6.00018-9

42. Singh, K., Guntuku, S.C., Thakur, A. and Hota, C. (2014) Big Data Analytics Framework for Peer-to-Peer Botnet Detection using Random Forests. Information Sciences, 278, 488-497. https://doi.org/10.1016/j.ins.2014.03.066
43. Jia, B., Ma, Y., Huang, X., Lin, Z. and Sun, Y. (2016) A Novel Real-Time DDoS Attack Detection Mechanism Based on MDRA Algorithm in Big Data. Mathematical Problems in Engineering, 2016, Article ID: 1467051. https://doi.org/10.1155/2016/1467051
44. Jin, W. and Yu, Z. (2016) The Analysis of Information System Security Issue Based on Economics. International Conference on Information Engineering and Communications Technology, Kunming, 21-22 2016. https://doi.org/10.12783/dtetr/iect2016/3801
45. Prasad, K.M., Reddy, R.A. and Rao, K.V. (2014) DoS and DDoS Attacks: Defense, Detection and Traceback Mechanisms—A Survey. Global Journal of Computer Science and Technology: E Network Web & Security, 14, 16-32.

CHAPTER 4

Generation of Labelled Datasets to Quantify the Impact of Security Threats to Cloud Data Centers

Sai Kiran Mukkavilli, Sachin Shetty, Liang Hong

Department of Electrical & Computer Engineering, Tennessee State University, Nashville, TN, USA

ABSTRACT

Anomaly based approaches in network intrusion detection suffer from evaluation, comparison and deployment which originate from the scarcity of adequate publicly available network trace datasets. Also, publicly available datasets are either outdated or generated in a controlled environment. Due to the ubiquity of cloud computing environments in commercial

Citation: Mukkavilli, S. , Shetty, S. and Hong, L. (2016), "Generation of Labelled Datasets to Quantify the Impact of Security Threats to Cloud Data Centers". *Journal of Information Security*, **7**, 172-184. doi: 10.4236/jis.2016.73013.

and government internet services, there is a need to assess the impacts of network attacks in cloud data centers. To the best of our knowledge, there is no publicly available dataset which captures the normal and anomalous network traces in the interactions between cloud users and cloud data centers. In this paper, we present an experimental platform designed to represent a practical interaction between cloud users and cloud services and collect network traces resulting from this interaction to conduct anomaly detection. We use Amazon web services (AWS) platform for conducting our experiments.

Keywords: Amazon Web Services, Anomaly Detection, Cloud Computing, Datasets, Intrusion Detection, Network Traces

INTRODUCTION

Intrusion detection is a very interesting topic among the researchers. In particular, anomaly detection is of high interest since it helps in detecting many novel attacks. However, there has not been a proper application of this system in the real world due to the complexity of these systems, as these require continuous testing and evaluation and proper tuning prior to deployment [1] . The most ideal methodology for running these systems is to train them with real labeled network traces which consist of comprehensive set of intrusions and abnormal behavior. Anomaly-based network intrusion detection systems (IDS) model patterns of normal activity and detect novel network attacks [2] [3] . However, these systems depend on the availability of normal profile pattern. But these patterns can change over a period of time due to various changes [2] [3] . This is a major challenge in itself as the availability of such datasets is very rare and the systems have to depend on one or more available datasets which lack understanding as they are heavily anonymized.

Another challenge is the comparison of IDS systems against one another. The lack of appropriate public dataset severely affects the evaluation of IDSs mainly affecting anomaly based detectors. Many existing datasets (KDD & DARPA etc.) [4] - [6] are static making them obsolete, unmodifiable, and irreproducible, despite being used widely. As with any other emerging internet technology, security is a major challenge for clouds especially for the migrating organizational data. These security risks can be well understood if we have access to the network traces in the cloud. To the best of our knowledge; there is no publicly available dataset which captures the normal and anomalous network traces in the interactions between cloud users and cloud data centers. Due to the ubiquity of cloud computing environments in commercial and government internet services; there is a need to assess the impacts of network attacks in cloud data centers. A systematic approach has been devised to design and develop an experimental platform designed to represent a practical interaction between cloud users and cloud services and collect network traffic traces resulting from this interaction to conduct anomaly detection. These network traces from the cloud are readily sharable and can be interchanged among collaborators and researchers without major privacy issues. This work has been geared towards reaching the aforementioned vision. This paper is organized as follows: Section 2 provides an insight into the related work; Section 3 emphasizes on cloud datacenter and its services; Section 4 & 5 talk about the execution and collection of normal and attack traces in detail; Section 6 emphasizes on ethics when performing experiments. And the paper concludes in Section 7 with details on future work and improvements to the dataset.

RELATED WORK

Cloud security issues have recently gained traction in the research community where the focus has primarily been on protecting servers on cloud providers (securing the low level operating systems or virtual machine implementations). Unsecured cloud servers have been proven to be crippled with novel denial-of-service attacks. Most existing work on network traffic generation has not focused on applicability in the area of network security and evaluation of anomaly based techniques. The authors in Sommer and Paxson [7] have made observations on anomaly based network intrusion detection mechanisms and have provided recommendations to further improve research in this field [7] . They indicate that in order to improve the intrusion detection systems, datasets play a crucial role to know the system behavior. They also acknowledge that to obtain these datasets is very difficult and to do so it must be done with some collaboration with network operators. We have tried to implement the same in our work.

DHS Predict is a distributed repository of many hosts and providers at major universities and other institutions. Datasets mainly include Domain Name System (DNS) data, Internet Traffic Flow, Border Gateway Protocol (BGP), Internet Topology Data, Intrusion Detection System (IDS) and Firewall Data, and Botnet Behavior. Access to this dataset is available to certain verified accounts at some locations. Despite the major contributions by DARPA (Lincoln laboratory) [6] and KDD (UC Irvine) [4] datasets, they have not been able to reproduce the real world scenarios which is criticized in

McHugh (2000) [8] and Brown et al. (2009) [9] . All these datasets are static making them obsolete, unmodifiable, and irreproducible, despite being used widely. Also the authors of the ISCX (2011) [10] dataset suggest a dynamic approach for generating the dataset, but this does not reflect the real world scenarios as the target servers they use are within the lab under the human assistance. Also, not much research has been done on the implication of vulnerabilities on the datacenter connecting the cloud user. In order to do so, datasets play a key role in demonstrating how well a system behaves. To the best of our knowledge, there is no publicly available dataset which captures the normal and anomalous network traces in the interactions between cloud users and cloud data centers. The systematic approach in this work addresses the flaws in the ISCX [10] dataset for generating a dataset dynamically and also shows the need for addressing the security issues in the cloud.

OVERVIEW OF CLOUD DATA CENTER & DATA-CENTER SERVICES

Cloud computing is a general term for anything that involves delivering hosted services over the Internet. It is a nascent technology. These services are broadly divided into three categories: Infrastructure-as-a-Service (IaaS), Platform-as-a-Service (PaaS) and Software-as-a-Service (SaaS). Supplying all those services at that scale requires can be achieved by expanding the hardware which makes up the datacenter. These services are delivered in various means (like private, public or hybrid cloud) by the cloud service providers (CSP) [11] - [16] . Examples include Amazon, Google, and Microsoft as shown in Table 1. A datacenter is usually a house of computers, and other components such as storage and network systems with other environmental supplies, backup power supplies and other security devices. Cloud Data centers are generally very huge, almost the size of multiple football fields (like Microsoft Azure datacenter). And maintaining them is a big issue too which costs millions of dollars [17] . So many companies lease space in large coalition facilities. Also many cloud regions are actually comprised of two or more distinct data centers (such as AWS in Sydney) [17] .

Amazon Datacenters

AWS is located in 9 geographical regions : US East (Northern Virginia), US West (Northern California), US West (Oregon), AWS GovCloud (US) Region, Sao Paulo (Brazil), Ireland, Singapore, Tokyo and Sydney [17] as shown in Figure 1 [18] . There is a dedicated GovCloud region located at Oregon, USA for US Government customers. All the data and the services stay within a designated region. When the user launches an instance the user can select an Availability zone or it is provided to him by Amazon. In order to prevent power outages within the zones they are isolated from each other. Our rented instances are located in the US-East (Northern Virginia) Region. We have chosen Amazon over other cloud providers for several reasons since Amazon's carriers (routers) security risks are lower compared to other carriers like Microsoft Azure [19] . Also Amazon has better pricing scheme (le carte pricing), where the users pay for what they use. There is couple of other benefits such as deployment speed, flexibility & performance.

Amazon Web Services (AWS)

Amazon web services (AWS) is an evolving and comprehensive cloud computing platform provided by Amazon.com. The first AWS was launched in 2006 to provide online services for websites. Sometimes web services are also known as remote or cloud services. AWS is distributed geographically into regions to ensure robustness and minimize the outages impact. The AWS offers many services like cloud drive, cloud search etc. [18] . These regions have central hubs located at Eastern USA, Western USA (two locations) Ireland, Australia, Singapore, Japan, and Brazil. Each region is divided into availability zones. Users of Amazon Web Services range from individual users (like students, professors etc.) to University research groups and small startup companies to large corporate businesses like Dropbox, Netflix. Etc. One of the main users of Amazon web service is the popular online storage service Dropbox which uses the IAAS (Infrastructure as a service) of the AWS. Once a file is added to Dropbox the file is transferred to Amazon S3 after encryption to various datacenters across USA. Similarly the download process is also the same. All AWS offerings are billed according to usage from service to service.

Table 1. Table showing cloud datacenter locations of Amazon, Google, Microsoft.

PROVIDER	REGION & SUBREGION
AWS US	US East (N Virginia)
AWS US	US West (N California)
AWS US	US West (Oregon)
AWS	GovCloud (Oregon)
AWS	South America (Sao Paulo)

AWS	EU (Ireland)
AWS	Asia Pacific (Singapore)
AWS	Asia Pacific (Tokyo)
AWS	Asia Pacific (Sydney)
Google	Central US (Council Bluffs, IA)
Google	Central US (Pryor Creek, OK)
Google	Europe (Europe)
Microsoft	Azure North-central US (Chicago, IL)
Microsoft	Azure South-central US (San Antonio, TX)
Microsoft	Azure West US (California)
Microsoft	Azure East US (Boydton, Virginia)
Microsoft	Azure East Asia (Hong Kong, China)
Microsoft	Azure South East Asia (Singapore)
Microsoft	Azure Northern Europe (Dublin, Ireland)
Microsoft	Azure West Europe (Amsterdam, Netherlands)

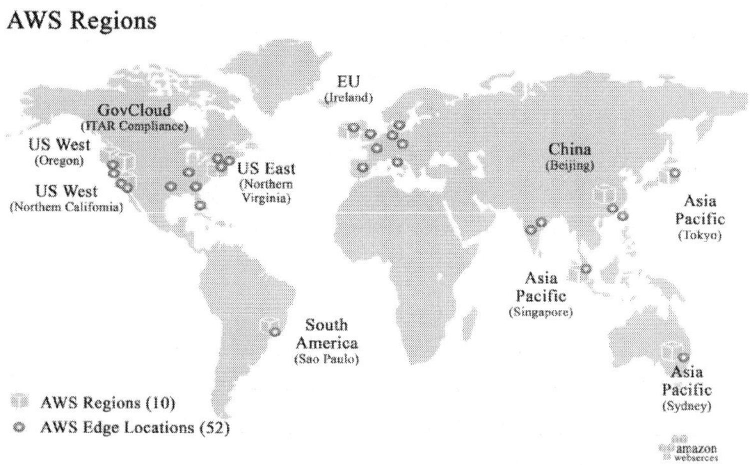

Figure 1. Map showing the location of Amazon cloud datacenters.

Cloud Users

Users access cloud computing using networked client devices, such as smartphones, desktop computers, laptops, tablets. The users are classified into two categories: Mobile cloud user's & Stationary cloud users. Mobile cloud users are the clients with access to mobile devices like smartphone, tablet etc. which use the resources of the cloud provider. Stationary users are the ones like desktop computers for accessing the cloud and also for performing research related to it. There are two main examples of stationary cloud users that are used for the research: PlanetLab, EmuLab. For our experiments we use PlanetLab nodes which mimic stationary cloud users. PlanetLab is a group of computers available as a test bed for computer networking and distributed systems research. PlanetLab is a great tool for performing large-scale Internet studies. Its power lies in that it runs over the common routes of the Internet and spans nodes across the world, making it far more realistic than a simulation. PlanetLab nodes utilize virtualization software, allowing applications to have full access to the system kernel [20] .

Network Traffic Datasets

During the last decade, anomaly detection has attracted the attention of many researchers to overcome the weakness of signature-based IDSs in detecting novel attacks. There are often limitations to test and evaluate a novel network concept/solution on a real network. Hence, most researchers rely on captured network traffic data to evaluate the performance of their proposed network concept/solution. Also there is a scarce commodity among network research community for a real network traffic dataset. Various network problems have been analyzed, evaluated & validated based on captured network traffic. Hence it is important to maintain the completeness and quality of the network traffic dataset. There are many examples of network datasets like KDD CUP-99 [4] , DARPA [6] , and LBNL [21] etc.

Signature Based IDS

Intrusion detection systems (IDS) are classified into Anomaly based & Signature based. Signature based detection involves searching the traces (packets & bytes) for malicious traffic. The advantage of this technique is that if you know the network behavior you are trying to identify it is easy to develop and understand the signatures.

GENERATION OF NORMAL CLOUD TRACES

One of the highest priorities of this work is to generate realistic background traffic. The main concern is to accurately reproduce the quantity and time distribution of flows for HTTP protocol (since majority of the traffic using the web is based on HTTP). To achieve this we have generated series of time instances which send web requests from the planet lab nodes to the EC2 server as shown in Figure 2. Table 2 shows the nodes that are used to generate the requests. Each node has JDK installed in it which runs the java script for the requests.

To model HTTP requests, several approaches are available. The majority of work in literature is based on well-known statistical distributions. These probability distributions are analytically well described and have the advantage of being compact and easy to evaluate. We have generated series of random time instances using mean (μ) and standard deviation (σ) which follow both normal and uniform distributions separately. These are used to generate series of web requests from the Planet Lab nodes to the EC2 server. Algorithm 1 explains in detail the mechanism for generating the web requests from normal nodes.

The algorithm (Algorithm 1) is executed in the PlanetLab nodes which are used as the clients for generating the web requests. For our experiments we chose 4 nodes for generating normal instances. Initially the start time (t{1}) of the node is calculated and then a time sequence (t) is read from the file. Then the thread is made to sleep for some time and then again the current system time (t{2}) is calculated.

The time difference (d) between current time (t{2}) and start time (t{1}) is calculated. Then the difference (d) is compared with the time sequence (t). If (d) is more than (t), this is the time to start the web request (t{3}). The node generates a request to the EC2 server to which the server responds. There is a TCP Handshake taking place between the node and the server. Then the file is downloaded onto the node. The end time (t{4}) is calculated after the web request response is completed.

The web response time (WRT) is the difference between the end time (t{4}) and start time (t{3}).

In this way WRT is calculated for one sequence. If (d) is less than (t) then the new time sequence is read from the file. Figure 2 shows the time instances generated using the normal distribution. These time instances are generated with a mean of 2.0216 and standard deviation of 0.3423. Similarly we generate time instances based on uniform distribution with a mean of 3.9209 and Standard deviation of 2.3446. The entire traffic is captured using the WIRESHARK running on the EC2 server.

GENERATION OF ATTACK CLOUD TRACES

Since the proposed dataset is intended for network security and intrusion detection purposes [8] , it would not be complete without a diverse set of attack scenarios. Attack traffic represents an attack scenario in an unambiguous manner.

Table 2. PlanetLab nodes for generating normal traces.

PlanetLab Nodes IP Address
pl2.eecs.utk.edu 160.36.57.173
plil-pa-6.hpl.hp.com204.123.28.57
planetlab2.unl.edu129.93.229.139
planetlab2.cesnet.cz195.113.161.83

Algorithm 1: HTTP wget request logic

```
begin:
Get current system time t1
t ← Get time instance from the file
thread.sleep()
Get current system time t2
while t.hasnext() do
    index i ← 0
    diff of time d ← t2-t1
    if d>t then
        time t3← start the wed request
        wget file from EC2
        time t4 ←end the web request
        Web Response time d ← t4-t3
    else
        thread.sleep()
    end if
end while
```

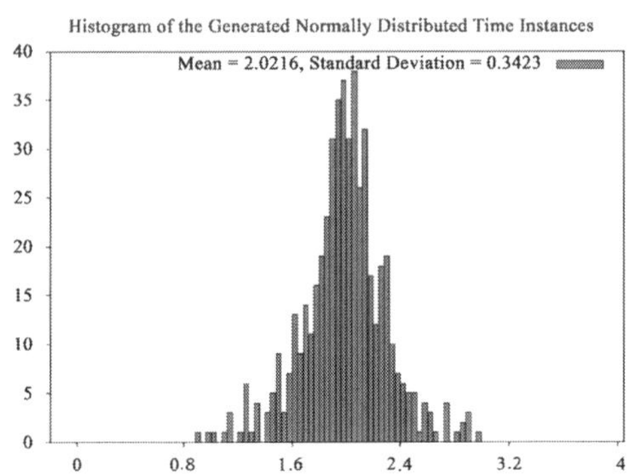

Figure 2. Time Instances based on normal distribution.

In the simplest case humans can carry out these attacks, and in the ideal case the autonomous agents can be used along with the compilers to carry out these attacks. Today, cloud computing systems are providing a wide variety of services and interfaces to the customers. There are various threats to these services which are explained in this paper. Our aim here is to mimic the actions of malicious hackers by performing multi-stage attack scenarios, each carefully crafted toward achieving a predefined set of goals [1]. The following are the common attacks that take place in the network. Denial-of-Service attack, Man-in-the-Middle Attack, Sniffer Attack, Portscan Application-Layer Attack etc. Out of these attacks we use the following three for the attacks in the cloud and for capturing traffic since these attacks deal with the Application layer protocols in the cloud and these best describe them and in capturing traffic.

- DDoS (Distributed denial of service)
- Man-in-the-Middle attack or ARP spoof
- Portscan

DDoS in Cloud

Distributed denial of service (DDoS) is an attack which many nodes systems attack one node all at the same time with a flood of messages. A distributed denial-of-service (DDoS) attack is one in which a multitude of compromised systems attack a single target, thereby causing denial of service for users of the targeted system [22] [23] . There are two types of DDoS attacks: a network-centric attack which overloads a service by using up bandwidth and an application-layer attack which overloads a service or database with application calls. For our experiments we use H-DOS in which we exploit seemingly-legitimate HTTP GET or POST requests to attack a web server. On July 17th 2013 a Distributed Denial-of-Service attack crippled the servers at hosting services firm Network Solutions, disrupting thousands of websites for several hours. DDoS attackers overwhelm servers by flooding a company's pipeline with unwanted network packets. Herndon, Va.-based Network Solutions, which manages more than 6 million domains, said on Facebook that its network security team was forced to respond to the attack. The outage is one of at least a dozen outages at cloud hosting providers impacting users in 2013. DDoS attacks are a common occurrence at hosting providers, e-commerce businesses and financial institutions [24] . In June, Network Solutions had its DNS servers hijacked and reconfigured to a malicious website after it botched efforts to thwart a DDoS attack.

Testbed Network Architecture for DDoS

The testbed network architecture for DDoS as shown in Figure 3 consists of 8 PlanetLab nodes which are distributed globally but are interconnected. They are loaded with fedora operating systems. Out of these few nodes are used to launch the attacks and few to generate normal traces. To perform the experiments we have rented an Amazon EC2 instance with Windows server 2008 as the operating system. Amazon provides various instances which vary based on price, performance etc. There are various kinds like General, Compute, Memory, Storage & GPU. Out of this we have selected the General category. In the general category we chose t1.micro for our experiments. T1 Micro instances (t1.micro) provide a small amount of consistent CPU resources and allow you to increase CPU capacity in short burst when additional cycles are available. They are well suited for lower throughput applications and websites that require additional compute cycles periodically [18] .

The rented instance is located in US-east region. The instance has the following configuration: Processor: Intel(R) Xeon(R) CPU E5430 @ 2.66 GHz RAM: 595 MB Cache: 6MB Address sizes: 38 bits physical, 48 bits virtual. Operating System: Windows Server 2008. The instance was launched and then an Apache Server 2.0 was setup to host our website. The website has a public IP of 72.44.46.206. We install and launch WIRESHARK in the same instance for capturing and storing the network traces. These traces are then moved to another system for monitoring and intrusion detection. The PlanetLab nodes used for the attack are shown in the Table 3 and for generating normal traces are shown in Table 2.

Security Groups in EC2

When launching an Amazon EC2 instance we need to specify its security group. The security group acts as a firewall allowing us to choose which protocols and ports are open to computers over the internet. We can choose to use the default security group and then customize it, or can create our own security group.

Configuring a security group can be done with code or using the Amazon EC2 management console [25] [26] .

The default security group allows all the incoming traffic and leaves most of the ports open. In order to make the experiment more realistic we have customized the security group in the following way. We have allowed the following protocols from the following ports as shown in Table 4.

SSH was used so that remote hosts could communicate with the EC2 server, HTTP was used for the website to be accessible; RDP was used so that the server could be launched from our system, DNS so that the server could be accessed with a DNS. All the other protocols were blocked.

Load Balancing & Round-Robin DNS in EC2

Load balancing is when the processes and communications are distributed evenly across a network. When it's difficult to predict the number of requests that will be issued to a server we use load balancing. Busy Web sites typically employ more than one web server in a load balancing scheme. If one server is full of requests, the requests are forwarded to another server with more capacity [27] .

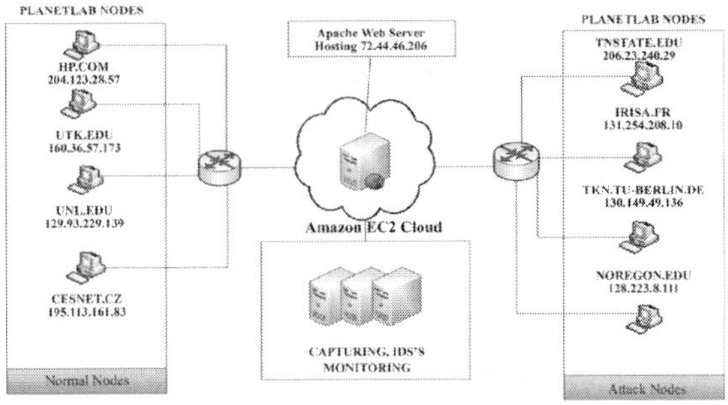

Figure 3. Testbed network architecture for DDoS [5.2].

Table 3. PlanetLab nodes for generating attack traces.

PlanetLab Nodes IP Address
peeramide.irisa.fr 131.254.208.10
planetlab01.tkn.tu-berlin.de 130.149.49.136
planetlab2.tsuniv.edu 206.23.240.29
planetlab1.cs.uoregon.edu 195.113.161.83

Table 4. Protocols allowed to communicate through EC2.

Protocols	Port
SSH	22
HTTP	80
RDP	3389
DNS	53

We use a popular tool available online 'lbd.sh' [28] to determine whether the web server is load balanced or not. Lbd (load balancing detector) detects if a given domain uses DNS and/or HTTP Load-Balancing (via Server: and Date: headers and differences between server answers). After running the script on EC2, it was shown that EC2 does load balancing. Also we have tested whether the EC2 uses the Round robin DNS scheme, wherein the server has one domain name but multiple IP addresses. After testing it was found that the EC2 has only one IP linked to one domain name.

Implementing DDOS on EC2

This attack is designed toward performing a stealthy, low bandwidth distributed denial of service attack without flooding the network. We will be using "slowloris" [29] as the main tool in this scenario as it has proven to make web servers completely inaccessible using a single machine. The slowloris starts by making a full TCP connection to the remote server. The connection is held open by the tool by sending valid & incomplete requests to the server at the regular intervals to keep the socket from closing. Since the web server capacity is limited, in a certain amount of time all the sockets are used up and no other connection is made. We start the attack by deploying the "slowloris" script in the attack nodes. The attack is planned in such a way that all the machines start the attack within the same time window with a minimum lag. The attack nodes start running the script with each script sending 110 numbers of requests and with a "tcpto" 5 to port 80 of the EC2 server. The attack takes place at random intervals while the normal behavior (traffic) keeps on running continuously. The attack is a stealthy one since the magnitude and the frequency of requests are made to look similar to the normal behavior.

The attack slowly overwhelms the server thereby bringing down the service completely. When the attack stops the server starts automatically again. Figure 4 & Figure 5 show the attack and normal behavior of the network traces following different distributions. The traffic is captured using the wireshark on the EC2 and then is moved to another system for monitoring and IDS (Intrusion detection system).

ARP Spoofing in EC2

ARP spoofing is a technique where spoofed messages are sent by the attacker into the LAN (Local area network). The attacker machine sits anonymized in between the host and the gateway and captures the traffic both ways. The technique it uses for capturing the traffic is IP forwarding. Many of today's networks are built on what is called the eggshell principle: hard on outside and soft on the inside. This means that if an attacker gains access to a host on the inside, she can then use the compromised host as a pivot to attack systems not previously accessible via the Internet such as a local intranet server or a domain controller. In our case we host two machines in the same virtual private cloud (VPC) in Amazon EC2, one machine acts as host and the second machine will be the attacker. The attacker machine will capture the traffic between the host and the gateway as shown in the Figure 6.

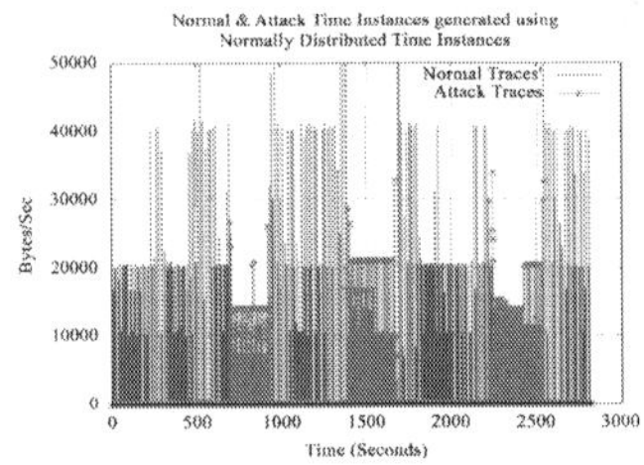

Figure 4. Network traces generated using normal time instances.

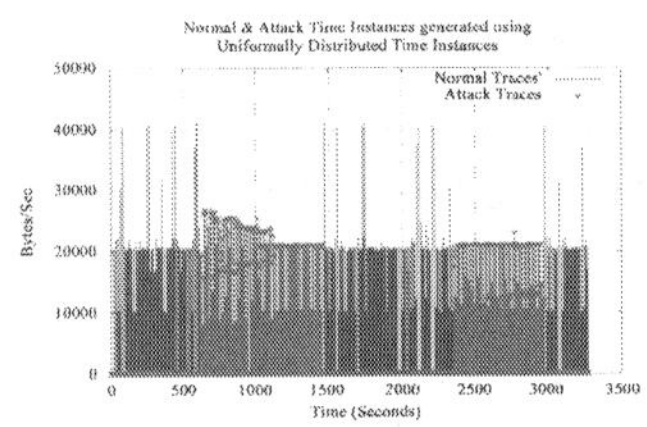

Figure 5. Network traces generated using uniform time instances.

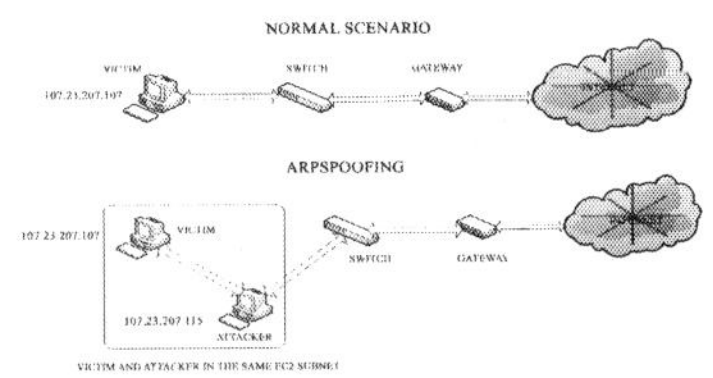

Figure 6. ARP spoofing in EC2.

For this experiment we consider the following: Two Windows 2008 server EC2 instances in the same subnet, Wire-shark, Ettercap-NG. We rent two instances with following configuration as shown in Table 5. The two instances are selected such that both are in the same subnet. For this experiment we first collect the traffic normally (in the absence of attacker) using wireshark. Then the well-known Spoofing software ETTERCAP-NG is installed in the attacker machine which listens to all the traffic between the victim machine and the gateway. Ettercap works by putting the network interface into promiscuous mode and by ARP poisoning the target machines. Thereby it can act as a "man in the middle" and unleash various attacks on the victims. For our experiment we have visited few websites like Facebook, Gmail etc. when the attacker is not present and again revisited the same websites in the presence of attacker. After collecting the traffic in both the attack and normal scenarios we convert it into user readable format (.arff) using tshark and then select the feature which best differentiates the normal and attack traffic. We have sorted the following feature from the list of features available "tcp.analysis.ack_rtt". This feature represents the round trip time. Figure 7 shows the difference between attack & normal traces using the above feature.

Port Scanning in EC2

Port scanning is a technique where the open ports of a server or website are probed. It is used by attackers as a means to compromise the services running on a system. We use Nmap which helps us in providing the open ports and the services running on the server. For our experiment we use Nmap to detect open ports and also any other operating system vulnerabilities by launching stealth attack as shown in Figure 8.

Table 5. Description of rented EC2 instances for ARP spoof attack.

Operating System	IP Address	Type
Windows Server 2008	IP:107.23.207.107	Victim
Windows Server 2008	IP:107.23.207.115	Attacker

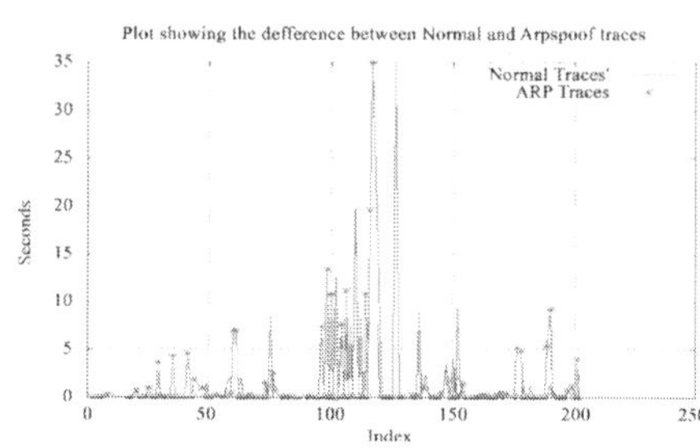

Figure 7. Difference between normal and ARP spoof traffic from same Planet-Lab nodes.

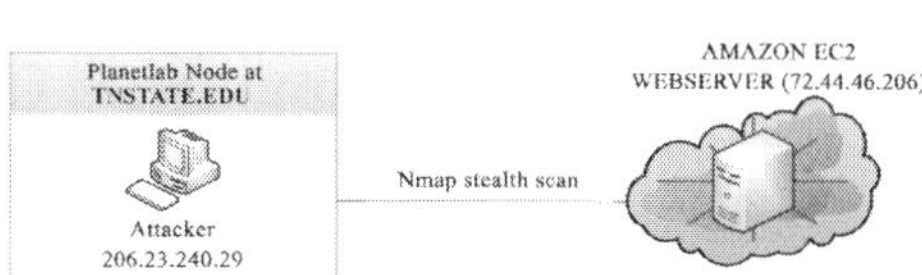

Figure 8. Portscanning using Nmap.

root@saikiran:~#sudo nmap -v -O --osscan-guess 72.44.46.206

Starting Nmap 4.52 (http://insecure.org) at 2014-11-01 18:10 UTC

Initiating Ping Scan at 18:10

Scanning 72.44.46.206 [2 ports]

Completed Ping Scan at 18:10, 0.07 s elapsed (1 total hosts)

Initiating Parallel DNS resolution of 1 host. at 18:10

Completed Parallel DNS resolution of 1 host. at 18:10, 0.08 s elapsed

Initiating SYN Stealth Scan at 18:10

Scanning ec2-72-44-46-206.compute-1.amazonaws.com (72.44.46.206) [1714 ports]

Discovered open port 3389/tcp on 72.44.46.206

Discovered open port 80/tcp on 72.44.46.206

Completed SYN Stealth Scan at 18:10, 34.46 s elapsed (1714 total ports)

Initiating OS detection (try #1) against ec2-72-44-46-206.compute-1.amazonaws.com (72.44.46.206)

Retrying OS detection (try #2) against ec2-72-44-46-206.compute-1.amazonaws.com (72.44.46.206)

Host ec2-72-44-46-206.compute-1.amazonaws.com (72.44.46.206) appears to be up ... good.

Interesting ports on ec2-72-44-46-206.compute-1.amazonaws.com (72.44.46.206):

Not shown: 1700 filtered ports

PORT STATE SERVICE

80/tcp open http

3389/tcp open ms-term-serv

6000/tcp closed X11

6001/tcp closed X11:1

6002/tcp closed X11:2

6003/tcp closed X11:3

6004/tcp closed X11:4

6005/tcp closed X11:5

6006/tcp closed X11:6

6007/tcp closed X11:7

6008/tcp closed X11:8

6009/tcp closed X11:9

6017/tcp closed xmail-ctrl

6050/tcp closed arcserve

Device type: general purpose

Running (JUST GUESSING): Microsoft Windows Vista|2008 (98%)

Aggressive OS guesses: Microsoft Windows Vista (98%), Microsoft Windows Server 2008 Beta 3 (96%), Microsoft Windows Vista Home Basic (91%)

No exact OS matches for host (test conditions non-ideal).

Uptime: 61.417 days (since Mon Sep 1 08:10:23 2014)

TCP Sequence Prediction: Difficulty = 262 (Good luck!)

IP ID Sequence Generation: Incremental

OS detection performed.

Nmap done: 1 IP address (1 host up) scanned in 38.886 seconds

Raw packets sent: 5194 (232.752 KB) | Rcvd: 36 (2092 B)

For the purposes of proper scanning and pinging we had to allow ICMP traffic through EC2. We had allowed this rule in the EC2 security groups. The first session is initiated from the PlanetLab node. Nmap is launched at the "tsuniv.edu" (206.23.240.29) PlanetLab node. It launches a stealth scan on the EC2 server which gives an approximation of the operating system and the number of open ports as shown above. The traffic is captured using the wireshark software [30] .

ETHICAL CONSIDERATION

Our experiments to implement the framework for generation and collection of network traces involve real world instances and systems. This usually raises an ethical debate as scanning remote network devices can sometimes lead to adverse attacks. At the same time, developing a robust framework for network traces without collecting data from the real world is very difficult. Simulation tools and performing experiments with a controlled lab environment cannot replicate the randomness of the real world network traffic. A recent journal article that discusses the ethics of security vulnerability research [31] , states that this type of zealous vulnerability research serves important social functions. Amazon EC2 provides students and researchers instances (Penetration Testing) that can be used for performing the experiments which involve attacks. For this the user has to get the permission from AWS before conducting any tests [32] . This approach is neither illegal nor unethical under the US laws. While accessing the instances to collect the vulnerability information we have taken utmost care not to disturb the host functions. We used minimum external resources to accurately collect the traces. The target networks in/24 blocks were scanned in a non-sequential order so that no organization is overwhelmed with our attacks. Also we did not scan any router or instance unnecessarily.

CONCLUSION & FUTURE WORK

Cloud computing offers many services to their clients including software, infrastructure etc., but they pose significant security risks to customer applications and data beyond what is expected using traditional on-premises architecture. These security risks can be well understood if we have access to the network traces in the cloud. Most of the network trace datasets are proprietary and cannot be shared due to privacy reasons; others are heavily anonymized and do not reflect current trends and lack certain statistical properties. Also, publicly available datasets are either outdated or generated in a controlled environment [1] . To the best of our knowledge; there is no publicly available dataset which captures the normal and anomalous network traces in the interactions between cloud users and cloud data centers.Due to the ubiquity of cloud computing environments in commercial and government internet services, there is a need to assess the impacts of network attacks in cloud data centers. We present a systematic approach to design and develop an experimental platform designed to represent a practical interaction between cloud users and cloud services and collect network traffic traces resulting from this interaction to conduct anomaly detection. Our results show statistical differences between normal and anomalous network traffic traces which can be exploited by anomaly detection systems to detect and isolate adversaries in the cloud data centers. In future, we plan to implement the captured traffic on the IDS (Intrusion Detection Systems) for better understanding of anomalies and also to reduce the false positives.

ACKNOWLEDGEMENTS

This work was partially supported by Department of Homeland Security (DHS) SLA grant 2014-ST-062- 000059 and Office of the Assistant Secretary of Defense for Research and Engineering (OASD(R&E)) under agreement number FAB750-15-2-0120.

REFERENCES

1. Shiravi, A., Shiravi, H., Tavallaee, M. and Ghorbani, A.A. (2012) Toward Developing a Systematic Approach to Generate Benchmark Datasets for Intrusion Detection. Computers & Security, 31.3, 357-374. http://dx.doi.org/10.1016/j.cose.2011.12.012
2. Mukkavilli, S.K., Shetty, S. and Hong, L. (2012) Mining Concept Drifting Network Traffic in Cloud Computing Environments. IEEE/ACM CCGRID, Ottawa, 13-16 May 2012, 721-722.
3. Shetty, S., Mukkavilli, S.K. and Keel, L.H. (2011) An Integrated Machine Learning and Control Theoretic Model for Mining Concept Drifting Data Streams. IEEE HST, Waltham, 15-17 November 2011, 75-80. http://dx.doi.org/10.1109/ths.2011.6107850
4. University of California-KDD Cup 1999 Data. http://kdd.ics.uci.edu/databases/kddcup99/kddcup99.html;2011
5. Tavallaee, M., Bagheri, E., Lu, W. and Ghorbani, A.A. (2009) A Detailed Analysis of the KDD CUP 99 Data Set. IEEE CISDA, Ottawa, 8-10 July 2009, 1-6.
6. MIT Lincoln Lab DARPA Data. http://www.ll.mit.edu/mission/communications/ist/corpora/ideval/index.html;2011
7. Sommer, R. and Paxson, V. (2010) Outside the Closed World: On Using Machine Learning for Network Intrusion Detection. IEEE Symposium on Security & Privacy, Oakland, 16-19 May 2010, 305-316.
8. McHugh, J. (2000) Testing Intrusion Detection Systems: A Critique of the 1998 and 1999 DARPA Intrusion Detection System Evaluations as Performed by Lincoln Laboratory. ACM Trans on Information System Security, 3, 264-294. http://dx.doi.org/10.1145/382912.382923
9. Brown, C., Cowperthwaite, A., Hijazi, A. and Somayaji, A. (2009) Analysis of the 1999 DARPA/Lincoln Laboratory IDS Evaluation Data with Netadhict. IEEE International Conference on Computational Intelligence for Security and Defense Applications, Ottawa, 8-10 July 2009, 1-7.
10. ISCX Datasets. http://www.unb.ca/research/iscx/dataset/iscx-IDS-dataset.html
11. Cloud vs. Traditional Data Center. http://www.businessnewsdaily.com/4982-cloud-vs-data-center.html
12. Classification of Data Center. http://www.datacenterknowledge.com/archives/2013/11/01/a-public-private-or-hybrid-cloud-debate-not-

really/

13. Data Center Types. http://research.gigaom.com/2012/10/4-types-of-data-centers/
14. CAIDA Data Centers. http://www.caida.org/
15. Cloud Platform. http://mindstormtools.com/2014/02/16/amazon-web-services-aws-and-the-new-google-cloud-platform/
16. Cloud Intrusion. http://www.di.unipi.it/~hkholidy/projects/cidd/
17. AWS Data Centers. http://www.turnkeylinux.org/blog/aws-datacenters
18. Amazon AWS Instances. https://aws.amazon.com/ec2/instance-types/
19. Reddy, S., Shetty, S. and Xiong, K. (2013) Security Risk Assessment of Cloud Carrier. 2013 13th IEEE/ACM International Symposium on Cluster, Cloud and Grid Computing (CCGrid), Delft, 13-16 May 2013, 442-449.
20. PlanetLab Nodes. http://www.planet-lab.org/status
21. LBNL-The Internet Traffic Archive. http://www.icir.org/enterprise-tracing/download.html
22. Specht, S.M. and Lee, R.B. (2004) Distributed Denial of Service: Taxonomies of Attacks, Tools and Countermeasures. Proceedings of 17th International Conference on Parallel and Distributed Computing Systems, San Francisco, 15-17 September 2004, 543-550.
23. Distributed Attack. http://searchsecurity.techtarget.com/definition/distributed-denial-of-service-attack
24. DDOS Attack. http://www.crn.com/news/security/240158492/ddos-attack-behind-latest-network-solutions-outage.htm
25. EC2 Instances. http://aws.amazon.com/ec2/
26. EC2 Security Groups. http://blog.learningtree.com/understanding-amazon-ec2-security-groups-and-firewalls/
27. Load Balancing. http://www.webopedia.com/TERM/L/load_balancing.html
28. Load Balancing Tool. https://packetstormsecurity.com/files/46871/lbd-0.1.sh.txt.html
29. Slowloris Tool. https://github.com/gkbrk/slowloris
30. Wireshark Tool. https://www.wireshark.org/
31. Benson, T., Akella, A. and Maltz, D.A. (2010) Network Traffic Characteristics of Data Centers in the Wild. Proceedings of the 10th ACM

SIGCOMM Conference on Internet Measurement, Melbourne, 1-3 November 2010, 267-280. http://dx.doi.org/10.1145/1879141.1879175

32. Penetration Testing Security. http://aws.amazon.com/security/penetration-testing/

SECTION 2
FRAMEWORKS FOR CLOUD SECURITY

CHAPTER 5

Towards a Comprehensive Security Framework of Cloud Data Storage Based on Multi Agent System Architecture

Amir Mohamed Talib, Rodziah Atan, Rusli Abdullah, Masrah Azrifah Azmi Murad

Faculty of Computer Science & IT, University Putra Malaysia UPM, Serdang, Malaysia

ABSTRACT

The tremendous growth of the cloud computing environments requires new architecture for security services. Cloud computing is the utilization of many servers/data centers or Cloud Data Storages (CDSs) housed in many different locations and interconnected by high speed networks. CDS,

Citation: A. Mohamed Talib, R. Atan, R. Abdullah and M. Azrifah Azmi Murad, "Towards a Comprehensive Security Framework of Cloud Data Storage Based on Multi Agent System Architecture," *Journal of Information Security*, Vol. 3 No. 4, 2012, pp. 295-306. doi: 10.4236/jis.2012.34036.

like any other emerging technology, is experiencing growing pains. It is immature, it is fragmented and it lacks standardization. Although security issues are delaying its fast adoption, cloud computing is an unstoppable force and we need to provide security mechanisms to ensure its secure adoption. In this paper a comprehensive security framework based on Multi-Agent System (MAS) architecture for CDS to facilitate confidentiality, correctness assurance, availability and integrity of users' data in the cloud is proposed. Our security framework consists of two main layers as agent layer and CDS layer. Our propose MAS architecture includes main five types of agents: Cloud Service Provider Agent (CSPA), Cloud Data Confidentiality Agent (CDConA), Cloud Data Correctness Agent (CDCorA), Cloud Data Availability Agent (CDAA) and Cloud Data Integrity Agent (CDIA). In order to verify our proposed security framework based on MAS architecture, pilot study is conducted using a questionnaire survey.

Rasch Methodology is used to analyze the pilot data. Item reliability is found to be poor and a few respondents and items are identified as misfits with distorted measurements. As a result, some problematic questions are revised and some predictably easy questions are excluded from the questionnaire. A prototype of the system is implemented using Java. To simulate the agents, oracle database packages and triggers are used to implement agent functions and oracle jobs are utilized to create agents.

Keywords: Cloud Computing; Multi-Agent System; Cloud Data Storage; Security Framework; Cloud Service Provider.

INTRODUCTION

Computer in its evolution form has been changed multiple times, as learned from its past events. However, the trend turned from bigger and more expensive, to smaller and more affordable commodity PCs and servers which are tired together to construct something called "cloud computing system". Moreover, cloud has advantages in offering more scalable, fault-tolerant services with even higher performance [1]. Cloud computing can provide infinite computing resources on demand due to its high scalability in nature, which eliminates the needs for cloud service providers to plan far ahead on hardware provisioning [2].

Cloud computing integrates and provides different types of services such as Data-as-a-Service (DaaS), which allows cloud users to store their data at remote disks and access them anytime from any place.

However, Determining data security is harder today, so data security functions have become more critical than they have been in the past [3]. However, there still exist many problems in cloud computing today, a recent research shows that cloud data storage security have become the primary concern for people to shift to cloud computing because the data is stored as well as processing somewhere on to centralized location called "data centers" or CDS. So, the clients have to trust the provider on the availability as well as data security. Even more concerning, though, is the corporations that are jumping to cloud computing while being oblivious to the implications of putting critical applications and data in the cloud. Moving critical applications and sensitive data to a public and shared cloud environment is a major concern for corporations that are moving beyond their data center's network perimeter defense. The problem of verifying correctness, confidentiality, integrity and availability for CDS security becomes even more challenging [4]. CDS systems are expected to meet several rigorous requirements for maintaining users' data and information, including high availability, reliability, performance, replication and data consistency; but because of the conflicting nature of these requirements, no one system implements all of them together. For example, availability, scalability and data consistency can be regarded as three conflicting goals. Security framework is proposed to facilitate the correctness, confidentiality, availability, and integrity of user' data cloud security. Data security on the cloud side is not only focused on the process of data transmission, but also the system security and data protection for those data stored on the storages of the cloud side. From the perspective of data security, which has always been an important aspect of quality of service, cloud computing inevitably poses new challenging security threats for a number of reasons:

- Firstly, cloud computing is not just a third party data warehouse. The data stored in the cloud may be frequently updated by the users, including insertion, deletion, modification, appending, reordering, etc. To facilitate storage correctness under dynamic data update is hence of paramount importance. However, this dynamic feature also makes traditional integrity insurance techniques futile and entails new solutions [4,5].
- Secondly, the deployment of cloud computing is powered by data centers running in a simultaneous, cooperated and distributed manner. Individual user's data is redundantly stored in multiple physical locations to further reduce the data integrity threats [4]. Therefore, distributed protocols for storage correctness assurance

will be of most importance in achieving a robust and secure cloud data storage system in the real world [5].

- Thirdly, CDS systems offer services to assure integrity of data transmission (typically through checksum backup). However, they do not provide a solution to the CDS integrity problem. Thus, the cloud client would have to develop its own solution, such as a backup of the cloud data items, in order to verify that cloud data returned by the CDS server has not been tampered with.
- Finally, there is lack of fine-grained cloud data access control mechanism to security-sensitive cloud resources [6].

To alleviate these concerns, a cloud solution provider must ensure that cloud users can continue to have the same security over their applications and services by providing evidence to these cloud users that their organization and cloud users are secure.

In order to achieve these problems we proposed a comprehensive security framework based on MAS architecture, our security framework has been built using two layers: agent layer and cloud data storage layer. The MAS architecture has five agents: Cloud Service Provider Agent (CSPA), Cloud Data Correctness Agent (CDCorA), Cloud Data Confidentiality Agent (CDConA), Cloud Data Availability Agent (CDAA) and Cloud Data Integrity Agent (CDIA).

The term "agent" is very broad and has different mean ings to different researchers [7-9]. Genesereth et al. [7], has gone so far as to say that software agents are application programs that communicate with each other in an expressive agent communication language.

A multi-agent system (MAS) consists of a number of agents interacting with each other, usually through exchanging messages across a network. The agents in such a system must be able to interact in order to achieve their design objectives, through cooperating, negotiating and coordinating with other agents. The agents may exhibit selfish or benevolent behavior. Selfish agents ask for help from other agents if they are overloaded and never offer help. For example, agents serving VIP (Very Important Person) cloud users for CSP service never help other agents for the same service. Benevolent agents always provide help to other agents because they consider system benefit is the priority. For example, agents serving normal cloud users for CSP service are always ready to help other agents to complete their tasks [6].

- The collaborative CDS environment elements are derived.
- Cloud users and CSPs are considered the main part of this framework, in which they have to make a SLA between them in term of facilitating the services by the CSP and renting these services to the cloud users.
- Agents will act as a tool to facilitate the security policies. The proposed security framework based on MAS architecture is formulated especially to facilitate the confidentiality, correctness assurance, availability and integrity of CDS and consists of four main components: layers, cloud users, CSPs and data flow. The layers consist of the collaboration tools of agents and CDS.

SECURITY FRAMEWORK

Figure 1 shows a schematic representation of security framework. The framework has been built by using two layers.

The functionality of those layers can be summarized as follows [4, 19]:

- Agent layer: This layer has one agent: the User Interface Agent. User Interface Agent acts as an effective bridge between the user and the rest of the agents.
- Cloud data storage layer: Cloud data storage has two different network entities can be identified as follows:
  - Cloud user: Cloud users, who have data to be stored in the cloud and rely on the cloud for data computation, consist of both individual consumers and organizations.
  - Cloud service provider (CSP): A CSP, who has significant resources and expertise in building and managing distributed cloud storage servers, owns and operates live cloud computing systems.

MAS ARCHITECTURE

In MAS architecture, we proposed five types of agents: Cloud Service Provider Agent (CSPA), Cloud Data Confidentiality Agent (CDConA), Cloud Data Correctness Agent (CDCorA), Cloud Data Availability Agent (CDAA) and Cloud Data Integrity Agent (CDIA) as illustrated in Figure 2. The rest of agents are described as follows:

Cloud Service Provider Agent (CSPA)

Is the users' intelligent interface to the system and allow the cloud users to interact with the security service environment. The CSPA provides graphical interfaces to the cloud user for interactions between the system and the cloud user. CSPA act in the system under the behavior of CSP. CSPA has the following actions [6,19]:

- Provide the security service task according to the authorized service level agreements (SLAs) and the original message content sent by the CDCorA, CDConA, CDAA and CDIA.

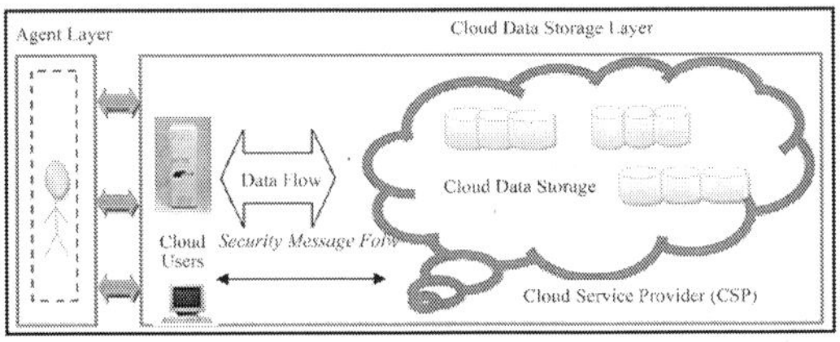

Figure 1. Proposed security framework.

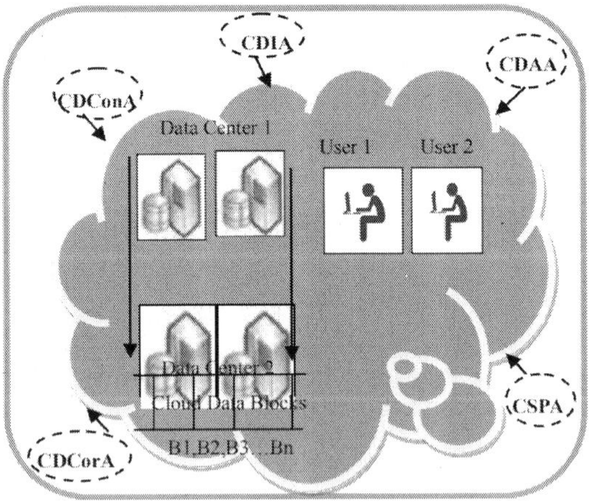

Figure 2. Proposed MAS architecture.

- Display the security policies specified by CSP and the rest of the agents.
- Designing user interfaces that prevent the input of invalid cloud data.
- Receive the security reports and/or alarms from the rest of other agents to respect.

- Translate the attack in terms of goals.
- Monitor specific activities concerning a part of the CDS or a particular cloud user.
- Creating security reports/alarm systems.

Cloud Data Confidentiality Agent (CDConA)

This agent facilitates the security policy of confidentiality for CDS. Main responsibility of this agent is to provide a CDS by new access control rather than the existing access control lists of identification, authorization and authentication. This agent provides a CSP to define and enforce expressive and flexible access structure for each cloud user [6]. Specifically, the access structure of each cloud user is defined as a logic formula over cloud data file attributes, and is able to represent any desired cloud data file set. This new access control is called as:

- Formula-based cloud data access control (FCDAC). This agent is also notifies CSPA in case of any fail caused of the techniques above by sending security reports and/or alarms.

Formula-Based Cloud Data Access Control (FCDAC) and also named as a SecureFormula it's an access policy determined by our MAS architecture, not by the CSPs.

It's also define as access is granted not based on the rights of the subject associated with a cloud user after authentication, but based on attributes of the cloud user. In our system, CDConA provide access structure of each cloud user by defining it as a logic formula over cloud data file attribute. SecureFormula is an additional confidentiality layer used by our system to verify that the cloud users' login page is a genuine.

If you are a cloud user, you are required to register first to the system and write your valid email and enter your SecureFormula during your first login. Your SecureFormula will be sent to your email. Be ensured that, your SecureFormula is not your password. Do not set your SecureFormula to be the same as your password! Sign in from your computer [6]:

- Enter your Cloud User ID;
- Verify that your SecureFormula image is correct;
- Confirm by entering your password.

Our confidentiality layer guaranteed that, even if your password is correct and your SecureFormula is incorrect, then you will not be able to login.

The architecture of CDConA consists of five modules, as shown in Figure 3. Cloud Communication Module provides the agent with the capability to exchange information with other agents, including the CDConA, CDCorA, CDAA, CDIA and CSPA. Cloud Register Module facilitates the registration function for CDConA. Cloud Request Management Module allows the agent to act as the request-dispatching center. Cloud Resource Management Module manages the usage of the cloud resources. Cloud Reasoning Module is the brain of the CDConA. When the request management module and resource management module receive requests, they pass those requests to reasoning module by utilizing the information obtained from the knowledge base and the confidentiality policy rule.

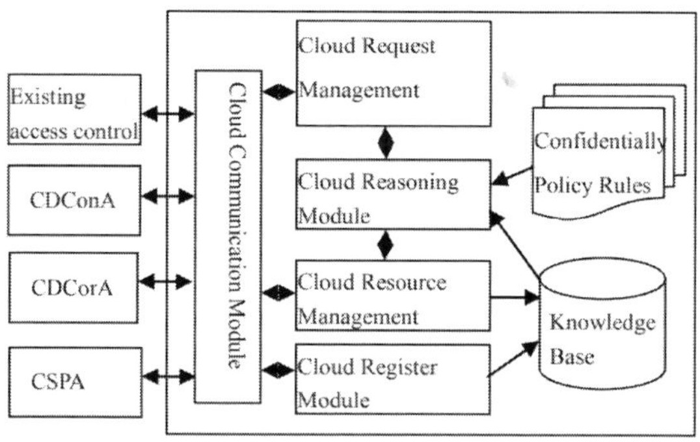

Figure 3. CDConA architecture.

Cloud Data Correctness Agent (CDCorA)

This agent facilitates the security policy of correctness assurance for CDS. Main responsibility of this agent is to perform various block-level operations and generate a correctness assurance when the cloud user performs update operation, delete operation, append to modify operation or insert operation. This agent notifies CSPA in case of any fail caused of the techniques above by sending security reports and/or alarms.

The architecture of the CDCorA consists of four modules, as shown in Figure 4. Cloud Communication Module provides the agent with the capability to exchange information with CSPA. Cloud Coordination Module provides the agent with the following mechanisms. If the data is updated then the data encryption is performed. If the data is deleted then the data encryption is performed. If the data is Append then the data encryption is performed. If the data is inserted then the data encryption is performed.

Cloud Reasoning Module calculates the necessary amount of cloud resources to complete the service based on the required service level agreements (SLA) by utilizing the information obtained from the knowledge base and the correctness assurance policy rule. Cloud Services Module performs the blocklevel operations of encryption and decryption when the cloud user update, delete, append and insert his/her data.

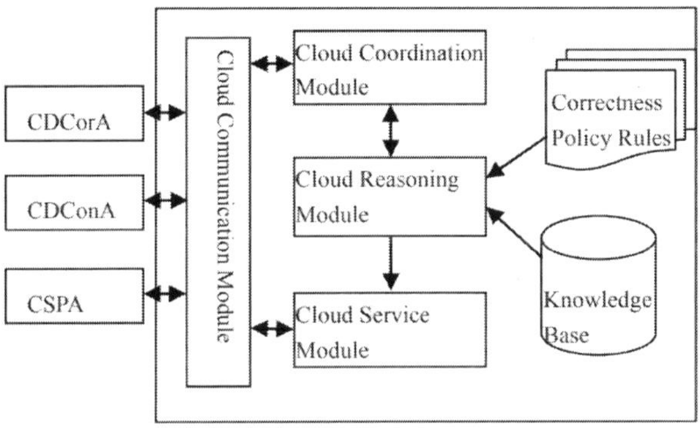

Figure 4. CDCorA architecture.

In CDS, there are many potential scenarios where data stored in the cloud is dynamic, like electronic documents, photos, or log files etc. Therefore, it is crucial to consider the dynamic case, where a cloud user may wish to perform various block-level operations of update, delete and append to modify the data. Our proposed correctness assurance protocol is not going to be genuine if there is absent of SecureFormula. So in case of: Update operation: The cloud user needs to enter his/her SecureFormula plus 00, Delete operation: The cloud user needs to enter his/her SecureFormula plus 01, Append operation: The cloud user needs to enter his/her SecureFormula plus 10 and Modify operation: The cloud user needs to enter his/her SecureFormula plus 11.

Cloud Data Availability Agent (CDAA)

This agent facilitates the security policy of availability for CDS. Main responsibility of this agent is to receive and display the security issues that offer by its sub-agents of CDDPA and CDRA. CDAA facilitate two new techniques of file distribution preparation and file retrieval. This agent is also notifies CSPA in case of any fail caused of the techniques above by sending security reports and/ or alarms.

Cloud data availability is to ensure that the cloud data processing resources are not made unavailable by malicious action. Our MAS architecture is able to tolerate multiple failures in cloud distributed storage systems. To ensure the availability, we explain the notions of global and local cloud attack blueprints. To detect intrusions, the CDAA receives a set of goals representing the global cloud attack blueprints. To recognize this global cloud attack blueprint, it must be decomposed in local cloud sub-blueprints used locally by the different agents distributed in the CDS. In general agents can detect only local cloud attacks because they have a restricted view of the CDS. So, we make a distinction between a global cloud attack blueprint and local cloud sub-blueprints. A global cloud blueprint is an attack blueprint, derived from the security policies specified at a high level by the CSPs, that the MAS must detect and the detection of this blueprint will be notified only to CDAA. A local cloud blueprint is a blueprint derived from the global cloud blueprint but that must be detected by local agents. For a CDAA overviewing the global cloud attack blueprint the probability of an attack is equal to 1, while for the local agent it is below 1.

The architecture of the CDAA consists of three modules, as shown in Figure 5. Cloud Communication Module provides the agent with the capability to exchange information with CDAA and CSPA. Cloud Servers Modules provides the agent with the following mechanisms: 1) Disperse the data file redundantly across a set of distributed servers; and 2) Enable the cloud user to reconstruct the original data by downloading the data vectors from the servers. Cloud Reasoning Module provides the CDAA with the specific misbehaving server(s) and server colluding attacks by utilizing the information obtained from the knowledge base and the availability policy rule.

Cloud Data Integrity Agent (CDIA)

This agent facilitates the security policy of integrity for CDS. It is used to enable the cloud user to reconstruct the original cloud data by downloading the cloud data vectors from the cloud servers. Main responsibility of this agent is backing up the cloud data regularly from "Cloud Zone" and sending security reports and/or alarms to CPSA when [20]:

- Human errors when cloud data is entered.
- Errors that occur when cloud data is transmitted from one computer to another.
- Software bugs or viruses.
- Hardware malfunctions, such as disk crashes.

Our proposed integrity layer named as “CloudZone”. In CloudZone, we introduce the first provably-secure and practical backup cloud data regularly that provide reconstruct the original cloud data by downloading the cloud data vectors from the cloud servers.

“CloudZone” Requirements

- “CloudZone” only backs up the MS SQL databases. It does not back up other MS SQL files such as program installation files, etc.
- “CloudZone” does not support component-based backup.
- “CloudZone” does not use Visual SourceSafe (VSS) for backup and restore.
- “CloudZone” supports backup and recovery of Windows Oracle 10 g.

With “CloudZone” Cloud Backup, you can select any of the following as backup objects:

- Oracle Server 10 g running on Windows.
- Microsoft SQL Server 2000, 2005 and 2008.
- Microsoft Exchange Server 2003 and 2007.

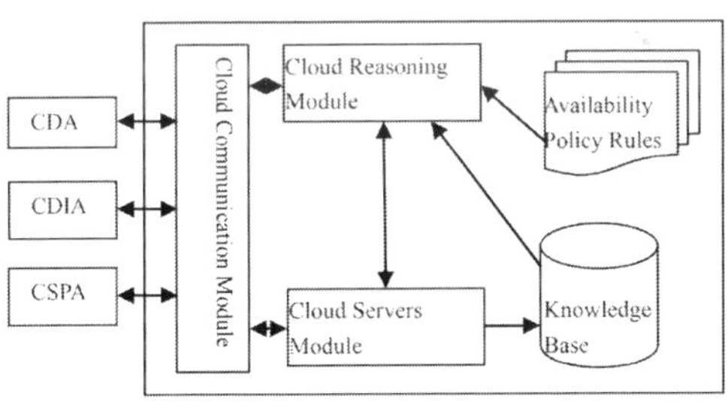

Figure 5. CDAA architecture.

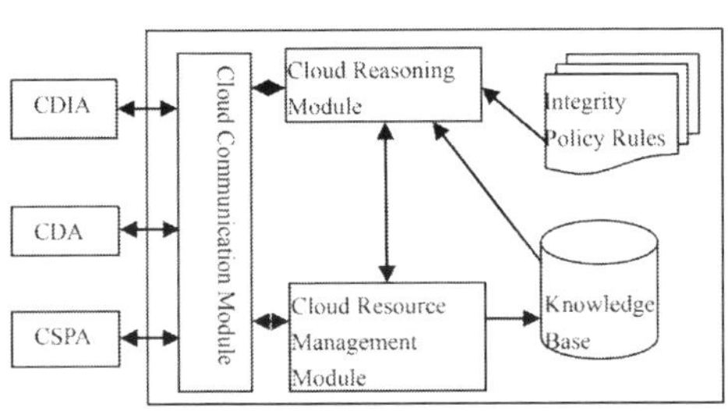

Figure 6. CDIA architecture.

The architecture of the CDIA consists of three modules, as shown in Figure 6. Cloud Communication Module provides the agent with the capability to exchange information with CDIA, CDConA, CDCorA, CDAA and CSPA. Cloud Resources Management Modules provides the agent with the following mechanisms. If the CDIA registered as CDIA-VIP then back-up of the data is performed successfully. If the CDIA did not register as CDIA-VIP, it asks the cloud user to back-up the data manually. Cloud Reasoning Module shows the reasons of in case the result of the back-up the data is failed by utilizing the information obtained from the knowledge base and the integrity policy rule [20].

IMPLEMENTATION GANAWA

Security as a Service (GSecaaS) has been implemented (~30.000 lines of JAVA code) with Oracle 11 g. The implementation was based on structure-in-5 MAS architectures described above. We briefly describe the GSecaaS implementation to illustrate the role of the agents and their interaction. To simulate the agents,

Oracle database packages and triggers are used to implement agent functions and Oracle jobs are utilized to create agents. Each agent is considered as an instance of the agent in the environment that can work independently, and can communicate with other agents in order to fulfill its needs or fulfill the others requests. To demonstrate the feasibility of the proposed system, a prototype is implemented using Java and PHP.

At the interface layer, the interaction of the system with the cloud user is based on a set of dialogues. These dialogues are implemented using Java and PHP. An example of an interface is shown in Figure 7.

PILOT STUDY

Result

The pilot data were tabulated and analyzed using WinSteps, a Rasch tool. The results of Person and Item summary statistics and measures are tabulated in Tables 1 and 2.

The results of the survey are analyzed in three parts; data reliability, fitness of respondent and items data and determination of component groups cut-off points.

Data Reliability

Summary statistics for respondents (persons) and items (questions) are depicted in Tables 1 and 2, respectively. 15 respondents returned the survey questionnaire. Out of which, Rasch identified an extreme score which will later be excluded from further analysis.

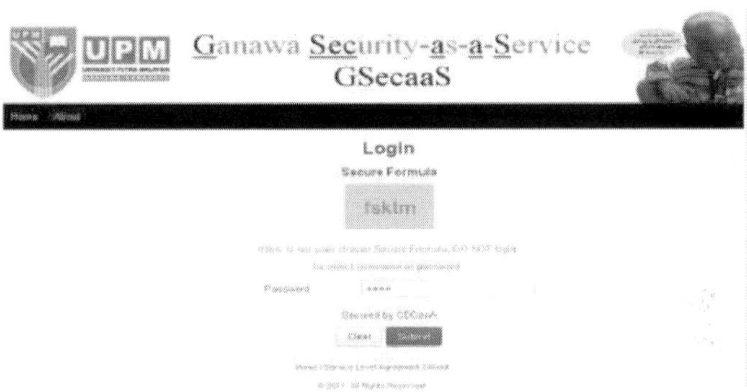

Figure 7. An example of interaction window with a cloud user (confidentiality layer).

Table 1. Summary of measured persons.

	Raw score	Count	Measure	Model error	Infit		Outfit	
					MNSQ	ZSTD	MNSQ	ZSTD
MEAN	133.8	42.8	0.49	0.27	1.02	−0.2	1.01	−0.2
S.D.	14.9	3.5	0.69	0.02	0.52	2.1	0.53	2
MAX.	167	45	2.64	0.34	3.14	6.4	3.37	6.7
MIN.	86	30	−0.65	0.25	0.28	−4.5	0.28	−4.4

Real RMSE 0.30 Adj. S.D. 0.62 Separation 2.10 Person reliability 0.82 Model RMSE 0.27 Adj. S.D. 0.64 Separation 2.35 Person reliability 0.85 S.E. of person mean = 0.11 Maximum extreme score: 1 Person valid responses: 95.0%.

From the summary of measured persons (Table 1), the spread of person responses is = 3.29 logit is fair. This is due to extreme responses by a participant. However, Reliability = 0.82 and Cronbach Alpha = 0.94 indicates high reliable data and hence the data could be used for further analyses

On the questionnaire items, the summary of 15 measured questionnaire items (Table 2) reveals that the spread of data at 2.36 logit and reliability of 0.74 are good and fair, respectively.

Table 2. Summary of measured items.

	Raw score	Count	Measure	Model error	Infit		Outfit	
					MNSQ	ZSTD	MNSQ	ZSTD
MEAN	119.8	38.3	0.02	0.3	1	0	1	0.1
S.D.	16.7	3.2	0.64	0.08	0.12	0.6	0.15	0.7
MAX.	150	40	1.16	0.6	1.29	1.5	1.4	1.9
MIN.	88	29	–1.2	0.2	0.83	–1.3	0.74	–1.3

Real RMSE 0.32 Adj. S.D. 0.54 Separation 1.69 Item reliability 0.74 Model RMSE 0.27 Adj. S.D. 0.64 reparation 2.35 Item reliability 0.75 S.E. of item mean = 0.09.

Details on each measured items are listed in Table 3. The acceptable limits are 0.4 < Acceptable Point Measure Correlation < 0.8 and 0.5 < Outfit Mean Square < 1.5, and –2.0 < Outfit z-standardized value < 2.0). The previous pilot study is therefore proven helpful in making the questionnaire more reliable.

Table 3. Items statistics—Measure order.

Item		Raw			Model	Infit		Outfit		Pt Mea
No.	Item	Score	Count	Measure	S.E.	MNSQ	ZStd	MNSQ	ZStd	Corr
				A cloud data storage (CDS)						
1	A1 roles	139	15	–1.18	0.3	0.98	0	1	0.1	0.31
2	A2 resources	127	15	0.12	0.22	0.88	–0.7	0.84	–0.8	0.44
3	A3 infrastructure	132	15	–0.32	0.26	0.88	–0.6	0.85	–0.7	0.43
4	A4 req analysis	128	14	–0.26	0.27	0.84	–0.8	0.81	–1	0.46
5	A5 sys analysis	129	15	–0.4	0.23	0.97	0	1.13	0.6	0.37
6	A8 implementation	124	14	–0.01	0.27	0.84	–0.7	0.84	–0.8	0.48
7	A7 domain	138	15	–0.82	0.28	1.04	0.3	1	0.1	0.28
				B cloud user						
8	B1 behavior	106	11	–0.56	0.39	1.06	0.3	1.1	0.4	0.24
9	B2 awareness	111	12	–0.53	0.28	1.19	0.6	1.27	0.9	0.13
10	B3 usage	94	11	0.05	0.26	0.9	–0.2	0.93	–0.1	0.48
				C cloud service provider (CSP)						
11	C1 facilitate	150	15	–0.72	0.38	0.89	–0.6	0.8	–0.7	0.31
12	C2 encourage	90	15	0.92	0.24	1.27	1.2	1.25	1.1	0.38
13	C3 provide	89	15	0.99	0.23	1.06	0.4	1.07	0.4	0.49
14	C4 trust	107	14	0.09	0.27	1.03	0.2	1	0.1	0.43
				D agent tools						
15	D1 definition	112	13	0.17	0.43	0.89	–0.2	0.88	–0.2	0.47
16	D2 characteristic	95	12	0.76	0.46	0.95	0	0.91	–0.1	0.31
17	D3 communication	126	10	0.2	0.6	0.83	–0.2	0.74	–0.3	0.56
18	D4 prosperity	128	12	0.76	0.46	0.95	0	0.91	–0.1	0.49
19	D5 goal	132	12	0.76	0.46	0.95	–0.2	0.94	–04	0.76
				E security goals in cloud computing						
20	E1 confidentiality	145	15	–0.09	0.34	0.86	–1.3	0.79	–1.3	0.39
21	E2 correctness assurance	137	15	0.81	0.34	0.9	0.9	0.87	1	0.41
22	E3 availability	126	15	–0.25	0.35	0.9	–0.3	0.87	–0.4	0.49
23	E4 integrity	116	15	0.75	0.26	0.95	–0.2	0.96	–0.2	0.45
24	E5 data privacy	131	39	1.13	0.35	1.1	0.8	1.14	0.9	0.26
25	E6 multi-tenancy	123	39	–0.5	0.39	1	0.1	1.05	0.3	0.4
26	E7 control	134	15	1.16	0.35	1	0	1.01	0.1	0.35
Mean		119.8	38.3	0.0	0.3	1.0	0.0	1.0	0.0	0.4
S.D.		16.7	3.2	0.6	0.1	0.1	0.6	0.2	0.7	0.1

Fitness of Respondent Data and Questionnaire Items Data

A Person-Item Differential Map (PIDM) is used to reveal the "easiest" and "hardest" questions answered by respondents. Based on the summaries and PIDM, a few observations could be concluded. Person SU1 is at the leftmost of the person distribution. Rasch provides the Person Item Distribution Map (PIDM), which is similar to histogram (Figure 8). PIDM allows both person and items to be mapped side-by side on the same logit scale to give us a better perspective on the relationship of person responses to the items. PIDM indicates a higher Person Mean (0.64) compared to the constrained Item Mean. This indicates tendency to rate higher importance to the prescribed questionnaire items.

PIDM is used to reveal the "easiest" and "hardest" questions answered by respondents. Based on the summaries and PIDM, a few observations could be concluded. Person SU1 is at the leftmost of the person distribution. As the Customer Service Director, it's lonely up there and not many want to share with him information, hence the pattern of answers. Item F1—"Cloud user must pay in order to get the cloud services", and F5—"Agents have the ability to pass the parameters among them" are on the rightmost and leftmost of the Item distribution, respectively. The question for F1 is on "Cloud user must pay in order to get the cloud services" Strategy and F5 is on "Agents have the ability to pass the parameters among them" strategy. We believe that respondents might not understand the terms "Cloud user must pay in order to get the cloud services" and "Agents have the ability to pass the parameters among them" in cloud computing concept and software agent concept. Layman-terms were used to better represent the questions. In this case, questions F1 and F5 were rephrased to F1—"both of these strategies the respondent must totally agreed". Determining the "Easy" questions is not as easy as portrayed in the Person-Item Variable map. It was envisaged that question F1 and F5 were revised.

Component Group Cut-Off Points

There are no hard and fast rules on how to determine which of the less important components should be excluded from the framework. The components are sorted into descending logit values. The list is then distributed to four experts from software engineering fields, and three cloud computing security experts.

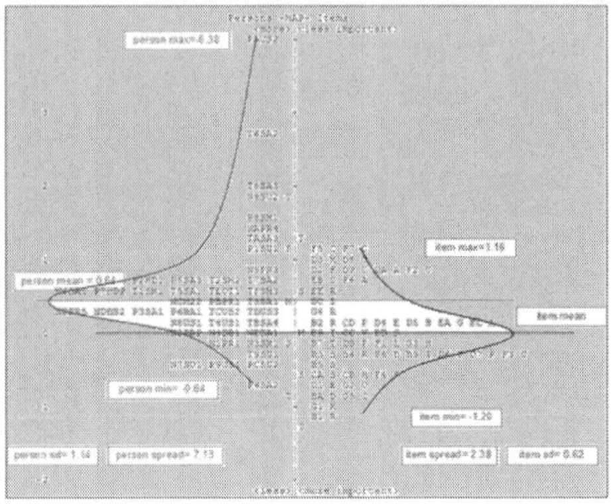

Figure 8. Person-item distribution map.

Discussion

Based on the overall experts' judgments, the following components are selected to be excluded from the model (Table 3):

- C2 Encourage/CSPs must encourage cloud users to use their trusted CDS.
- D1 CSPA—Provide the security service task according to the authorized service level agreements (SLAs)/ different area.
- E5 Data privacy/different area.
- E6 Multi-tenancy/different area.
- E7 Control/different area.

Based on the above reduced components, the revised framework is depicted in Figure 1 and its MAS architecture in Figure 2. Based on the Pilot study results, the revised security framework based on MAS architecture is directly driven from the initial framework. This is because the most of the components are common and used to identify the respondent in the questionnaire.

The proposed security frameworks to facilitate security of CDS are based on Wang et al. [4], Talib et al. [5], Takabi et al. [14], Yu et al. [15], Du et al. [16] and Venkatesan and Vaish [17], they all runs in six main parts layers, functions, security goals, infrastructures, approaches, technologies and applications and overlaps on some specific components are architectures and collaborations. The major comparison on the major components of all above frameworks is depicted in Table 4.

CONCLUSION

In this paper, we investigated the problem of data security in cloud computing environment, to ensure the confidentiality, correctness assurance, availability and integrity of users' data in the cloud; we proposed a security framework and MAS architecture to facilitate security of CDS. This security framework consists of two main layers as agent layer and cloud data storage layer. The propose MAS architecture includes five types of agents: CSPA, CDConA, CDCorA, CDAA and CDIA. To formulate the security framework for collaborative CDS security, the components on MAS, cloud user and CSP are compiled from various literatures. An initial model of modified MAS components for collaborative CDS security is proposed. The relationships between these components are used to construct the questionnaire, which were tested in a pilot study. Rasch model was used in analyzing pilot questionnaire. Item reliability is found to be poor and a few respondents and items were identified as misfits with distorted measurements. Some problematic questions are revised and some predictably easy questions are excluded from the questionnaire. A prototype of the system (GSecaaS) is implemented using Java and PHP. The use of this system has shown how the system could be used to facilitate the security of the CDS.

Table 4. Comparisons between the frameworks.

Item/Framework	Wang *et al.* [4]	Talib *et al.* [5]	Takabi *et al.* [14]	Yu *et al.* [15]	Du *et al.* [16]	Venkatesan and Vaish [17]
Layer	Y	Y	Y	NA	Y	NA
Function	Y	Y	Y	NA	Y	Y
Security goal	Y	Y	Y	Y	Y	Y
Infrastructure	Y	Y	Y	Y	Y	Y
Approach	NA	Y	Y	Y	Y	Y
Technology	Y	Y	Y	Y	Y	Y
Application	Y	NA	Y	Y	Y	NA
Architecture	NA	Y	NA	NA	Y	Y
Collaboration	Y	Y	Y	Y	Y	Y

REFERENCES

1. M. Zhou, R. Zhang, W. Xie, W. Qian and A. Zhou, "Security and Privacy in Cloud Computing: A Survey," Proceedings of the Sixth International Conference on Semantics Knowledge and Grid (SKG), Beijing, 2010, pp. 105- 112.
2. C. S. Aishwarya, "Insight into Cloud Security Issues," UACEE International Journal of Computer Science and Its Applications, 2011, pp. 30-33.
3. J. W. Rittinghouse and J. F. Ransome, "Cloud Computing: Implementation, Management, and Security (Chapter 6)," 2009.
4. C. Wang, Q. Wang, K. Ren and W. Lou, "Ensuring Data Storage Security in Cloud Computing," IEEE, Vol. 186, No. 978, 2009, pp. 1-9.
5. A. M. Talib, R. Atan, R. Abdullah and M. A. A. Murad, "Formulating a Security Layer of Cloud Data Storage Framework Based on Multi-Agent System Architecture," TGSTF International Journal on Computing, Vol. 1, No. 1, 2010, pp. 120-124.
6. A. M. Talib, R. Atan, R. Abdullah and M. A. A. Murad, "Towards New Access Data Control Technique Based on Multi Agent System Architecture for Cloud Computing in Software Engineering and Computer Systems Part II," In: V. Snasel, J. Platos and E. El-Qawasmeh, Eds., Springer Series: Communications in Computer and Information Science 189, Springer-Verlag, pp. 268-279.
7. M. R. Genesereth and S. P. Ketchpel, "Software Agents," Communication of the ACM, Vol. 37, No. 7, 1994, pp. 48-53.
8. E. H. Durfee, V. R. Lesser and D. D. Corkill, "Trends in Cooperative Distributed Problem Solving," IEEE Transactions on Knowledge and Data Engineering, 1989, pp. 63- 83.
9. H. Mouratidis, P. Giorgini and G. Manson, "Modelling Secure Multi-Agent Systems," ACM, 2003, pp. 859-866.
10. S. Ramgovind, M. M. Eloff and E. Smith, "The Management of Security in Cloud Computing," Information Security for South Africa (ISSA), Sandton, Johannesburg, 2010, pp. 1-7.
11. K. D. Bowers, A. Juels and A. Oprea, "HAIL: A HighAvailability and Integrity Layer for Cloud Storage," 2009. http://eprint.iacr..org/2008/489.pdf
12. D. Zissis and D. Lekkas, "Addressing Cloud Computing Security Issues," Future Generation Computer Systems, Vol. 28, No. 3, 2010,

pp. 583-592.

13. J. Yang and Z. Chen, "Cloud Computing Research and Security Issues," International Conference on Computational Intelligence and Software Engineering (CiSE), 2010, pp. 1-3.
14. H. Takabi, J. B. D. Joshi and G. J. Ahn, "SecureCloud: Towards a Comprehensive Security Framework for Cloud Computing Environments," 34th Annual IEEE Computer Software and Applications Conference Workshops, 2010, pp. 393-398.
15. H. Yu, N. Powell, D. Stembridge and X. Yuan. "Cloud Computing and Security Challenges," ACM, 2012, pp. 298-302.
16. J. Du, W. Wei, X. Gu and T. Yu, "RunTest: Assuring Integrity of Dataflow Processing in Cloud Computing Infrastructures," ASIACCS'10, Beijing, 13-16 April 2010, pp. 293-304.
17. S. Venkatesan and A. Vaish, "Multi-Agent Based Dynamic Data Integrity Protection in Cloud Computing," 2011, pp. 76-82.
18. A. A. Aziz, A. Mohamed, A. Zaharim, S. Zakaria, H. A. Ghulman and M. S. Masodi, "Evaluation of Information Professionals Competency Face Validity Test Using Rasch," Proceedings of the 4th Pacific Rim Objective Measurement Symposiom (PROMS), 2008, pp. 396-403.
19. A. M. Talib, R. Atan, R. Abdullah and M. A. A. Murad, "Security Framework of Cloud Data Storage Based on Multi Agent System Architecture: Semantic Literature Review," Computer and Information Science, Vol. 3, No. 4, 2010, p. 175.
20. A. M. Talib, R. Atan, R. Abdullah and M. A. A. Murad, "CloudZone: Towards an Integrity Layer of Cloud Data Storage Based on Multi-Agent System Architecture," ICOS, 2011, pp. 127-132.

CHAPTER 6

Control Framework for Secure Cloud Computing

Harshit Srivastava[1], Sathish Alampalayam Kumar[2]

[1]Information Technology, Maharaja Agrasen Institute of Technology, New Delhi, India

[2]Computer Science and Information Systems, Coastal Carolina University, Conway, USA

ABSTRACT

Cloud computing is touted as the next big thing in the Information Technology (IT) industry, which is going to impact the businesses of any size and yet the security issue continues to pose a big threat on it. The security and privacy issues persisting in cloud computing have proved to be an obstacle for its widespread adoption. In this paper, we look at these issues from a business

Citation: Srivastava, H. and Kumar, S. (2015), "Control Framework for Secure Cloud Computing". *Journal of Information Security*, **6**, 12-23. doi: 10.4236/jis.2015.61002..

perspective and how they are damaging the reputation of big companies. There is a literature review on the existing issues in cloud computing and how they are being tackled by the Cloud Service Providers (CSP). We propose a governing body framework which aims at solving these issues by establishing relationship amongst the CSPs in which the data about possible threats can be generated based on the previous attacks on other CSPs. The Governing Body will be responsible for Data Center control, Policy control, legal control, user awareness, performance evaluation, solution architecture and providing motivation for the entities involved.

Keywords: Cloud computing, Security, Privacy, Organization, Control, Governance, Framework, Cloud Provider

INTRODUCTION

National Institute of Standards and Technology (NIST) defines cloud computing as a computing model for enabling ubiquitous, convenient, on-demand network access to a shared pool of configurable computing resources (e.g., networks, servers, storage, applications, and services) [1] . These services can be rapidly provisioned and released with minimal management effort or service provider interaction. NIST also defines that the cloud computing can be achieved through three service models: Software as a Service (SaaS), Platform as a Service (PaaS) and Infrastructure as a Service (IaaS). Cloud computing can be implemented by the four deployment models: Private Cloud, Community Cloud, Public Cloud and Hybrid Cloud. This emerging paradigm allows an organization to reduce costs and develops highly scalable solutions [2] . Cloud promises customers with the benefits of a more convenient way of provisioning IT resources at a faster speed and with a lower cost, compared to traditional IT processes and systems.

Cloud computing has been regarded as the next big thing in the Information Technology (IT) industry. It is predicted that it will have a global impact on how people store and access their data. Apart from storage, it also provides other services which can be utilized from anywhere and at any time. The only concern, however, with cloud computing is the security and privacy issues. As people put their valuable data on the cloud, they are completely dependent on the Cloud Service Provider (CSP) to ensure proper security for their data. Due to large amount of attacks on the data on the cloud, many people have lost their important data and moreover, the confidentiality of their data has been compromised. Therefore, security and privacy are big concern in cloud computing. These issues have been impeding the growth of cloud computing and are proving to be a major obstacle for its widespread adoption.

Cloud service providers try to provide cloud services with built-in security features. They try to build a cloud infrastructure that can withstand any sort of failure whether it is technical, logical or physical. However, there are many factors that can harm the security and reliability of the Cloud infrastructure despite of taking all the necessary steps.

They are generally categorized in the following three layers, in which an organization takes control of the security. These are as follows:

- Physical Layer: The physical layer of security encompasses many factors.

1) Data Center: This deals with the geographical location of the data center. Locations are chosen in such a way that they are not prone to natural or man-made disasters. No data center will be successful in withstanding severe earthquakes, cyclones, volcanic eruptions etc. and it is best to keep the data center in a place that is less vulnerable to be affected by these factors. Also, location of data centers is kept confidential so that it does not fall prey to external attacks.
2) Biometric Scanning: There are methods such as finger-print scan or retina-scan which allow only selected employees to enter the data center. There are usually very few people that are allowed physical entry inside the area where the data are actually stored.
3) Building: The buildings are generally designed to be a data center from the start. They are built in such a way that they can withstand fires. There are cameras all around the place and alarms that go off in case of emergency. Employees and security guards are present in the data center 24 × 7.

- Logical Layer: Logical Layer of security deals with the design of the network that is used for providing cloud services. The network is kept secured with the help of firewalls, anti-virus and intrusion detection systems. Companies that provide cloud services do not want to compromise with the quality of the software used, since it would harm their reputation and affect their business. The hypervisors are generally of high standards and these systems are centrally managed and protected.

- Methodology Layer: This concerns with the security method used at local level in a cloud service provider and it may differ from one organization to another. The main concept of this layer is to assure that various other aspects of security is taken care of. The password that every employee has is made to be very secure and difficult to crack as opposed to some preposterous passwords like "1234" which do not really help in making the system secure. The environment inside a data center is generally very secure and only a few trusted staff members are allowed to make significant changes in the system. The cloud service providers try to give the tasks to trusted staff members instead of outsourcing the tasks.

Organizations are playing a vital role in determining the course of Cloud Computing. If the security and privacy issues continue to remain, then future of Cloud Computing might be in danger. We have to find solutions and controls to the security, privacy and reliability problems in order to make cloud computing a trustworthy paradigm.

COMPANIES INVOLVED IN CLOUD COMPUTING

As cloud computing offers exciting new opportunities to the companies to expand their Infrastructure, some companies took it to the next level and started providing cloud services. The big names in cloud service providing industry are Amazon, Google and of late, IBM and Microsoft. Oracle/Sun and HP are also not far behind. Google has built the largest Cloud Computing infrastructure with Data Centers existing in Taiwan, Singapore, Finland, Belgium and Ireland apart from various US states. Amazon, besides being a huge online shopping site, is also a big mover in cloud computing revolution. With Microsoft Azure, Microsoft has also entered the Cloud Computing industry. Oracle/Sun, IBM and Rack Space have also tied their future to Cloud Computing. However, the security issues existing in cloud computing also reflects upon the security breaches and attacks to the Data Centers of these companies.

There have been many instances where the Data Centers of the Cloud Service Providers have slowed down or have stopped working altogether. In June 2012, a big storm in North Virginia affected the Amazon's Data Center. As a result, websites like Netflix, Instagram, Pinterest, and Heroku were down for few hours because they relied on Amazon's cloud service [3] . In another incident, a flawed storage software update over Google triggered an unexpected bug In March 2011. Around 150,000 Gmail accounts were affected and all their messages were deleted in the wake of that software bug [4] .To overcome such security threats, cloud providers try to minimize the risk of attacks by various ways. The whole process of deployment of security is also governed by how they deploy the technology of cloud computing in the first place. The way each cloud service provider deploys the cloud is different from one to another. Therefore, the techniques followed by them are significantly different. For example, as per Cloud Security Alliance Guide [5] , Amazon's AWS EC2 infrastructure, as an example, includes vendor responsibility with respect to security and privacy lies only at the physical security, environmental security, and virtualization security level. The user is responsible for security controls at the operating system, applications, and data level. As an example of how the cloud service providers differ from one another, Salesforce.com's Customer Relationship management (CRM) is a SaaS offering and provides entire service to the user. Hence the provider is not only responsible for the physical and environmental security controls, but it must also address the security controls on the infrastructure, the applications, and the data.

According to a recent survey [6] , the total number of records containing sensitive personal information involved in security breaches in the United States is more than 600 million records in about 4000 data breaches since January 2005. Recent surveys reveal that human errors and systems glitches caused nearly two-thirds of data breaches globally in 2012, while malicious or criminal attacks are the most costly everywhere at an average of $157 per compromised record.

Some surveys show that malicious attacks (defined as a combination of hacking and insider theft) accounted for nearly 47 percent of the recorded breaches in 2012 in the United States. Hacking attacks were responsible for more than one-third (33.8 percent) of the data breaches recorded [6] .

According to a survey by Open Security Foundation [7] , there were more than 2000 cloud related data breach incidents globally since 2012. Surveys done on some randomly selected companies show that 82% of those companies saved money moving to cloud while only 14% downsized their IT after cloud adoption.

LITERATURE REVIEW

As we discussed earlier, the main concern in cloud computing is of security and the security issues in cloud computing remain the chief obstacle that may prevent its widespread adoption. As more and more data is being migrated to the cloud, there have been more attacks, such as Denial of Service and Authentication attacks. For example, the increase of Internet-capable devices creates opportunities for remote hacking and data leakage. More cloud adopters have been at the receiving end of cloud infrastructure security incidents as compared to traditional IT infrastructure security events. These security incidents and data breaches can have financial consequences on a corporate organization [8] . Despite the decrease in the cost of data breaches in the last year, data breaches are still reported to have cost British and German organizations on average between $2.7 million and $4.4 million [8] . In addition to the economic and financial troubles, security breaches and threats can lead to damaged reputations, loss of customers, delayed software releases and a reduction in investor confidence [9] .

Cloud computing vs. Outsourcing

In traditional outsourcing, service providers are commissioned to handle data, system and process actively for the user according to the organization's mandate. However, cloud computing has a self-service nature, where users pay for pre-packaged IT resources made available by the cloud providers, using which they process data or other jobs on their own in a self-service fashion. In such cases, the users use infrastructure/resources supplied by the provider, and don't need to own them. Unlike outsourcing, service providers who act actively, cloud providers can be considered as agents who help users to process data and perform other jobs. Cloud providers can, at most, store data passively that the users decide to store on the provider's infrastructure, which is readily retrieval as and when needed.

Shared infrastructure/environments and economies of scale are what drive the public cloud computing providers instead of tailor-made infrastructure to fit the needs of every customer. Though customization of the service is possible in some cases, it would cost additional time and money.

The organization exercises better control over the service provider in traditional outsourcing due to the body of knowledge related to process and systems. Due to one size fit all nature and type of service in the cloud, it's often seen that organization lose control on the cloud providers and struggle with the use of resources on the cloud.

Although, a substantial number of studies already exist on Cloud Computing, it is still unclear how or whether CC differs from the traditional concept of Information Technology Outsourcing. The risks that persisted in IT Outsourcing has just been transferred to Cloud Computing. Security is a prime concern while outsourcing the IT resources of a company and the third party organization that provides outsourcing cannot be trusted blindly with confidential data. Although many service providers are scrupulous about securing their facilities but there may still be risks persisting. The facility has to be secured both on the physical as well as the logical level. All these security risks and privacy concerns can be associated with the issues persisting in cloud computing.

Eric and Yuanyuan [10] believe that contracting to cloud computing include the standard risks of Outsourcing of any kind with 3 major issues being

- Vendor Lock-in: The risk of interoperability persists in cloud computing. Client find themselves locked-in to a specific cloud provider, unable to transition from one provider to another, or finding a lack of interoperability between their existing in-house infrastructure and cloud based services.
- Security and privacy of data: The data that is stored on the client's servers, the client retains control over the security of the servers. But where client data is given to the cloud provider to store, it is stored by the cloud provider in multiple data centres across multiple jurisdictions. Google, for example, has data centres in the US, Europe, Russia, South America and across Asia. Whilst storage across multiple locations may distribute the risk of a single point of failure, it also creates multiple possible points for intrusion.
- Undermining of the confidential data: Concerns regarding security, privacy and integrity of data are further exacerbated by little and/ or inconsistent regulatory framework regarding the privacy and security of data. In some countries laws give government agencies a right to inspect data held there and privacy law safeguards are unknown. This clearly undermines the confidentiality of the data stored in the cloud.

Deployment of Security in Cloud Environment

Compared to traditional IT environment, security deployed at every level in the cloud environment must be different while considering the security needs for each level. Chow et al., [11] think that traditional in-house authorization and authentication framework that were employed previously cannot be extended to the cloud environment and would probably need some modification to be compatible to the services of cloud computing. Subashini and Kavitha [12] highlighted security issues applicable to various layers of the cloud computing environment while noting that security needs will vary for each delivery model. The biggest threat to the cloud environment that exists today is of unauthorized access. The users put their confidential data on the cloud hoping that their data will remain safe but due to unauthorized access, the confidentiality of the data is undermined. As a result, users are reluctant to migrate their data to the cloud.

Security Issues in Cloud Environment

Per our literature review, common security issues that arise in cloud computing can be classified broadly into six areas:

- Infrastructure: This concern is mainly related to the physical security provided by the cloud service provider. Cohen [13] states that from physical security perspective, the security issues might be more vulnerable in cloud computing as compared to traditional in-house security techniques. Security of the data centers provisioned by the cloud service providers would fall under infrastructure area. This concerns the amount of surveillance that exists inside the data center. There must be enough security guards and cameras present so as to reduce the risk of external intrusion or attacks. Moreover, this security control must be consistent across all the cloud providers. Cloud provider should ensure that the data center security is well-planned out and this might just alleviate the security risks which are larger as it is.
- Data: The 2011 Ernst and Young Global Information Security Survey [14] reported that 36% of respondents were currently using cloud computing services or deploying applications and storing data in cloud environments, as compared to 23% from the previous year. Furthermore, this report goes on to state that 25% of respondents are currently evaluating or investigating the use of cloud services in the subsequent year. Cloud computing services are also being utilized by governments in order to reduce costs and improve the efficiency of IT solutions within their agencies [15] . With more and more organizations moving to cloud and storing their data in the cloud, there is more data available than there ever has been before. Therefore the surface area of the attacks is also larger. As a result, unauthorized data accesses are common

attacks that occur. These attacks weaken the trust of the users and they feel that their data is insecure. Users also raise other issues that might be possible with the type of data security provided by cloud providers. These include the security of Application Program Interfaces (API) provided by them. Users would want to know whether the software used and the machines present are reliable and the way in which they are used, such that it is sufficient to ensure data security. Cloud Providers are reluctant to provide this kind of information as giving all the details about security they will make themselves vulnerable to more attacks. This creates a lack of transparency between the users and the Cloud Providers.

- Access: Jansen and Grance [16] stated that one of the biggest concerns for an organization, considering the adoption of cloud computing, is preventing unauthorized access to resources. It has been demonstrated that the unauthorized access of data compromises the confidentiality of the data stored access [16] . Cloud computing promises availability i.e. users can access the same data from any device. Question is if this would impact security? If there would be any unauthorized access of someone's data, it will not be from the same device that the user uses to access it but from a remote location and obviously from a different device. In that case, it is essential to ensure that the user is genuine. Therefore, a default device should be assigned to a user by the cloud provider and if the user tries to access the data from another device, one would need to give proper verification and authentication in order to prove his identity. Google follows the location based access technique but not all the cloud providers follow this [15] . Hence an organization should ensure that all the providers consistently follow these controls.
- Availability: To ensure availability to all the users, that try to access their account or data, the cloud service must scale itself according to the number of users. The number of servers increase or decrease to keep up with the traffic. This scalability feature is performed either automatically by the cloud providers' servers through knowledge learning or manually by prompting the administrator to do this. This however, will not ensure that a cloud can handle any amount of traffic that comes its way. SAP's CEO, Leo Apotheker stated: "There are certain things that you cannot

run in the cloud because the cloud would collapse. Don't believe that any utility company is going to run its billing for 50 million consumers in the cloud." This raises another issue that in case of huge traffic caused by DoS attacks, the cloud might just collapse and for that time the users will not be able to access their data.

- Compliance: Several organizations such as SAS 70 and ISO 27001 put forth regulations from the security audits, operation traceability and data location perspective. Cloud providers are supposed to follow these rules & regulations in order to ensure security of the cloud. Users need to be completely aware of what all rules and regulations are followed by their cloud provider. There have been many instances such as the case of Google Docs in March 2009, where full security and data safety audit reports were not made public and data integrity was allegedly compromised by improper access [17] .
- Role of Users: The customers also play an important role in determining the course of cloud computing. Cloud adopters need to trust the cloud providers and understand that until the technology is fully matured, that cloud computing customers will need to make every effort to protect the information consciously. Reed and Bennett [18] provide key guidelines on how to make best use of secure cloud services and a concise guide to cloud computing. The key points of their discussion are:

1) The biggest risk that the technology faces today is Users.
2) Shadow IT is an on-going risk and generally introduced by such employees who have no concerns beyond their own role in considering the risks involved in the solution provided.
3) Experienced teams often roll out new technologies, but there still exists the risk when traditional security practices are ignored or adapted to the new environment.
4) Attackers will always go after the valuable things and it may not be money itself.
5) A single security standard is unlikely to save you.

Related Solutions Proposed in Literature: There are few organizational control perspective solutions proposed in the literature to address the issues discussed earlier. Organizational control will help to manage the overall services of the cloud service provider and in return, reduce the security and reliability issues of cloud computing. The cloud computing governance model by Guo, Song and Song [19] addresses requirements and objectives of service, policy, security, risk and compliance management in cloud computing and supplements detailed descriptions and important information on the required system design. Their main contribution lies in the development of an architecture for Risk and Compliance Management (RCM), which focuses on controlling of services and policies (compliance regulations) by means of monitoring cloud computing Services. An overview of RCM in Cloud Computing is provided by Chaput and Ringwood [20] . They discuss different types of RCM regulations like laws and industry regulations affecting the adoption of Cloud Computing. Four key features discussed are security methods like data classification, access control, authentication and authorization, risk management methods like business impact analysis and business continuity, certifications and auditing standards.

In the territory of compliance management, Matthews et al. [21] propose virtual machine contracts, which extend the open virtual machine format. These electronic contracts describe and formalize technical requirements such as firewall rules, transport protocols, source and destination addresses as well as source and destination ports, to configure the virtual machines for a particular network segment. Kamara and Lauter [22] present methods and architectures for the encryption of cloud storage. One objective is to secure storage services for regulatory compliance by encrypting the data on-premise to avoid access to the data by a third party. They argue that this approach reduces the legal exposure and in return reduces the risk factors. Brandic et al. [23] provides an extension of Service Level Agreements (SLA) with regard to compliance issues. They introduce Compliance Level Agreements (CLA) and develop a detailed architecture for compliance management in Cloud Computing.The security risks in cloud computing can be reduced by specifically outlining the attacks and threats which may be considered as malicious. Ristenpart et al. [24] believes that security guidelines are also needed to address and mitigate risks associated with hypervisor-level attacks including cross-virtualization attacks. An insecure hypervisor can allow a malicious user to gain access to data stored in virtual machines hosted on a vulnerable hypervisor. Standards and guidelines can specify how the organization accomplishes a Virtual Machine Image (VMI) [25] . Wei et al. [26] suggest that a framework is developed to manage VMI creation, storage and destruction procedures. This framework is likely to contain controls such as filters to remove sensitive information from an image prior to publishing and a mechanism to track changes performed on a specific image to mitigate malicious image modification.

Another organizational control is punishment, which is carried out to reduce the undesirable behavior of employees such as non-compliance to the safety regulations and rules. Punishment is generally considered as a very effective way to produce behavior change. As a management tool within organizations, punishment is defined as "the application of a negative consequence to, or the withdrawal of a positive consequence from, an employee" [27] . Mohammad I. Merhi & Punit Ahluwalia [28] state that some employees in general tend to repeat actions that do not produce negative outcomes and prefer to avoid those actions that lead to negative actions; thus reducing likelihood of punishment. The rationale behind this argument is that punishment creates an anxiety in minds of employees which forces them to change their behaviors towards organizational policies.

All the solutions mentioned above are very limited and specific to some particular areas of the cloud computing industry. Acting on these specific details from outside will be very painstaking and time consuming. Therefore, we need to come up with such a solution that integrates all these methods and binds them into a unit that will control all the proceeding in the cloud environment. We will call it the Governing Body. This will help to bring some kind of Organizational Control in the cloud environment and reduce the security and reliability issues persisting in cloud computing.

GOVERNING BODY

There is a need for the cloud providers to hide some security related information, as they need to keep all the information about the security procedures confidential in order to minimize any security breaches. Do we have any reference to substantiate this claim This lack of transparency results in the cloud customers losing trust on the cloud providers. As a result, customers are reluctant to store their valuable data on the cloud, which undermines the potential of cloud computing. Our framework approach to solve these issues is by the formation of a governing body which will act as an interface between the cloud providers and cloud end users and provide organizational control. The governing body in our framework is unique compared to the existing infrastructure due to the following reasons: This governing body will be an independent unit and will not be influenced by any of the two entities involved. It will be responsible for any and every actions that take place inside the cloud environment. Various cloud providers will need to register themselves to the governing body and then that body will assess all the procedures and methodologies involved in the technology.

In general, this Governing Body will be responsible for risk assessment & management, security performance evaluation, policy, audit and compliance with respect to the deployment of cloud layer. The Governing Body is different from the existing infrastructure as it will not be limited to just assessing the conditions. In addition, it will also provide solutions and alternatives to the customers in case of any issues that takes place in the cloud environment whether it is due to technology failure or any external factors.

As shown in Figure 1, the governing body is an interface that provides formal control and governance between cloud provider and customer, to ensure that there is a smooth working and a well-coordinated system. The governing body will be responsible for the following functionalities, which the cloud provider cannot provide on their own.

Data Center Control

Governing body will be responsible for the operations inside the cloud environment. By migrating applications to the cloud, the risk factors increase. The traditional data control methods need to be modified in order to cope with the security and privacy challenges associated with the cloud environment. The entity that is at most risk inside the cloud environment is data center. The data center is a centralized location, where the entire customer's data are stored. Hence, cloud providers need to ensure that no security breaches take place inside the data center. To achieve this, the governing body should continuously monitor the possible security related threats and the products/solutions available to counter those threats, procure and implement them. For instance, some of the solutions include data replication facilities with hot site disaster recovery service. The governing body would need to ensure that the data centers are safe and secure and that all the data that resides inside it, must be backed up to ensure the business continuity in case of disaster. Disaster recovery and business continuity is one thing that every cloud provider promises. However, to ensure it gets implemented and operates in a right manner, there needs to be a centralized authority to get them implemented.

Policy Creation and Control

The security features that are included in the cloud environment are very important to determine the level of security present in the cloud. The security policy that will be drafted by the governing body will be responsible for all the layers of the security features that will be included in the cloud. For example, the security policy shall specify the use of firewalls, anti-virus, type of virtualization and the hyper-visor used to achieve the secure cloud functionality.

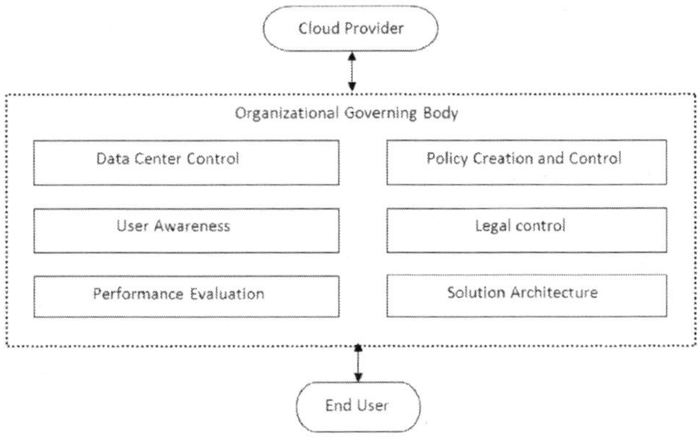

Figure 1. Organizational control through governing body.

It is to be noted that the above features may vary depending upon the budget of the cloud provider, which in turn will reflect in the use and adoption of that cloud.

We suggest that the governing board and the cloud provider would jointly determine the security features to be included. Only an outline of the features will be discussed between the two and once the cloud is deployed, the governing body would validate to see if all the features discussed before have been implemented.

User Awareness

The governing body will need to specify all the procedures and methods that a cloud provider and user follow to ensure the security and privacy of the cloud.

The governing body needs to filter and provide information to users in such a way that the users are aware of the security features and at the same time, no confidential information is leaked. Our automated control framework described in next section, ensures that based on triggers, central body convey right information at right time to right parties involved in the environment in an automated fashion. This will ensure removal of the lack of transparency in communicating security features, such that users are able to trust the cloud providers.

Legal Control

There are a number of jurisdictions and laws that apply to cloud computing. Laws vary from place to place and generally the data centers of a cloud provider are located in different countries or may be different continents. To gain knowledge and abide by all the laws of different location can be very difficult to cope with. For example US Patriot Act can be applied to foreign organizations that use U.S based cloud provider. Per US Patriot Act the Governmental authorities only may access cloud data pursuant to the Patriot Act to 1) "obtain foreign intelligence information not concerning a United States person" or 2) "protect against international terrorism or clandestine intelligence activities". Even a single law broken may affect the organization in many different ways. These laws and jurisdiction vary from geographical locations to the methods involved in the cloud computing and allowing the personnel to enter or work in the facility. Complying with all the jurisdiction and laws is a very time consuming job and may reflect in the efficiency of the cloud. Therefore, by outsourcing and letting the governing body take care of all the legal matters, the cloud provider can redirect the resources to ensure their cloud services are safe, secure and efficient and at the same time ensure all the jurisdictions and laws are followed.

Performance Evaluation

One of the parameters to evaluate the performance of the cloud is the number of security breaches and attacks to determine the performance of the cloud. Governing body should assess the performance of the cloud environment based on the security parameters and draft a report that will determine the efficiency of the cloud. This will help users in determining what all security features are being ignored by the cloud provider and help them make decisions by providing the right choices. The performance evaluation of the providers would motivate the good providers to increase their trust score with the governing body, compared to those providers who can try to negatively affect the organization. This will also help the governing body to rank the providers based on the provider's trust score. The cloud providers will also benefit from this evaluation, as they will get to know the limitations and the disadvantages in their implementation of security controls in the cloud computing environment and redirect the resources where the attention is needed. With the help of the performance evaluation functionality, the factors that caused attacks and threats can be identified and response strategies cab be applied to remove those threats and attacks, to ensure the cloud is safe and reliable.

Solution Architecture

The governing body shall not only be responsible for the policy, monitoring, evaluation and legal controls but also responsible for providing solutions to the customers: providers and end users. For example, following are some of the problem samples that the governing body shall be responsible for providing solutions: 1) Customers lost their data or are unable to access their data due to the occurrence of mishap in the cloud environment. 2) If a Cloud Provider goes bankrupt or due to some other factors and decides to shut down some of the data centers, many users' data will be at risk. At that point of time, the governing body will be responsible for providing alternative solutions to the users. The solution might range from migration of data to some other cloud provider or giving all the data back to the user so that they can manage it themselves in their internal IT environment. This results in tighter organizational control for the resources, which is the governing body's mandate.

In a large organization that caters to the needs of millions of customers, there could be many unsatisfied customers, who often file legal complaints or threaten to damage the reputation of the organization in some way or the other. Disputes and conflicts may also arise between two or more cloud providers, due to the disagreement over the issues. Disputes in IT industry are very common and there have been a number of incidents where some company adopted someone else's ideas to develop their own product. For instance, recently Microsoft sued Salesforce.com for the cloud computing patent infringement. In this case, the governing body will make sure that the conflicts and disputes are solved through our framework. This is done with the help of threat index, which we introduced in our framework. The threat index is computed by the security parameters, of which conflicts and disputes are part of it.

Motivation for the Entities Involved

The proposed framework ensures that the entities involved: Cloud provider, governing body and the end user are motivated to participate in the operations. The motivation for the governing body is in the satisfaction on its leadership service to control the cloud operation between the cloud provider and the end user successfully in a secure manner. The Governing Body will also hold the power to send a warning or shut-down a cloud provider if the cloud provider fails to comply with most of the regulations set by the Governing Body. The cloud provider can also be warned if its recent methods to secure the cloud are proving to be ineffective or even dangerous. In this case, the cloud providers might be reluctant to support the Governing Body and might even question its existence as it is harming them in one way. On the other hand however, by complying with all the regulations set by the Governing Body, they will ensure quality in their functioning and therefore will attract a large number of customers. In this way, the Governing Body can prove to be a negative factor to those who aren't securing their technology properly and can also prove to be massively beneficial for those who are abiding by all the rules and regulations of the Governing Body.

As a result, the cloud providers who are detrimental to the needs of the user are marginalized and the cloud providers who are sensitive to the secure operations of the cloud become successful in their operations. This also ensures that the provider works collaboratively with the governing body to ensure its success in its existence.

Thus the governing body provides organizational control to the cloud environment by keeping track of all the activities going on and providing solutions as and when required. By establishing a central body, cloud computing will become organized and managed by ensuring right information is conveyed at right time to right parties. Thus, through this governance control framework enabled governing body, which is trusted by both the cloud provider and the end user, we can eliminate the lack of transparency that exists between the user and the cloud provider. As the end users perceive security and transparency in the communications, with minimal conflicts and disputes, they would be motivated to participate in the clouds computing activities (Table 1).

ORGANIZATION CONTROL FRAMEWORK

The functionalities that were discussed earlier can be achieved by our framework, as shown in Figure 2. Security parameters indicated in Figure 2 include technical, legal and policy parameters. In this framework, Threat Index (TI) calculates the vulnerability of a cloud environment based data center to threats and attacks. This threat index is calculated based on the parameters from cloud based data center security control, legal control, policy control perspectives. By calculating the threat index, performance trend of a cloud provider can be identified and communicated to the user. Threat Index can be calculated over a specified period of time and that can be compared with the benchmark index thresholds obtained with the help of historical training [29] -[32] . Historical training is done by collection of data, with and without attacks, with and without legal control, with and without policy control over a long period of time. The comparison of the index threshold with the threat index helps the organization to gain knowledge of the current security, policy and legal trends. This will help the organization and the cloud provider to increase or decrease the controls from technical, legal and policy perspective with the help of solution architecture framework. It will also help them pointing out the methodologies that are flawed, if any, and help them improve it in order to increase the reliability of the cloud.

Table 1. Proposed methods to handle security challenges.

Security Challenges	**Method(s)**
Data Centre	1. Design a basic layout for the Data Centre such that secure cloud services are provided by cloud provider to the user 2. Continuously monitor security related threats and provide solutions such as data replication and hot-site recovery service, if the need arises
Policy Creation and Control	1. Security policy will be drafted by Governing Body to ensure the security at all layers 2. Cloud Provider and Governing Body will collaborate to implement and control the features in the security policy.
User Awareness	1. The governing body will need to specify all the procedures and methods that a cloud provider and user need to follow 2. Filter the information and make the users aware of the security features without leaking any confidential information. 3. central body convey right information at right time to right parties involved in the environment in an automated fashion
Legal Control	1. Governing body would acquire global laws pertaining to the cloud operation and take care of all the legal matters related to global cloud operations so that the Cloud Provider can focus its resources on making the cloud safe, secure and efficient.
Performance Evaluation	1. Assess the performance of the cloud provider based on the security parameters and estimate the efficiency and the threat index of the provider's operations. 2. Governing Body will then rank all the cloud providers based on their efficiency.
Conflict and Dispute Resolution	1. This will be done with the help of threat index that computes security parameters of which, conflicts are a part. 2. If the cloud provider is found guilty in a dispute, its license will be revoked.

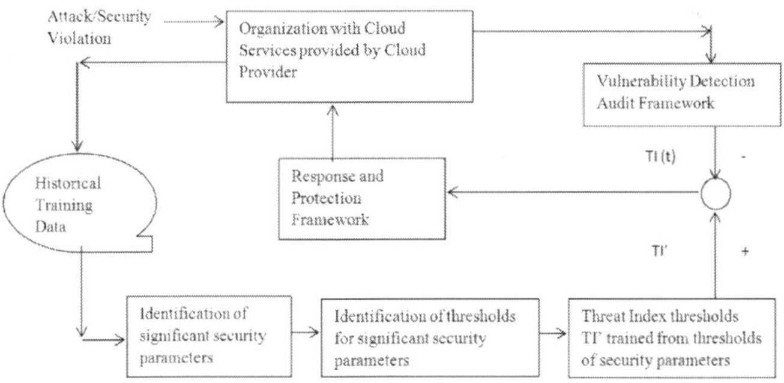

Figure 2. Organization control framework for cloud services.

SUMMARY AND CONCLUSION

Cloud computing is purported to be the future of the IT industry. Cloud computing marks a true paradigm shift in how the computing would happen in the future and cloud computing is likely to have the same impact on IT industry that foundries have had on the manufacturing industry. However, one thing that proves to be the biggest obstacle in its course is security issue.

Security issues vary from physical and legal level involving data centers and geographical locations to methodological level involving the policy and logic used in deploying the cloud to technical level involving the technology involved in implementing the cloud. This has prevented cloud computing from its widespread adoption.

Harshit Srivastava, Sathish Alampalayam Kumar From an organizational control perspective, we provided an automated control framework comprised of independent governing body that will mediate between the cloud provider and the user. Governing body will be responsible for ensuring the security of cloud based data center, implementation of a secure policy & control, increase the user awareness about security methods deployed, handling the legal matters, resolution of disputes, evaluation of performance and providing solutions for the end user. We have described a framework, which computes threat index based on the security parameters, that the governing body could apply to fulfill their responsibilities and use in the planning the implementation of the security policy to keep the organization in control from the cloud computing security and privacy issues.

REFERENCES

1. Mell, P. and Grance, T. (2011) The NIST Definition of Cloud Computing. NIST Special Publication 800-145, National Institute of Standards and Technology, Gaithersburg. [Citation Time(s):1]
2. Armbrust, M., Fox, A., Griffith, R., Joseph, A.D., Katz, R., Konwinski, A., Lee, G., Patterson, D., Rabkin, A., Stoica, I. and Zaharia, M. (2009) Above the Clouds: A Berkeley View of Cloud Computing. Technical Report No. UCB/ EECS-2009-28, University of California, Berkeley. [Citation Time(s):1]
3. Morgan, T.P. (2014) Amazon Cloud Knocked out by Violent Storms in Virginia. http://www.theregister.co.uk/2012/06/30/amazon_cloud_storm_outage/ [Citation Time(s):1]
4. Mah, P. (2014) The Big Gmail Crash and the Lesson for Email Administrators. http://www.theemailadmin.com/2011/03/the-big-gmail-crash-and-the-lesson-for-email-administrators [Citation Time(s):1]
5. Cloud Security Alliance Guide (2013). https://www.cloudsecurityalliance.org/csaguide.pdf [Citation Time(s):1]
6. Symantec (2014). http://www.symantec.com/connect/blogs/data-breach-trends [Citation Time(s):2]
7. Open Security Foundation Dataloss DB [Data File] (2014). http://www.symantec.com/connect/blogs/data-loss-db-breach-data-breaches-classified-source [Citation Time(s):1]
8. Glisson, W.B., McDonald, A. and Welland, R. (2006) Web Engineering Security: A Practitioner's Perspective. Proceedings of the 6th International Conference on Web Engineering, ACM, Palo Alto. [Citation Time(s):2]
9. Ponemon Institute LLC (2011) The 2011 Cost of Data Breach Study: Global. Symantec. [Citation Time(s):1]
10. Clemons, E.K. and Chen, Y.Y. (2011) Making the Decision to Contract for Cloud Services: Managing the Risk of an Extreme Form of IT Outsourcing. 44th Hawaii International Conference on System Sciences (HICSS), Kauai, 4-7 January 2011, 1-10, http://dx.doi.org/10.1109/HICSS.2011.292 [Citation Time(s):1]
11. Chow, R., Golle, P., Jakobsson, M., Shi, E., Staddon, J., Masuoka, R. and Molina, J. (2009) Controlling Data in the Cloud: Outsourcing Computation without Outsourcing Control. Proceedings of the 2009 ACM Workshop on Cloud Computing Security, Chicago, 13 November

2009, 85-90. [Citation Time(s):1]

12. Subashini, S. and Kavitha, V.A. (2011) Survey on Security Issues in Service Delivery Models of Cloud Computing. Journal of Network and Computer Applications, 34, 1-11. http://dx.doi.org/10.1016/j.jnca.2010.07.006 [Citation Time(s):1]
13. Cohen, M. (2012) Forecasting the First Steps of Cloud Adoption. eWEEK, 14, 1-3. [Citation Time(s):1]
14. Ernst & Young Advisory Services (2011) Into the Cloud, out of The Fog—The 2011 Global Information Security Survey. Ernst & Young, Zimbabwe. [Citation Time(s):1]
15. Willcocks, L., Venters, W., Whitley, E. and Hindle, J. (2012) Cloud on the Landscape: Problems and Challenges. The New IT Outsourcing Landscape: From Innovation to Cloud Services. Palgrave Macmillan, Basingstoke. [Citation Time(s):2]
16. Jansen, W. and Grance, T. (2011) Guidelines on Security and Privacy in Public Cloud Computing. NIST Technical Report-SP-800-144. [Citation Time(s):2]
17. Vascellaro, J.E. (2013) Wall Street Journal Article. http://blogs.wsj.com/digits/2009/03/08/1214/ [Citation Time(s):1]
18. Bennett, R.G. (2010) Silver Clouds, Dark Linings: A Concise Guide to Cloud Computing. Prentice Hall, Upper Saddle River. [Citation Time(s):1]
19. Guo, Z., Song, M. and Song, J. (2010) A Governance Model for Cloud Computing. IEEE Proceedings of the International Conference on Management and Service Science, Wuhan, 24-26 August 2010, 3759-3764. [Citation Time(s):1]
20. Chaput, S.R. and Ringwood, K. (2010) Cloud Compliance: A Framework for Using Cloud Computing in a Regulated World. In: Antonopoulos, N. and Gillam, L., Eds., Cloud Computing Principles Systems and Applications, Springer, Heidelberg, 241-255. [Citation Time(s):1]
21. Matthews, J., Garfinkel, T., Hoff, C. and Wheeler, J. (2009) Virtual Machine Contracts for Datacenter and Cloud Computing Environments. ACDC'09 Proceedings of the 1st Workshop on Automated Control for Datacenters and Clouds, Barcelona, 19 June 2009, 25-30. http://dx.doi.org/10.1145/1555271.1555278 [Citation Time(s):1]
22. Kamara, S. and Lauter, K. (2010) Cryptographic Cloud Storage. Proceedings of the 1st Workshop on Real Life Cryptographic Protocols and Standardization,

Canary Islands, 28 January 2010, 1-14. [Citation Time(s):1]

23. Brandic, I., Dustdar, S., Anstett, T., Schumm, D., Leymann, F. and Konrad, R. (2010) Compliant Cloud Computing (C3): Architecture and Language Support for User-Driven Compliance Management in Clouds. IEEE Proceedings of the 3rd International Conference on Cloud Computing, Miami, 5-10 July 2010, 244-251. [Citation Time(s):1]
24. Ristenpart, T., Tromer, E., Shacham, H. and Savage, S. (2009) Hey, You, Get off of My Cloud: Exploring Information Leakage in Third-Party Compute Clouds. Proceedings of the 16th ACM Conference on Computer and Communications Security, Chicago, 9-13 November 2009, 199-212. [Citation Time(s):1]
25. PCI Security Standards Council (2011) Information Supplement: PCI DSS Virtualization Guidelines. [Citation Time(s):1]
26. Wei, J., Zhang, X., Ammons, G., Bala, V. and Ning, P. (2009) Managing Security of Virtual Machine Images in a Cloud Environment. In: Oprea, A., Ed., ACM Workshop on Cloud Computing Security, ACM, New York. [Citation Time(s):1]
27. Trevino, L.K. (1992) The Social Effects of Punishment in Organizations: A Justice Perspective. Academy of Management Review, 17, 647-676. [Citation Time(s):1]
28. Merhi, M.I. and Ahluwalia, P. (2013) Information Security Policies Compliance: The Role of Organizational Punishment. Proceedings of the 19th Americas Conference on Information Systems, Chicago, 15-17 August 2013, 1-7. [Citation Time(s):1]
29. Alampalayam, S.P. and Kumar, A. (2003) Security Model for Routing Attacks in Mobile Ad Hoc Networks. Proceedings of IEEE VTC, Louisville, 6-9 October 2003, 2122-2126. [Citation Time(s):1]
30. Alampalayam, S.P. and Kumar, A. (2007) Statistical Based Intrusion Detection Framework Using Six Sigma Technique. International Journal of Computer Science and Network Security, 7, 333-342.
31. Alampalayam, S.P. and Kumar, A. (2004) Predictive Security Model Using Data Mining. Proceedings of IEEE Globecom, Louisville, 29 November-3 December 2004, 2208-2212.
32. Alampalayam, S.P. and Srinivasan, S. (2009) Intrusion Recovery Framework for Tactical Mobile Ad Hoc Networks. The International Journal of Computer Science and Network Security, 9, 1-10.

CHAPTER

7

Security Model for Preserving Privacy over Encrypted Cloud Computing

Jassim R. Mlgheit[1], Essam H. Houssein[2], Hala H. Zayed[1]

[1]Faculty of Computers and Informatics, Benha University, Benha, Egypt

[2]Faculty of Computers and Information, Minia University, Minia, Egypt

ABSTRACT

In our today's life, it is obvious that cloud computing is one of the new and most important innovations in the field of information technology which constitutes the ground for speeding up the development in great size storage of data as well as the processing and distribution of data on the largest scale. In other words, the most important interests of any data owner nowadays are related to all of the security as well as the privacy of data, especially in the case of outsourcing private data on a cloud server publicly which has not

Citation: Mlgheit, J. , Houssein, E. and Zayed, H. (2017), "Security Model for Preserving Privacy over Encrypted Cloud Computing". *Journal of Computer and Communications*, **5**, 149-165. doi: 10.4236/jcc.2017.56009.

been one of the well-trusted and reliable domains. With the aim of avoiding any leakage or disclosure of information, we will encrypt any information important or confidential prior to being uploaded to the server and this may lead to an obstacle which encounters any attempt to support any efficient keyword query to be and ranked with matching results on such encrypted data. Recent researches conducted in this area have focused on a single keyword query with no proper ranking scheme in hand. In this paper, we will propose a new model called Secure Model for Preserving Privacy Over Encrypted Cloud Computing (SPEC) to improve the performance of cloud computing and to safeguard privacy of data in comparison to the results of previous researches in regard to accuracy, privacy, security, key generation, storage capacity as well as trapdoor, index generation, index encryption, index update, and finally files retrieval depending on access frequency.

Keywords: Cloud Computing, Multi-Keyword Query, Ranked Query, Trapdoor, Privacy Preserving, Encrypted Cloud Data, Top-K Query, Cloud Security

INTRODUCTION

We can refer to cloud computing as being a remarkable and outstanding IT innovation in today's life. It is mainly based on the fact that cloud can produce resources and services of computing since it is a modern and distinguished technique. The services provided by cloud computing are numerous and can be classified into the following: Infrastructure-as-a-Service (IaaS), Platform-as-a-Ser- vice (PaaS) as well as Software-as-a-Service (SaaS) [1] . These services are also offered on the largest data canters scale such as Amazon, Google, and even Microsoft which draws the attention of several numbers of customers around the globe. As regards minor as well as medium size businesses, cloud computing relocation develops noteworthy and big savings from the economic perspective. As a matter of fact, cloud computing relocation is mainly dependent on the model of "pay per use" in respect with prices, as the payment by the user is based on his using or consuming the available resources [2] . And in spite of all the advantages offered by the cloud computing relocation, there are however some obstacles and problems which may occur such as inter-provider data portability problem, energy conservation problem, as well as security problem [3] .

Several methods are mainly proposing to provide a precise protection of data privacy upon outsourcing storage on the Cloud Server Provider (CSP) [4] - [9] [11] [12] [13] . These methods use certain cryptographic mechanisms so as to enhance the policies used for access control. Hence, the users are allowed to get the keys for the items of data to which they have access. Theoretically, we have too many cryptographic techniques which can be used to achieve this objective [12] .

Furthermore, the next important issue regarding the encryption as well as access control is known as key management as the mechanisms used for key management mechanisms may provide good access control to the data that are being outsourced on CSPs [4] . There are many methods suggested for exploiting the hierarchical together with other relationships taking place among several items of data so as to minimize the number of distributed keys and make key management more simple [4] [5] [7] [8] [11] . In other words, in the event of changing access control policies for these methods or approaches, the key distribution should be carried out once again in order to ascertain that authorized users are only allowed to access. Also, one only feature be easy to run on the computer of the user, i.e. cloud computing systems interface software. It must be as simple as the commonly used web browser, and the cloud network shall be responsible for the rest [12] [13] .

In addition, there are several approaches which are suggested mainly so as to assess the security of cloud computing and therefore propose a "trusted the third party" with the aim of making sure that security considerations are complied with in any cloud computing environment [14] [15] . So as to confront the disclosure of data, a typical solution shall be private data encrypting prior to their upload onto the cloud server. Firstly, we must verify that any data are invisible for the external users as well as administrators of the cloud. Secondly, we have some strict limitations of processing on encrypted data. For instance, standard searching algorithms of plain text are no longer in use nowadays. So as to carry out a keyword-based query, we should decrypt all data set regardless of the tiny matching result set.

In this paper, we will propose a new scheme to improve the performance of cloud computing and to safeguard privacy of data in comparison to the results of previous researches in regard to accuracy, privacy, security, key generation, storage capacity as well as trapdoor, index generation, index encryption, index update, and finally files retrieval depending on access frequency.The paper will be organized as follows. In Section 2, we will present the works related to ours. In Section 3, we will present the Problem formulation. Section 4 we will describe Precision and rank privacy. Section 5 we will evaluate our model through Performance analysis. Finally, Section 6 will be the Conclusion.

RELATED WORK

This section will cover a detailed review of the related works which are referred for to formulate our proposed model.

Kamara, S., & Lauter, K. [23] , have submitted their proposal of a conceivable architecture design to be used in a cryptographic cloud storage. As soon as the data are being prepared for storage onto the cloud, the owner of data will create certain indexes as well as encrypt such data using a specific scheme for symmetric encryption (e.g., AES) by means of a unique key. Therefore, the indexes are being encrypted by means of a scheme of searchable encryption to further encrypt such unique key by a scheme of attribute-based encryption following the proper policy. Eventually, all of the encrypted data as well as indexes are being encrypted in a manner which can be verified afterward by the data verifier to check if they are integral by means of a storage proof. As such, this identical strategy is also used in several types of research. In their turn, all of Fu, Z., et al. [24] , have also proposed the application of a deterministic algorithm for encryption with the aim of keywords' encryption, as well as using stream ciphers so as to carry out security post-encrypt keywords. Furthermore, Han, F., et al. [25] , gave their proposal of a new technique for transforming the Key-Policy Attribute-Based Encryption (KP-ABE) to be Attribute-Based Encryption instead using the feature of Keyword Search (ABEKS). In order to render transformation feasible, the researchers were keen on defining the feature of weak anonymity, which is known as attribute privacy that is also incurring slight computational transparency. The so-called cipher text-policy Attribute-Based Encryption (CP-ABE) is be used for the first while the aim of implementing a thorough control known as "priority access". In the next step, the fundamental or principal scheme "KP-ABE" applied for supporting encrypted data search facility. Nevertheless, the ABEKS is somewhat vulnerable to security violation as it is not providing the adequate or satisfactory feature of Access Control Aware Search (ACAS); however, it may leak such a volume of documents which includes the checked words. As well, it may be of less efficiency compared to such methods depending on the search based on the index. This would perform a complete decryption of documents so as to recover the documents that are requested; while the methods of search based on the index are only decrypting documents' identifiers which include but not limited to such the keywords to be searched. As far as Chen, R., et al. [26] , are concerned, Asymmetric Searchable Encryption is proposed in this respect in which they introduced Public Key Encryption with keyword Search (PEKS), that is dependent on the assumption of Bilinear Diffie -Hellman (BDH). The schemes of Asymmetric Searchable Encryption are suitable for to any situation in which the part which is searching onto data cloud differ from the generating one. The principal drawback in this regard is related to the weak security control.

According to Liu, Q., et al. [27] , there is a newly proposed a scheme of Secure as well as Privacy Preserving Keyword Search (SPKS), that is especially allowing the Cloud Service Provider (CSP) to partake decipherment process, to retrieve files which contain certain keywords that are only specified by users, with the objective of lowering all of the computational as well as communication overhead to be decrypted for users, with one condition that user data are being preserved and their as well as user querying privacy are maintained. The thorough analysis of performance reveals that SPKS scheme is fit to be applied in any cloud environment. Furthermore, Shiba Sampat Kale, P., & Lahane, S. R. [28] , have proposed a plain idea related to Multi-keyword Ranked Search over Encrypted cloud data (MRSE) which is mainly dependent on protected inner product computation in addition to effective similarity for coordinate matching. Then, there are two meaningfully significant improved schemes of MRSE so as to attain numerous strict privacy preconditions using two different threat models. Also, the assignment of anonymous ID is to be used by the user in order to maintain and secure the utmost security of data onto the cloud server. So as to improve the experience of data search and the search service in general, there should be more advanced extension using both schemes in order to support as much more as possible search semantics. As well, all of Xia, Z., et al. [29] , have proposed a semantic multi-keyword ranked search scheme over the encrypted cloud data (MRSE) that is concurrently meeting some stringent privacy requirements. First of all, the researchers have used "Latent Semantic Analysis (LSA)" so as to show the existing relationship between all of the terms as well as documents. This relationship between terms is inevitably taken. In the second place, they scheme we use is employing secure "k-nearest neighbor (k-NN)" so as to achieve secure search functions. According to this proposed scheme, the exact matching files are not only returned, but also this feature extends to returning the files which include terms latent semantically related to query keyword.

Also, Madane, S. A., & Patil, B. M. [30] , have discussed in detail the multiple- keyword ranked search over encrypted cloud data problem and also constructed various security settings which are required. Based on various concepts of multi- keyword, the researchers selected an efficient principle for coordinate matching. Also, they started in the first place to suggest a secure inner data computation feature. As well, the researchers could achieve efficient ranking result by means of k-nearest neighbor method that is used as well in order to help the server encrypt the document by RSA Algorithm and also convert encrypted document to be a Zip file having an activation code, then this activation code shall send to user a request for download. Finally, Barde, C. R., et al. [31] , firstly executed a plain idea of Single Keyword Search over Encrypted Data as well as Multi-key- word Ranked Search over Encrypted cloud data (MRSE) which is mainly dependent on protected inner product computation in addition to the effective similarity of coordinate matching. In other words, several matches are being used with the aim of capturing the data documents relevance of in relation to the search query. Then, there are two meaningfully significant improved schemes of MRSE so as to attain numerous stringent privacy preconditions using two different threat models. Also, the assignment of anonymous ID is to be used by the user in order to maintain and secure the utmost security of the data onto the cloud server. So as to improve the experience of data search and the search service, there should be more advanced extension using both schemes in order to support as much more as possible search semantics.

PROBLEM FORMULATION

In this research paper, we will propose a new (SPEC) model with the aim of improving the previously used models as well as results of the previous researches in this field, mainly document keyword collection which represents as index, encrypted index as well as secure index, multi-keyword query, trapdoor which is an encrypted version of a query. We will describe hereinafter the threat model, abbreviations as well as the proposed model architecture, and eventually the proposed model construction.

Threat Model

In our proposed model architecture, we consider that the cloud server is "honest-but-curious" which is typically adopted by most previous searchable encryption schemes. In other words, the cloud server is implementing honestly the protocol and then returns back the search results in a correct manner, however, it is curious as well to deduce some important information while performing the execution of the protocol. In the well-established cipher text, the encrypted dataset, encrypted search query and the searchable index are made are available to the cloud server [16] . We have two main parts, first model "Ciphertext Model" which supposes that the CSP can see encrypted files as well as indexes. Second "Background Model", in which CSP can collect intentionally queries' statistical data (trapdoors). Therefore, CSP is capable of calculating the file containing keyword [17] .

Proposed Model Architecture

The entire architecture of cloud data service system which involves four entities, is shown in Figure 1. The data owner, data user, administration server and cloud server.

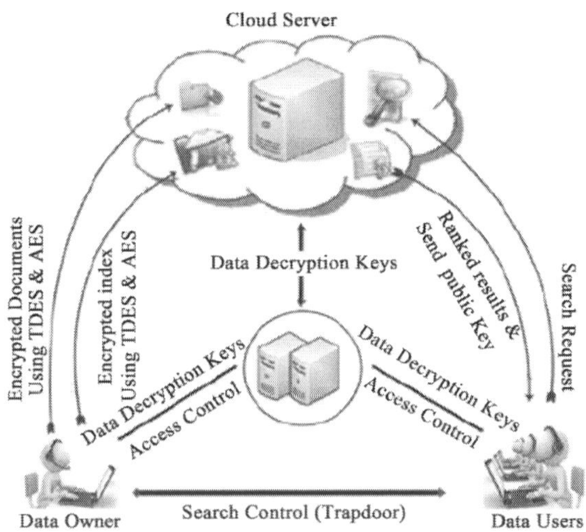

Figure 1. Architecture model of the search over encrypted cloud computing.

A data owner has a data documents collection for outsourcing them to the cloud server in an encrypted form. So as to activate search capability over encrypted document collection for effective data utilization, the data owner before outsourcing, will be requested to build an encrypted searchable index from documents, he outsources to the index as well as the encrypted document collection to cloud server. For searching over the encrypted documents, the approved user will acquire a corresponding through search control mechanisms as he first obtains the trapdoor firstly, i.e., the "encrypted" version of the search keyword, from the data owner, then submits the trapdoor to the cloud server. As soon as trapdoor is received from the data user, a cloud server is in charge of searching the index and returning the corresponding collection of encrypted documents. In order to improve document retrieval accuracy, search result must be ranked by cloud server in accordance with certain ranking criteria such as (coordinate matching). Furthermore, in if we would like to minimize communication cost, data user will send an optional number along with the trapdoor, and then, a cloud server is only sending back top-k documents which are relevant to the search query. At the end, access control mechanism used for managing decryption given to users as well as updating data collection by inserting new documents, updating existing ones, deleting existing ones.

Proposed Model Construction

In this section, we will present a detailed description of our proposed model which will be based on the following logarithms:

Key Generation

Our proposal is based mainly upon the following: a key generator which is able to generate new keys depending on three part (M1, M2, and S) and a set of operations. Results are merged to check the size of output equal the size of the plain text. In case the size of the output is equal to the size of plain text, therefore, merged key can be entered as a secret key. Algorithm 1. Illustrates the steps of the key generation proposal.

Algorithm 1. Secret Key generation

1. Procedure: Secret Key generation
2. The secret key consists of three parts.
3. Converting first part to square matrix A.
4. Making transpose to matrix A and stored in a

Matrix B.

5. Multiplying the A to B.
6. Storing result in M_1
7. Converting second part to square matrix C.
8. Making transpose to matrix C and store in

Matrix D.

9. Multiplying the C to D.
10. Storing result in M_2
11. Making reverse to the third part and store in E.
12. Making Xor operation between the third part

And E.

13. Storing result in S.

14. Merging the three-part to present the new key in

The following form:

15. S connect M_1 connect M_2

16. The new key possible to enter the master key.

17. End

Build Index

Having generated the key pairs, then the owner will build a file collection index. In general, we will utilize Kuzu, M., et al. [18] scheme to be the basis on which our index is built. Then, building the index will be shown in detail hereinafter in Algorithm 2.

Algorithm 2. Build Index

1. Procedure: Build Index
2. K_{id} = Keygen(ψ)
3. For all Di ∈∈ D do
4. F_i = extract features of Di
5. for all f_{ij} ∈∈ F_i and g_k ∈∈ g do
6. If g_k (f_{ij}) ∉ bucket identifier list then
7. Add g_k (f_{ij}) to the bucket identifier list
8. end if
9. end for
10. end for
11. for all B_k ∈∈ bucket identifier list do
12. Y_{Bk} = EncK_{id} (B_k)
13. add Y_{Bk} to I
14. end for
15. return I

where D is data document collection; g is composite hash functions; ψψ is security parameter.

Encryption Index

Having built the index, the owner will encrypt index so as to ensure the privacy of index. So far as there is limited computing power on data owner's part, we will have encrypts index [19] . Our process of encryption process will be detailed hereinafter in Algorithm 3.

Algorithm 3. Encryption index

1. Procedure: encryption index
2. Split the index I into two vectors {I', I"}
3. for each element ij ∈∈ I
4. set I'j = I"j = Ij if sj ∈∈ S is 1
5. Otherwise I'j = 1/2 Ij + r, I"j − 1/2 Ij - r
6. Encrypt {I', I"} with (M1, M2) into $\{M_1^t \cdot I', M_2^t \cdot I''\}$
7. Output Enc SK (I) = $\{M1^t \cdot I', M2^t \cdot I''\}$ as the secure index.

Where r is a random number

Encryption and Decryption of Data

Having uploaded the data onto the cloud server, the owner will encrypt file collection so as to make sure of the privacy files. Meanwhile, the data owner is only having a limited computing power, and we have used *Tripple Data Encryption Standard* (TDES) and Advanced Encryption Standard (AES-128) Algorithms in order to encrypt files with the aim of ascertaining data privacy. Having received the matched documents from CSP for the purposes of search request corresponding, the approved user will decrypt such files by means of the private key as well as receive plain text using Tripple DES algorithm in order to decrypt the document. TDES takes a 64-bit long plaintext data block 56-bit input and in the meantime will generate a 64-bit block output. We conduct the same DES algorithm for three times on each of the data blocks. It is often extending DES key size of as per the algorithm to be applied three times successively by means of 3 different keys [20] [21] . Prior to the use of 3TDES, the user will generate and distribute a 3TDES key K firstly, that is composed of three main DES keys K_1, K_2 and K_3. It means however that actual 3TDES key has length $3 \times 56 = 168$ bits. The process of encryption will be detailed hereinafter in two Algorithms

Algorithm 4.1. Tripple Des of Encryption and Decryption

We can describe the encryption and decryption process as follows:-

1. Procedure: Encryption and Decryption
2. Encrypt the documents or files using single DES with first Key that is called K1.
3. Then, decrypt the output from Encrypt process with first key using single DES

   With second key that is called K2.
4. Finally, encrypt the output from decrypt process with second key using

   Single DES with third key that is called K3.
5. The output from encrypt process with third key is encrypted document.

Decryption process of encrypted documents or files is a reverse process. The user will firstly, decrypt of documents or files using third key that is called K3, then encrypt it using second key that is called K2, and finally, decrypt of documents or files using first key that is called K1.

Algorithm 4.2. AES-128bits of Encryption and Decryption

We describe in detail the rounds of Advanced Encryption Standard (AES-128) Algorithms in order to encrypt files or documents and each round consist of four sub-processes as follows

1. Procedure: Encryption and Decryption
2. SubBytes:

Byte Substitution is a nonlinear byte substitution that operates independently on each byte by looking up on a fixed table is called (S-box) and the result of the 16 input bytes is a matrix of as well as four columns as well as four rows.

3. ShiftRows:

is shifted to the left for each the four rows of the matrix and transformation operates on the rows , it cyclically shifts on bytes in each row and bytes that fall off of the row are reinserted on the right side of the same row. The shift is carried out as follows:

- unchanged of The first row.
- shifted one byte (one positions) to the left of The second row.
- shifted two byte (two positions) to the left of The third row.
- shifted three byte (three positions) to the left of The fourth row.
- the output is a novel matrix containing the same byte but shifted.

4. MixColumns:

MixColumns is transformed process of all the columns that containing four bytes by means of certain mathematical function. that Such a function takes for each column four bytes as input and the result is four totally novel bytes, and novel bytes is replace with original bytes ,The result is a novel matrix containing 16 new bytes. This step is not executed in the final round.

5. Add round key:

In this Add Round Key operation which executed (XOR) operation to the 128 bits of the round key. If this is the final round then the result is encrypted documents or files. Executed XOR operations on results from mix column and round keys. For AES 128,128 bit XOR operations are executed. Otherwise, the resulting 128 bits are interpreted as 16 bytes and then we begin another similar round.

Trapdoor Generation

Having sorted the data in the cloud, if authorized user is looking forward to retrieving any file containing some keywords, he will compute the trapdoor (Twi) for keywords wi ∈∈ w and then resend it to the cloud server provider (CSP) in the form of search request [19] . The process of computing trapdoor will be detailed hereinafter in Algorithm 5.

Algorithm 5. Trapdoor generation

1. Procedure: Trapdoor
2. Compute Trapdoor
3. Send trapdoor to the (CSP)
4. The user gets the trapdoor information from the data Owner
5. For inserted keywords, the user computes the trapdoor
6. Then, the user sends trapdoor (Twi, k) to the CSP

Where k is an optional value, Twi is a compute trapdoor.

Ranked Search

Data user will send the trapdoor to the CSP. Having the information, first of all, the CSP will determine the files that may be accessed by data consumer (DC), and he will compute afterward matching score of each authorized file in the encrypted index set. Then the CSP will sort results depending on scores and will return back the top k files in the resulting set to the DC. In our trapdoor algorithm, whenever keyword access frequency is regarded, values of locations in the query vector are very likely to be determined by their corresponding access frequency. The process of ranked search will be detailed hereinafter in Algorithm 6.

Algorithm 6. Ranked search

1. Procedure: Ranked Search
2. for every level i from 1 to n do
3. If (I' (wi)== Twi)
4. Rank (Ri)/higher level which is matching query
5. end if
6. end for
7. Cloud server ranks matched documents according to rank.
8. Then, it sends top-k documents that have most relevant to the user R = {r1, r2 … rk} Where R is relevant documents, Twi is Trapdoor.

PRECISION AND RANKED PRIVACY

The definitions of commonly used performance metrics will be used herein, which is precise to measure search result in an accurate manner as well as the rank privacy which can count the information leakage of search results. In order to assess the effect on search result accuracy, we use the definition "precision" [22] . In other words, "precision" of a top-k search will be defined as Pk = Ḱ/k whereas Ḱ represents the number the real top-k documents which are returned by cloud server. Meanwhile, we will assess the "rank privacy". The definition "rank privacy" is also used [22] , i.e., the rank privacy at point k is calculated as P=∑ki=1i/K2P=∑i=1ki/K2 Ṕ. For every document in the returned top-k documents, we will define the rank perturbation as Ṕ i=|ci′−ci|i=|ci′−ci| where ci′ is the ranking of document di in the retrieved top-k documents, and it is set to k if greater than k, ci is the actual ranking of document di in the data set and k denotes the number of top-k retrieved documents.

PERFORMANCE ANALYSIS

We have executed our own schemes using a laptop or a PC provided with Intel Core i5 processor of 3.3 GHz capacity as well as 4 GB RAM memory. The total number of simulation code is 5637 lines written in java (JDK) language with Sql yog, NetBeans IDE 7.1.2, Mozilla Firefox, using simple

File *Transfer Protocol* (FTP) protocols and apache-tomcat server of similar computation power using Amazon EC2 M1 Medium instance. So as to generate ranked keyword query, we use on a random basis, a letter from a certain keyword, then it will be replaced with another one. We will allow mostly two ranked query of keywords. In the next section, we will give a detailed description charts which show our research results.

Generation Time and Storage Space of Secret Key

On the superior features of SPEC in comparison to previous solutions is that it can naturally extend keyword dictionary set at the minimal cost. In our experiments, we will firstly compare time consumption to generate secret keys of proposed Extended-Keygen algorithm with MKQE and MRSE algorithm when new keywords are introduced in the dictionary. Then, we compare storage consumption performance.

We can observe from Figure 2(a) that SPEC is more efficient than MKQE and MRSE. Basically, whenever original dictionary size is up to 1000, MRSE,

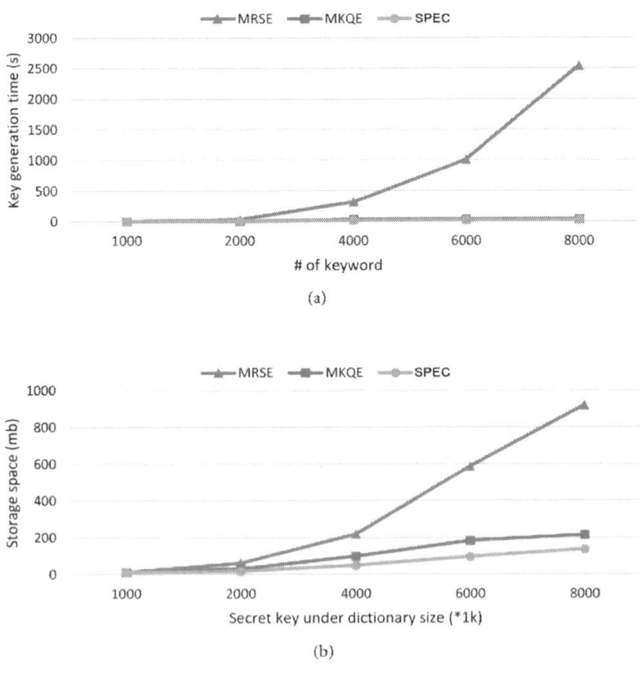

Figure 2. (a) Secret key generation overhead (s), starting from 1000 keywords; (b) the storage comparison under the same dictionary size.

MKQE as well as SPEC will use the same algorithm in order to generate secret keys, thus their performances are the same. The overhead for secret key generations in MRSE is gradually increasing compared to MKQE and SPEC. SPEC is better than MKQE and MRSE and the difference is minimal. Thus, the time consumption in MRSE is higher than MKQE and SPEC. Furthermore, the performance gap becomes even wider as more and more keywords are added. Apparently, SPEC has a better performance than MRSE and MKQE since it reuses an original set of indexes during keyword expansion. A number of elements required to be produced in matrices is too much smaller than MKQE as well as MRSE respectively.

Also, we compare storage consumption to update keyword dictionary as well as other data structures in our scheme with MKQE and MRSE. Result in Figure 2(b) indicates that SPEC consumes less space. As the size of the dictionary increases, SPEC saves, even more, storage spaces than MKQE and MRSE. The reason is that in SPEC, we use partitioned matrices and a great quantity of unused elements which are not stored. Due to the help of linked matrix list, SPEC can make sure that the space consumption grows linearly according to the expansion of dictionary.

Time of Trapdoor and Index

In order to evaluate the SPEC performance, we are going to analyze as well time consumption in regard to various operations. In our experiments, we will assess the index construction time, trapdoor construction time, index update time and the finally Index encryption time.

In Figure 3(a) we notice index generation time for the index, the generation time which is increasing in a linear manner with respect to a number of inserted keywords. Trapdoor generation time is almost the same as index generation time because of the identical procedure.

In Figure 3(b) a comparison is held between trapdoor generation time consumption of MRSE, MKQE on the one hand and SPEC on the other hand. As per results, we can observe that it shows in all scenarios, SPEC outperforms MKQE and MRSE, and therefore performance gap is larger with the increase in keyword dictionary size.

As per Figure 4(a) results of time consumption metric as soon as the dictionary is extended. In this set of experiments, we compare time spending on index update operation in SPEC with the time to MKQE the complete set of file indexes as well MRSE since the dictionary expands. Also based on this result, we can observe that if keyword number in the dictionary increases,

SPEC achieves better performance than previous strategies. In other words, when the dictionary becomes larger, our proposed system achieves better performance than the two existing systems.According to Figure 4(b) a comparison is held between the time consumption to generate the encrypted file indexes with different sizes of keyword dictionary. As shown in the results, SPEC takes less time to generate the indexes in all scenarios. As per Figure 4(b), we can see that if the number of keywords in the dictionary becomes larger, the time of encryption index increases gradually and then SPEC outperforms all of MKQE and MSRE.

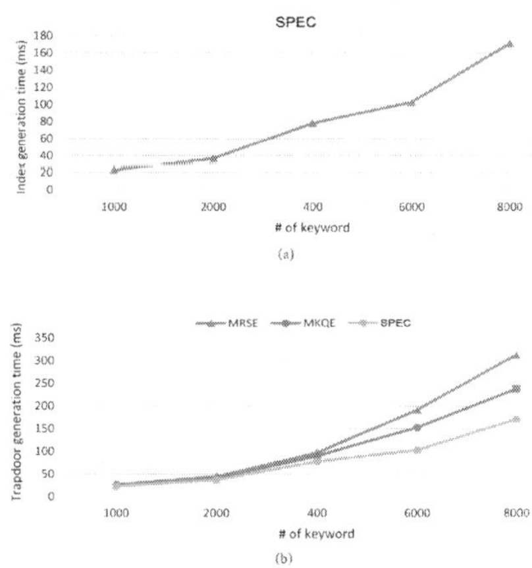

Figure 3. (a) The generation time of index for single file v.s. # of the keywords; (b) Time consumption comparison on trapdoor generation (ms).

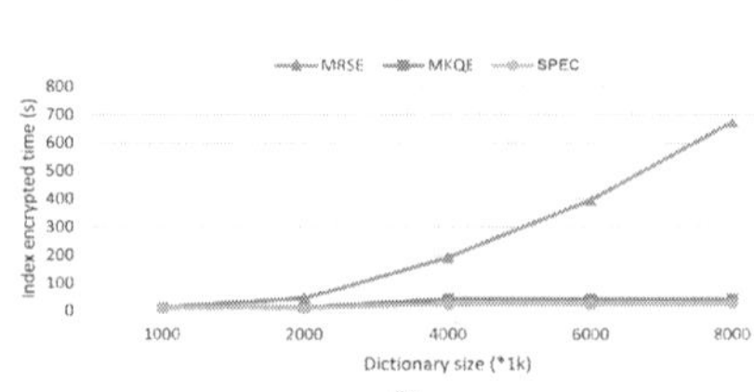

Figure 4. (a) update index time starting with 1000 with update index; (b) Index encryp- tion time comparison with 1000 file indexes encrypted.

Keyword access Frequency Analysis

In this set of experiments, we compare the query results in SPEC, MRSE, and MKQE when taking the access frequency of keyword into account. The keywords that have high access frequency appear in the top k position in the matching result set. When we set k = 40, it means that the first 40 files having the highest scores will be returned for each query.

Figure 5 shows the results of the keywords that have high access frequency or Wight appear in the top k position in the matching result set and also the results search are ranked based on the history and the number of times the document id is present in the buckets as well as results query must be rank based on rank when return to the user as search results.

We can conclude from Figure 5. With take into account popular a keyword, our proposed system will achieve better performance than the existing systems, a keyword with a larger access frequency has a higher probability to appear in result set.

CONCLUSION

In the present paper, our main objective is to find an effective solution to the problems of multi-keyword ranked query over encrypted cloud computing. First of all, we gave a definition or a formulation of the problem, to analyse the solutions in hand and then we will use a new scheme called (SPEC) in order to solve this problem and therefore improve the performance of cloud computing and to safeguard privacy of data in comparison to the results of previous researches in regard to accuracy, privacy, security, key generation, storage capacity as well as trapdoor, index generation, index encryption, index update, and finally files retrieval depending on access frequency. Then, we have designed a new trapdoor generation algorithm, which may be able to solve finally out-of-order problem in the returned result set without affecting the accuracy and privacy of data.

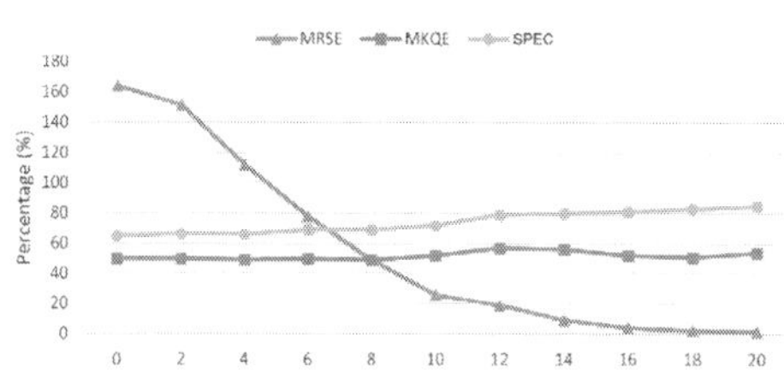

Figure 5. Percentage of files containing highest access frequency. Keywords in the top 20 locations.

Moreover, the access frequency of keywords is considered as well in ranking algorithm when generating a query and must be rank based on rank. We have used Tripple Data Encryption Standard (TDES) and Advanced Encryption Standard (AES-128) Algorithms in order to encrypt files with the aim of ascertaining data privacy. We confirm that DC will be highly capable of retrieving files they really need. In view of simulation experiments, we can finally reveal that our model can be of better performance than previous ones and will have a good security level as well.

REFERENCES

1. Wang, C., Ren, K., Yu, S. and Urs, K.M.R. (2012) Achieving Usable and Privacy-Assured Similarity Search over Outsourced Cloud Data. INFOCOM, Orlando, 25-30 March 2012, 451-459. https://doi.org/10.1109/infcom.2012.6195784
2. Buyya, R. and Dastjerdi, A.V. (2016) Internet of Things: Principles and Paradigms. Elsevier, New York.
3. Rong, C., Nguyen, S.T. and Jaatun, M.G. (2013) Beyond Lightning: A Survey on Security Challenges in Cloud Computing. Computers & Electrical Engineering, 39, 47-54.
4. Zhang, R., Liu, J., Han, Z. and Liu, L. (2011) RBTBAC: Secure Access and Management of EHR Data. International Conference on Information Society, London, 27- 29 June 2011, 494-499.
5. Zhang, R., Liu, L. and Xue, R. (2014) Role-Based and Time-Bound Access and Management of EHR Data. Security and Communication Networks, 7, 994-1015. https://doi.org/10.1002/sec.817
6. Nabeel, M., Bertino, E., Kantarcioglu, M. and Thuraisingham, B. (2011) Towards Privacy Preserving Access Control in the Cloud. 7th International Conference on Collaborative Computing: Networking, Applications and Work Sharing, Orlando, 15-18 October 2011, 172-180. https://doi.org/10.4108/icst.collaboratecom.2011.247061
7. Nabeel, M. and Bertino, E. (2012) Privacy Preserving Delegated Access Control in the Storage as a Service Model. 13th International Conference on Information Reuse and Integration, Las Vegas, 8-10 August 2012, 645-652.
8. Nabeel, M. and Bertino, E. (2014) Privacy Preserving Delegated Access Control in Public Clouds. IEEE Transactions on Knowledge and Data Engineering, 26, 2268- 2280. https://doi.org/10.1109/TKDE.2013.68
9. Nabeel, M., Shang, N. and Bertino, E. (2013) Privacy Preserving Policy-Based Content Sharing in Public Clouds. IEEE Transactions on Knowledge and Data Engineering, 25, 2602-2614. https://doi.org/10.1109/TKDE.2012.180
10. Raykova, M., Zhao, H. and Bellovin, S.M. (2012) Privacy Enhanced Access Control for Outsourced Data Sharing. International Conference on Financial Cryptography and Data Security, Kralendijk, 27 Februray-2 March 2012, 223-238. https://doi.org/10.1007/978-3-642-32946-3_17

11. Kaur, G. and Mahajan, M. (2013) Analyzing Data Security for Cloud Computing Using Cryptographic Algorithms. International Journal of Engineering Research and Applications, 3, 782-786.
12. Zissis, D. and Lekkas, D. (2012) Addressing Cloud Computing Security Issues. Future Generation Computer Systems, 28, 583-592.
13. Han, J., Susilo, W. and Mu, Y. (2013) Identity-Based Data Storage in Cloud Computing. Future Generation Computer Systems, 29, 673-681.
14. Boutet, A., Frey, D., Guerraoui, R., Jégou, A. and Kermarrec, A.M. (2016) Privacy-Preserving Distributed Collaborative Filtering. Computing, 98, 827-846. https://doi.org/10.1007/s00607-015-0451-z
15. Fu, Z., Wu, X., Guan, C., Sun, X. and Ren, K. (2016) Toward Efficient Multi-Keyword Fuzzy Search over Encrypted Outsourced Data with Accuracy Improvement. IEEE Transactions on Information Forensics and Security, 11, 2706- 2716. https://doi.org/10.1109/TIFS.2016.2596138
16. Fahl, S., Harbach, M., Muders, T. and Smith, M. (2012) Confidentiality as a Service—Usable Security for the Cloud. 11th International Conference on Trust, Security and Privacy in Computing and Communications, Liverpool, 25-27 June 2012, 153-162.
17. Harbach, M., Fahl, S., Brenner, M., Muders, T. and Smith, M. (2012) Towards Privacy-Preserving Access Control with Hidden Policies, Hidden Credentials, and Hidden Decisions. 10th Annual International Conference on Privacy, Security and Trust, Paris, 16-18 July 2012, 17-24. https://doi.org/10.1109/pst.2012.6297915
18. Kuzu, M., Kantarcioglu, M., Thuraisingham, B., Khan, L. and Schweitzer, H. (2013) Practical Privacy Preserving Record Integration and Search. The University of Texas, Austin.
19. Wang, C., Cao, N., Ren, K. and Lou, W. (2012) Enabling Secure and Efficient Ranked Keyword Search over Outsourced Cloud Data. IEEE Transactions on Parallel and Distributed Systems, 23, 1467-1479. https://doi.org/10.1109/TPDS.2011.282
20. Singh, M. and Singh, N.S. (2014) Implementation of Triple Data Encryption Standard Using Verilog. International Journal of Advanced Research in Computer Science and Software Engineering, 2277, 667-670.
21. Kakkar, A., Singh, M.L. and Bansal, P.K. (2012) Comparison of Various Encryption Algorithms and Techniques for Secured Data Communication. International Journal of Engineering and Technology, 2, 87-92.

22. Cao, N., Wang, C., Li, M., Ren, K. and Lou, W. (2014) Privacy-Preserving Multi-Keyword Ranked Search over Encrypted Cloud Data. IEEE Transactions on Parallel and Distributed Systems, 25, 222-233. https://doi.org/10.1109/TPDS.2013.45
23. Kamara, S. and Lauter, K. (2010) Cryptographic Cloud Storage. International Conference on Financial Cryptography and Data Security, Tenerife, 25-28 January 2010, 136-149. https://doi.org/10.1007/978-3-642-14992-4_13
24. Fu, Z., Ren, K., Shu, J., Sun, X. and Huang, F. (2016) Enabling Personalized Search over Encrypted Outsourced Data with Efficiency Improvement. IEEE Transactions on Parallel and Distributed Systems, 27, 2546-2559. https://doi.org/10.1109/TPDS.2015.2506573
25. Han, F., Qin, J., Zhao, H. and Hu, J. (2014) A General Transformation from KP-ABE to Searchable Encryption. Future Generation Computer Systems, 30, 107- 115.
26. Chen, R., Mu, Y., Yang, G., Guo, F., Huang, X., Wang, X. and Wang, Y. (2016) Server-Aided Public Key Encryption with Keyword Search. IEEE Transactions on Information Forensics and Security, 11, 2833-2842. https://doi.org/10.1109/TIFS.2016.2599293
27. Liu, Q., Wang, G. and Wu, J. (2012) Secure and Privacy Preserving Keyword Searching for Cloud Storage Services. Journal of Network and Computer Applications, 35, 927-933.
28. Shiba Sampat Kale, P. and Lahane, S.R. (2014) Privacy Preserving Multi-Keyword Ranked Search with Anonymous ID Assignment over Encrypted Cloud Data. International Journal of Computer Science and Information Technologies, 5, 7093- 7096.
29. Xia, Z., Chen, L., Sun, X. and Wang, J. (2013) An Efficient and Privacy-Preserving Semantic Multi-Keyword Ranked Search over Encrypted Cloud Data. Advanced Science and Technology Letters, 31, 284.
30. Madane, S.A. and Patil, B.M. (2015) Comparison of Privacy Preserving SingleKeyword Search and Multi-Keyword Ranked Search Techniques over Encrypted Cloud Data. International Journal of Computer Applications, 126, 34-38.
31. Barde, C.R., Katkade, P., Shewale, D. and Khatale, R. (2014) Secured MultipleKeyword Search over Encrypted Cloud Data. International Journal of Emerging Technology and Advanced Engineering, 4, 528-532.

CHAPTER 8

Trusted Heartbeat Framework for Cloud Computing

Dipen Contractor[1], Dhiren Patel[1], Shreya Patel[2]

[1]Department of Computer Engineering, NIT, Surat, India

[2]Department of Computer Engineering, CKPCET, Surat, India

INTRODUCTION

Outsourcing computation to cloud can reduce IT expenditure spent by companies. Still, most of them are not willing to do so, due to security concerns with cloud computing environment and services. As per survey [1] , it is found that despite of huge benefits, fear is still there about security threats like loss of control of data and integrity of systems. Computing nodes (virtual machines) can be tampered with or ill configured to produce wrong results. E.g. Assigned Hadoop task (related to financial data consolidations)

Citation: Contractor, D. , Patel, D. and Patel, S. (2016), "Trusted Heartbeat Framework for Cloud Computing". *Journal of Information Security*, **7**, 103-111. doi: 10.4236/jis.2016.73007. .

may generate incorrect result due to few malfunctioning nodes [2] . Due the large size of data and its processing, the error is very hard to identify in collective results, and it may result in huge loss.

Malfunctioning Nodes and Infrastructure Attacks

In a public cloud infrastructure, malfunctioning nodes may infringe security requirements specified by service consumer. They may produce malicious outputs, which may violate the privacy and integrity ofcomputation. This may result in disclosure of users' confidential data, and profile users' behaviors (and preferences) for privacy analysis. Moreover, software flaws, bugs and mis-configurations can lead to incorrect results or un- intended information leakage.

Malicious or tempered nodes may eavesdrop the communication between other nodes, in order to disclose confidential data, enforce malicious privacy profiling [3] , launch replay attacks [3] , and Man-In-the-Middle attacks [2] [4] in the cloud system. They may also impersonate the Master to steal other node's data, or vice versa. Moreover, malicious node can launch Denial of Service attacks [5] . Growing number of vulnerabilities uncovered in cloud platform has prompted the move towards implementing trust based solutions incorporated with hardware support. The Trusted Computing's (TC) [6] initiative and adoption of trusted platform module (TPM) [7] has been gaining attestion from industry as well as acadamic. Hardware manufacturer is also participating to accelerate the adoption of TC across varios platform.

We consider a cloud system, which takes a user task, distributes among computing nodes, and gathers its output as shown in Figure 1. We propose a framework for integrity verification of cloud. We use three proce- dure viz: for registration, for verification and for detection of virtual machine. TPM based node registration process will initially establish trust. Attested heartbeat procedure periodically verifies the trustworthiness of every node in the system. Tampered or misconfigured nodes can be identified quickly by reputation based decision procedure.

Rest of the paper is organized as follows: In Section 2, we discuss background and related work on Heartbeats and TPM. In section 3, we propose the Trusted Heartbeat infrastructure. Section 4 shows usage model of proposed framework with conclusion and references at the end.

BACKGROUND AND RELATED WORK

Hadoop

Apache Hadoop [8] is framework that facilitates the data intensive distributed processing of massive data sets across clusters machines. It supports extension of processes from a single to thousands of machines. Designed with a fundamental assumption that hardware failure is common, making it the software's responsibility to identify and handle failures at the application layer. It replicates data across multiple nodes with rapid data transfer facility. Hadoop implementation essentially consists of two major components: (i) Hadoop Distributed File System (HDFS) [9] : A file system that manages all the nodes in a cluster for data storage, and (ii) Map- Reduce [10] : The framework that allocate work to nodes in a cluster. Hadoop Cluster can be designed in various ways. One of which includes a single master and multiple worker nodes. The master node consists of a Job- Tracker, TaskTracker, NameNode and DataNode. A worker node acts as both a DataNode and TaskTracker, it depends on avalability of physical or virtual resources (Figure 2).

Heartbeat in Hadoop Environment

Heartbeat [11] is a communication mechanism that provides a efficient; yet simple way for a Hadoop system to monitor performance and make that information available to external observers. Applications can use heartbeat information to automatically add or subtract resources from their pool.

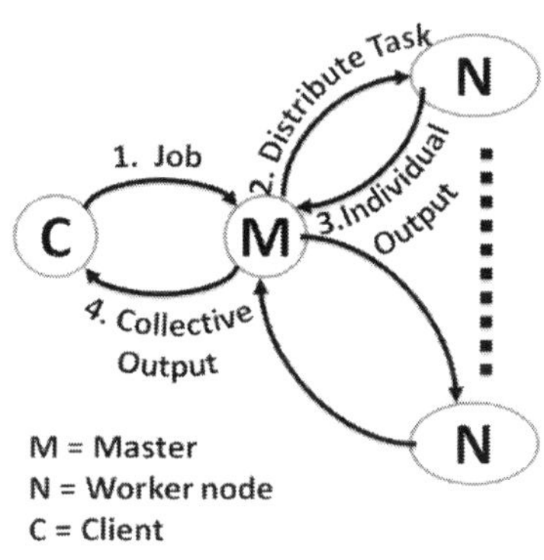

Figure 1. Cloud computing scenario.

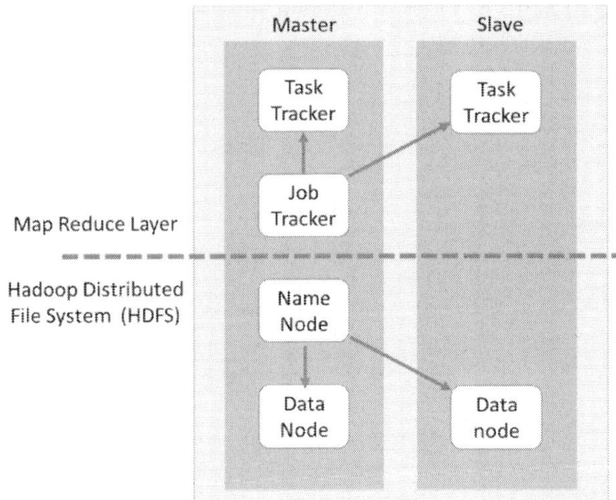

Figure 2. Hadoop cluster adopted from [10] .

HDFS replicates file blocks for fault tolerance. An application can specify the number of replicas of a file at the time it is created. The NameNode makes all decisions concerning block replication. Each DataNode sends heartbeat messages timely to its NameNode, so the later can identify loss of connectivity if it stops receiving these messages. The NameNode marks such node as dead DataNode (not responding to heartbeats) and desists from sending requests to it. Data stored on such node is no longer available to a client (Figure 3).

Trusted Platform Module (TPM)

The trusted computing group consortium has developed specifications for the trusted platform module. The TPM is a special purpose microcontroller on a motherboard. By incorporating a physical facility for secure generation and storage of cryptographic keys, the TPM becomes the core supporter for creating an interoperable "trusted computing" environment. These capabilities that every TPM provides include hashing by SHA-1 algorith, random number generation, asymmetric key generation as well as encryption and decryption by RSA algorithm. Following in Table 1; is the list of different types of keys can be created with TPM with their properties.

Integrity verification of the software components to support mitigation of security concerns related to cloud computing infrastructure. Though, it does not actually provide absolute assurance, trusted computing improves the complexity for attackers by operating at hardware level. With a correct implementation, an attacker would need physical access to the hardware in order to subvert the TPM [13] . In our proposed work, we use TPM to prevent Man-In-The-Middle attack and verify the integrity of Virtual machine via attestation.

Related Work

There have been many attempts to enhance the fault tolerance and trust based mechanisms to preserve integrity of cloud system in open distributed environment [14] . For sensitive data in open distributed systems, Airavat [15] is developed. It incorporates mandatory access control to detect privacy violation. Verification-based Integrity Assurance Framework [16] is based on the idea of replication and quiz related methods. It can detect malicious and normal task trackers in Hadoop system with the help of predefined set of questionnaires. Authors in article [17] , proposed algorithm named Longest Approximate Time to End (LATE). LATE finds the slow tasks in a homogeneous environment. LATE first estimates the remaining time for each tasks, then assigns the speculative tasks for those with the longest remaining time to end and maintains integrity of the system. Terra [18] provides an attestation ability that allows a remote party to reliably detect whether the host is running a platform that the remote party trusts. As elaborated by Bercher et al. [19] , for encrypted communication between all the nodes in the HDFS system, a key must be securely exchanged in advance. However, there are issues with how the key is shared. As seen in [20] ; key exchange is done frequently by heartbeat messages and attacker can pretend to be a data node and can many chunks of data.

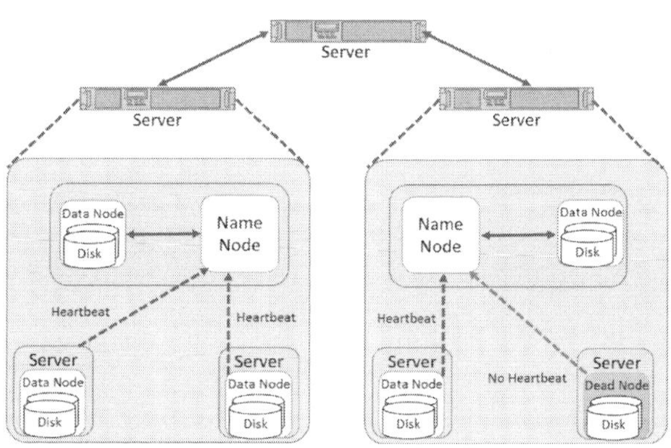

Figure 3. Heartbeat in Hadoop environment adopted from [12] .

Table 1. TPM Key types with their pupose [7].

Key Name	Purpose
Endorsement Key (EK)	A key-pair based on RSA algorithm; imposed by TPM manufacturer to identify uniquely TPM.
Storage Root Key (SRK)	A non-transferable key generated by the platform owner to serve as the root key in the hierarchy of keys associated with the TPM.
Attestation Identity Key (AIK)	Used for attestation and identification of a TPM (i.e. activated mode). Trusted third party can create identity certificate by signing public key part of AIK.
Signing Key	Used by the system to sign messages.
Storage Key	Used to encrypt and decrypt other keys. (using RSA)
Identity Key	Used for operations that requires TPM identity.
Binding Key	Used for Unbind operations to decrypt a data.

We propose a scheme to determine whether a particular VM is trustworthy or not. Only attested and trusted VMs can get the tasks and collaborate in network. Negative reputation is assigned if node does not generate output (or produce malicious output).

TRUSTED HEARTBEAT FRAMEWORK

In this framework, we assume TPM communication cannot temper, and storage is not exposed. The main intention of TPM is to repel most of the attacks on the software, we presume that trusted platform can assess each and every software module loaded on platform in terms of hash code [7] . In addition, we assume Master node works as a trusted party which performs attestations as suggested by TC [21] .

For better understanding of our framework, we denote job tracker as a master node and task tracker as simple node. Proposed framework is as shown in Figure 4. The Task scheduler present at every node executes tasks assign to them. Trust collector is attached to each node to manage assessments and support the attestation service. In master node, the task scheduler deploys jobs to nodes and collects their outcomes. Task manager stores node information and their assign task information. In addition, trust and reputation collector manages the trust information of nodes, and Trust Verifier performs attestations to them. The collected security properties (Endorsement Key and Attestation Identity Key) are stored in the Trust storage.

Trust manger binds evidence generated with accordance to TC's notation as trusted data. Moreover, users can get such information to assess the security properties of the worker node at any time, for the entire processing cycle. The Trust & reputation collector collects such properties of nodes and stores them with corresponding values. These values are kept in the trust storage for future score calculation. Following are the three main procedures for our proposed system.

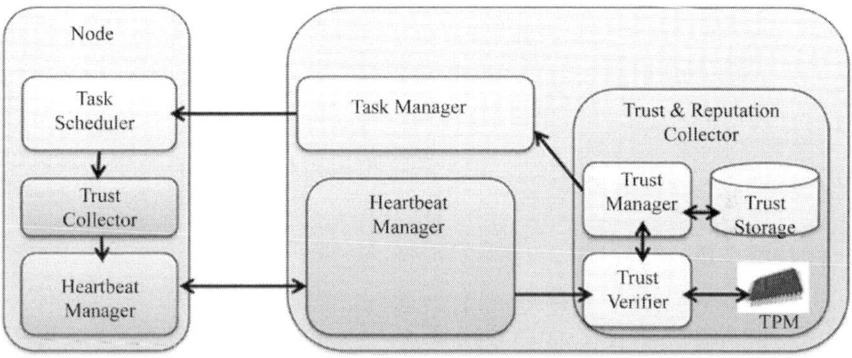

Figure 4. Architecture of trusted heartbeat framework.

(a) Initial Node Registration

Initially, when a data node joins a network, node registration takes place. It identifies a genuineness of TPM and exchanges keys for sealing and binding operations. The genuineness of TPM is identified by its public EK key.

Every time a worker node initiate connection request to the master node, an initial attestation procedure will be executed by master node. Verifier has collected all the properties of each node whose information is stored at the storage. Therefore, only registered node with allowed properties will be included to the list of the task Manager (for completing tasks). TC credentials and public session keys are stored at trust storage.

In Trusted Heartbeat framework, every node (N) is identified with its corresponding and unique AIK, and the Master (M) facilitates as the Privacy-CA defined by TC infrastructure [22] , for registering and identifying all these AIKs. Whenever a new node is included to the Hadoop based cloud system, it is first get registered at the Master and assigned with AIK key credentials. Figure 5 shows steps for node registration. As suggested earlier, only registered node can communicate with master and can get tasks with genuine TC credentials. Node registration procedure is more elaborated in Figure 6. In our Trusted Heartbeat framework implementation, the Trust & Reputation Collector is added to Master node and Trust collector to every node. Their exchanged messages are incorporated into the heartbeat protocol via Heartbeat manager. To simplify our protocol, we assign manually AIK credentials to node.

Time to time collector and trust storage updates the nonce information, and initiate the attestation procedure by invoking the TPM Quote from TPM instruction with the fresh nonce. As shown in Figure 9(a), latest generated nonce and reputation is then added to the request and sent to the Master. The verifier collects and maintains the public credentials of individual nodes. When a request in heartbeat message; with genuine AIK credentials is received, verifier will first perform verification followed by registration of that node. The properties indicated from the worker node's Stored Message Logs (SML) are inspected with security policies which are defined earlier and stored in Trust storage (shown in Figure 9(c)), and only the expected worker node can be added in future. As shown in node registration procedure (Figure 6), Trust verifier maintains nonce information in a cache (i.e. for faster execution) and revise cache value by execution the SHA-1 hash operation to get the new value. Time interval between each received messages and the stored information of the cache together determines the longer time for a heartbeat to be valid (Figure 7).

(b) Verification of Heartbeats

The verifier from trust and reputation collector is invoked each time, when a heartbeat message with attestation request reaches to the master node. It examines the nonce value in the cache; received through recent heartbeat (last_nonce) message. If verifier does not find that nonce value, it invalidates the connection request through heartbeat message. Once more when worker node sends heartbeat message with valid new_nonce, it can continues to communicate the master and get the task. The trust verifier can verifies the received signature and quote of PCR values using the TPM_Verify [7] set of instructions of TPM. If the verifier finds any mismatch in hash value, it will put that node to gray list and that node has to again start with node initialization procedure (As shown in Figure 9). Difference in PCR values shows variation in node software status, therefore a new assessment requires to be initiated. After successful completion of verification, the new worker node's assessment information is updated for further communication.

Procedure Node Registration
N(Node)$_i$ → M(Master node) : Certificate(K_{EKi}), {K_{AIKi}}
M (Master node) → N(Node)$_i$:{Certificate(K_{AIKi}),N(Node)ID$_i$},Certificate(K_M), N_a

Figure 5. Node registration procedure.

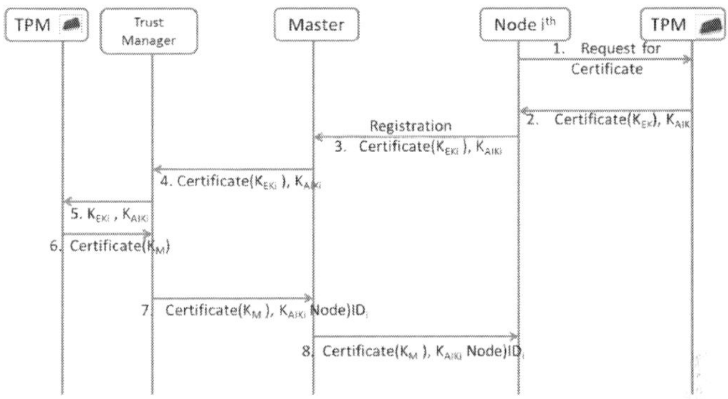

Figure 6. Step by step node registration procedure.

Procedure for Verification of Heartbeat

Variable definition:

new_nonce: Represent the received nonce of the node from heartbeat.

last_nonce: Represent the received nonce of the node from previous heartbeat.

procedure vah
//input: *Heartbeat_Received*: Symbolize the received heartbeat
//output: Grey list
new_nonce = Nounce.get(*Heartbeat_Received*)
new_nonce ← $nonce_{last}$
updated_nonce ← *(current_time – last_time)*
for *i=1* → *updated_nonce* do
new_nonce ← *compute hash of new_nonce*
insert*new_nonce* into *nonce_cache*
end for

if *Heartbeat.nonce* $\notin$ *nonce_cache* then
return false (*Heartbeat_Received* is Invalid)
end if
if *Verify_Sig(nonce, AIK)= false* then
return false (*Heartbeat_Received* Invalid)
end if
if *hash(PCRs)* $\notin$ *node_PCRHash values* then perform attestation
if Attestation is correct then
insert *PCRHash values*
add(*time_current*, *PCRHash*) to *Master_PCRHash*
return true
else
return false (node may be malicious)

```
    Put that node credentials in gray list.
        end if
    end if
end Procedure
```

Figure 7. Verifying heartbeat procedure.

(c) Reputation based detection

Reputations are gathered with each Heartbeat message received from Master. Calculated reputations, which are lower than a pre-defined threshold, master node, will unregister that node or mark it as a lost one. The threshold value can be computed based on the number of nodes and previously stored information available at trust storage.

The Black list is one that contains a list of all such failed nodes. Similarly, Gray list is one that contains a probable list of nodes that have faced some decrements in reputations (Figure 8).

Every susceptible node comes in Graylist first and then after inactivity it will be in Blacklist (shown in Figure 9(d)). Since reputations are collected in same cluster only, detecting a failed or malicious node is faster compared to collecting all reputations from all the nodes as depicted in Reputation based decision procedure.

Procedure for reputation based decision
Variable definition: *From_rep*: Symbolize the reputation of the sender of a worker node. *To_rep*: Symbolizethe reputation of the malicious node.

procedure rbd
//input: *Heartbeat_Received*: Represent the received heartbeat
//Output: *Heartbeat_Sent*: Represent heartbeat to sent
From_rep = Reputation.get(*Heartbeat_Received*)
If *From_rep*<*Threshold*
From_rep = *From_rep* + 1 //gain reputation
endif
If found heartbeat in Greylist
for each node in Greylist

```
            Sent Heartbeat_To with penalty
                If not received any Heartbeat_From from that node
                    If (To_rep< Minimum Reputation)
                        Put node in Black list and Inform other nodes in same cluster
                Lostnode(Heartbeat_Sent)
                endif
            endif
        end foreach
    endif
end procedure
```

Figure 8. Procedure for reputation based decision.

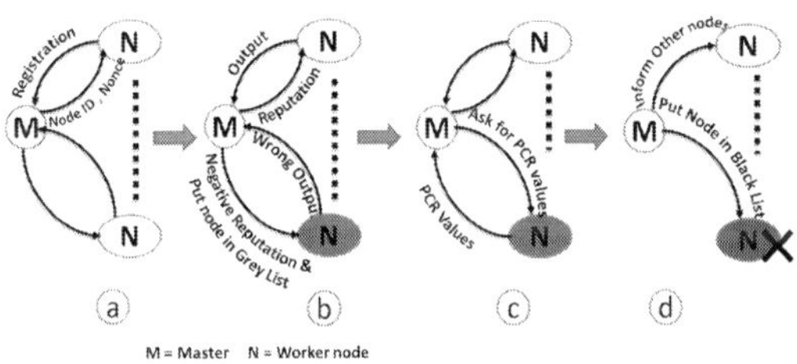

Figure 9. Working of our framework.

A worker node can receive its reputation or penalties through heartbeat messages. Master node increases reputation of a worker node each time when it gets heartbeat messages with hash values. The Trust & reputation based detector has a upper bound for the maximum reputation, After reaching that value, initialization process begins. However, when node comes in graylist then it starts receiving penalties if it does not reply.

Figure 9 shows general step by step working of Trust and Reputation Collector with the procedures. All tasks performed by the Master node are indicated in it.

CONCLUSION

In this paper, we propose Trusted Heartbeat framework; that creates a collaborative network among virtual machines. With remote attestations and heartbeat messages, a Master node can define the exact status (working or malfunctioning) of its nodes. This proposed framework identifies the genuine worker node using trusted computing facilities. Heartbeat interval time is very important parameter in our system. Trust and reputation based detector improve Hadoop like distributed systems in detecting malicious nodes quickly. This framework shows utilization of common messages to establish trust among all the corresponding nodes in distributed environment.

REFERENCES

1. (2012) What's Holding Back the Cloud. http://www.intel.in/content/dam/www/public/us/en/documents/reports/whats-holding-back-the-cloud-peer-research-rep ort2.pdf
2. Khan, S.M. and Hamlen, K.W. (2012) Hatman: Intra-Cloud Trust Management for Hadoop. CLOUD'12: Proceedings of 5th International Conference on Cloud Computing, Honolulu, 24-29 June 2012, 494-501. http://dx.doi.org/10.1109/cloud.2012.64
3. Feng, J., Chen, Y., Ku, W. and Liu, P. (2010) Analysis of Integrity Vulnerabilities and a Non-Repudiation Protocol for Cloud Data Storage Platforms. ICPPW'10: Proceedings of 39th International Conference on Parallel Processing Workshops, San Diego, 13-16 September 2010, 1-8. http://dx.doi.org/10.1109/icppw.2010.42
4. Sujitha, G., Varadharajan, M., Rao, Y.V., Sridev, R., Gauthaum, M.K.S., Narayanan, S., Raja, R.S. and Shalinie, S.M. (2013) Improving Security of Parallel Algorithm Using Key Encryption Technique. Information Technology Journal, 12, 2398. http://dx.doi.org/10.3923/itj.2013.2398.2404
5. Contractor, D. and Patel, D. (2012) Trust Management Framework for Attenuation of Application Layer DDoS Attack in Cloud Computing. IFIPTM 2012: 6th IFIP WG 11.11 International Conference on Trust Management, 374, 201- 208. http://dx.doi.org/10.1007/978-3-642-29852-3_14
6. Futral, W. and Greene, J. (2013) Introduction to Trust and Intel Trusted Execution Technology. Intel Trusted Execution Technology for Server Platforms, 1-14.
7. TPM Software Stack (TSS) Specification, Version 1.2. http://www.trustedcomputinggroup.org/resources/tcg_software_stack_specification_tss_12_faq
8. White, T. (2012) Hadoop: The Definitive Guide. O'Reilly.
9. Dean, J. and Ghemawat, S. (2008) MapReduce: Simplified Data Processing on Large Clusters. Communications of the ACM, 51, 107-113. http://dx.doi.org/10.1145/1327452.1327492
10. Borthakur, D. (2007) The Hadoop Distributed File System: Architecture and Design. In hadoop.apache.org, 2007. http://hadoop.apache.org/docs/r0.18.0/hdfs_design.pdf
11. Hoffmann, H., Eastep, J., Santambrogio, M.D., Miller, J.E. and

Agarwal, A. (2010) Application Heartbeats for Software Performance and Health. ACM Sigplan Notices, 45, 347-348. http://dx.doi.org/10.1145/1837853.1693507

12. Hanson, J. (2011) Hadoop Heartbeat. http://www.ibm.com/developerworks/library/wa-introhdfs/
13. Krautheim, F.J., Phatak, D.S. and Sherman, A.T. (2010) Introducing the Trusted Virtual Environment Module: A New Mechanism for Rooting Trust in Cloud Computing. TRUST '10: Proceedings of 3rd International Conference on Trust and Trustworthy Computing, Berlin, 21-23 June 2010, 211-227. http://dx.doi.org/10.1007/978-3-642-13869-0_14
14. Scales, D.J., Nelson, M. and Venkitachalam, G. (2010) The Design of a Practical System for Fault-Tolerant Virtual Machines. ACM SIGOPS Operating Systems Review, 44, 30-39. http://dx.doi.org/10.1145/1899928.1899932
15. Roy, I., Setty, S.T.V., Kilzer, A., Shmatikov, V. and Witchel, E. (2010) Airavat: Security and Privacy for MapReduce. Proceedings of the 7th USENIX Symposium on Networked Systems Design and Implementation (NSDI), 10, 297-312.
16. Wang, Y. and Wei, J. (2011) VIAF: Verification-Based Integrity Assurance Framework for MapReduce. CLOUD'11: Proceedings of IEEE International Conference on Cloud Computing, Washington DC, 4-9 July 2011, 300-307. http://dx.doi.org/10.1109/cloud.2011.33
17. Zaharia, M., Konwinski, A., Joseph, A.D., Katz, R.H. and Stoica, I. (2008) Improving MapReduce Performance in Heterogeneous Environments. OSDI, 8, 7.
18. Garfinkel, T., Pfaff, B., Chow, J., Rosenblum, M. and Boneh, D. (2003) Terra: A Virtual Machine-Based Platform for Trusted Computing. SIGOPS Operating System Review, 37, 193-206. http://dx.doi.org/10.1145/1165389.945464
19. Becherer, A. (2010) Hadoop Security Design Just Add Kerberos? Really. iSEC PARTNER, 1-10.
20. Devi, S. and Kamaraj, K. (2014) Architecture for Hadoop Distributed File Systems. International Journal of Enhanced Research in Management & Computer Applications, 3, 13-19.
21. Ko, S.Y., Hoque, I., Cho, B. and Gupta, I. (2010) Making Cloud Intermediate Data Fault-Tolerant. Proceedings of the 1st ACM

Symposium on Cloud Computing, Indianapolis, 2010, 181-192. http://dx.doi.org/10.1145/1807128.1807160

22. Schiffman, J., Moyer, T., Vijayakumar, H., Jaeger, T. and McDaniel, P. (2010) Seeding Clouds with Trust Anchors. Proceedings of the 2010 ACM Workshop on Cloud Computing Security Workshop, Chicago, 2010, 43-46.

CHAPTER 9

Education Technology Cloud Platform Framework Establishment and Security

Guoqiang Hu, Yanrong Yang, Li Li

Network and Education Technology Center, Northwest A&F University, Yangling, China

ABSTRACT

With more educational business absorbed into information management system at universities, traditional information management platform seems unable to provide efficient service for tea- ching and research. Some universities then resort to cloud computing platform. In view of the problems existing in the traditional information platform, this study presented an information management framework designed with cloud technology, and introduced the security techniques for its protection.

Citation: Hu, G. , Yang, Y. and Li, L. (2016), "Education Technology Cloud Platform Framework Establishment and Security". *Journal of Computer and Communications*, **4**, 7-14. doi: 10.4236/jcc.2016.47002.

Keywords: Cloud Platform, Framework, Security

INTRODUCTION

As the digital campus construction of Northwest Agriculture & Forestry University keeps advancing, great achievements have been made in network construction, information services and educational technology. Through years of relentless exploration, the university's digital campus has built up a traditional information platform integrating the network construction, information services and educational technology. However, a number of problems have been discovered during the actual application of the traditional information platform in recent years, so how to solve these problems has become a top priority for the construction of the digital campus.

PROBLEMS IN THE TRADITIONAL INFORMATION PLATFORM

Huge Quantity and Great Variety of Equipment Make Equipment Management Harder and Harder

At present, the wireless internet covers 80% of our campus with over 1200 network devices and more than 50,000 points of access information. Private networks for finance, campus cards, libraries, video surveillance and control system, and medical treatment have been set up, but it is difficult for the existing network platform to incorporate more network devices.

Equipment Installation and Maintenance Are Mainly Carried Out by Stand-Alone Operation, Which Is Troublesome and Onerous

Public network services that have been built up and in operation in our university includes: The domain name service (http://nwsuaf.edu.cn/, the platform for public resources (the network for educational resources, FTP, PT, etc.), the website groups (including about 100 websites such as the university's homepage, the secondary website and the websites for special topics), e-mail system (with over 33,000 users), the mobile portal, VOD, VPN, IPTV, the recording and broadcasting system, and the system for releasing campus information. Every service is installed on an independent server, the software installation and debugging of which are mainly carried out by stand-alone operation. Therefore, it takes a large amount of time-consuming maintenance in the event of a failure. In addition, the application of the virtual technology is confined to a single physical host with little use of resource pooling, leading to a low utilization.

The Storage Resource Is Insufficient and Is Greatly Wasted When Allocated

There are mainly two storage devices in the university, respectively IBM DS4800 (24TB) and IBM DS5100 (130TB). With the data of the digital campus increasing, the storage resource of 154TB is severely insufficient with low utilization.

It Is Difficult to Satisfy Teachers and Students' Personalized Needs and the Support for (Long-Distance) Mobile Working Is Far from Enough

There are many problems in the traditional platform, which considerably restrain the growth of the Data Center and the development of the university's educational informatization. The expansion speed of the Network and Educational Data Center being faster than the growth of the traditional infrastructure has become a major bottleneck for the current development of the Center. And a new educational information platform is needed for the expansion of businesses and the diverse development of educational technologies in the future.

Cloud computing as a new model for resource utilization and delivery is bringing a profound and extensive revolution for electronic information technology.

Virtualization-based cloud computing boasts the technical advantages of high reliability, on-demand service, and high scalability. In consideration of them, this paper designs a cloud computing platform to solve the problems existing in traditional platforms. The new platform built with cloud computing not only can solve the problems in the traditional platform, but have an improved data protection system.

IN THE BUILDING OF COULD PLATFORM, THE WORK THAT I HAD DONE INCLUDES: CLOUD PLATFORM FRAMEWORK DESIGN OBJECTIVES

More Convenience for Providing Educational Resources

Different physical and virtual resources can be classified and released dynamically according to the needs of teachers and students, and resources can be provided quickly and flexibly by adding available resources to match the newly added demands; if the users no longer use this part of resources they will be released.

Cloud computing conveniently provides users with computing resources, realizing the expandability of educational resource utilization.

Customizable Self-Services

Cloud computing provides users with self-help resource services so that users are able to obtain self-help computing resources without needing to be face-to-face with the providers. Meanwhile, the cloud system provides certain application server directories for the users to choose service items and content to meet their needs on their own.

More Convenience for Teachers and Students

The components and overall structure of cloud computing are integrated by SDN and provide services for tea- chers and students through network.

Campus users can visit educational and book resources they are interested in with different end devices through 3G/4G or wireless network at any places inside the campus while users outside campus can visit educational resources through VPN. In this way, cloud services for education are ubiquitous.

Quantifiable Services

When providing cloud services for users inside and outside campus, the resources are monitored and controlled in real-time to automatically control and optimize their allocation for different types of services provided for users, and thus to ensure that every user's requirements are met timely.

Resource Pooling and Transparency

For the teachers at Network and Educational Data Center, computing resources, storage resources, network resources and educational resources can be collectively managed and coordinated, becoming a "resource pool" to provide services for teachers and students; for other teachers and students, they only need to be concerned about whether their needs are met, rather than knowing about the resources and the internal operation process by themselves [1] .

Framework Building of Cloud Platform

Generally, cloud computing provides services according to the usage amount of users. This kind of service model provides a configurable shared pool of computing resources (including networks, servers, storage and application software) for the users in time by offering available, convenient and on-demand network accesses. With a little of management and few interactions with service providers, users can get the service resources they need.

The cloud computing platform is composed of a series of resources that can be shared, upgraded dynamically and virtualized, and users can simply use the resources on the cloud computing platform according to their own requirements without needing to master technologies related to cloud computing.

Based on the levels of the services, the cloud computing is divided into three categories, i.e. SaaS, PaaS and IaaS [2] . IaaS, Infrastructure-as-a-Service, includes resources such as computing resources (physical and virtual machines), storage resources, network resources, load balancing and firewalls. PaaS, Platform-as-a-Service, includes operating systems, operating environment for programming languages, database, Web Server and WebSphere Application Server. SaaS, Software-as-a-Service, provides software services (for WEB, WAP, Android/IOS/WP) through the Internet.

The cloud platform in our university consists of 3 sub-platforms, respectively the application cloud platform, the application-based cloud platform and the campus-based cloud platform according to their services models. By combining this with practical application services, the framework for campus cloud platform is proposed in this paper.

Layer of Infrastructure

This layer is corresponded to the IaaS in the cloud computing service model, which mainly integrates and uniformly allocates hardware resources through virtualization technology with infrastructure resources of digital campus as its core. With a series of unified management services such as optimal management, storage management and security management, all heterogeneous and loose nodes are integrated into a tight "virtual super computers" with a single image [3] .

Users can deploy and operate the operating systems and software applications on the cloud platform composed of all the hardware resources. When doing this, rather than being concerned about the deployment and management of the infrastructure layer, users only need to obtain their service resources through the service interface provided for them. In this paper, the infrastructure layer is sorted into four layers, i.e., layer of resource pools, layer of virtualization, layer of management support and layer of service. The detailed design is as shown in Figure 1.

1) Layer for resource pools

This layer is mainly composed of computing resources (service cluster related to cloud computers), network resources (a large network consisting of NPE, NCE, gateways, routers and switches) and storage resources (disk arrays). It is to provide hardware and software support for the cloud platform.

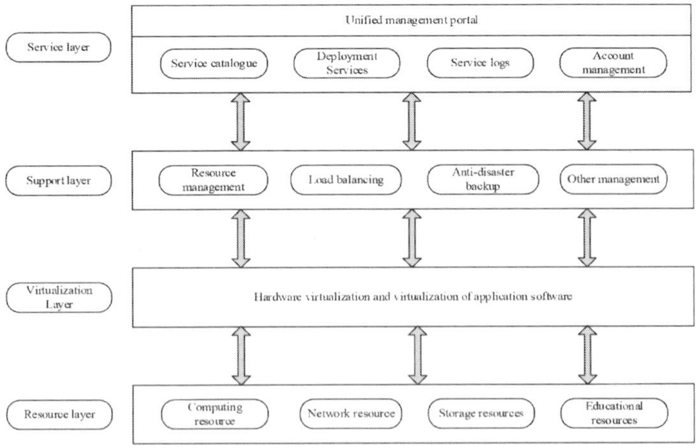

Figure 1. The framework for infrastructure layer.

2) The layer of virtualization

The technology of virtualization is used to integrate various kinds of heterogeneous resources that are originally irrelevant to form the unified and controllable resource pools. Teachers and students with authentication and authorization can therefore use the resources in the resource pool dynamically.

3) Layer of management support

This layer is designed for achieving the dynamic and security management of virtualized resources optimizing resources scheduling management, the purposes of which are to effectively lower resource costs, improve resource utilization, and ensure the availability, safety and liability of resource services by means of backup and disaster recovery and security isolation.

4) Layer of service portal

Users are provided with a unified interface for applying for and using the computing, storage and network services, and for safety, a unified authentication management portal is adopted by the Center. The users need to log onto the platform before applying for services.

The Layer of Basic Services for Digital Campus Cloud Platform

This layer is corresponded to the PaaS in the cloud computing service model. Different kinds of application services are effectively managed in this layer to ensure the stable operation of the campus cloud platform.

With the support of other relevant services, the interactions and service sharing between application systems can be realized in this layer.

It is subdivided into platform resource services layer, platform data management layer, platform security management layer and user management. The detailed design is as shown in Figure 2.

1) Layer of platform resource services

It includes database management, virtual machine management, and the technologies of middleware pro- cessing and parallel processing, which provides technical support for the normal operation of the services.

2) Layer of platform database management

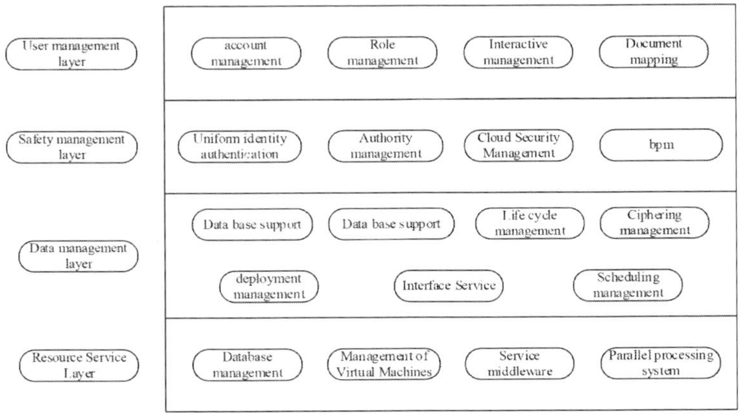

Figure 2. The structure for basic services layer.

Data generated by each sub-system are processed and analyzed in this layer. With data scheduling, data caching, data sharing and data security, the liability and stability of data storage are guaranteed.

3) Layer of platform safety management

It is mainly composed of services related to the platform security. The authentication system and permission administration allow the teachers and students to visit the resources and customize the services in a secured way.

4) Layer of platform user management

It mainly manages user accounts and user permissions. Self-services are provided for the teachers and students so that they can modify their passwords, pay their fees, and check the record application resources on the cloud platform.

Layer of Application Services on the Digital Campus Cloud Platform

This layer is to provide software applications for the users, and all the application software needs the support of the application-based cloud platform and the campus-based cloud platform. Uses are able to choose specific applications based on their permissions. The cloud platform of the university is mainly designed to provide various kinds of software services for teachers and students who can also customize different applications to meet their demands in their work and scientific researches.

SECURITY ISSUES IN THE USING OF THE CLOUD PLATFORM

Whine providing users and companies with storage resources, software resources and computing resources at a low cost with extremely great convenience, safety issues may pose one of the biggest challenges for cloud computing. By the multi-layered and multidimensional real-time monitoring and off-line analyses of the traditional platform, it is found that the campus cloud platform is faced with security threats in terms of business, information and operation and maintenance, which have basically covered all the safety issues in Internet applications. Only by effectively prevent the cloud platform from these three kinds of safety threats can it provide liable security protection for different applications for the teachers and students. To solve security issues, the following measures are adopted.

To Set up an Operation and Maintenance Platform to Safeguard Daily Safety

As to Hosting applications, the teachers and students are generally concerned more about whether it is safe or not to deploy the code on the campus servers. To protect the applications of them, the cloud computing platform should be given security and protection strategies from different levels like system, network, data and passwords [4] .

1) Resource isolation

Isolation of hardware resources can be divided into CPU isolation, network isolation and disk I/O isolation. The strategy for CPU isolation: To bind all the virtual CPUs and the Domain-0 to physical CPUs.

The strategy for network isolation: iptables+tc is used for network isolation, with strategy limits on the incoming traffic implemented and HTB traffic control for bridge devices conducted. Network isolation providing security for data transfer has become a mechanism applied extensively in financial areas such as e-banking and e-payment. The other ways to ensure network security and isolation includes VLAN technology, VPN technology and HTTP/SSL technology [5] .

Disk I/O isolation: dm-ioband is used with a principle of setting only the proportion yet no absolute cap.

The strategy of access quarantine is used between different businesses to prevent safety issues caused by internal malicious access between applications.

2) Security reinforcement

The reinforcement of operating systems and software: the configuration of the operating systems and the server software is consolidated to prevent security holes at the operating system level, and the developers will be informed in time to deal with them accordingly. All the servers attached to the platform should receive timely software upgrades so as to patch the software that has vulnerabilities and to even change the secondary websites or the software that has powerful vulnerabilities.

Database reinforcement: to install operating systems and data files in the database programs onto different NTFS partitions; to install database programs and files onto non-system volumes; to install the components necessary for the businesses instead of those unnecessary ones such as upgrade tools, development tools, code samples and online books; to restrict the client computers to link to the scope of the protocols that can be used by the database servers and ensure the safety of these protocols, like limiting using TCP/IP only; to restrict the client computers to link to the specific ports that are used by the data servers without using default ports.

3) Network security

The powerful defense system of the Network Education Center is made full use of to help the applications resist network attacks and intrusions. The Center will clear abnormal traffic and monitor botnets at a regular interval, will hide the surveillance and financial intranets and isolate the security domains, and will set up firewalls respectively at the exits of each intranet. An IPS is deployed on the cloud platform, which can interrupt, adjust and isolate some abnormal internet transfer immediately. The anti-virus server is deployed on the cloud computing system to manage anti-virus software; the safety patch server is deployed on the management node on the cloud computing platform to automatically install patches, test and roll back, which helps the teachers and students to install patches with automatic tools.

4) Data security

The most advanced technology of virtualized mass storage has been adopted to store and manage data resources so as to back up timely and extensively and store various kinds of core data resources reliably for a long time. Corresponding safety mechanism includes data encryption, data isolation, data verification, data backup and disaster recovery. The data between different applications are isolated because teachers and students with development demands are only able to access the data under their corresponding accounts after they apply for the virtual machines. Through the end-to-end VLAN isolation, the data isolation in terms of management level, business level and storage level is realized, and thus to avoid the impact that the mutual effects between each aspect have on the data security.

In addition, with regard to the data upload and download between the Internet and the intranet, the campus cloud computing platform should provide special passage for the upload and download on FTP and run a security scan for the applications so as to prevent the test code or code that has safety holes from being published to the Internet.

5) Password safety

The unified identity authentication platform based on LDAP can manage the campus users and permissions in a unified and centralized way, so the users only need to log onto the campus information portal to visit all the systems inside the campus. When campus users log onto the servers directly, multifactor authentication is used to guarantee the safety of passwords effectively and carry out multi-level fine authorization.

6) Daily scanning of security vulnerabilities

The applications are scanned for security holes so as to discover them in time and give an alert. With regard to hosting applications, the security server daemon will run a safety scan for the applications deployed on the server and regularly send audit reports to the email boxes of the teachers and students who apply for servers. The secondary portal sites will be regularly scanned for safety holes which will be delivered in time to the website maintainers.

Business Safety

The cloud platform should provide a one-stop security platform to check, manage and operate the security information. The business security platform includes two modules:

1) Open API audit information check module

The security server daemon will automatically analyze the data that the applications call from the

Open API, and will identify applications with abnormal accesses based on dimensions of active users, user visits, frequency and abnormal IP to give an alert.

2) Anti-addiction module

The "anti-addiction system" is a system launched by the government in 2005 to prevent juveniles from addicting to online games by limiting their times online playing games with technical means so as to protect their mental and physical health [6] . More and more students have lost themselves in the Internet when they no longer receive the strict regulation from parents and society. Moreover, "anti-addiction" is not limited to juveniles. An "anti-addiction system" should be developed specially to restrict college students from surfing online.

Information Security

The cloud platform should introduce information filtering and detecting mechanism. The technology of Internet spam detection and filtration can identify and filter malicious information on the dimensions of character recognition, user behavior analysis and credit system, ensuring the coverage while effectively reducing misjudge rate. The information security can be divided into three parts:

1) To improve information classification and management and strictly control users' access rights to information.

Combining the setting of permission, universities can strictly control user's access rights by classifying the information and users according to a certain sequence and based on information security level and category of the information needed by users. Besides, the identity authentication system should be linked so that only the users who are permitted by the authentication system can visit the educational resources on the cloud. For the cloud computing is environmentally dynamic, cross-organizational, and diverse in services, the technologies of the unified identity authentication platform and access control are used to strictly control the teachers and students or visitors' access to the information, and thus the information security is effectively ensured.

2) To protect the integrity of information during transmission by using encryption technologies

In order to make sure that the information on the "educational cloud" won't be illegally intercepted, tampered or maliciously damaged during storage and transmission, the cloud platform should combine the technologies of encryption, digital signature and information hiding to protect the confidentiality and integrity of data so as to create a safe cloud platform for teachers and students.

3) To take proactive actions to ensure information security

The provider of the cloud platform should adopt the technology of proactive defense by publishing the newest methods to prevent Trojan viruses on the one hand and warning users when they are visiting malicious webpages or virus programs on the other hand.

CONCLUSION

This paper has designed the framework of for the cloud platform of educational technology, which mainly includes layer of infrastructure, layer of basic services and layer of application services. The cloud platform designed based on the framework has completely solved the problems in the traditional information platforms. Besides, prevention strategies are proposed to address the security issues in the using of new platform, thus making sure that users can use the cloud platform of educational technology safely.

ACKNOWLEDGEMENTS

The authors wish to thank the helpful comments and suggestions from my leaders in Network and Education Technology center. This work is supported by Research project of teaching reform of higher education in Shaanxi (No.13BY13).

REFERENCES

1. Miller, T.D. and Crawford, I.L. (2010) System and Method for Allocating Computing Resources for a Grid Virtual System. US, US7765552.
2. Celesti, A., Tusa, F., Villari, M. and Puliafito, A. (2011) An Approach to Enable Cloud Service Providers to Arrange IaaS, PaaS, and Saas Using External Virtualization Infrastructures. 2011 IEEE World Congress on Services (SERVI- CES), Washington DC, 4-9 July 2011, 607-611. http://dx.doi.org/10.1109/SERVICES.2011.92
3. T.A. (2011) DNA Sequence Patterns—A Successful Example of Grid Computing in Genome Research and Building Virtual Super-Computers for the Research Commons of e-Societies. 8th International Desktop Grid Foundation (IDGF) Workshop, Max Planck Institute for Gravitational Physics, Hannover, 17 August 2011.
4. Godhankar, P.B. and Gupta, D. (2014) Review of Cloud Storage Security and Cloud Computing Challenges. International Journal of Computer Science & Information Technology, 5, 528-533.
5. Jiang, Y. (2014) To Explore the Application of Vlan Technology in Network Security and Access Control and Practice. Network Security Technology & Application, 7, 18-19.
6. Van Melderen, L. and De Bast, M.S. (2009) Bacterial Toxin-Antitoxin Systems: More than Selfish Entities? PLoS Genet, 5, Article ID: e1000437.

SECTION 3
ENHANCING SECURITY IN THE CLOUD

CHAPTER

10

Design and Development of a Novel Symmetric Algorithm for Enhancing Data Security in Cloud Computing

Mohammad Anwar Hossain, Ahsan Ullah, Newaz Ibrahim Khan, Md Feroz Alam

Department of Computer Science and Engineering, World University of Bangladesh, Dhaka, Bangladesh

ABSTRACT

Cloud computing is a kind of computing that depends on shared figuring assets instead of having nearby servers or individual gadgets to deal with applications. Technology is moving to the cloud more and more. It's not just a trend, the shift away from ancient package models to package as service has steadily gained momentum over the last ten years. Looking forward, the following decade of cloud computing guarantees significantly more

Citation: Hossain, M. , Ullah, A. , Khan, N. and Alam, M. (2019), "Design and Development of a Novel Symmetric Algorithm for Enhancing Data Security in Cloud Computing". *Journal of Information Security*, **10**, 199-236. doi: 10.4236/jis.2019.104012.

approaches to work from anyplace, utilizing cell phones. Cloud computing focused on better performances, better scalability and resource consumption but it also has some security issue with the data stored in it. The proposed algorithm intents to come with some solutions that will reduce the security threats and ensure far better security to the data stored in cloud.

Keywords: Data Security, Cloud Computing, Encryption, Decryption, Secret Key, Symmetric Algorithm, 192 Bits, Hashing, Permutation, SHA-512

INTRODUCTION

Research Background

Cloud computing is a general term for anything that involves delivering hosted services over the Internet [1] . These services are broadly divided into three categories: Infrastructure-as-a-Service (IaaS), Platform-as-a-Service (PaaS) and Software-as-a-Service (SaaS). There are total three principles of cloud computing and they are, on demand computing resources, founding a pay-as-you-go business model for computing and information technology services that can be used for elastic scaling, and elimination of up-front capital and operational expenses [2] .

As the rate of cybercrimes increasing rapidly throughout the internet, and cloud computing is an enchanting target for many reasons that's why data security plays the most key role in the cloud and the major concern over the internet in order to serve all the services and benefits of it. Data secrecy over the network could be achieved by using cryptographic technique that is the process of encryption and decryption.

Encryption is the method by which plaintext is converted from a readable form to an encoded version (cipher text) that can only be decoded by another entity if they have access to a decryption key. Decryption is the reverse process encryption to convert the encrypted text into plain text. There are three most common types of encryption and decryption methods and they are Symmetric, asymmetric, and hybrid algorithms that can be used to encrypt and decrypt data in cloud computing storage [3] .

Symmetric encryption is an encryption system in which the sender and receiver of a message share a single common key that is used to encrypt and decrypt the message. Symmetric algorithm that is used in cloud computing are Data Encryption Standard (DES), Advanced Encryption Standard

(AES). Asymmetric Encryption uses two distinct yet related keys, one key is a Public key which is used for encryption and the other key is the Private key used for decryption.

The private key is intended to be private so that only the authenticated recipient can decrypt the message. An example of asymmetric algorithm used in cloud computing is RSA algorithm. Hybrid encryption is a method of encryption that combines two or more encryption schemes and includes a combination of symmetric and asymmetric encryption to take advantage of the strengths of each type of encryption [4] .

It's a research where authors are developing novel a symmetric algorithm which will be used for the encryption and decryption of data stored in the cloud thus enhancing the data security of the cloud. In this paper, authors used several permutation to increase the complexity and security.

The reason behind choosing symmetric encryption is that symmetric key encryption doesn't require as many CPU cycle as asymmetric key encryption, so it can be said that it's generally faster. Thus, when it comes to speed, symmetric is much faster than asymmetric.

For encrypting private and sensitive data or information symmetric encryption trumps the asymmetric encryption, as symmetric encryption uses the same key for both encryption and decryption. So unless the sender himself tells the secret key to the receiver, the receiver will never be able to decrypt the message.

Objective

To design and develop a symmetric algorithm for enhancing data security in cloud.

Justification of Study

Cloud computing is perhaps the most flamboyant technological innovation of the 21st Century. Because Cloud computing facilitates the access of applications and data from any location worldwide and from any device with an internet connection.

But the security of client's data is a major responsibility of a cloud provider. To be secured information needs to hidden from unauthorized access (Confidentiality), protected from unauthorized change (integrity), and available to the authorized entity when it is needed (availability). And it not uncommon that many cloud servers have been under attack by hackers and lost valuable data for the lack of security.

As the world progresses people are becoming more and more dependent on these sort of services to store their data and information and it has become utmost important to protect the data that are stored in the cloud. Our algorithm mainly works to improve the security and overcome these problems.

The most important services that our algorithm will provide are:

*Confidentiality: The algorithm aims to unauthorized disclosure of the protected data.

*Integrity: Protect against illegal modification and deletion.

*Authorization: Algorithm will prevent the access of unauthorized users.

By providing these services, algorithm ensures more security in cloud computing.

Scope of Study

Data security is one of the biggest challenges at the current time. The security of client's data is major responsibility of cloud provider. Cloud computing is likely to suffer from a number of known and unknown vulnerabilities, enabling attackers to either obtain computing services for free or steal information from cloud. To solve this problem, we have proposed a symmetric algorithm that will provide safest data security and will prevent the unauthorized access of dada. It will provide data to the authorized user without any loss of data or theft of data.

Contribution of the Proposed Work

The main contribution of the proposed work in terms of encrypting data of the cloud is that the algorithm can encrypt up to 192 bits of data at a time. So in cases of encrypting a large amount of data the algorithm works efficiently saving more time.

Each of the rounds and the algorithm itself has been designed in such a way that it is impossible to crack or decipher the encrypted texts without the key. Each round of encryption and decryption process has several customize permutation which makes the algorithm more secure from theft. By using a secure encryption and decryption process and a large key size of 192 bits and a secure SHA-512 as hash function, the proposed algorithm achieves the cryptographic goals which are confidentiality, integrity and authentication. So it provides robust security to the data stored in cloud for which it has been designed for.

Brief Introduction of the Paper

In the literature review chapter, the authors have reviewed the existing related works that have been done by other authors and also showed the key difference. In the methodology section, the authors have written about the method of the proposed work. In the research design and analysis section the authors talk about the SHA-512 for message authentication, encryption and decryption process, the flowchart of encryption and decryption and has theoretically proven the algorithm. There is also a security analysis of the algorithm and the implementation of the algorithm which is done in Java is showed. The author also showed a model to use the algorithm in cloud. The next section is the result discussion, where the authors compare the proposed algorithm with existing algorithm. The next section is the conclusion.

LITERATURE REVIEW

Cloud Computing is transforming information technology. As information and processes are migrating to the cloud, it is transforming not only where computing is done, but also fundamentally, how it is done. As increasingly more corporate and academic worlds invest in this technology, it will also drastically change IT professionals' working environment. Cloud Computing solves many problems of conventional computing, including handling peak loads, installing software updates, and, using excess computing cycles.

Cloud computing has significantly impacted every section of our lives and business structure. Securing the cloud data is the major concern in the cloud computing environment. Many research works are being proposed to secure cloud data.

In [5] , the author proposed a hybrid cryptography model for cloud data security which combines the symmetric key (AES) and asymmetric key (Hyper Elliptic Curve Cryptography (HECC)) techniques. The AES and HECC algorithms are used for the key generation, encryption and decryption processes. To enhance the level of data security in cloud she used Hyper Elliptic Curve Cryptography (HECC). The HECC in cloud environment typically have encrypted with the public key and decrypted with a private key. The reviewed paper works with block size of 128 bit whereas the proposed work provides the facility to take 192 bits as block size.

In [6] , the authors have developed a hybrid hashing security algorithm for data storage on cloud computing which makes the data more secure from theft. In this work, they used hybrid algorithm (RSA and AES) and hash functions for securing cloud data storage. In this work, they proposed a new Hybrid-SHA256 algorithm. They used different data input sizes (34, 67, and 93) kb, for both the Hybrid and Hybrid-SHA256 algorithms. Their model provides more secure encryption than Hybrid model because the model used hashing and digital signature concept. The reviewed work used hybrid algorithm (RSA and AES) whereas our algorithm is totally new. The reviewed work used SHA-256 and digital signature concept, on the other hand, the proposed algorithm used SHA-512 for message authentication.

In [7], the authors proposed a model to secure user data in cloud computing using encryption algorithms in which they used different algorithms. They proposed several different algorithms to eliminate the concerns regarding data loss, segregation and privacy. They used RSA, DES, AES and Blowfish algorithm to encrypt and decrypt data in cloud and compare the accuracy of each algorithm. They use different key size for each algorithm. The key length of DES algorithm is 56 bits. The key size of AES algorithm is 128, 192 and 256 bits. The key size of Blow-fish algorithm is 128 - 448 bits. The key size of RSA algorithm is 1024 bits. They found that AES algorithm takes the least time to execute cloud data. Blowfish algorithm has the least memory requirement. DES algorithm takes least encryption time. RSA takes longest memory size and encryption time. The reviewed work did a survey on four different algorithms by comparing them considering their advantages and disadvantages, on the other hand, the proposed algorithm specifically works for encrypting data in cloud in a secure way.

In [8] , the authors developed an encryption algorithm to enhance data security in cloud storage. Their algorithms suggest the encryption of the files to be uploaded on the cloud. The security of the data uploaded by the user is ensured by doubly. The algorithm encrypts the data as well provides access to the data only on successful authentication. In this algorithm, the uploaded file will be encrypted by using AES algorithm. The AES key is encrypted by RSA Algorithm. The reviewed algorithm works for encrypting file and store it in cloud but the proposed work encrypt text and store it in cloud.

In [9] , the authors have developed an algorithm to enhance data security in cloud computing. They developed a Lightweight cryptographic algorithm. The algorithm mainly works in three steps. Firstly, key exchange. This step has two parts: key generation and key exchange. Secondly, Data storage in which the encrypted data is stored in cloud. Thirdly, data access by which the user requests the data from the cloud storage. To do this the authors used asymmetric and symmetric cryptographic algorithm. The data is encrypted by a symmetric algorithm and then the symmetric key distribution between cloud provider and the user is done by using an asymmetric algorithm. The reviewed paper used a Light weight cryptographic algorithm which works in three steps where the proposed algorithm is a customized symmetric algorithm.

In [10] , the authors proposed an encryption technique for the information security in cloud computing which can prevent the attacks on the data. The algorithm consists of three layers. Firstly-Authentication layer, Secondly-Encryption and confidentiality, thirdly-Data store. Authentication layer provides authentication by constructing a secret key from the user password and by digital signature. Encryption and confidentiality layer encrypt the user data by using AES. Then the Data store layer stores the user data. The reviewed paper uses AES for encryption whereas the proposed algorithm is a new customize concept of symmetric encryption.

In [11] , the authors have developed a model to prevent the threats in cloud. They build a model to share data in cloud using RSA and for data integrity used MD5 algorithm.

The difference between the reviewed work and the proposed work is that they used RSA for encryption and MD-5 for integrity, on the contrary, a new symmetric algorithm and SHA-512 is used for encryption and integrity in this proposed work.

In [12] , the authors proposed a simple data protection model where data is encrypted using Advanced Encryption Standard (AES) before it is launched in the cloud, thus ensuring data confidentiality and security, a privacy-preserving public auditing system for data storage security in cloud computing is intended, although the computational time is increased but the privacy is preserved where data is stored in the cloud by using the most prominent algorithm AES.

The difference between the reviewed work and the proposed work is that the reviewed work used a data protection model before storing data in cloud which takes more time than the proposed algorithm.

In [13] , the authors proposed a model where they provide architecture and guidelines to increase the security as well as the privacy of the data owner by transferring the process of encryption and decryption from the cloud to self. For maximizing the security of data, user segments and encrypts the data using a secured co-processor. This work provides guideline and architecture to increase security using a secured co-processor and the proposed work uses a symmetric algorithm to secure the cloud data.

In [14] , the authors proposed a model for a privacy-preserving public auditing system for data storage security in cloud computing is intended, although the computational time is increased but the privacy is preserved where data is stored in the cloud by using the most prominent algorithm AES. The reviewed work is based on a model for privacy-preserving public system where the privacy is presented using AES algorithm. The proposed work uses a totally new symmetric encryption for encrypting and decrypting cloud data.

In [15] , the authors proposed a model for data security in cloud computing using AES under Heroku cloud. The implementation for deploying Heroku as a cloud platform consists of several steps. Then, they implement a website as an application to data security. In the website, they implement AES as data security algorithm. The performance evaluation shows that AES cryptography can be used for data security. Moreover, delay calculation of data encryption shows that larger size of data increases the data delay time for encrypting data. The reviewed algorithm used AES algorithm under Heroku cloud whereas the proposed algorithm is not specified for any cloud platform.

In [16] , the authors proposed a system to achieve secure data sharing for dynamic groups in the cloud, they expect to combine the group signature and dynamic broadcast encryption techniques. Specially, the group signature scheme enables users to anonymously use the cloud resources, and the dynamic broadcast encryption technique allows data owners to securely share their data files with others including new joining users. Unfortunately, each user had to compute revocation parameters to protect the confidentiality from the revoked users in the dynamic broadcast encryption scheme, which results in that both the computation overhead of the encryption and the size of the cipher text increase with the number of revoked users. The reviewed work is a system for securely sharing data in dynamic group of cloud. The proposed algorithm is for securely storing data in cloud.

In [17] , the author proposed ploud architecture is enhanced security model for data storage within cloud environment. It consists of various users with local availability of mail server and cryptographic application. A cryptographic application installed on client side will connect user with storage and allows for encryption and decryption operation on data. As the cryptographic application is installed on client's machine it will increase speed-up ratio and mean processing for encryption and decryption process. The authentication server used for authenticating users to enter into server environment and use available functionalities. The reviewed work allows a limited number of user having a local availability of email server and cryptographic application to store data in cloud where the proposed algorithm has no limitation on user to store data in cloud.

In [18] , the authors proposed that cloud customers may form their expectations based on their past experiences and organizations needs. They are likely to conduct some sort of survey before choosing a cloud service provider. Customers are expected also to do security checks that are centered on three security concepts: confidentiality, integrity and availability. Access controls to ensure that only authorized users gain access to applications, data and the processing environment and is the primary means of securing cloud-based services. Service providers are able to inspect activity in their environment and provide reports to clients. Ya-Qin Zang proposed that Computing. The reviewed work provides security to cloud according to customers expectation based on their experience. On the contrary, the proposed algorithm is developed based on all the risk factors and threats on cloud data.

In [19] , the authors proposed cloud security data model which based on a three-layer system structure, in which each layer performs its own duty to ensure the data security of cloud layers. The first layer is responsible for cloud user authentication. It is designed as OTP authentication module and uses digital certificates issued by the appropriate users and also manage user permissions. The second layer manages the user's data encryption by using AES algorithm, which is the most secured and faster encryption algorithm. For sensitive data such as one's personal information (ex. credit card number) should be encrypted and sent to the cloud. Data integrity is provided by using algorithms like MD5 and RSA. For non-sensitive data such as one's local information (ex. address details), it should be protected by using digital signatures and sent to the cloud. It also protects the privacy of users based on fine-grained attribute-based access control policies through access control policy algorithms. Access control mechanisms are tools to ensure authorized user can access and to prevent unauthorized access to information systems. Such mechanisms should cover all stages in the lifecycle of user access, from the initial registration of new users to the final de-registration of users who no longer require access to information systems and services. Special attention should be given, where appropriate, to the need to control the allocation of privileged access rights, which allow users to override system controls. The third layer supports the faster user data recovery by using Byzantine fault tolerance algorithm methods. The reviewed work is a three layer-based cloud security data model. The proposed algorithm is a data encryption algorithm for enhancing data security in cloud.

In [20] , the authors proposed a model to protect the data from attackers by using two essential processes. These processes are listed as Encryption and Decryption. Encryption is the process of converting the data to stop it from attackers to read the original data clearly. Encryption involves conversion of plain text to unreadable format.

It is known as cipher text. The user cannot read the above format. Hence, the next process that is carried out by the user is Decryption. In the world of computing, there exist security issues for storing the data in cloud.

In order to secure data in cloud AES encryption technique is used in this project. Advanced Encryption Standard is a block cipher with a block length of 128 bits. It permits three different key lengths: 256, 192,128 or bits. The reviewed work uses AES algorithm for encrypting and decrypting data. The proposed algorithm uses a new symmetric algorithm that is more secure and less time consuming than AES.

The main difference between the proposed work and the existing related works that have been reviewed this section are that most of these papers work with block size of maximum 128 bits. Whereas, the proposed algorithm works with 192 bits. The key size of the proposed algorithm is also 192 bits where the maximum reviewed papers work with key size of 128 bits.

METHODOLOGY

In this research paper, authors used 5 phases to describe the procedure. These phases are planning, requirement analysis, proposed algorithm, implementation, testing and result. Figure 1 shows the method of the proposed work.

Planning

A successful research begins with a proper planning. So the authors started this process of research with a proper plan. The plan includes the topic of the research and the working process. First of all, the authors went through many research works of similar topic.

Then the authors selected the title based on the knowledge gained from those papers. While going through those papers the authors found out that there were few limitations in every work. So the authors planned the research to overcome those limitations, also keeping a uniqueness to the work.

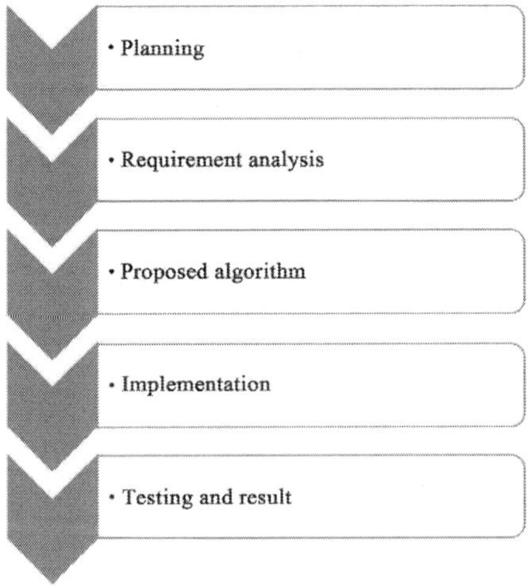

Figure 1. Proposed methodology.

Requirement Analysis

Every work has some requirements according to needs. The proposed work does require some specific resources.

1) System Requirements: system requirement can be isolated into two types:
    a) Software requirement.
    b) Hardware requirement.

- • Software Requirements

i) Language—Java.
ii) Environment—JDK and JRE.
iii) Operating System—Windows, Linux, MAC.
iv) Cloud Server.
v) External Algorithm—AES, DES, SHA.

- Hardware Requirements

i) Laptop or Desktop with processor.
ii) USB cable.

2) User Requirements: user requirement includes what the user expects from the system. For this, the user wants the security of data including integrity, confidentiality and authentication.

Proposed Algorithm

The proposed algorithm works in Block wise. The proposed algorithm takes a plain text of up to 192 bits block of data and converts it into a cipher text.

This algorithm includes many specific methods for encryption and decryption. For both the encryption and decryption, the key size is same which is 192 bits.

The algorithm encrypts and decrypts the data in 12 rounds. Each round uses the same key to encrypt and decrypt the data. A hash value is also generated for authentication. The goal of the proposed algorithm is to secure and enhance the protection of data stored in cloud.

Implementation

The programming language used to design the proposed algorithm is java. In java, for encrypting data, the algorithm works in two steps.

At first, it takes input, secondly it requires a 192-bit secret key to encrypt, after providing key, the algorithm encrypts the data and gives a cipher text as output and a hash code is also generated.

For decrypting data, the algorithm works in three steps, at first, it receives the cipher text, secondly it requires the same secret key and thirdly it receives the hash code and then it decrypts the data and provides the original text. After implementing the algorithm in java, the authors propose to use the algorithm in cloud.

Testing and Result

After implementation, the authors got the result that satisfies the conditions. After that, they compared it with other similar existing algorithm and found that the algorithm fulfills all the conditions of enhancing security of the cloud in a better way than the other existing algorithm.

RESEARCH DESIGN AND ANALYSIS

In Figure 2, the authors showed the overview of Encryption and Decryption Process:

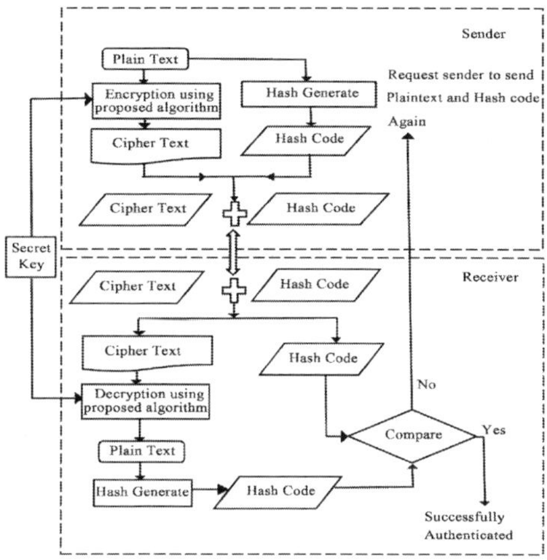

Figure 2. Flowchart of encryption and decryption process overview.

Hashing

SHA 512 Logic

SHA 512 is a cryptographic hashing algorithm that input as a message with a maximum length of less than 2^{128} and provides output as a 512-bit massage digest. The algorithm process the input in 1024 bits blocks. Figure shows the overall processing of a message to produce a digest [21] .

Features of SHA-512 Hashing Algorithm

- Plaintext Block Size = 1024 bits.
- No. of Rounds/steps = 80.
- Each Round-Qword = 64 bits.
- Each Round-constant K Buffer—8 buffers (a, b, c, d, e, f, g, h).
- Store Intermediate result.
- Each buffer size—64 bits.

Message Digest Generation Using SHA-512-

Step 1: Append padding bits—pad the bits 100… so that length of plain text is 128 < multiple of 1024 bits.

Step 2: Append length—append 128-bit representation of original plain text such that length = Multiple of 1024 bits.

Step 3: Initialize hash buffer—initialize the buffers (a, b, c, d, e, f, g, h) in 64 bit in Hexadecimal.

Step 4: Process each block of plain text in 80 rounds.

Step 5: Output—hash code of 512 bits.

In Figure 3 and Figure 4, the authors showed how message digest generation and processing of a single 1024-bit block data in SHA-512.

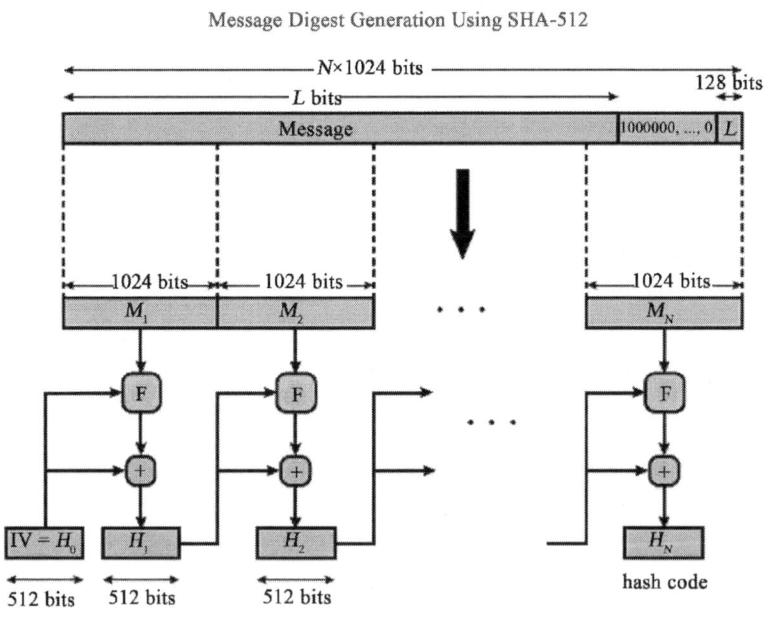

Figure 3. Message digest generation using SHA-512 ("message digest generation using SHA 512-Google search") [22] .

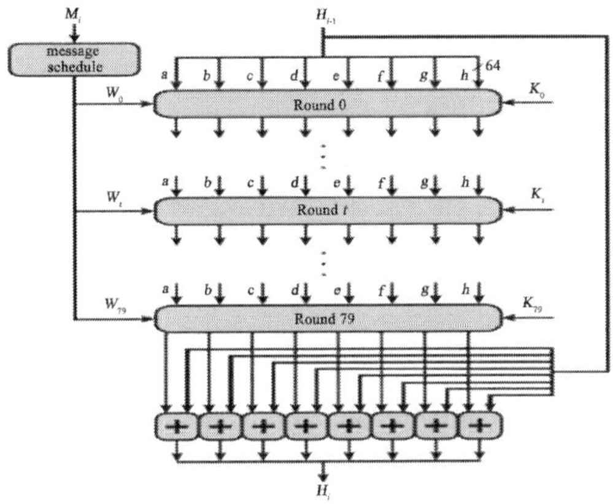

Figure 4. Processing of a single 1024-bit block in SHA-512 ("processing of a Single 1024-bit block in SHA 512-Google search") [23] .

Encryption Process

Encryption Process Flow Chart

Figure 5 shows the encryption process flowchart.

Block Diagram of Encryption Process Round Function

In Figure 6, the authors showed the round function of encryption process.

Encryption Process Description

1) Take an input or plaintext message of any size and key text of 24 bytes.
2) Generate 4 * 6 block matrix, which is denoted by M, Initially i = 0, j = 0, which is shown in Table 1.
3) Convert the messages characters into ASCII equivalent.
4) Perform Shift Rows using following steps:

*Row 1 (R1)—3 bit Left circular shift.

*Row 2 (R2)—2 bit Left circular shift.

*Row 3 (R3)—1 bit Left circular shift.

*Row 4 (R4)—0 bit Left circular shift.

5) Enact Permutation 1 using following steps:

Step i: Interchange column-C1 by C2 and C2 by C1.

Step ii: Interchange column-C3 by C4 and C4 by C3.

Step iii: Interchange column-C5 by C6 and C6 by C5.

Step iv: Interchange Row-R1 by R3 and R3 by R1.

Step v: Interchange Row-R2 by R4 and R4 by R2.

6) Reverse the whole block of matrix.

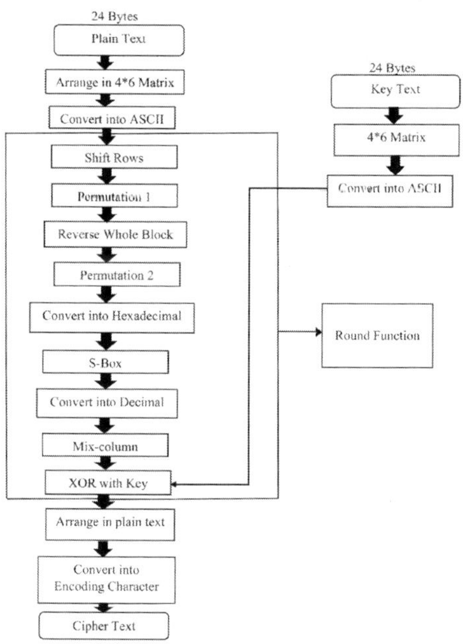

Figure 5. Encryption process flowchart.

Table 1. Generation of 4 * 6 matrix.

		C1	C2	C3	C4	C5	C6
M=	R1	$A_{i,j}$	$A_{i,j+1}$	$A_{i,j+2}$	$A_{i,j+3}$	$A_{i,j+4}$	$A_{i,j+5}$
	R2	$A_{i+1,j}$	$A_{i+1,j+1}$	$A_{i+1,j+2}$	$A_{i+1,j+3}$	$A_{i+1,j+4}$	$A_{i+1,j+5}$
	R3	$A_{i+2,j}$	$A_{i+2,j+1}$	$A_{i+2,j+2}$	$A_{i+2,j+3}$	$A_{i+2,j+4}$	$A_{i+2,j+5}$
	R4	$A_{i+3,j}$	$A_{i+3,j+1}$	$A_{i+3,j+2}$	$A_{i+3,j+3}$	$A_{i+3,j+4}$	$A_{i+3,j+5}$

7) Enact Permutation 2 using following steps:

Step i: Interchange column-C5 by C6 and C6 by C5.

Step ii: Interchange Row-R1 by R4 and R4 by R1.

Step iii: XOR between column C1 and column C3 i.e. C1 ⊕ C3 = X.

Step iv: XOR between column C2 and column C4 i.e. C2 ⊕ C4 = Y.

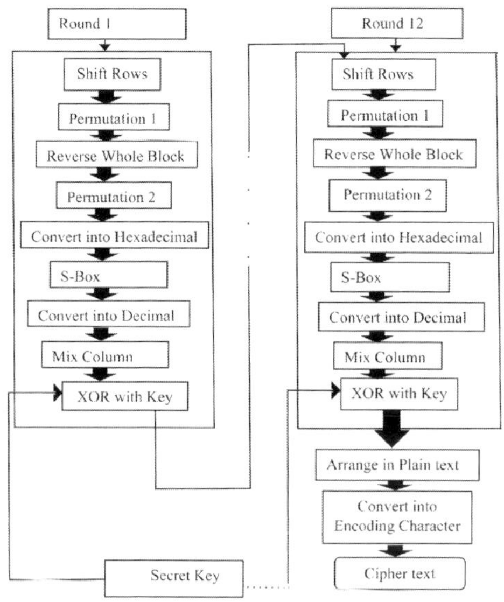

Figure 6. Round function of encryption process.

Step v: Replace C1 by X and C2 by Y.

8) Convert the values into equivalent Hexadecimal value.
9) Apply Substitution Box (S-box).
10) Convert the values into ASCII equivalent.
11) Perform mix column operation that is to XOR the constant matrix with the result of step 10. Table 2 shows the predefined constant matrix.
12) Calculate the key using the following steps:

* Generate 4 * 6 block matrix from key text which contains fixed-length size of 24 bytes or (192 bits) each.

* Convert the key characters into ASCII equivalent.

13) Perform XOR between the resultant mix column and the calculated key matrix.
14) Arrange the matrix values as plain text.
15) Convert the plain text into corresponding encoding characters

using base 64 encoders [24] .

- AES SubBytes transformation Table.

Table 3 provides value of Rijndeal S-box [25] .

Table 2. Constant matrix.

Constant Matrix=	2	3	1	1	2	3
	1	2	3	1	1	2
	1	1	2	3	1	1
	3	1	1	2	3	1

Table 3. AES SubBytes transformation ("Rijndeal S-box", 2019) [25] .

	0	1	2	3	4	5	6	7	8	9	A	B	C	D	E	F
0	63	7C	77	7B	F2	6B	6F	C5	30	01	67	2B	FE	D7	AB	76
1	CA	82	C9	7D	FA	59	47	F0	AD	D4	A2	AF	9C	A4	72	C0
2	B7	FD	93	26	36	3F	F7	CC	34	A5	E5	F1	71	D8	31	15
3	04	C7	23	C3	18	96	05	9A	07	12	80	E2	EB	27	B2	75
4	09	83	2C	1A	1B	6E	5A	A0	52	3B	D6	B3	29	E3	2F	84
5	53	D1	00	ED	20	FC	B1	5B	6A	CB	BE	39	4A	4C	58	CF
6	D0	EF	AA	FB	43	4D	33	85	45	F9	02	7F	50	3C	9F	A8
7	51	A3	40	8F	92	9D	38	F5	BC	B6	DA	21	10	FF	F3	D2
8	CD	0C	13	EC	5F	97	44	17	C4	A7	7E	3D	64	5D	19	73
9	60	81	4F	DC	22	2A	90	88	46	EE	B8	14	DE	5E	0B	DB
A	E0	32	3A	0A	49	06	24	5C	C2	D3	AC	62	91	95	E4	79
B	E7	C8	37	6D	8D	D5	4E	A9	6C	56	F4	EA	65	7A	AE	08
C	BA	78	25	2E	1C	A6	B4	C6	E8	DD	74	1F	4B	BD	8B	8A
D	70	3E	B5	66	48	03	F6	0E	61	35	57	B9	86	C1	1D	9E
E	E1	F8	98	11	69	D9	8E	94	9B	1E	87	E9	CE	55	28	DF
F	8C	A1	89	0D	BF	E6	42	68	41	99	2D	0F	B0	54	BB	16

Theoretical Proof of Encryption Process

The proposed algorithm encrypts the data in 12 rounds. For theoretical proof, the authors showed the calculation of just one round.

Insert a plaintext.

→ Anwar Newaz Feroz from 34c.

Arrange the plain text in 4 * 6 matrix (see Table 4).

Convert into equivalent ASCII value (see Table 5).

Perform Shift Rows (see Table 6).

Enact Permutation 1:

Interchange column-C1 by C2 and C2 by C1 (see Table 7).

Interchange column-C3 by C4 and C4 by C3 (see Table 8).

Interchange column-C5 by C6 and C6 by C5 (see Table 9).

Interchange Row-R1 by R3 and R3 by R1 (see Table 10).

Interchange Row-R2 by R4 and R4 by R2 (see Table 11).

After Permutation 1 the result is (see Table 12).

Reverse the whole block of matrix (see Table 13).

Table 4. 4*6 matrix of plaintext.

A	n	w	a	r	N
e	w	a	z	F	e
r	o	z	_	f	r
0	m	3	4	c	.

Table 5. ASCII conversion.

65	110	119	97	114	78
101	119	97	114	70	101
114	111	122	32	102	114
111	109	51	52	99	46

Table 6. Shift Row operation.

C1	C2	C3	C4	C5	C6
97	114	78	65	110	119
97	122	70	101	101	119
111	122	32	102	114	114

111	109	51	52	99	46

Table 7. Interchange column.

C1	C2	C3	C4	C5	C6
114	97	78	65	110	119
122	97	70	101	101	119
122	111	32	102	114	114
109	111	51	52	99	46

Table 8. Interchange column.

C1	C2	C3	C4	C5	C6
114	97	65	78	110	119
122	97	101	70	101	119
122	111	102	32	114	114
109	111	52	51	99	46

Table 9. Interchange column.

R1	114	97	65	78	119	110
R2	122	97	101	70	119	101
R3	122	111	102	32	114	114
R4	109	111	52	51	46	99

Table 10. Interchange row.

R1	122	111	102	32	114	114
R2	122	97	101	70	119	101
R3	114	97	65	78	119	110
R4	109	111	52	51	46	99

Table 11. Interchange row.

122	111	102	32	114	114
109	111	52	51	46	99
114	97	65	78	119	110

122	97	101	70	119	101

Table 12. Result of permutation 1.

122	111	102	32	114	114
109	111	52	51	46	99
114	97	65	78	119	110
122	97	101	70	119	101

Table 13. Reverse the whole block.

C1	C2	C3	C4	C5	C6
101	119	70	101	97	122
110	119	78	65	97	114
99	46	51	52	111	109
114	114	32	102	111	122

Enact Permutation-2:

Interchange column-C5 by C6 and C6 by C5 (see Table 14).

Interchange Row-R1 by R4 and R4 by R1 (see Table 15).

Perform C1 $\oplus$ C3 = X (see Table 16).

Perform C2 $\oplus$ C4 = Y (see Table 17).

Replace C1 by X and C2 by Y (see Table 18).

After Permutation-2 the result is (see Table 19).

Convert into equivalent Hexadecimal Value (see Table 20).

Replace the value using S-Box (see Table 21).

Convert into equivalent Decimal Value (see Table 22).

Mix column operation (see Table 23).

Tables 24-29 show the XOR operation between each column of Mix column operation.

Resultant mix column (see Table 30).

Key Generation

Key text: → This key is symmetric.

Table 14. Interchange column.

R1	101	119	70	101	122	97
R2	110	119	78	65	114	97
R3	99	46	51	52	109	111
R4	114	114	32	102	122	111

Table 15. Interchange row.

C1	C2	C3	C4	C5	C6
114	114	32	102	122	111
110	119	78	65	114	97
99	46	51	52	109	111
101	119	70	101	122	97

Table 16. C1 ♁ C3.

114	♁	32	=	82
110		78		32
99		51		80
101		70		35

Table 17. C2 ♁ C4.

114	♁	102	=	20
119		65		54
46		52		26
119		101		18

Table 18. Value exchange.

82	20	32	102	122	111
32	54	78	65	114	97

80	26	51	52	109	111
35	18	70	101	122	97

Table 19. Result of permutation 2.

82	20	32	102	122	111
32	54	78	65	114	97
80	26	51	52	109	111
35	18	70	101	122	97

Table 20. Hexadecimal conversion.

52	14	20	66	7A	6F
20	36	4E	41	72	61
50	1A	33	34	6D	6F
23	12	46	65	7A	61

Table 21. Value replacement using S-box.

00	FA	B7	33	DA	A8
B7	05	2F	83	40	EF
53	A2	C3	18	3C	A8
26	C9	5A	4D	DA	EF

Table 22. Decimal conversion.

0	250	183	51	218	168
183	5	47	131	64	239
83	162	195	24	60	168
38	201	90	77	218	239

Table 23. Mix column.

0	250	183	51	218	168	♁	2	3	1	1	2	3
183	5	47	131	64	239		1	2	3	1	1	2
83	162	195	24	60	168		1	1	2	3	1	1
38	201	90	77	218	239		3	1	1	2	3	1

Table 24. XOR operation.

0	♁	2	=	2
183		1		182
83		1		82
38		3		37

Table 25. XOR operation.

250	♁	3	=	249
5		2		7
162		1		163
201		1		200

Table 26. XOR operation.

183	♁	1	=	182
47		3		44
195		2		193
90		1		91

Table 27. XOR operation.

51	♁	1	=	50
131		1		130
24		3		27
77		2		79

Table 28. XOR operation.

218	⊕	2	=	216
64		1		65
60		1		61
218		3		217

Table 29. XOR operation.

168	⊕	3	=	171
239		2		237
168		1		169
239		1		238

Table 30. Result of Mix column operation.

2	249	182	50	216	171
182	7	44	130	65	237
82	163	193	27	61	169
37	200	91	79	217	238

Arrange this plaintext in a 4 * 6 matrix table (see Table 31).

Convert into equivalent ASCII value (see Table 32).

Back to Encryption

XOR between the last resultant mix column table and the key text table (see Table 33).

Tables 34-39 show the XOR between the last resultant mix column table and the key text table.

Resultant matrix is (see Table 40).

Arrange in plain text:

86 145 223 65 248 192 211 126 12 235 50 205 33 218 172 118 88 221 87 161 56 97 233 222.

Convert into Cipher text:

ODYgMTQ1IDIyMyA2NSAyNDggMTkyIDIxMSAxMjYgMTIgMjM1
IDUwIDIwNSAzMyAyMTggMTcyIDExOCA4OCAyMjEgODcgMTYx

IDU2IDk3IDIz MyAyMjI=.

Table 31. 4*6 matrix of key text.

T	h	i	s	_	k
e	y	_	i	s	_
s	y	m	m	e	t
r	i	c	.	0	0

Table 32. ASCII conversion.

84	104	105	115	32	107
101	121	32	105	115	32
115	121	109	109	101	116
114	105	99	46	48	48

Table 33. XOR between resultant mix column and key text table.

2	249	182	50	216	171	⊕	84	104	105	115	32	107
182	7	44	130	65	237		101	121	32	105	115	32
82	163	193	27	61	169		115	121	109	109	101	116
37	200	91	79	217	238		114	105	99	46	48	48

Table 34. XOR operation.

2	⊕	84	=	86
182		101		211
82		115		33
37		114		87

Table 35. XOR operation.

249	♁	104	=	145
7		121		126
163		121		218
200		105		161

Table 36. XOR operation.

182	♁	105	=	223
44		32		12
193		109		172
91		99		56

Table 37. XOR operation.

50	♁	115	=	65
130		105		235
27		109		118
79		46		97

Table 38. XOR operation.

216	♁	32	=	248
65		115		50
61		101		88
217		48		233

Table 39. XOR operation.

171	♁	107	=	192
237		32		205
169		116		221
238		48		222

Table 40. Resultant matrix.

86	145	223	65	248	192
211	126	12	235	50	205
33	218	172	118	88	221
87	161	56	97	233	222

Decryption Process

Decryption Process Flow Chart

Figure 7 shows the decryption process flowchart.

Block Diagram of Decryption Process Round Function

In Figure 8, the authors showed the round function of decryption process.

Decryption Process Description

1) Received the cipher text from the encryption process.
2) Decode the cipher text using base 64 decoders [24] .
3) Generate 4 * 6 block matrix of the decoded value, which is denoted by M_d. Initially I = 0, j = 0, which is shown in Table 41.
4) Calculate the key using following steps:

*Generate 4 * 6 block matrix from key text which contains fixed-length size of 24 bytes or (192 bits) each.

*Convert the key characters into ASCII equivalent.

5) Perform XOR between the result generated block matrix M_d and the calculated key matrix.
6) Perform mix column operation that is to XOR the constant matrix with the result of step 5.

Table 42 shows the predefined constant matrix:

7) Convert the matrix values into equivalent Hexadecimal.
8) Apply Reverse Substitution Box (S-Box).
9) Convert the Hexadecimal values into Decimal value.
10) Enact Permutation 4 using following steps:

Step i: XOR between column C1 and column C3 i.e. $C1 \oplus C3 = X$.

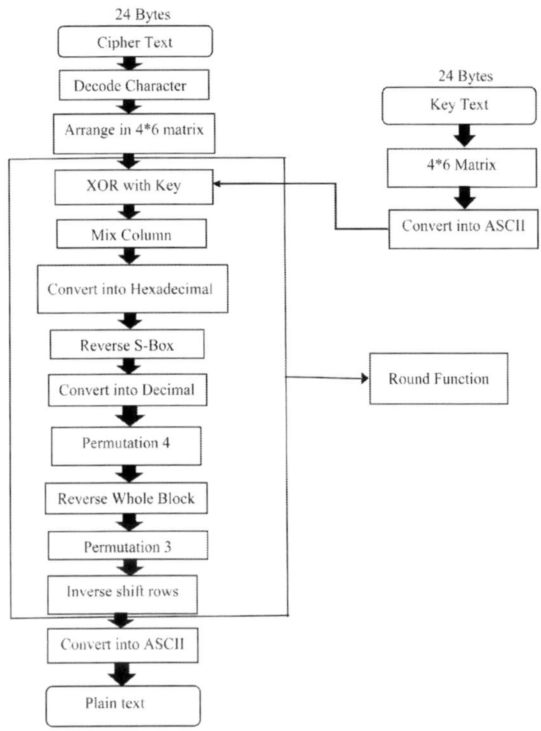

Figure 7. Decryption process flowchart.

Table 41. Generation of 4 * 6 matrix.

		C1	C2	C3	C4	C5	C6
M_d=	R1	$A_{i, j}$	$A_{i, j+1}$	$A_{i, j+2}$	$A_{i, j+3}$	$A_{i, j+4}$	$A_{i, j+5}$
	R2	$A_{i+1, j}$	$A_{i+1, j+1}$	$A_{i+1, j+2}$	$A_{i+1, j+3}$	$A_{i+1, j+4}$	$A_{i+1, j+5}$
	R3	$A_{i+2, j}$	$A_{i+2, j+1}$	$A_{i+2, j+2}$	$A_{i+2, j+3}$	$A_{i+2, j+4}$	$A_{i+2, j+5}$
	R4	$A_{i+3, j}$	$A_{i+3, j+1}$	$A_{i+3, j+2}$	$A_{i+3, j+3}$	$A_{i+3, j+4}$	$A_{i+3, j+5}$

Table 42. Constant matrix.

Constant Matrix=	2	3	1	1	2	3
	1	2	3	1	1	2
	1	1	2	3	1	1
	3	1	1	2	3	1

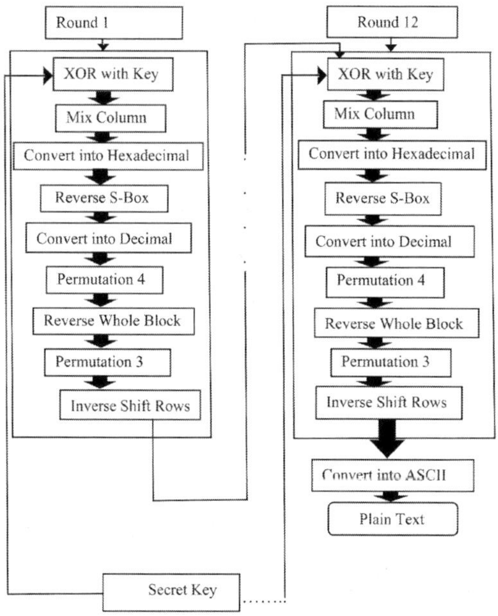

Figure 8. Round function of decryption process.

Step ii: XOR between column C2 and column C4 i.e. C2 ⊕ C4 = Y.

Step iii: Replace C1 by X and C2 by Y.

Step iv: Interchange Row-R1 by R4 and R4 by R1.

Step v: Interchange column-C5 by C6 and C6 by C5.

11) Reverse the whole block of matrix.

12) Enact Permutation 3 using the following steps:

Step i: Interchange Row-R2 by R4 and R4 by R2.

Step ii: Interchange Row-R1 by R3 and R3 by R1.

Step iii: Interchange column-C5 by C6 and C6 by C5.

Step iv: Interchange column-C3 by C4 and C4 by C3.

Step v: Interchange column-C1 by C2 and C2 by C1.

13) Perform inverse Shift Rows.

14) Convert the decimal values into equivalent ASCII character.

15) Finally Arrange the ASCII equivalent into plaintext.

- AES inverse SubBytes transformation table.

Table 43 provides the value of Rijndeal inverse S-box [25] .

Table 43. AES Inverse SubBytes transformation ("Rijndeal S-box", 2019) [25].

	0	1	2	3	4	5	6	7	8	9	A	B	C	D	E	F
0	52	09	6A	D5	30	36	A5	38	BF	40	A3	9E	81	F3	D7	FB
1	7C	E3	39	82	9B	2F	FF	87	34	8E	43	44	C4	DE	E9	CB
2	54	7B	94	32	A6	C2	23	3D	EE	4C	95	0B	42	FA	C3	4E
3	08	2E	A1	66	28	D9	24	B2	76	5B	A2	49	6D	8B	D1	25
4	72	F8	F6	64	86	68	98	16	D4	A4	5C	CC	5D	65	B6	92
5	6C	70	48	50	FD	ED	B9	DA	5E	15	46	57	A7	8D	9D	84
6	90	D8	AB	00	8C	BC	D3	0A	F7	E4	58	05	B8	B3	45	06
7	D0	2C	1E	8F	CA	3F	0F	02	C1	AF	BD	03	01	13	8A	6B
8	3A	91	11	41	4F	67	DC	EA	97	F2	CF	CE	F0	B4	E6	73
9	96	AC	74	22	E7	AD	35	85	E2	F9	37	E8	1C	75	DF	6E
A	47	F1	1A	71	1D	29	C5	89	6F	B7	62	0E	AA	18	BE	1B
B	FC	56	3E	4B	C6	D2	79	20	9A	DB	C0	FE	78	CD	5A	F4
C	1F	DD	A8	33	88	07	C7	31	B1	12	10	59	27	80	EC	5F
D	60	51	7F	A9	19	B5	4A	0D	2D	E5	7A	9F	93	C9	9C	EF
E	A0	E0	3B	4D	AE	2A	F5	B0	C8	EB	BB	3C	83	53	99	61
F	17	2B	04	7E	BA	77	D6	26	E1	69	14	63	55	21	0C	7D

Theoretical Proof of Decryption Process

The proposed algorithm decrypts the data in 12 rounds. For theoretical proof, the authors showed the calculation of just one round.

Cipher text:

ODYgMTQ1IDIyMyA2NSAyNDggMTkyIDIxMSAxMjYgMTIgM-jM1IDUwIDIwNSAzMyAyMTggMTcyIDExOCA4OCAyMjEgODcgM-TYxIDU2IDk3IDIz MyAyMjI=.

Decode Character:

86 145 223 65 248 192 211 126 12 235 50 205 33 218 172 118 88 221 87 161 56 97 233 222

Arrange the cipher text into 4 * 6 matrix table (see Table 44).

Key Generation

Key text:

→ This key is symmetric.

Arrange this plaintext in a 4 * 6 matrix table (see Table 45).

Convert into equivalent ASCII value (see Table 46).

Back to Decryption

XOR between the arranged cipher text matrix table and the key text table (see Table 47).

Tables 48-53 show the XOR between the arranged cipher text matrix table and the key text table.

Resultant matrix is (see Table 54).

Table 44. 4 * 6 matrix of decoded value.

86	145	223	65	248	192
211	126	12	235	50	205
33	218	172	118	88	221
87	161	56	97	233	222

Table 45. 4 * 6 matrix of key text.

T	h	i	s	_	k
e	y	_	i	s	_
s	y	m	m	e	t
r	i	c	.	0	0

Table 46. ASCII conversion.

84	104	105	115	32	107
101	121	32	105	115	32
115	121	109	109	101	116
114	105	99	46	48	48

Table 47. XOR between arranged cipher text and key text table.

86	145	223	65	248	192	⊕	84	104	105	115	32	107
211	126	12	235	50	205		101	121	32	105	115	32
33	218	172	118	88	221		115	121	109	109	101	116
87	161	56	97	233	222		114	105	99	46	48	48

Table 48. XOR operation.

86	⊕	84	=	2
211		101		182
33		115		82
87		114		37

Table 49. XOR operation.

145	⊕	104	=	249
126		121		7
218		121		163
161		105		200

Table 50. XOR operation.

223	⊕	105	=	182
12		32		44
172		109		193
56		99		91

Table 51. XOR operation.

65	⊕	115	=	50
235		105		130
118		109		27
97		46		79

Table 52. XOR operation.

248	⊕	32	=	216
50		115		65
88		101		61
233		48		217

Table 53. XOR operation.

192	⊕	107	=	171
205		32		237
221		116		169
222		48		238

Table 54. Resultant matrix.

2	249	182	50	216	171
182	7	44	130	65	237
82	163	193	27	61	169
37	200	91	79	217	238

Mix column operation (see Table 55).

Tables 56-61 show the XOR operation between each column of Mix column operation.

Resultant mix column (see Table 62).

Convert into equivalent Hexadecimal Value (see Table 63).

Replace the value using Reverse S-Box (see Table 64).

Convert into equivalent Decimal Value (see Table 65).

Enact Permutation-4:

Perform C1 ⊕ C3 = X (see Table 66).

Perform C2 ⊕ C4 = Y (see Table 67).

Replace C1 by X and C2 by Y (see Table 68).

Interchange Row-R1 by R4 and R4 by R1 (see Table 69).

Interchange column-C5 by C6 and C6 by C5 (see Table 70).

After Permutation 4 the result is (see Table 71).

Reverse the whole block of matrix (see Table 72).

Enact Permutation 3:

Interchange Row-R2 by R4 and R4 by R2 (see Table 73).

Table 55. Mix column.

2	249	182	50	216	171	⊕	2	3	1	1	2	3
182	7	44	130	65	237		1	2	3	1	1	2
82	163	193	27	61	169		1	1	2	3	1	1
37	200	91	79	217	238		3	1	1	2	3	1

Table 56. XOR operation.

2	⊕	2	=	0
182		1		183
82		1		83
37		3		38

Table 57. XOR operation.

249	⊕	3	=	250
7		2		5
163		1		162
200		1		201

Table 58. XOR operation.

182	$\oplus$	1	=	183
44		3		47
193		2		195
91		1		90

Table 59. XOR operation.

50	$\oplus$	1	=	51
130		1		131
27		3		24
79		2		77

Table 60. XOR operation.

216	$\oplus$	2	=	218
65		1		64
61		1		60
217		3		218

Table 61. XOR operation.

171	$\oplus$	3	=	168
237		2		239
169		1		168
238		1		239

Table 62. Result of mix column operation.

0	250	183	51	218	168
183	5	47	131	64	239
83	162	195	24	60	168
38	201	90	77	218	239

Table 63. Hexadecimal conversion.

00	FA	B7	33	DA	A8

B7	05	2F	83	40	EF
53	A2	C3	18	3C	A8
26	C9	5A	4D	DA	EF

Table 64. Value replacement using reverse s-box.

52	14	20	66	7A	6F
20	36	4E	41	72	61
50	1A	33	34	6D	6F
23	12	46	65	7A	61

Table 65. Decimal conversion.

C1	C2	C3	C4	C5	C6
82	20	32	102	122	111
32	54	78	65	114	97
80	26	51	52	109	111
35	18	70	101	122	97

Table 66. C1 ♁ C3.

82	♁	32	=	114
32		78		110
80		51		99
35		70		101

Table 67. C2 ♁ C4.

20	♁	102	=	114
54		65		119
26		52		46
18		101		119

Table 68. Value exchange.

R1	114	114	32	102	122	111

R2	110	119	78	65	114	97
R3	99	46	51	52	109	111
R4	101	119	70	101	122	97

Table 69. Interchange row.

C1	C2	C3	C4	C5	C6
101	119	70	101	122	97
110	119	78	65	114	97
99	46	51	52	109	111
114	114	32	102	122	111

Table 70. Interchange column.

101	119	70	101	97	122
110	119	78	65	97	114
99	46	51	52	111	109
114	114	32	102	111	122

Table 71. Result of permutation 4.

101	119	70	101	97	122
110	119	78	65	97	114
99	46	51	52	111	109
114	114	32	102	111	122

Table 72. Reverse the whole block.

R1	122	111	102	32	114	114
R2	109	111	52	51	46	99
R3	114	97	65	78	119	110
R4	122	97	101	70	119	101

Table 73. Interchange row.

R1	122	111	102	32	114	114
R2	122	97	101	70	119	101
R3	114	97	65	78	119	110
R4	109	111	52	51	46	99

Interchange Row-R1 by R3 and R3 by R1 (see Table 74).

Interchange column-C5 by C6 and C6 by C5 (see Table 75).

Interchange column-C3 by C4 and C4 by C3 (see Table 76).

Interchange column-C1 by C2 and C2 by C1 (see Table 77).

After Permutation-3 the result is (see Table 78).

Perform inverse shift rows (see Table 79).

Convert into equivalent ASCII value (see Table 80).

Arrange in Plain text/Decrypted text:

Anwar Newaz Feroz from 34c.

Table 74. Interchange row.

C1	C2	C3	C4	C5	C6
114	97	65	78	119	110
122	97	101	70	119	101
122	111	102	32	114	114
109	111	52	51	46	99

Table 75. Interchange column.

C1	C2	C3	C4	C5	C6
114	97	65	78	110	119
122	97	101	70	101	119
122	111	102	32	114	114
109	111	52	51	99	46

Table 76. Interchange column.

C1	C2	C3	C4	C5	C6
114	97	78	65	110	119
122	97	70	101	101	119
122	111	32	102	114	114
109	111	51	52	99	46

Table 77. Interchange column.

97	114	78	65	110	119
97	122	70	101	101	119
111	122	32	102	114	114
111	109	51	52	99	46

Table 78. Result of Permutation 3.

R1	97	114	78	65	110	119
R2	97	122	70	101	101	119
R3	111	122	32	102	114	114
R4	111	109	51	52	99	46

Table 79. Inverse shift row operation.

65	110	119	97	114	78
101	119	97	122	70	101
114	111	122	32	102	114
111	109	51	52	99	46

Table 80. ASCII conversion.

A	n	w	a	r	N
e	w	a	z	F	e
r	o	z	_	f	r
o	m	3	4	c	.

Security Analysis

Cloud is being used for storing sensitive and important data so it is very important to use a strong key that will provide security to the data stored in cloud. If we used a key of 10 characters using alphanumeric character. There are total 26 alphabets in English and if we count the upper and lower cases the total numbers are 26 + 26 = 52 and if we count the numeric digits the total number is 62. For a 10 character key, it will be 62^{10} or 8.39 * 10^{17} or 8.4 quintillion combination almost. A computer would take almost 257,201,646.091 years to crack a 10 digits key. A super computer will take 800,000,000 seconds or 133,333,333.333 minutes or 2,222,222.22222 hours or simply we can say it will take almost 257 years to crack the key. This calculation is for 10 digits key and if we take 48 digits key also count the special characters then it will take a numerous amount of time to crack the key which sounds almost impossible.

Implementation of the Algorithm in Java

Figure 9 shows the Starting of the program:

When a user wants to encrypt a text, he had to type his text in "Input: (Text/ Encrypted Text)" panel. Then he had to give a secret key of 192 bits in "Key:" panel. Then he had to click on "Encrypt" button (see Figure 10).

After clicking on "Encrypt" button the encryption will be done and user will get a "Cipher text" as output in "Output: (Text/Encrypted Text)" panel and a "Hash code" is also generated in "Hash:" panel (see Figure 11).

To get the plain text from the cipher text, user had to copy the cipher text from "Output: (Text/Encrypted Text)" and paste it in "Input: (Text/Encrypted Text)" panel and copy and paste the "Hash code" in "Hash:" panel.

After that he had to enter the same secret key in "Key:" panel and then he had to click on "Decrypt" button (see Figure 12).

After clicking on "Decrypt" button, the decryption process will be done and user will get the original text in "Output: (Text/Encrypted Text)" panel (see Figure 13).

User also can see the execution time of the encryption and decryption process.

Proposed Model of Data Storage in Cloud Using the Proposed Algorithm

In Figure 14, the authors provide a view of using the algorithm in cloud platform in which data will be encrypted and decrypted using the proposed algorithm. The proposed algorithm takes data from sender, encrypts it and stored the cipher text in cloud, the key and hash code are stored in a database which is also stored in cloud.

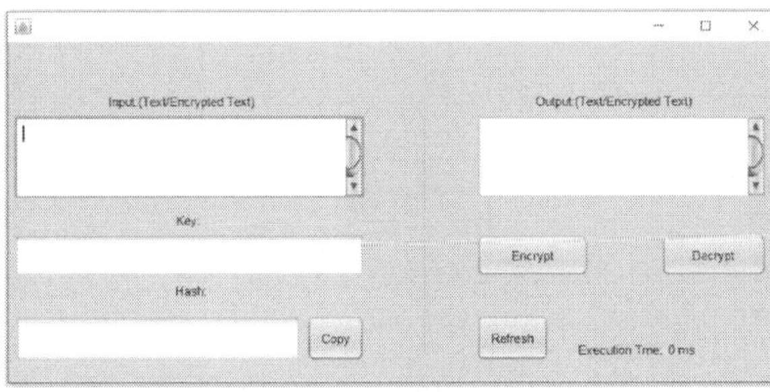

Figure 9. Interface of the algorithm in JAVA.

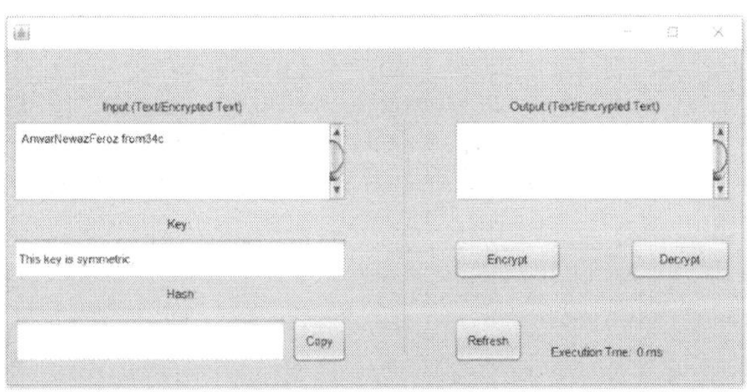

Figure 10. Encryption of data in Java interface.

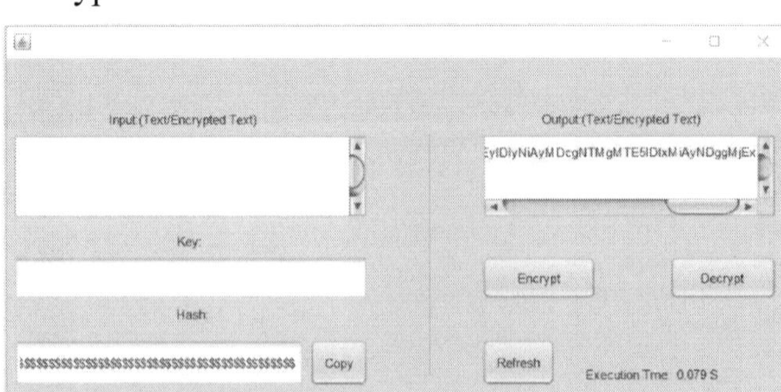

Figure 11. Encrypted text and hash value.

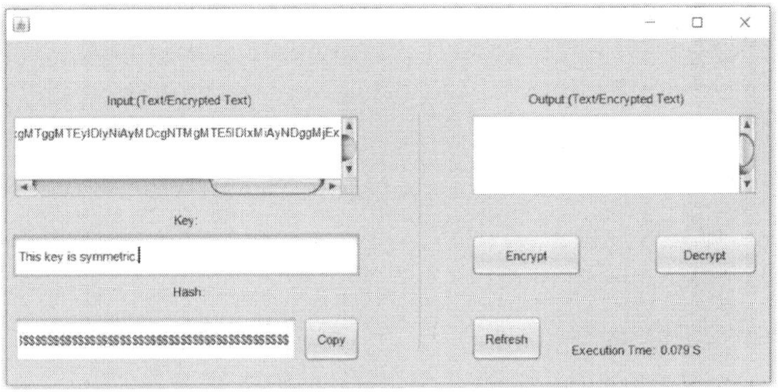

Figure 12. Decryption of encrypted text in Java interface.

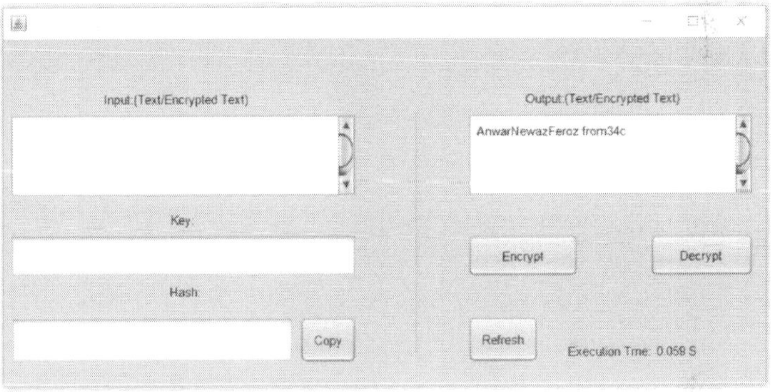

Figure 13. Original plain text.

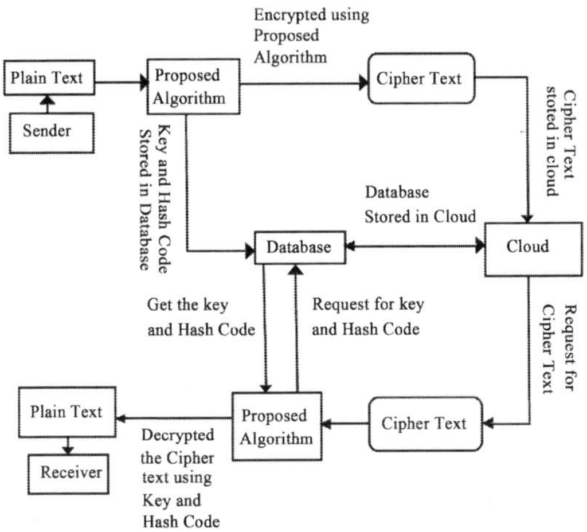

Figure 14. Proposed model of data storage in cloud using the proposed algorithm.

When a receiver request the data, he gets the cipher text from cloud, then he request for key and hash code from data base, after getting the hash code and key, the receiver decrypts the data using the proposed algorithm and gets the original plain text.

RESULT DISCUSSION

The result has tested by:

Windows 10Pro64-bit.

Intel®Core™i5-7200UCPU@2.50 GHz 2.71 GHz.

8 GB RAM.

In Table 81, the authors analyze the algorithm with the same key and same message size for different types of data.

In Table 82, the authors compare the algorithm with AES, DES.

Graphical Representation of Encryption and Decryption time for 192-bit data among the proposed algorithm, AES and DES (see Figure 15).

Graphical Representation of Encryption and Decryption time for 384-bit data among the proposed algorithm, AES and DES (see Figure 16).

Graphical Representation of Encryption and Decryption time for 576-bit data among the proposed algorithm, AES and DES (see Figure 17).

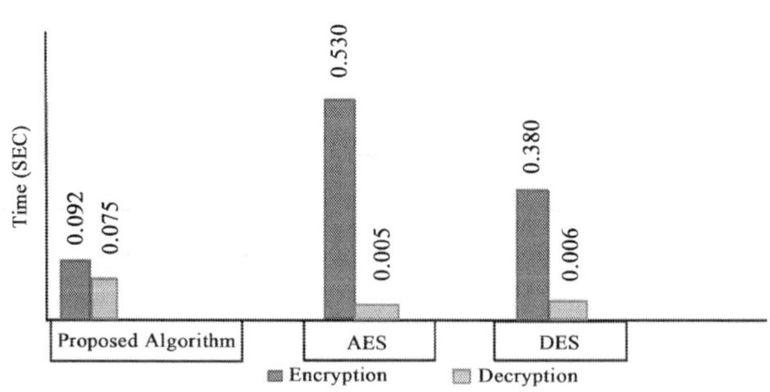

Figure 15. Encryption and decryption for 192-bit data.

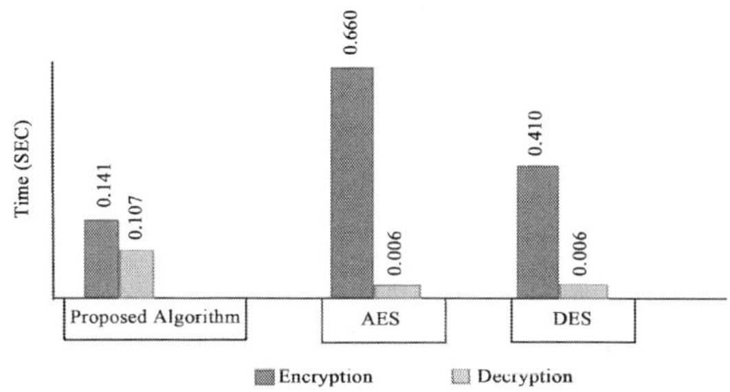

Figure 16. Encryption and decryption for 384-bit data.

Table 81. Algorithm analysis with the same key and same message size.

Data			Key size	Runtimes (sec)			
Type	No	Size		Encryption		Decryption	
					Average		Average
Numeric	1	192-bit	192-bit	0.089 s	0.086 s	0.056 s	0.053 s
	2	192-bit	192-bit	0.090 s		0.051 s	
	3	192-bit	192-bit	0.081 s		0.052 s	
Alphabetic	1	192-bit	192-bit	0.092 s	0.086 s	0.074 s	0.080 s
	2	192-bit	192-bit	0.086 s		0.085 s	
	3	192-bit	192-bit	0.078 s		0.078 s	
Alphanumeric	1	192-bit	192-bit	0.087 s	0.088 s	0.082 s	0.081 s
	2	192-bit	192-bit	0.086 s		0.078 s	
	3	192-bit	192-bit	0.092 s		0.085 s	

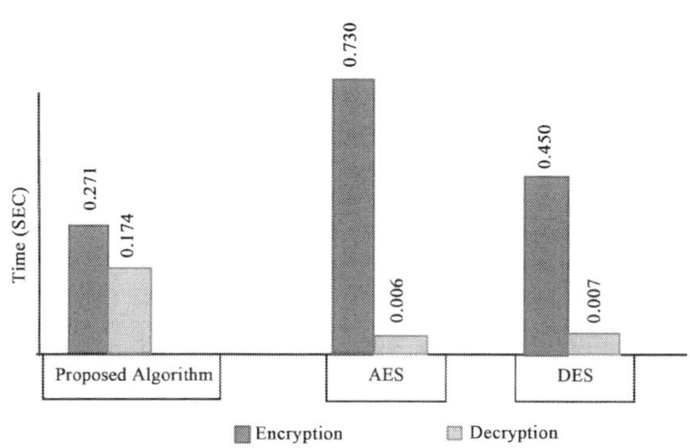

Figure 17. Encryption and decryption for 576 bit data.

Table 82. Comparison of proposed algorithm with AES, DES.

Data		Key Size	Run Time	
Algorithm	Message Size		Encryption	Decryption
Proposed Algorithm	192-bit	192-bit	0.092 s	0.075 s
	384-bit		0.141 s	0.107 s
	576-bit		0.271 s	0.174 s
AES	192-bit	128-bit	0.530 s	0.005 s
	384-bit		0.660 s	0.006 s
	576-bit		0.730 s	0.006 s
DES	192-bit	64-bit	0.380 s	0.006 s
	384-bit		0.410 s	0.006 s
	576-bit		0.450 s	0.007 s

CONCLUSIONS

Conclusion

The main purpose of the algorithm is to provide security to data stored in cloud. For this purpose, the authors used a symmetric algorithm. They used various methods to further enhance the algorithm which can easily be used for encrypting data stored in cloud. The algorithm works on block wise. The algorithm takes up to 192 bits block of data at a time and encrypts them into cipher text. The algorithm encrypts and decrypts the data in 12 rounds. The algorithm used 192-bit key that's why it provides better security. Symmetric algorithms are used widely around the world to store private data and since this algorithm will also be used to encrypt private data, that's why authors thought of using a symmetric algorithm. The algorithm developed by the authors ensures data confidentiality, integrity and authenticity for data stored in cloud.

Limitations

1) It works on text format data only.
2) Key and Hash code exchange is not much secure.

Future Works

1) Audio, video, image and file encryption.
2) Providing better security on Key and Hash code exchange.

REFERENCES

1. Definition of Cloud Computing. https://searchcloudcomputing.techtarget.com/definition/cloud-computing
2. What Is Cloud Computing. https://searchcloudcomputing.techtarget.com/definition/cloud-computing
3. What Is Encryption and Decryption. https://www.tutorialspoint.com/internet_technologies/data_encryption
4. What Is the Types of Encryption Technique. https://www.zettaset.com/blog/types-of-encryption-underlying-algorithms
5. Selvi, S. (2017) An Efficient Hybrid Cryptography Model for Cloud Data Security. International Journal of Computer Science and Information Security, 15, 307-313.
6. AbdElnapi, N.M.M., Omara, F.A. and Omran, N.F. (2016) A Hybrid Hashing Security Algorithm for Data Storage on Cloud Computing. International Journal of Computer Science and Information Security, 14, 175-181.
7. Arora, R. and Parashar, A. (2013) Secure User Data in Cloud Computing Using Encryption Algorithms. International Journal of Engineering Research and Applications, 3, 1922-1926.
8. Kartit, Z. and El Marraki, M. (2015) Applying Encryption Algorithm to Enhance Data Security in Cloud Storage. Engineering Letters, 23, 277-282.
9. Belguith, S., Abderrazak, J. and Attia, R. (2015) Enhancing Data Security in Cloud Computing Using a Lightweight Cryptographic Algorithm. The 11th International Conference on Autonomic and Autonomous Systems, Rome, 24-29 May, 98-103.
10. Singh, N. and Singh, N.K. (2014) Information Security in Cloud Computing Using Encryption Techniques. International Journal of Scientific & Engineering Research, 5, 1111-1113.
11. Agarwal, A. and Agarwal, A. (2011) The Security Risks Associated with Cloud Computing. International Journal of Computer Applications in Engineering Sciences, 1, 257-259.
12. Pancholi, V.R. and Patel, B.P. (2016) Enhancement of Cloud Computing Security with Secure Data Storage Using AES. International Journal for Innovative Research in Science & Technology, 2, 18-21.
13. Sachdev, A. and Bhansali, M. (2013) Enhancing Cloud Computing

Security Using AES Algorithm. International Journal of Computer Applications, 67, 19-23. https://doi.org/10.5120/11422-6766

14. ArulJothy, K., Sivakumar, K. and Delsey, M.J. (2017) Efficient Cloud Computing with Secure Data Storage Using AES and PGP Algorithm. International Journal of Computer Science and Information Technologies, 8, 582-585.
15. Lee, B.-H., FaridWajdi, M. and Dewi, E.K. (2018) Data Security in Cloud Computing Using AES under HEROKU Cloud. 27th Wireless and Optical Communications Conference, Hualien, 30 April-1 May 2018.
16. Sathana, V. and Shanthini, J. (2014) Automated Security Providence for Dynamic Group in Cloud. International Journal of Innovative Research in CE, 2.
17. BhavaniBai, B. (2014) Ensuring Security at Data Level in Cloud Using Multi Cloud Architecture. International Journal of Science and Technology.
18. Mounica, D. and Rani, R. (2013) Optimized Multi-Clouds Using Shamir Shares. International Journal for Development of Computer Science & Technology, 1, 83-87.
19. Jose, N. and Kamani, C. (2013) A Data Security Model Enhancement in Cloud Environment. Journal of Computer Science and Engineering, 10, 1-6.
20. Delfin, S., et al. (2018) Cloud Data Security Using AES Algorithm. International Research Journal of Engineering and Technology, 5, 1189-1192.
21. Hash Function.pdf, n.d
22. Message Digest Generation Using SHA 512. https://www.google.com/search?client=firefox-b-d&channel=trow&biw=1536&bih=750&tbm=isch&sa=1&ei=mbZBXfvJNdHhz7sP6d-SyAM&q=message+digest+gener ation+using+SHA+512+&oq=message+digest+generation+using+SHA+512+&gs_l =img.3..35i39.2548.3808..4778...0.0..0.148.2391.8j14......0....1..gws-wiz-img.zrg5K-XsXAU&ved=0ahUKEwi7-pWkv9_jAhXR8HMBHemvBDkQ4dUDCAY&uact=5#img rc=piLEnVVNqsKcMM
23. Processing of a Single 1024-Bit Block in SHA 512. https://www.google.com/search?q=Processing+of+a+single+1024-+bit+block+in+SHA+512-&client=firefox-b-d&channel=trow&source=lnms&tbm=

isch&sa=X&ved =0ahUKEwidv6a-v9_jAhVp8XMBHfUQAToQ_AUIEigC&biw=1536&bih=750#im grc=SUvuOD_TXhzHvM
24. Base64 Encoder and Decoder. https://www.base64encode.org
25. Rijndeal S-Box, 2019. Wikipedia.

CHAPTER

11

Enhancing Mobile Cloud Computing Security Using Steganography

Hassan Reza, Madhuri Sonawane

School of Aerospace Sciences, Department of Computer Science, University of North Dakota, Grand Forks, ND, USA

ABSTRACT

Cloud computing is an emerging and popular method of accessing shared and dynamically configurable resources via the computer network on demand. Cloud computing is excessively used by mobile applications to offload data over the network to the cloud. There are some security and privacy concerns using both mobile devices to offload data to the facilities provided by the cloud providers. One of the critical threats facing cloud users is the unauthorized access by the insiders (cloud administrators) or

Citation: Reza, H. and Sonawane, M. (2016), "Enhancing Mobile Cloud Computing Security Using Steganography". *Journal of Information Security*, **7**, 245-259. doi: 10.4236/jis.2016.74020.

the justification of location where the cloud providers operating. Although, there exist variety of security mechanisms to prevent unauthorized access by unauthorized user by the cloud administration, but there is no security provision to prevent unauthorized access by the cloud administrators to the client data on the cloud computing. In this paper, we demonstrate how steganography, which is a secrecy method to hide information, can be used to enhance the security and privacy of data (images) maintained on the cloud by mobile applications. Our proposed model works with a key, which is embedded in the image along with the data, to provide an additional layer of security, namely, confidentiality of data. The practicality of the proposed method is represented via a simple case study.

Keywords: Cloud Computing, Mobile Computing, Software Security, Software Privacy, Data Hiding, Steganography, Encryption

INTRODUCTION

Cloud computing refers to popular method of accessing services and resources via network connections on demand [1] . The popularity of cloud computing, for most part, can be attributed to fee for service and flexibility of providing services and resources to the customer whenever they these services are needed. The cloud paradigm has significantly eased up front infrastructural and operating cost. However, there are many issues and concerns remained to be addressed when migrating to cloud computing. Examples of these issues include security, scalability, privacy, portability, etc.

The growth of the number of the mobile devices in the past few years has shown that there is a high demand for mobile applications [1] . Mobile devices are considered to be low-end computing. As such, they have limited storage and computing capability compared to the traditional computing platforms such as desktops. Cloud computing has been used as a durable alternative to compensate the inherent limitations of mobile devices by mobile industry [2] . The current approach to increase security and privacy of data work encryption algorithms, negatively affects the performance [3] .

Mobile cloud computing (MCC) acting as clients, is benefitting from the cloud computing platform acting as server [4] [5] . Mobile devices and apps became very popular over the past two decades [6] . This is very evident by the exponential growth in the development of mobile devices and systems such as, android, smart phones, PDA's with a variety of mobile computing, networking and security technologies. Mobile computing has three major components [3] : hardware, software and communication.

In mobile cloud computing, the user data are stored on device or cloud. As the internet enabled mobile usage to continue growing, web-based malicious security threat is a serious issue. In this paper, we discuss the working concepts of mobile cloud computing and its various security issues.

In this work, we attempt to address security of mobile cloud computing using mobile devices, because it is very important for customers and providers to retrieve, transmit and retain the data on cloud without breaking any type of secrecy [7] . As discussed in [5] [7] , existing security standards and policies [4] are meant to assure the data and access security, but no standards/requirements currently exit to prevent unauthorized access of customer data by the cloud providers. Toward this goal, we have applied techniques from steganography to secure data maintained by the cloud provide. Steganography has been used to hide messages [8] inside some kinds of contents like image, audio or video in such a way that it does not allow anyone to detect that there is a secret message present. Due to today's advanced modern technology, stenography is used on image, text, audio and video [9] . Efficiency of the application is based on the medium used and the maximum data capacity to hide information inside medium.

BACKGROUND: CLOUD AND MOBILE COMPUTING

Cloud computing is one of the popular methods for the users to host and deliver services over the Internet by dynamically providing computing resources [1] . Cloud computing eliminates the overhead of planning ahead for acquiring different resources. The National Institute of Standards and Technology (NIST) defines cloud computing as "a model for enabling convenient, on-demand network access to a shared pool of configurable computing resources that can be rapidly provisioned and released with minimal management effort or service provider interaction" [1] . According to NIST, the key characteristics of cloud computing are:

- On-demand self-service: The users have access and the power to change cloud services online. User can add, delete, or change storage networks and software as needed.
- Broad network access: User can access cloud services using their Smartphone, tablets, laptops, or desktop computers. These devices can be used, wherever they are connected with online access point.

- Resource pooling: The cloud computing enables users to enter and use data within the software, hosted in the cloud at any time, and from any location.
- Elasticity: The cloud computing is flexible and scalable according to the user's needs. User can easily add or remove other users, resources or software features.
- Measured service: Cloud provider can measure storage levels, processing, the number of user accounts and the user are billed accordingly.
- Pricing: Cloud computing cost is based on amount of resources used by the user. Cloud computing is transparent to capture for accurate billing information.
- ▪ Quality of service: Cloud computing guarantees, best performance, adequate resources and on round-the- clock availability service for the users.

Cloud Computing services can be classified into three layered service models. These models are: 1) Infrastructure as a service (IaaS), 2) Platform-as-a-Service (PaaS), 3) Software-as-Service (SaaS) [2] . The IaaS model is based on the provisioning of processing, storage, networks and other fundamental computing resources which are more hardware oriented [10] [11] . This service is mainly used by the system managers. The consumer is able to deploy and run arbitrary software. With infrastructure as a service, the user itself is able to run and manage own operating systems and applications by using virtualization technologies user can also make use of storage systems and/or network devices. The infrastructure management of is done by the service provider of the cloud but still the user has full control of operating systems, applications, storage and partial control over network devices. The advantage IaaS is that there is no need to purchase a server and manage physical data storage, networking manually. Examples: Amazon EC2 for computation power and Amazon S3 for storage provisioning.

The PaaS model allows users to run applications on the infrastructure offered by the service providers. The PaaS requires that the applications are created with programming languages or tools that are supported by the service provider. The management of the infrastructure and operating systems is in the hands of the service provider. While on other hand user has full administrative control over the applications he wants to host on the cloud system [12] . This service provides pre- built application components known as Application Programmable Interface (API). It is commonly used by developers to build the higher level applications. Examples of this model include: Google Application Engine, Force.com.

The SaaS model allow applications and software service are being used on demand The management of the infrastructure, operating systems and the configuration of the application is completely achieved by the service provider. This service is commonly used by the business users. It provides the complete customizable within the limits applications. It is mainly used for achieving specific business task with mainly focusing on end-user requirements. Examples: Google Docs, Microsoft Office Web Applications.

Cloud deployment models refer to how cloud infrastructure are operated and utilized by users, and organizations. According to NIST, cloud deployment models are public cloud (services available to public), private cloud (services are exclusively available to the member of a single organization), community cloud (services are exclusively available to the member of multiple organizations), and hybrid cloud (share feathers of both public and private clouds).

Mobile cloud computing (MCC) refers to the computing paradigm that combines the capability of low end computing devices such as smart phones with the capabilities provided by the cloud computing using network connectivity. The key characteristics of mobile cloud computing are Reliability, Scalability, Security, Agility, device independence, reduced cost of mobiles and mobile services and reduced maintenance [12] . Moreover, mobile cloud computing provides auto-upgrade services to the users devices based on the service demand by the user.

Figure 1 represents the architecture of MCC. In this mode, mobile devices takes the advantages of the services provided by cloud computing. In Figure 1, the main components of the MCC architecture are mobile user, mobile device, network connectivity, and cloud service provider [14] . User is responsible for accessing mobile, installing mobile applications, upgrading the applications and operating systems, creating the backup files, downloading and/or uploading information from or to cloud. Cloud service provider mainly provides various services, such as applications and storage, etc. User's data (e.g., images) can be offloaded to the cloud via the mobile network.

Cloud Computing Security Breaches and Issues

The objective of the mobile cloud computing is to make process convenient for mobile user to access and receive data from the cloud [12] .

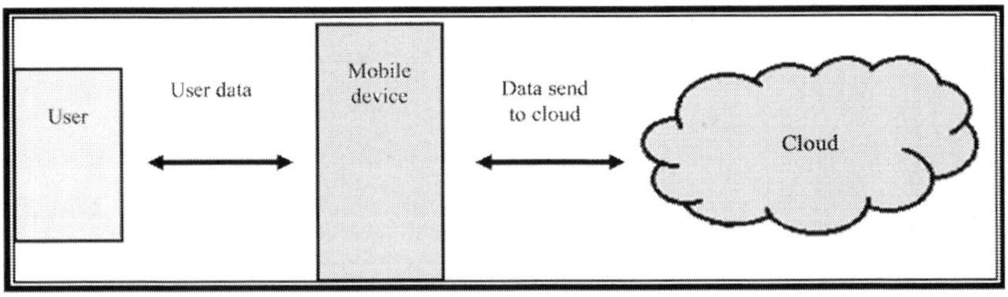

Figure 1. Mobile cloud computing model.

In spite of many advantages provided by the mobile cloud computing, there are some security challenges exist in the area of mobile and cloud computing. According to [15] , major security issues include: 1) Data ownership, which means the legal rights and complete control over data elements, 2) Data privacy, which is the right of an organization (or individual) to determine what data can be shared by who, 3) Data security, which refers to protecting data from malicious use.

Other important issue is the notion of security of data stored in the data storage provided by cloud computing provider. To secure data on the cloud, cloud providers are required to follow security standards and measures [12] . These data security standards are supposed to implement operational security policies and procedures Examples of these policies include: access control, encryption, content assurance, data authentication procedures, and account and user management [16] .

In general, when data is stored and offloaded to the cloud, mobile devices may be exposed to the following security threads: 1) In case the mobile device gets stolen or lost, the transmission of un-encrypted data between cloud computing and mobile devices [6] [12] [17] - [20] , which may be subject to man-in-the-middle attacked, or data security breach by insider (i.e., cloud administrator).

In case when the mobile devices are stolen (or lost), data from the devices, can be avoided by wiping of mobile device from remote location. To handle man-in-the-middle attack, majority of mobile manufacturers provide feature or security application [2] [5] . In regard to the insider attack by cloud administrator, there are not any viable protection exist. In this work, we are trying to provide additional layer of protection against insider attack. To this end, we are utilizing steganography to enhance the data security offload to the cloud computing.

RELATED WORK

There are many different approached of storing data securely over the cloud, using mobile computing such as end-to-end encrypted data transmission, dynamic credential generation, steganography etc.

The stored application or information on cloud raises security issues which are discussed in Bilogrevic [21] . To increase the storage capacity of mobile device, mobile users use cloud storage services. The mobile users do not have any control on the information store on the cloud which causes security and privacy issues [22] - [24] .

C. Saravankumar and C. Arun [5] explain cloud computing issues and proposed new cloud computing security model. An important issue of the mobile cloud computing is to secure the user data is addressed in this paper. There are many security standards and policies are available to secure the data such as data privacy, authenticated access to data, third party data protection, but these standards are exist only at the cloud end. It is a critical for the customer as well as provider to store, retrieve and transmit the data over the cloud network in a secure manner. To provide secure system, the authors have proposed the algorithm [5] to develop a customer owned security model. This algorithm is able to send the encrypted data to the provider. The provider can also apply the security by encryption over the customer's data by using the algorithm. The customer's data is secure at both the end. The proposed algorithm uses ASCII and BCD security with steganography that stores the encrypted data in an image file which will be send to the provider end. The security algorithm is using CDM (Common Deployment Model) which also provides an interoperable security services over the cloud. The main objective of the proposed algorithm is to control and send the data in an encrypted manner by the customer to the provider. The provider also maintains the data with a security algorithm to protect the data from unauthorized access.

Z. Al-Khanjari and A. Alani proposed a steganography scheme architectural model to protect data in cloud. Cloud computing systems needs to satisfy interoperability, security, safety, dependability, performance and many other parameters [25] . Security is one of the important issues, discussed and resolved in this paper using protected access control technique which can prevent security problems. Authors are proposing steganography to secure the data in cloud computing. The paper explains that how to hide the data through security pipeline channel. This provides protected access to the data. Steganography will provide safety, dependability, performance, integrity and confidentiality to the data for exchanging data over the network. It is hiding the data when data is requested and displayed. This steganography scheme uses text properties to hide the data, text properties includes font, font metrics, font styles, color and their RGB values, and the x, y location to display data. This steganography architecture supports cloud computing to provide security from unauthorized access. The architecture contains 3 layers physical Layer, data Layer, security Layer [25] . Security layer hides the data through security pipeline channel.

S. Brohi, M. Bamiah, S. Chuprat and J. Manan provide a solution for data privacy issue [26] . In some organization such as healthcare and payment card industry, have a user's personal data which is very important factor, these organizations can store data on cloud but malicious attackers may steal, view or manipulate client's data. To provide privacy to cloud data storage, authors propose an improved technique which consists of five contributions [26] : resilient role-based access control mechanism; partial homomorphic cryptography; efficient third- party auditing service; data backup and recovery process.

This technique maintains client's data intact and protects them from malicious attackers.

Resilient Role-based Access Control Mechanism - The process starts from this phase and it is responsible for generation of private and public keys by requesting the cloud server for data communication over the internet.

Using Partial Homomorphic Cryptography, data inside the file will be homomorphic-ally encrypted during the uploading process and stored on the cloud in the encrypted format [26] . Whenever this file is required, server needs client's private key to decrypt the selected file. This technique not allows the client to process the data on cloud while it is in the encrypted format [26] . To change the encrypted data, client needs to decrypt the data prior to processing. Here author has used the security features of asymmetric algorithms, he has implemented the homomorphic version of RSA algorithm to encrypt, decrypt and process the encrypted data on cloud.

STEGANOGRAPHY: BACKGROUND

Now a day's sender can send the secret data openly using encrypted mail or files to receiver with no fear of reprisals. However there are often cases when this is not allowed when sender or receiver is working for a company that does not allow encrypted email or the local government does not allow encrypted communication. This is where steganography can play a key role. In the simplest form, steganography refers to the method of writing hidden messages in a manner that no one other person but sender and receiver would be able to securely understand and communicate the information hidden in the means of communications (e.g., images) [6] [13] [27] - [29] . The steganography is a channel of communication through which secret data can be transmitted in total secrecy to avoid misuse of data. To this end, steganography covers secret data into some kind of medium like images, audio or video and transmits them in total secrecy from sender to receiver to avoid suspicious attacks. In this paper, we propose a text steganography method for hiding secret textual data and uploading it over cloud.

Figure 2 shows the architecture of steganography. The model consists of the following components: users, who interact with system by inputting data and the key, original image that the sender will use to embed the data, stego-image, which is the image contains embedded key and data, and finally, steganography application, which receives as an input stego-image and user key.

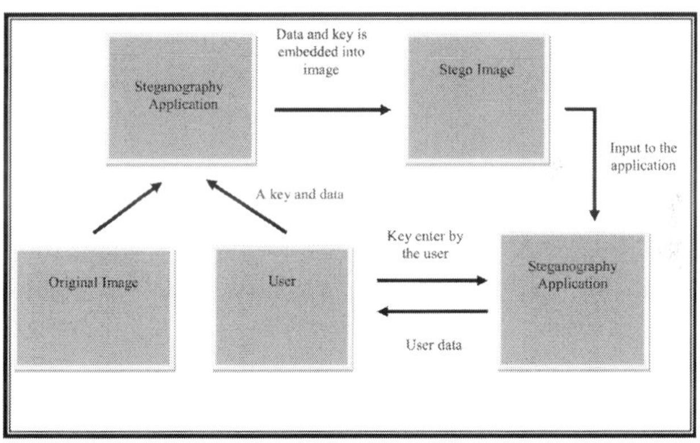

Figure 2. The architecture of Steganography.

In the steganography model, the user is responsible for selecting any 24-bit image and entering data and the key. In steganography, the classified information aretypically stored in the least significant bits of a digitized file, that means those bits that can be changed in subtle way and hence cannot be detected by the human eye.

After accepting input from the user, the steganography application embeds the key and data into the image selected by the user; this image is called a stego-image. To retrieve data from the image, the stego-image acts as an input to the steganography application. The steganography application retrieves the key from the stego-image and compares it with the user entered image; if both keys are matched then the application displays the embedded data to the user.

Steganography can be classified as: 1) pure steganography, 2) symmetric steganography and 3) asymmetric steganography [30] . Pure steganography does not require any exchange of information. Symmetric steganography does not require exchange of keys prior to sending the messages. Asymmetric steganography does not require to exchange keys prior to sending the messages.

Steganography, for the most part, is dependent on the type of medium being used to hide the information. Medium being commonly used include text, images, audio or video used in network transmissions. Image steganography is generally more preferred media because of its easiness, harmlessness and attraction. Technology advancement in cameras and digital images being saved in cameras and then transfer to PCs [15] has also enhanced many folds. Another thing is the text message hidden in the images does not distort the image. There are some techniques available which change only one bit of an image whose effects is almost negligible on its quality and image looks like unchanged. There are some methods are used to hide information in the media/medium selected for steganography. Some methods are as follows [28] : 1) embedding secret message in text/documents, 2) embedding secret message in audio/video, 3) embedding secret message in images.

To farther enhance secure communication, it is common practice to encrypt the hidden message before placing it in the cover message. However, the hidden message does not need to be encrypted to qualify as steganography. The hidden message can be in plain English. If steganographer decides to have the extra layer of protection then the encryption should provide that extra level of protection. In case, the hidden message is found by unauthorized person (thief), then encryption provides additional level of data protection.

In what follows, we explain the method of embedding secret message in images using pure Steganography approach.

THE METHOD USING STEGANOGRAPHY

For the mobile users, data security and privacy are key concerns. Cryptography and steganography are basic but popular methods to protect data. Using cryptography, the data is transformed using well-defined algorithm that hopefully makes it hard to read encrypted data without having proper keys.

On the other hand, steganography operates by hiding the message in some kind of medium to transfer to another user in such a way that no one will be able to see or guess the exchange of messages. Some steganography methods are hybrid method combining cryptography and steganography. Combination of cryptography and steganography method may enhance the security of the communication, may affect the performance because these technique demand additional processing that may affect energy consumption. To ease the power consumption, our proposed application applies steganography with an embedded key.

In what follows, we outline the overall process to apply steganography. The process consists of the following steps:

1) Encryption (Optional): The media file which is supposed to be processed will be encrypted in some binary codes. These binary codes depend on the nature of media file. This encryption is different for different files.
2) Data chunking: The encrypted media file is chunked in various parts and this file is to be proceeding for further steganography.
3) Applying steganography: The steganography is done on the chunked encrypted files. Sending chunked files - The chunked files to be sent to receiver and these files will be in the hidden form. This all files are received by the receiver and then are proceed to get the original data.
4) File recombination: The chunked files are recombined to get the whole file so that the receiver can get the original file.
5) Decryption (optional): The previously recombined file is decrypted to get the original file which is sent from the sender.

Images are the most popular medium to use as a cover for steganography. In the simplest form, an image is a collection of pixels that contains different light intensities [31] . These pixels are referred by numeric forms of a grid and displayed horizontally. Most images are in rectangular shape of pixels and represented as bits and color of the pixel. Each pixel has 8-bits to describe the color [31] . There are different image formats exist and for these different image formats, different steganography algorithms exist. There are mainly three types of image files are used for steganography, 16-bit, 24-bit and 32-bit. Digital color images are usually 24-bit files and uses RGB color model it is also known as true color. RGB color model of the 24-bit image are derived from three primary colors: red, green and blue and each color is represented by 8-bits.

Information can be hidden in many different ways in images. Message insertion in images means simply embed every bit of information in the image. More complex encoding can be done by embedding the message only in "noisy" areas/pixels of image that will attract less attention. The message may also scattered on pixels randomly throughout the cover image.

In general, the most common approaches for information hiding are [8] are: 1) Least Significant Bit (LSB) insertion, 2) Masking and filtering techniques, 3) Algorithms and Transformation.

The least significant bit [15] (LSB) insertion is considered as a common, simple, and efficient algorithm for embedding information in an image [31] . The least significant bit is also called as 8th bit of the bytes inside an image which is changed to a bit of the information which is to hide.

Using a 24-bit image, a bit of each of color (red, green and blue) corresponding to each pixel of image can be used to embed the data, which means each pixel store 3 bytes with 8-bits in each. The message is embedded into the first 8 bytes of the grid and in each byte only the 3-bits are changed to embed the information. So only half of the bits in an image is needed to be modified in order to hide a secret data [9] [29] . Since there are 256 different possible intensities of each color, changing the least significant bit of a pixel should result in small changes in the intensity of the colors. These changes, in turn, cannot be identified by human eye and allows the message to be successfully hidden, stored, and finally transmitted over Internet. When modifying the LSB bits in 8-bit image pointer to enter in the palette are changed. It is really important to remember that a change of even one bit could mean the difference in a shade of red and shade of blue. Change of shades sometimes would be noticeable on displayed image. While in other-hand grey-scale palettes shades is not as pronounced

The main benefit of LSB insertion approach is that the data can be inserted in the pixels but still the human eye would be unable to notice it. While using LSB approach on 8-bit images, more care needs to be taken, as 8-bit format changes can be detected by human eyes as 24-bit format are not. Also, additional care needs to be taken in the selection of the cover image in a way that changes to the data will not be visible in the stego-image. Commonly known images, painting such as the Mona Lisa should be avoided. In most cases, a simple picture of (e.g., dog) would be ideal.

Masking and filtering techniques hide the information by marking the image in a manner similar to paper watermarks. This technique can be applied on 24-bit gray-scale or colored images. Watermarking techniques are more integrated into the image; they may be applied without fear of image destruction. The human visual system cannot detect changes in JPEG images.

The algorithms and transformations technique, on the other hand, use mathematical functions to hide the least bit coefficients in the compression algorithms which reduce the size of images.

Proposed Approach to Secure Data from Cloud Provide

The proposed solution allows a customer to protect its own data by maintained by cloud provider. Although, mobile devices are increasingly essential part of human life, but they are considered as low-end computing with limited processing capability, energy supply, data protection, and storage capacity. As noted previously, it is imperative to consider these inherent limitations of mobile devices when one is attempting to provide additional layer of data protection.

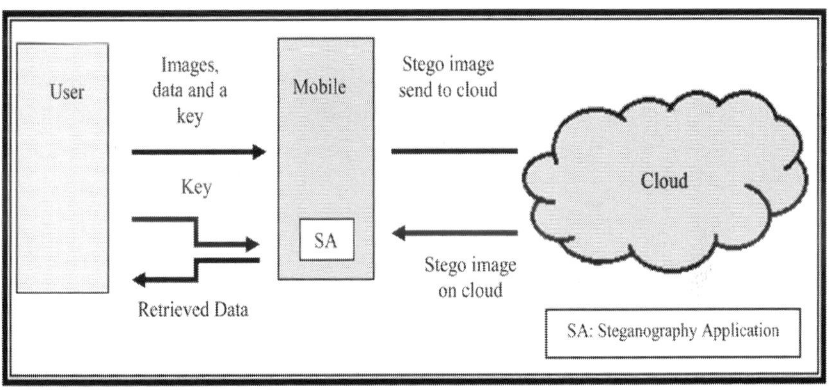

Figure 3. Proposed system.

Figure 3 shows the software architecture of the proposed system with the steganography application (SA). The key elements of our model include the following components: User, who select an image and enters key and data, 2) Mobile device (smartphone), which works as an intermediate device bridging the gap between the sender and receiver's information on which the steganography application is running, 3) Steganography application (SA), which is a mobile-application (app) running on the mobile device to embed data and the key in the image given by the user; it then generates a stego-image and retrieves data from the image if user entered key matches, 4) Cloud computing provider providing various service (e.g., SaaS).

The proposed architectural model is based on Client-server architecture [32] ; the system is combines the essential features of cloud computing and steganography. As noted previously, in this model, this is the user who is responsible for selecting an image, entering the data and the keys as the input; the input are used by the steganography application, which is configured on the user's mobile device. The steganography application processes all these inputs and creates as an output the stego-image to be stored on the cloud. It is assumed that the mobile device has a connection via internet to access the data maintained on cloud. At the time of data retrieval, the image is fetched from the cloud and again processed by the steganography application to display data to the user if the user entered key matched with the embedded key.

There exists a large body of work aiming at hiding sensitive information in images. Our proposed approach uses 24-bit image steganography to embed data and a key into an image. Different methods of hiding messages work with different types of images. For example, one technique lacks in payload capacity whereas the other approach lacks in robustness.

In this research we have used the least significant bit technique to hide information, which makes the mobile cloud computing application robust and less prone for image distortion. We used 24-bit images because 24-bit images can display more than 16,000 k different combinations that can easily hide data in a way that it will be hard to detect any difference between the modified image and the original image.

To add additional layer of protection, encryption algorithms are used but if the user wants to embed large amounts of information, these algorithms may increase the load on the processor as well as the response time. To overcome this problem, we have used the concept of a key to provide more secure data storage. Using a key, the key first is embedded into an image together with the payload (data). The system will use a specific algorithm to calculate those bytes' location where the key has been stored. Because this app is deployed and used on the user's side, therefore only the user of the system needs to remember this key. As such, we do not need to be concerned about key exchange between the sender and receiver.

The digital image is represented by an array of pixels. These pixels represent the intensities of the three colors: red, green and blue (also known as RGB). In RGB model, a value of each color describes a pixel. In our case, we are using Least Significant Bit (LSB) approach for hiding information into the image.

In what follows, we show how the data embedding process of using LSB is performed. Assuming that the user wants to embed letter "A" into a 24-bit image and the binary value of "A" is 10000011. In 24-bit image each pixel has eight bits for each color in RGB model that is red, green and blue. The user needs to change the least significant bits that require only 3 pixels for hiding 8 bits letter "A". The original three pixels are represented in Table 1. Each row of the table represents each pixel and each column represents RGB value of each pixel.

Table 1. Represents 24-bit word.

	Red	Green	Blue
Pixel 0	00100111	11101001	11001000
Pixel 1	00100111	11001000	11101001
Pixel 2	11001000	00100111	11101001

Table 2. Represents 24-bit word after inserting the letter A.

	Red	Green	Blue
Pixel 0	00100111	11101000	11001000
Pixel 1	00100110	11001000	11101000
Pixel 2	11001001	00100111	11101001

After embedding the binary value of "A" that is 10000011 into the three pixels, starting from the top left byte in the table and going to the right end. Following the same sequence for each row would generate result represented in Table 2. For red byte of the pixel 0, last bit is replaced with first bit of letter A and process is continued till the last bit of the letter 'A'. In this example, we have used an 8-bits letter 'A' to replace 9 bytes; the blue byte of pixel 2 remains unchanged. The underline values are the ones which are modified by the LSB transformation method.

The most important features of this application are, the user can use different keys for different information, so even if the thief guesses the key for one stego-image he won't be able to use same key for other images, which reduces the chances of data theft, and if the user loses the mobile device, then the user can access cloud data from any other mobile by simply downloading the "Mobile Cloud Computing" application on that mobile device.

CASE STUDY

In recent year's mobile with digitalized applications are widely used and popular due to flexibility and feasibility of the wireless internet. Most of the daily work can be performed easily with the help of mobile internet such as modern ways of communication like Messenger, Whats App, Facebook and Email, handling banking accounts using mobile e-banking.

Now a day's who owns a mobile, text or call more often than directly going to someone's house to convey the message even if house is really close. Email's has replaced for mails. Paper signed up or registration has replaced by online forms etc.

For any kind of online work, we mostly have to sign up and open new account with personal detail so that you can access your account later with username and password. Due to the popularity and comfort of mobile wireless internet access, user prefers opening and accessing new accounts using mobile phones. In this case it is highly possible that user have many accounts and there is high chance of forgetting credentials of those accounts. Hence to be on the safe side, users write down some important information or pass phrase somewhere. This written information may be read or access by another user or it is also possible that user kept this information at house and wanted to access that from remote location which is not possible. To handle this issue, we have proposed solution in which user can store limited amount of information on cloud, by mobile using steganography, which will protect user data from cloud administrator. If user is storing their information on cloud then they can access data from any location without any strain of losing important data on mobile device or any unauthenticated data access.

This application works for small amounts of data per image with low processing power and less battery usage, which eventually increases the performance of the overall application and the mobile device. This approach combines and enhances the trust in mobile computing as well as the efficiency of cloud computing.

Figure 4 shows the Mobile Cloud Computing Application's main page, where a user can select an input and output image path, and enter data and a key to embed into an image. Figure 5 explains how a user can enter information and an encryption key to embed in the selected image.

Figure 6 shows that using mobile cloud computing application; a user is able to browse for the file location of the original image as well as the file location of the stego-image (message embedded image) using the provided "Browse" button. Figure 7 and Figure 8 display a message shown by the application after pressing the “Embed” button. This message box represents that the process of message encoding and key into the specified image is completed successfully.”Browse” button to select the stego-image and enter the key. After pressing the “Retrieve” button, information is retrieved if the entered encryption key matches with the retrieve key from the stego-image.

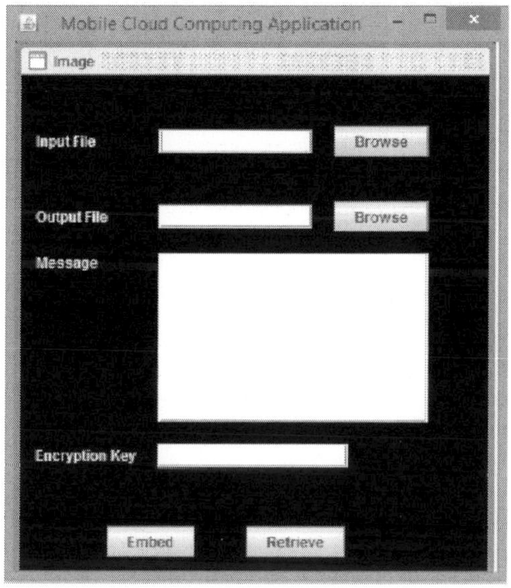

Figure 4. Main page.

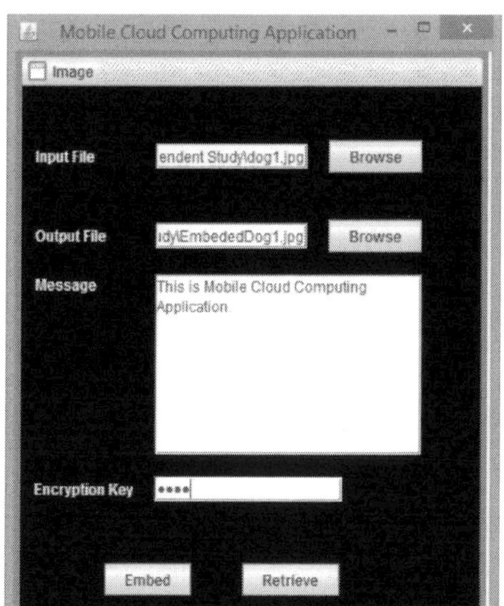

Figure 5. Data acceptance page.

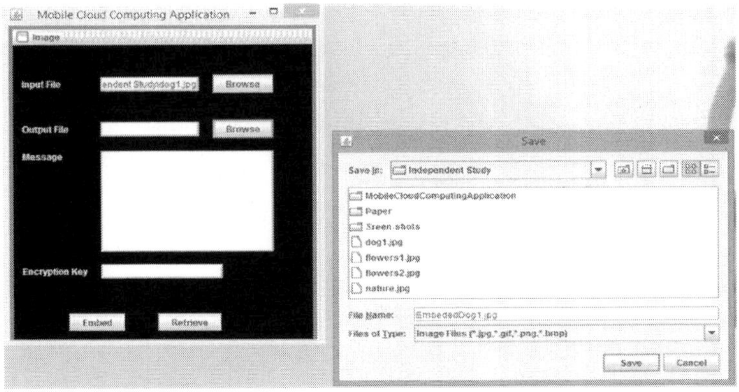

Figure 6. File selection page.

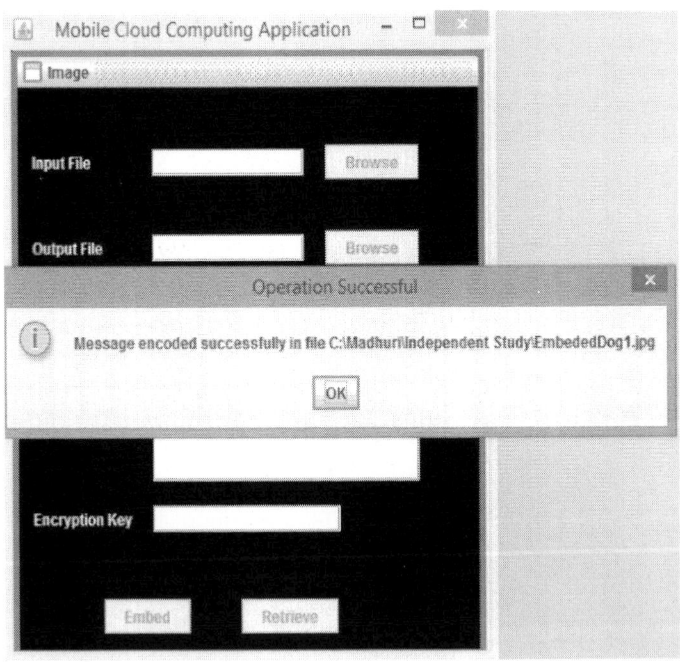

Figure 7. Operation successful message box.

Figure 9 and Figure 11 are the original images and Figure 10 and Figure 12 are the stego-images created after embedding secret message and the key. This figures shows that the images look same before and after embedding the message and key into the image. Image is little distorted but it cannot be recognized by human eyes.

CONCLUSION AND FUTURE WORK

Mobile cloud computing is one of the mobile technology trends which combine the advantages of both mobile computing and cloud computing, and provides optimal services for mobile devices. Cloud computing is a transformative technology that can change the nature of computing so often, specifically for business purposes. It offers on-demand network access for configurable computing resources like networks, servers, storage, applications, and different cloud services that can be rapidly installed and uninstalled with minimal management effort.Many applications are supported by mobile cloud computing such as mobile commerce and mobile healthcare, which contain user sensitive data. Security to this sensitive data is a more important factor in the mobile cloud computing. Due to memory storage issues, this data are usually stored on the cloud. Cloud data are secured against invalid data access and data theft, but technologies are still lacking behind due to the cloud administrator's invalid data access.

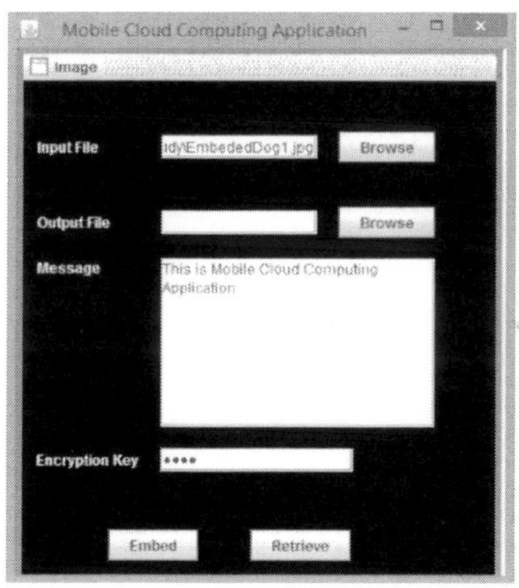

Figure 8. Data retrieval page.

Figure 9. Before using SA.

Figure 10. After using SA.

Figure 11. Before using SA.

Figure 12. After using SA.

Hence, to resolve this issue, we have proposed a "Mobile Cloud Computing" application, which provides secured data storage through mobile on the cloud against the cloud administrator by using steganography application which improves performance of mobile cloud computing. This steganography application can be used on networks for data security without using third party interference. The mobile cloud computing application is able to embed only limited amounts of data into images. In the future, we can extend this capability from a few words to huge data files by replacing the steganography medium that is, images with audio or video files. The proposed system will work perfectly as long as a user remembers the key, but if he loses the key, then the system does not have any provision for recovering or guessing the key, so in this case a user might lose the data. This issue will have to be addressed in the future. The proposed system is efficient and legal for the client as long as the cloud administrator doesn't have restrictions about a client's data. As this system is hiding the original data, a user may abuse this feature and can store illegal or unethical data. As of now, the proposed system does not have any remedy for this issue. In the future, cloud management systems and proposed models may work in parallel for smooth and legal data storage function.

REFERENCES

1. Gupta, P. and Gupta, S. (2012) Mobile Cloud Computing: The Future of Cloud. International Journal of Advanced Research in Electrical Electronics and Instrumentation Engineering, 1, 134-145.
2. Bheda, H. and Lakhani, J. (2013) Application Processing Approach for Smart Mobile Devices in Mobile Cloud Computing. International Journal of Software Engineering and Knowledge Engineering, 3, 1046-1055.
3. Buyya, R., Yeo, C. and Venugopal, S. (2008) Market-Oriented Cloud Computing: Vision, Hype, and Reality for Delivering it Services as Computing Utilities in High Performance Computing and Communications. The10th IEEE International Conference on IEEE, 5-13.
4. Donald, C. and Arockiam, O.L. (2013) Mobile Cloud Security Issues and Challenges: A Perspective. St. Joseph's College Tiruchirappalli, Department of Computer Science, Tamil Nadu.
5. Saravankumar, C. and Arun, C. (2014) An Efficient ASCII-BCD Based Steganography for Cloud Security Using Common Development Model. Journal of Theoretical and Applied Information Technology, 65, 1992-8645.
6. Prasad, R., Gyani, J. and Murti, P. (2012) Mobile Cloud Computing: Implications and Challenge. Journal of Information Engineering and Applications, 2, 7-15.
7. Juneja, M. and Singh, P. (2014) Improved LSB Based Steganography Techniques for Color Images in Spatial Domain. International Journal of Network Security, 16, 366-376.
8. Kumar, A. and Pooja, K. (2010) Steganography: A Data Hiding Technique. International Journal of Computer Applications, 9, 975-8887. http://dx.doi.org/10.5120/1398-1887
9. Ross, A. and Fabien, P. (1998) On the Limits of Steganography. IEEE Journal of Selected Areas in Communications, 16, 474-481.
10. Foster, I., Zhao, Y., Raicu, I. and Lu, S. (2008) Cloud Computing and Grid Computing 360-Degree Compared. Grid Computing Environments Workshop, 2008, 1-10. http://dx.doi.org/10.1109/gce.2008.4738445
11. Buyya, R., Yeo, C., Venugopal, S., Broberg, J. and Brandic, I. (2009) Cloud Computing and Emerging IT Platforms: Vision, Hype, and Reality for Delivering Computing. The 5th Utility Future Generation

Computer Systems, 25, 599- 616. http://dx.doi.org/10.1016/j.future.2008.12.001

12. Bahar, A., Habib, M. and Islam, M. (2013) Security Architecture for Mobile Cloud Computing. International Journal of Scientific Knowledge, 3, 11-17.
13. Nasab, M. and Shafiei, B. (2011) Steganography in Programming. Australian Journal of Basic and Applied Sciences, 5, 1496-1499.
14. Shamim, S., Sarker, A. and Bahar, A. (2015) A Review on Mobile Cloud Computing. International Journal of Computer Applications, 113, 4-9. http://dx.doi.org/10.5120/19908-1883
15. Kekre, H.B., Athawale, A. and Halarnkar, P.N. (2008) Increased Capacity of Information Hiding in LSB's Method for Text and Image. International Journal of Electrical, Computer, and Systems Engineering, 2, 246-249.
16. Sahu, D., Sharma, S., Dubey, V. and Tripathi, A. (2012) Cloud Computing in Mobile Applications. International Journal of Scientific and Research Publications, 2, 1-9.
17. Huang, D., Zhou, Z., Xu, L., Xing, T. and Zhong, Y. (2011) Secure Data Processing Framework for Mobile Cloud Computing. IEEE Conference on Computer Communications Workshops (INFOCOM WKSHPS), Shanghai, 10-15 April 2011, 620-624. http://dx.doi.org/10.1109/infcomw.2011.5928886
18. Satyanarayanan, M. (1996) Fundamental Challenges in Mobile Computing. 15th Annual ACM Symposium on Principles of Distributed Computing, Philadelphia, 23-26 May 1996, 1-7. http://dx.doi.org/10.1145/248052.248053
19. Oberheide, J., Veeraraghavan, K., Cooke, E., Flinn, J. and Jahanian, F. (2008) Virtualized In-Cloud Security Services for Mobile Devices. 1st Workshop on Virtualization in Mobile Computing, Breckenridge, 17-20 June 2008, 31-35. http://dx.doi.org/10.1145/1622103.1629656
20. Portokalidis, G., Homburg, P., Anagnostakis, K. and Bos, H. (2010) Paranoid Android: Versatile Protection for Smartphones. 26th Annual Computer Security Application Conference (ACSAC), Los Angeles, 5-9 December 2016, 347-356. http://dx.doi.org/10.1145/1920261.1920313
21. Bilogrevic, I., Jadliwala, M., Kumar, P., Walia, S., Hubaux, J., Aad, I. and Niemi, V. (2011) Meetings through the Cloud: Privacy-Preserving Scheduling on Mobile Devices. Journal of Systems and Software, 11,

1910-1927. http://dx.doi.org/10.1016/j.jss.2011.04.027

22. Ren, W., Yu, L., Gao, R. and Xiong, F. (2011) Lightweight and Compromise Resilient Storage Outsourcing with Distributed Secure Accessibility in Mobile Cloud Computing. Tsinghua Science and Technology, 16, 520-528. http://dx.doi.org/10.1016/S1007-0214(11)70070-0
23. Yang, J., Wang, H., Wang, J., Tan, C. and Yu, D. (2011) Provable Data Possession of Resource Constrained Mobile Devices in Cloud Computing. Journal of Networks, 6, 1033-1040. http://dx.doi.org/10.4304/jnw.6.7.1033-1040
24. Tysowski, P. and Hasan, M. (2011) Re-Encryption-Based Key Management towards Secure and Scalable Mobile Applications in Clouds. IACR Cryptology Eprint Archival, 668-678.
25. Al-Khanjari, Z. and Alani, A. (2014) Developing Secured Interoperable Cloud Computing Services. The European Interdisciplinary Forum 2014 (EIF 2014), Vilnius, 18-19 June 2014, 341-350.
26. Brohi, S., Bamiah, M., Chuprat, S. and Manan, J. (2014) Design and Implementation of a Privacy Preserved Off-Premises Cloud Storage. Journal of Computer Science, 10, 210-223. http://dx.doi.org/10.3844/jcssp.2014.210.223
27. Bassil, Y. (2012) A Text Steganography Method Using Pangram and Image Mediums. International Journal of Scientific & Engineering Research, 3, 2229-5518.
28. Bender, W., Gruhl, D., Morimoto, N. and Lu, A. (1996) Techniques for Data Hiding. IBM Systems Journal, 35, 313- 336. http://dx.doi.org/10.1147/sj.353.0313
29. Wang, H. and Wang, S. (2004) Cyber Warfare: Steganography vs. Steganalysis. Communications of the ACM, 47, 76- 82. http://dx.doi.org/10.1145/1022594.1022597
30. Mahajan, S. and Singh, A. (2012) A Review of Methods and Approach for Secure Steganography. International Journal of Advanced Research in Computer Science and Software Engineering, 2, 484-488.
31. Johnson, N. and Jajodia, S. (1998) Exploring Steganography: Seeing the Unseen. Computer, 31, 26-34. http://dx.doi.org/10.1109/MC.1998.4655281
32. Shaw, M. and Garlan, D. (1996) Software Architecture: Perspective on an Emerging Discipline. Prentice Hall, Upper Saddle River.

CHAPTER

12

Data Security of Mobile Cloud Computing on Cloud Server

Mohammad Waseem, Abdullah Lakhan, Irfan Ali Jamali

Department of Computer Science and Engineering, Southeast University, Nanjing, China

ABSTRACT

Mobile Cloud computing is a technology of delivering services, such as software, hardware (virtual as well) and bandwidth over the Internet. Mobile devices are enabled in order to explore, especially Smart phones. The mobile cloud computing technology is growing rapidly among the customers and many companies such as Apple, Google, Facebook and Amazon with rich users. Users can access their data at any time, at any place, even with any device including mobile devices by using the cloud storage services, although

Citation: Waseem, M. , Lakhan, A. and Jamali, I. (2016), "Data Security of Mobile Cloud Computing on Cloud Server". *Open Access Library Journal*, **3**, 1-11. doi: 10.4236/oalib.1102377.

these properties offer flexibility and scalability in controlling data, however, at the same time it reminds us with new security threats. These security issues can be resolved by proper handling of data. The cloud server provider can secure the data by applying the encryption and decryption techniques while storing the data over the cloud. In this paper, we proposed some encryption and decryption methods for securing the data over the cloud so that an unauthorized person or machine cannot access the confidential data owing to encrypted form.

Keywords: Amazon Cloud Server, Cloud Computing, Security, Data Security, AES Encryption, Eclipse IDE, JSON API

Subject Areas: Cloud Computing, Information and Communication: Security, Privacy, and Trust, Mobile Computing Systems

INTRODUCTION

To have an in-depth understanding of Mobile Cloud Computing (MCC), it is necessary to get a complete grasp on cloud computing [1] . Cloud computing is a new market-oriented business model which offers high quality and low cost information services [2] . Generally, cloud computing resources are provided in the form of services such as Infrastructure as a Service (IaaS), Data storage as a Service (DaaS), Communication as a Service (CaaS), Security as a Service (SecaaS), Hardware as a Service (HaaS), Software as a Service (SaaS), Business as a Service (BaaS), and Platform as a Service (PaaS). There are various layered architectures available for cloud computing to provide the aforementioned services as a utility [3] . User can consume these services based on SLA (Service Level Agreement) which define their QoS (Quality of Service) parameters on a pay-per-use basis as well as users can access their data any time, at any place, even with any computing device including mobile devices.

Cloud computing with resource constraint mobile devices, ubiquitous wireless infrastructure, mobile web, and location-based services provides a ground for a new computing paradigm called Mobile Cloud Computing (MCC) [4] . The ultimate goal of the MCC is to enable execution of rich mobile applications on a plethora of mobile devices, with a rich user experience [5] . According to the consumer and enterprise market, cloud-based mobile applications are expected to rise to $9.5 billion by 2014. Due to increase in the number of users, there are numerous challenges existing in the field of MCC, including data replication, consistency, limited scalability, unreliability, unreliable availability of cloud resources, portability (due to the lack in cloud provider standard), trust, security and privacy. To attract more potential consumers, the cloud service provider has to target all the security issues to provide a completely secure environment [6]. Many commercial cloud storage services protect user's data stored in server storages by introducing client-based or server-based data encryption.

The objective of this paper is to draw attention to many important issues and challenges concerning with security as well as privacy in mobile cloud application development. This paper also proposes some data encryption and decryption solutions for MCC. The rest of the paper is organized as follows. Section 2 presents the research background and overview. Section 3 researches methodology. Section 4 presents the software and tools and Section 5 concludes the paper with a summary of our contributions.

RESEARCH BACKGROUND AND OVERVIEW

The term "cloud" is used as a symbol of the Internet and other communications systems as well as an idea of the underlying infrastructures involved.

Cloud computing commonly refers as the result of an evolution of the widespread adoption of virtualization, service-oriented architecture, autonomic, and utility computing. The Details of location of infrastructure or component devices are unknowns to most of the end-users, User doesn't need to thoroughly understand or control the technology infrastructure that supports their computing activities and the users do not necessarily have their own resources. Following is a brief history of this evolution.

Mobile devices such as Smartphone, Tablets are increasingly becoming an integral part of modern life and culture as the connectivity, communication and sharing have turned out to be easier and convenient among people. Mobile applications (apps) for that matter reduce the performance of a task in a span of minutes and help deliver accurate results. Today mobile apps are built up not merely for communication, but also to learn, recrea- tion, and to earn unlike traditional mobile apps such as ringtone editor, grid based games etc. Technology is progressing at a speedy rate.

Cloud Computing Service

Cloud service providers offer their services mainly in three different ways, such as Software as a Service (SaaS), Platform as a Service (PaaS) and Infrastructure as a Service (IaaS). Figure 1 describes these three layers of services which are provided by cloud service providers.

Infrastructure as a Service

IaaS mostly offers Utility computing, which allows users to get infrastructure from cloud service providers as virtual resources as need basis. Virtual hardware, raw processors, storage software platforms include computers.

In spite of having physical hardware in their offices placed in the 'cloud' and information is accessed through the internet. The basic idea behind IaaS is not new, but this type of cloud computing is getting new life from big providers like Sun, Amazon, Rackspace, according to architecture showing in Figure 1, IBM and Google. The main benefit is that there is no need to procure a server or execute physical data center equipment like storage, networking, etc. [7] . They have organized over the applications and Operating Systems they install on top of the rented computing resources [8] . The user can't handle or control the underlying cloud infrastructure but it has had power over operating systems, deployed applications, storage, and maybe limited [9].

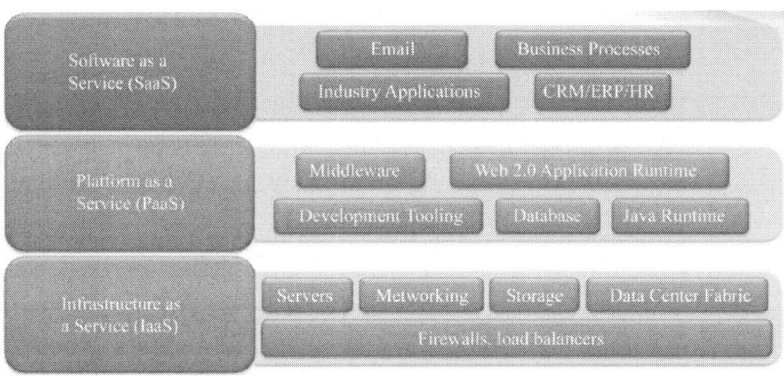

Figure 1. Cloud architecture.

The company of IaaS provides off line storage, server and networking hardware as per rental basis and can be accessed over the cloud [10] . The customers need not to procure the necessary servers, data center or the network resources. A key advantage here is that clients need to pay only for the time period and they can use the cloud service [11] .

Software as a Service

SaaS mostly offers executed applications on demand for users. Software executes over the cloud and serve to many end-users or client organizations. This is the model of software deployment where an application is hosted over the Internet and serves to the tenants. This way eliminates the need to install and execute the application on the customer own computer, These applications are accessible from various customer devices because of a thin client interface such as a web browser (e.g., web enabled e-mail). This type of service provides complete applications to the clients which is customizable within the confines [12] . SaaS model service delivery, clients procures cloud-based applications from service providers. A SaaS provider cannot store the unencrypted client data [13]. Network-based access and management of commercially offered software that are handled from centralized locations and enabling clients to access these applications which is remotely over the Internet.

RESEARCH METHODOLOGY

The paper involves different research approaches; first a literature study is conducted to gain a fundamental understanding of cloud computing and usage of its services in the architectural development of software. It also includes research articles of different researchers who have covered data storage techniques and have applied in different areas. Secure data storage by different researchers is also included in this literature study.

Next, few case studies are also referred in this context in which we will try to find the pros and cons of different variations conducted and implemented at various organizations, such as: encryption algorithms like—AES, DES, RSA and blowfish to ensure the security of data in cloud. The research will be conducted using Java runtime of Google App Engine, i.e. JDK 1.6 Eclipse IDE, Google App Engine SDK 1.6.0 or higher. Following are the steps for proposed work plan.

There are many advantages in mobile cloud ecosystem. However, there are some issues and challenges in mobile cloud computing such as data ownership, privacy and Data Security and other Security Issues. There are some possible solutions are presented for Cloud-access protection strong authentication method ensures that only legitimate user with authorization can access cloud-based services embedded device identity protection. It is possible to embed a personalized configuration profile on each employee's mobile device, thereby implementing a credential or personal security token on their mobile device. There are some other security features and policies that can be enforced to maximize the security on mobile devices, especially in a corporate context.

Security is an important factor in cloud deployment and by building in the capabilities described in these six steps, organizations can better manage and protect their customer data over the cloud.The team will also refer to the reports published by IEEE, SEI, ACM and other renowned research forums. This method will give us the understanding for implementation of mobile cloud computing as point of security view.

SOFTWARE AND TOOLS

Implement secure data storage over the cloud.

A. Android

B. Google API

C. Eclipse

D. JSON

E. JAVA

F. Amazon AWS Cloud server

E. Unit Testing

F. EC2 cloud database

PREVIOUS WORK

According to paper [14] , there are many issues in mobile cloud computing due to limitations of mobile devices. Security is the main concern in mobile cloud computing. In Mobile Cloud Computing data of owner is stored on the cloud, which is not secured.

According to paper [15] , due to the feature of resource-constrains, security in mobile devices have potential challenges in cloud accessing, consistent accessing, data transmission, and so on. Such challenges can be solved using: special application (service) and middle-ware (provide a platform for all mobile cloud computing systems).

According to paper [15] , the security applying on client side of mobile cloud computing are also inherited in mobile cloud computing with the additional limitations of resource constrained mobile devices such as time consuming.

According to paper [16] , mobile cloud computing architecture for code offloading in MCC applications, addressing both energy and performance issues due to time constraint.

According to paper [17] , all processing in MCC is performed on the mobile side. So there are some issues related to the data travelling such as Bandwidth, latency, availability and heterogeneity.

KEY COMPONENTS

DDOS Attack

Denial of Service is such type attacks over the cloud that prevents the clients from receiving the service from the cloud. The attacker is continuously attack to the target server to get the server busy make a machine or network resource unavailable to its intended users, so that clients might not be able to receive the service from the server, because server will busy servicing the attack. There are many techniques to perform DOS attack. Like SYN flood. The SYN flood exploits the TCP 3-way handshake with the help of requesting connections to the target server and ignoring the acknowledgement (ACK) from the server. Attacker applies attack to the server. This makes the server to wait for the ACK, wasting time and resources. Eventually, the servers do not have any resources to provide services to the clients. This type of attack can be prevented by authorizing strict access to the cloud and may using cryptographic protocols to make sure that the right personnel are accessing the cloud [17] .

There are different technology products have been released to prevent and detect DDOS attacks, the security breach had been growing at a shocking rate both in the cloud computing environments and enterprise.

XML SIGNATURE ELEMENT WRAPPING

Customers are typically capable to connect to cloud computing via a web browser or web service, web service attacks also affect cloud computing. XML signature element wrapping is the familiar attack for web service. Cloud security uses XML signature to protect an element's name, attributes and value from unauthorized person, it is not able to protect the information in the document. The attacker is able to control a SOAP message through copying the target element and inserting any value the attacker can insert the original element to everywhere else on the SOAP message. This technique can scam the web service to procedure the malicious message created by the attack.

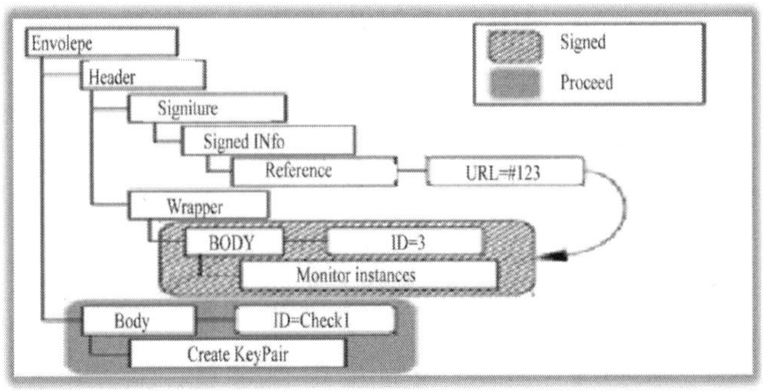

Figure 2. XML data security.

According to Figure 2, customer send data but it is open body. If the attacker intercept and alters the SOAP message by inserting the same element as the customer but attackers send request 456 in place of 123. After web service receives the message, web service will send the 456 send back to the customer. Another possible scenario attack may be in the form of e-mail web service application. When the attacker intercepts the SOAP message and changes the receiver's e-mail address to the attacker's email address, then web service will forward the e-mail to the attacker.

XML signature wrapping attacks are possible because of the fact that the signature does not convey any information to where the referenced element is placed. This attack was introduced for the first time, in 2005 by McIntosh and Austel, stating different kinds of this attack, including Simple Context, Optional Element, Optional Element in security header (sibling value) and Namespace injection (Sibling order). This attack happens in SOAP message, which transfers the XML document, over the Internet.

Malware Attack

Malware attack executes this attack, an intruder is necessary to produce his own malicious application, service or virtual machine instance and then the intruder has to attach it to the cloud system. When malicious software will be added to the cloud system, the attacker has to trick the cloud system to treat with malicious software as a valid instance. Another scenario is this that may be attacker try to upload a virus or Trojan program to the cloud. Once the cloud system treats it as a valid service, if the virus program execute automatically over the cloud infects the virus which can damage to the cloud. Due to this attack virus damages the hardware of the cloud system, other cloud instances running on the same hardware may affect the virus program because they share the same hardware. Attacker may plan to use a virus program to attack other users on the cloud system. When customer requests the malicious program case, the cloud system sends the virus over cloud to the customer and then run on the customer's machine. Client's computer will be impure via virus. The type of attack could be possible, performing a service instance integrity verifying for incoming requests. The hash value may be used to store over the original service instance's image file and compare this value with the hash values of all new service instance images. The result of using the hash values, an attacker needs to create a valid hash value comparison in order to trick the cloud system and inject a malicious instance over the cloud system.

The term malware refers to any malicious software that could intentionally perform malicious tasks on a computer system or on networked systems. The following covers some basic definitions of the malware problem.

Virus is a program that is designed to replicate itself and to spread from one machine to another using an infected carrier host program. That is a malicious program copy itself into a program. Once an infected program is executed, the virus starts its functionality, infects and damages the machine. Thus, viruses attempt to spread and infect within the infected machine.

Trojan Horse

Trojan horse is a program that is believed to be useful but which has a harmful intention towards the host machine. Some hidden parts of this type of malware contain a malicious payload that may exploit or damage the host system. Trojan horses can also be spyware because of their malicious actions such as the unauthorized collection of a user's data.

MOBILE TERMINAL SECURITY ISSUES

Mobile terminal security issues still originated from mobile clients. Firstly, mobile customers are usually lacks security awareness; and un-confidentiality. Secondly, mobile customers may not use themselves properly. So it is needed to find out abnormality of customers owing to troubleshooting above in mobile terminal attacks can cause privacy disturbance leads leakage, irregularity of information and devices damaged by several attacks which is deleterious for clients because of disclosure of data on cloud can be hacked [17].

RELATED WORK

Data Storage Issues

In [17] previous paper according to Figure 3 discussed about security inside the mobile device before submitting the data on cloud, but we found out the issue about battery consuming, time taking, and because of limited bandwidth some time encryption and decryption performance go down.

According to Table 1, the data stored in cloud or stored in other places is similar, need to consider three different aspects of information security: confidentiality, integrity and availability by using xml web services. Possible solution for data confidentiality is data encryption. In order to ensure encryption this is necessary to consider both encryption algorithm and key strength as cloud computing environment involves large amount of data transmission, storage and handling. Also needs to consider processing time and efficiency of encryption of huge amount of data.

Cloud is extremely powerful to perform computations while computing ability of mobile devices has a limit so many issues occur to show how to balance the differences between these two. So there are some issues in implementing cloud computing for mobile. These issues can be related to limited resources, related to network, related to security of mobile users and clouds. Some issues are explained as follows.

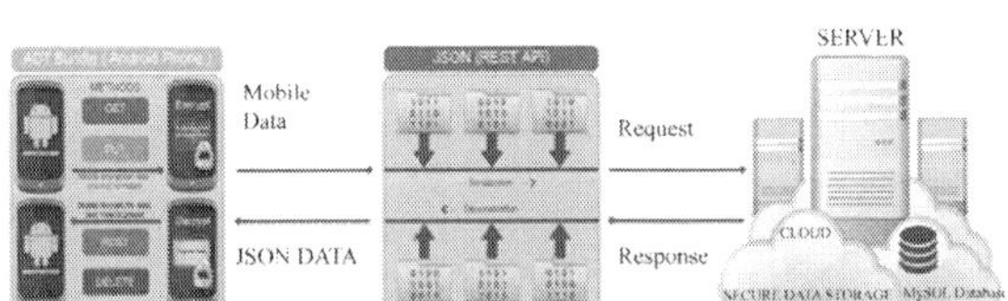

Figure 3. Mobile cloud computing data security.

Table 1. Security Issues in XML.

Issues	**Reason**
Encryption/Decryption	Time Consuming
Brute Force Attack	Because of open body
Resolve the external entity	Because XML 1.0/1.1 Stand

Implicit trust of internal DTD	Declaring the general entity notation
Configuration catalogs	Entity resolve catalogs
Trust the external schema	External schema definition
UTF-8/UTF-16	Malformed
Sure the trust entity	Import and include construct

PROPOSED WORK

According to Figure 4, the data of mobile computing travel to cloud computing through JSON object, that is trusted because it has serialize format of data into JSON object, then cloud server will encrypted all data into cryptography, finally it will store in cloud data storage.

According to Figure 5, replace the xml web services REST API, and solve the above all problems of "XML", and according to Figure 5 now data security will be manipulated at cloud server and proposed work for secure data storage in Mobile cloud computing, wrote AES (Advanced Encryption Standards)

Encryption and Decryption algorithm in Java (JDK and JRE). Now deploy encryption into Amazon Elastic Compute Cloud (EC2). There are three block ciphers consisted on AES, AES-128, AES-192 and AES-256. Every cryptographic key using 128-, 192- and 256-bits, listed automatically to encrypt and decrypt data in the blocks. Secrete key or symmetric is using for encryption and decryption. Both sender and receiver must know while using same secret key. Consider, all key lengths are enough to protect classified information up to the "Secret" Level with "Top Secret" information, and must require 192- or 256-bit key lengths. There are bits listed below for every round:

1. 10 rounds for 128-bit keys
2. 12 rounds for 192-bits keys
3. 14 rounds for 256-bits keys

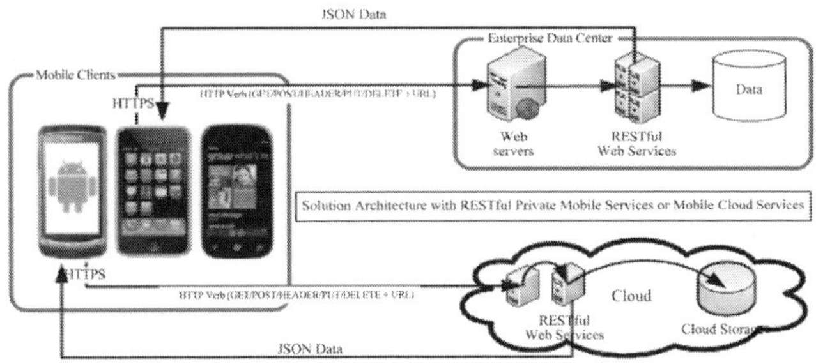

Figure 4. Complete solution mobile cloud computing security on server.

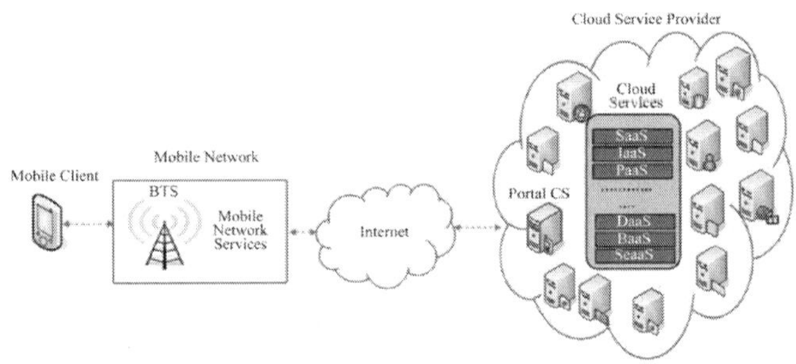

Figure 5. Mobile communication with cloud domain and servers.

Every round consists of many processing steps that include interchange, transposition and mixing of the input plain text and transform it into the final output of cipher text. Cipher text is a text which cannot be understandable by everyone.

Suggested Research Methodology

According to this research methodology user can manipulate the cloud Amazon services with RESTFUL API integrate cloud service with full security, in our previous work [17] we already mentioned about how to apply security in mobile computing before going to cloud computing, but due to battery consuming and time consuming. This model shows how to overcome the problems by using same methodology and without effect of "QOS".

Server Side Mathematical Model Encryption Model

A public-key cryptography algorithm which uses prime factorization as the trapdoor one-way function, defines

$$N= pq \tag{1}$$

for p and q primes. Also define a private key d and a public key e such that

$$de = 1\left(\bmod \varnothing(n)\right) \tag{2}$$

$$\left(e, \varnothing(n)\right) = 1 \tag{3}$$

where $\varnothing(n)$ is the quotient function; (a, b) denotes the greatest common divisor (so (a, b) =1 means that a and b are relatively prime), and a = b mod(a) is a congruence. Let the message be converted to a number M. The sender then makes n and e public and sends

$$E = M^{e}\left(\bmod n\right) \tag{4}$$

To decode, the receiver (who knows ^{d}) computes

$$E^{d} = \left(M^{e}\right)^{d} = M^{e\,d} = M^{N}\varnothing(n)+1 = M\left(\bmod n\right) \tag{5}$$

since ^{N} is an integer. In order to crack the code, ^{d} must be found. But this requires factorization of ^{n} since

$$\varnothing(\varnothing) = (p-1)(q-1) \tag{6}$$

Both p and q should be picked so that $p \pm 1$ and $q \pm 1$ are divisible by large primes, since otherwise the Pollard p − 1 factorization method or Williams p + 1 factorization method potentially factor ^{n} easily. It is also desirable to have $\varnothing(\varnothing(pq))$ large and divisible by large primes.

It is possible to break the cryptosystem by repeated encryption if a unit of $z/\varnothing(n)z$ has small field order (Simmons and Norris 1977, Meijer 1996), where Z/Z^{s} is the ring of integers between 0 and $^{s-1}$ under addition and multiplication (mod^{s}). Meijer (1996) shows that "almost" every encryption exponent ^{e} is safe from breaking using repeated encryption for factors of the form

$$P = 2p1 + 1 \tag{7}$$

$$q = 2q1 + 1 \tag{8}$$

Whereas another equation joined this equation

$$P = 2p2 + 1 \tag{9}$$

$$q = 2q2 + 1 \tag{10}$$

and p, p1, p2, q, q1, and q2 are all primes. In this case,

$$\varnothing(n) = 4\ p1\ q1 \qquad (11)$$

$$\varnothing(\varnothing(n)) = 8\ p1\ q1 \qquad (12)$$

Meijer (1996) also suggests that p2 and q2 should be of order 10^{75}.

Using the RSA system, the identity of the sender can be identified as genuine without revealing his private code.

The Model provides full security using JSON - REST API and performing GET, PUT, POST and DELETE (CRUD) operation by JAVA. Java provides the strong encryption method. We applied encryption in JAVA code to plain text and converted it into cipher text. The cipher text is the encrypted file. It's purely secure. And that file sent to cloud server.

IMPLEMENTATION

According to Figure 5, the application of cloud is possible in many domains. One of the domains of our current interest is that of mobiles. Hence, we will be focusing on utility of cloud computing environment for mobile usage and how can a cloud add value to the overall functionality and performance of mobile devices?

According to [9] as depicted in Figure 2, MCC is a service that allows resource constrained mobile users to adaptively adjust processing and storage capabilities by transparently partitioning and offloading the computationally intensive and storage demanding jobs on traditional cloud resources by providing ubiquitous wireless access.

According to Figure 5, this architecture is showing the mobile data first step go to private cloud server, which is responsible for data encryption and cryptography. Then encrypted data will go to cloud server that is public and responsible for data storage on cloud database that is EC2 database storage.

The relationship between mobile cloud computing is now secure, the security exist on cloud server that is located privately and safely and public cloud only responsible for storage the encrypted data into data storage. This way user can safely share their important data on cloud server without any hindrance. This concept may be some time taking but very secure for mobile cloud computing.

Authentication and authorization are useful for this architecture, now security flows can occur throw this architecture.

DEPLOYED APPLICATION

Build an Android app using the IBM Mobile Data for Blue mix cloud service

Store, delete, update, and query objects stored in the cloud

Step-1 Add some grocery list items

Step-2 Restart the application

Notice that your data items have persisted. You now have data on the cloud!

Step-3 See your data on the cloud

Log in to Blue mix.

Click your application in the Dashboard view.

Step-4 On the Manage Data tab, you can see encrypted Data Classes being stored in the cloud, as well as the instances of each Data Class being persisted

Step-5 You can reverse decrypted your data when you again access the data into mobile

Click the Mobile Data Service. Interface for application.

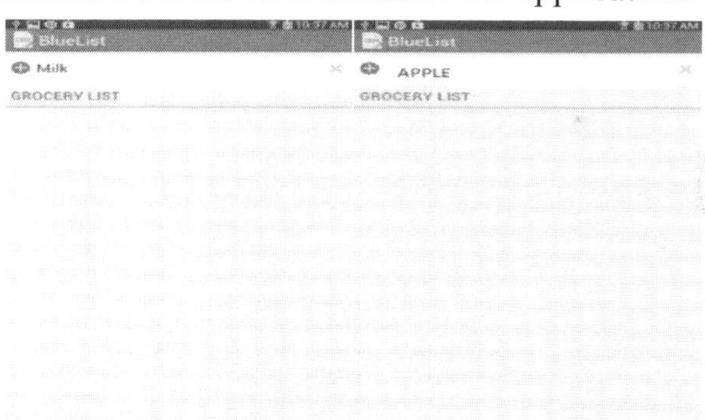

Dashboard

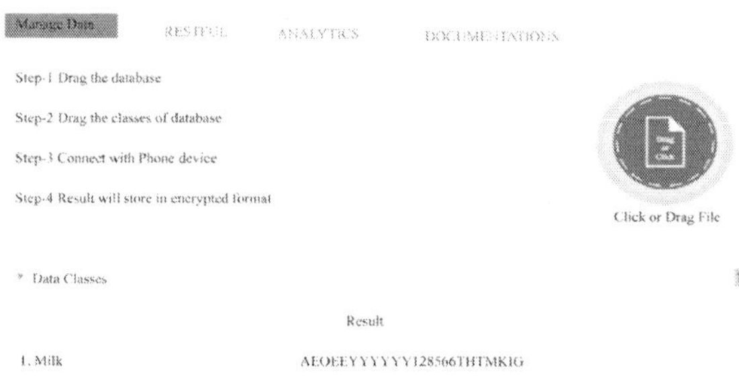

CONCLUSIONS

The concept of cloud computing provides a great opportunity to users to utilize their services by on-demand basis. The requirement of mobility in cloud computing gave birth to Mobile cloud computing. MCC provides more possibilities for access services in convenient manner. It is expected that after some years a number of mobile users will go to use cloud computing on their mobile devices.

There are many issues in mobile cloud computing due to limitations of mobile devices. Security is the main concern in mobile cloud computing. In Mobile Cloud Computing, data of owner is stored on the cloud, which is not secured.

This paper has provided the description about the basics of Mobile Cloud Computing and issues associated with it. Mainly it discussed about security of data stored in cloud and importance of data security. This paper has explored a number of mechanisms for providing data security so that Mobile Cloud Computing can be widely accepted by a number of users in future. It also proposed a mechanism to provide confidentiality, access control as well as integrity to mobile users.

ACKNOWLEDGEMENTS

This is the team work, whose help, suggestions, knowledge, experience and encouragement helped to reached research on final results. Team members work hard to try to reduce the problems of client and server side security.

FUTURE WORK

In this paper, we present a prototype of the secure data processing model for mobile cloud computing. In the future, we will focus on the follow research: 1) investigate more application scenarios that require data sharing between cloud private domain and public domain; 2) investigate the robustness of the Tri-rooted ESSI solution; and 3) investigate the security monitoring, auditing, and misuse detection in the mobile cloud system.

REFERENCES

1. Abrishami, S. and Naghibzadeha, M. (2012) Deadline-Constrained Workflow Scheduling Algorithms for Infrastructure as a Service Clouds.
2. Armbrust, M., Fox, A., Griffith, R., Joseph, A.D., Katz, R.H., Konwinski, A., Lee, G., Patterson, D.A., Rabkin, A., Stoica, I. and Zaharia, M. (2013) Above the Clouds: A Berkeley View of Mobile Cloud Computing. Technical Report, EECS Department University of California, Berkeley. http://www.eecs.berkeley.edu/Pubs/TechRpts/2009/EECS-2009-28.html
3. http://nvlpubs.nist.gov/nistpubs/Legacy/SP/nistspecialpublication800-145.pdf
4. John, R. (2005) DoD Directive 3020.40, Mobile Cloud Computing Defense Critical Infrastructure Program. 19 Aug, p. 13. http://www.dtic.mil/whs/directives/corres/pdf/302040p.pdf
5. Ouyang, X.Z. (2011) Cloud Computing in Mobile Communication Networks. Emerging Technologies of Future Multimedia Coding, Analysis and Transmission, No.1. http://wwwen.zte.com.cn/endata/magazine/ztecommunications/2011Year/no3/articles/201110/t20111029_260205.html
6. Li, X.P., Qian, L.H. and Yang, J. (2015) Workflow Scheduling with Deadline and Time Slots Constraints in Mobile Cloud Computing. IEEE 19th International Conference on Computer Supported Cooperative Work in Design (CSCWD), Calabria, 6-8 May 2015, 606-613. http://ieeexplore.ieee.org/stamp/stamp.jsp?tp=&arnumber=7231027
7. (2011) Adrian Otto's Blog. What Is a Cloud Platform? http://adrianotto.com/2011/02/cloud-platform/
8. Pooja, N.D. and Ramteke, P.L. (2013) Mobile Cloud Computing. International Journal of Science and Research.
9. Hampton, T.J. (2011) A Quick Guide to Cloud Terminology. 11 August. http://www.thehostingnews.com/a-quick-guide-to-cloud-terminology.html
10. Lakhan, A. (2015) Security and Data Privacy Using Mobile Cloud Computing.
11. Rahman, M. and Hassan, R. (2015) Adaptive Workflow Scheduling for Dynamic Grid and Cloud Computing Environment.
12. Singh, R. (2015) Workflow Scheduling in Cloud Computing Using

Spot Instance.

13. Kaur, N. (2015) Comparison of Workflow Scheduling Algorithms in Cloud Computing.
14. Kaur, A. (2015) A Review of Workflow Scheduling in Cloud Computing Environment.
15. Singh, L. and Singh, S. (2015) A Survey of Workflow Scheduling Algorithms and Research Issues.
16. Lakhan, A. and Hussain, F. (2015) Data Security and Privacy for Cross Platform Using Mobile Cloud Computing.
17. Lakhan, A.A. (2015) Integration of Dual Data Security Algorithm for Mobile Private Cloud Computing.

CHAPTER

13

New Proposed Robust, Scalable and Secure Network Cloud Computing Storage Architecture

Fawaz S. Al-Anzi, Ayed A. Salman, Noby K. Jacob

Compute Engineering Department, Kuwait University, Kuwait City, Kuwait

ABSTRACT

Cloud computing describes highly scalable computing resources provided as an external service via the internet. Economically, the main feature of cloud computing is that customers only use what they need, and only pay for what they actually use. Resources are available to be accessed from the cloud at any time, and from any location via the internet. There's no need to worry about how things are being maintained behind the scenes—you simply purchase the IT service you require. This new, web-based generation

Citation: Al-Anzi, F. , Salman, A. and Jacob, N. (2014), "New Proposed Robust, Scalable and Secure Network Cloud Computing Storage Architecture". *Journal of Software Engineering and Applications*, 7, 347-353. doi: 10.4236/jsea.2014.75031.

availability, several reports related to privacy of data have been outward in recent years. To ensure the security of the customer data, we distributed data among available service providers rather than storing whole data on single service provider site.

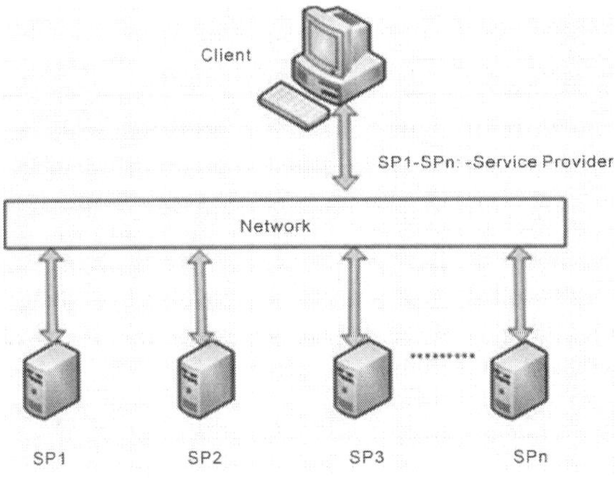

Figure 1. Proposed RSSNS architecture for cloud data storage.

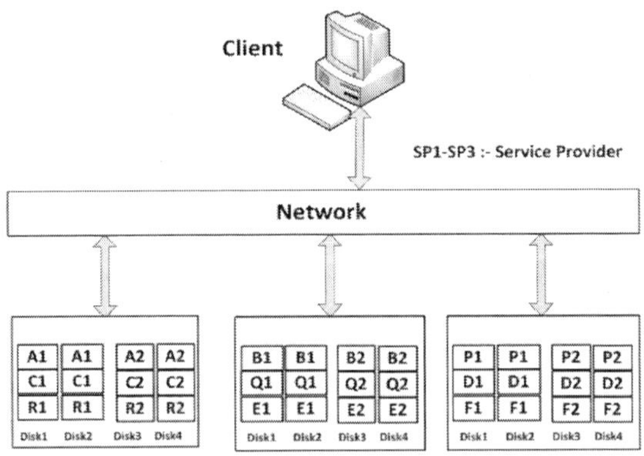

Figure 2. Proposed RSSNS architecture with three service providers.

Suppose customer data D is to be outsourced. In the centralized storage scheme, the whole data are stored on single service provider. So data are insecure in centralized storage scheme. As a security concern, in the proposed architecture, original data D is encrypted to D' and split into cipher blocks A and B as shown in Figure 5. Let us assume that two cloud service providers are available say SP1 and SP2. The encrypted data are distributed among service providers in such a way that cipher block A is stored on SP1 and B is stored on SP2.Proposed architecture use RAID 10 for storage. Therefore blocks A and B are again striped and mirrored (A: A1, A2 and B: B1, B2). The splitting of data blocks is done in such a way that, a single service provider cannot able to retrieve any information from the data stored in his network. The other security threat encountered is the cloud service provider might collude together to reconstruct and access the customer's stored data.

Here in this approach, the encryption and distribution is carried out in such a way that, data reconstruction is not possible, even though couple of service provider will collude each other. It guarantees the security of the proposed architecture.

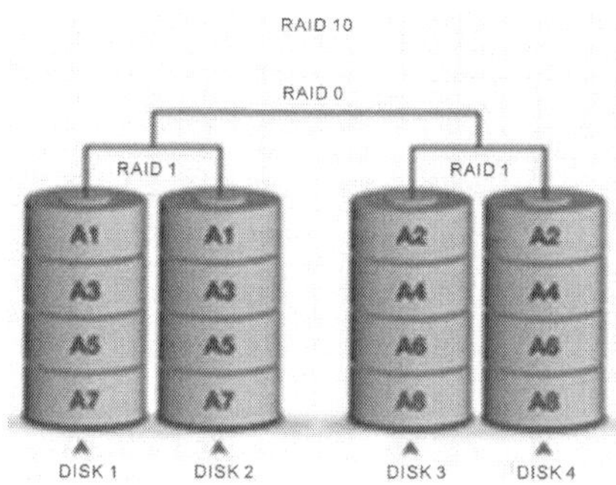

Figure 3. RAID 10 storage scheme.

Figure 4. Parity scheme.

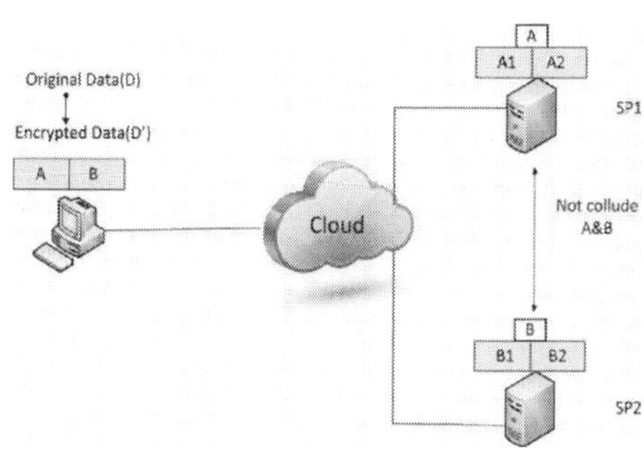

Figure 5. Security of the proposed architecture.

Data availability is achieved through redundancy involving where the data are stored and how it can be reached. Availability of the data stored on any storage device depends on how fast the data are accessed. Bandwidth of the network channel depends on availability. So high speed network cables are used for data retrieval. The RAID level implementation of the proposed architecture also offers better availability of the data.

ANALYSIS OF OUR PROPOSED SCHEME

In this section, we analyze security and performance properties of our proposed architecture.

Security: Ensuring the security of the data stored in the cloud storage is one of the major challenges. The Service provider might be honest, but malicious users creates security problem. This is a severe threat for critical data such as medical or financial records, as cloud service provider employees has physical access to the hosted data. To tackle the security issue we encrypt the original data and later by distributing the fragments transparently across multiple service providers. This way, none of the storage vendors is in an absolute possession of the client's data.

Availability: Management of computing resources as a service by a single Service provider implies the risk of a single point of failure. This failure depends on many factors such as hardware, software or network failure In July 2008, for instance, Amazon storage service S3 was down for 8 hours because of a single bit error. Our solution addresses this issue by storing the data on several cloud storage providers—whereby no single entire copy of the data resides in one location, and only a subset of providers needs to be available in order to reconstruct the data.

Reliability: The reliability of the proposed architecture is achieved by the parity scheme, by enabling the application to retrieve data correctly even if some of the providers corrupt or lose the entrusted data.

The proposed cloud storage architecture based on RAID technology outperforms the muti-cloud storage architecture proposed by Singh et al. [1] in terms of security, availability and reliability.

CONCLUSION AND FUTURE DIRECTIONS

In this paper we proposed a new, web-based generation of computing utilizes remote servers for data storage and management. The model which addresses the challenging issue tackled in the cloud computing is the security of data stored in the service providers' site. The new architecture for secure data storage allows users' data to be encrypted and split into various cipher blocks and distributed among different service providers site rather than solely depend on single provider for data storage. This architecture ensures better reliability, availability, scalability and security.

Fawaz S. Al-Anzi, Ayed A. Salman, Noby K. Jacob Future directions of this research are to investigate the reliability of such model as well as reliability, availability, scalability, performance and robustness. Another important point to investigate is to build a business model for a fair customer charge of such storage services by the SPs.

REFERENCES

1. Singh, Y., Kandah, F. and Zhang, W. (2011) A Secured Cost-Effective Multi-Cloud Storage in Cloud Computing. IEEE INFOCOM Workshop on Cloud Computing, Tainan, 16-18 December 2010, 619-624.
2. Chen, P.C., Freg, C.P., Hou, T.W. and Teng, W.G. (2010) Implementing RAID-3 on Cloud Storage for EMR System. IEEE International Computer Symposium, Tainan, 16-18 December 2010, 850-853.
3. Joshi, S., Patwardhan, U. and Deshpande, P. (2010) RAID 5 for Secured Storage Virtualization. IEEE International Conference on Data Storage and Data Engineering, Bangalore, 9-10 February 2010, 278-282.
4. Dijk, M. and Juels, A. (2010) On the Impossibility of Cryptography Alone for Privacy-Preserving Cloud Computing. HotSec'10 Proceedings of the 5th USENIX Conference on Hot Topics in Security, Article No. 1-8.
5. Olivera, P.F., Lima, L., Barros, J. and Medard, M. (2010) Trusted Storage over Untrusted Networks. IEEE Global Telecommunication Conference, Miami, 6-10 Decemebr 2010, 1-5.
6. Amazon.com (2008) Amazon Web Services (AWS). http://aws.amazon.com
7. http://en.wikipedia.org/wiki/Cloud_computing
8. Sun, J. and Yue, S.-S. (2011) The Application of Cloud Storage Technology in SMEs. International Conference on E- Business and E-Government (ICEE 11), Shanghai, 6-8 May 2011, 1-5.
9. Deng, J., Hu, J., Liu, A.C.M. and Wu, J. (2010) Research and Application of Cloud Storage. 2nd International Workshop on Intelligent Systems and Applications (ISA 10), Wuhan, 22-23 May 2010, 1-5.
10. Wu, J., Ping, L., Ge, X., Wang, Y. and Fu, J. (2012) Cloud Storage as the Infrastructure of Cloud Computing. International Conference on Intelligent Computing and Cognitive Informatics (ICICCI 10), Kuala Lumpur, 22-23 June 2010, 380-383.
11. Zhang, D., Sun, F., Cheng, X. and Liu, C. (2011) Research on Hadoop-Based Enterprise File Cloud Storage System. 3rd International Conference on Awareness Science and Technology (iCAST 11), Dalian, 27-30 September 2011, 434- 437.
12. Zhang, X., Du, H., Chen, J., Lin, Y. and Zeng, L. (2011) Ensure Data

Security in Cloud Storage. International Conference on Network Computing and Information Security (NCIS 11), Guilin, 14-15 May 2011, 284-287.

13. Koletka, R. and Hutchison, A. (2011) An Architecture for Secure Searchable Cloud Storage. International Conference on Information Security South Africa (ISSA 11), Johannesburg, 15-17 August 2011, 1-7.
14. Hao, L. and Han, D. (2011) The Study and Design on Secure-Cloud Storage System. International Conference on Electrical and Control Engineering (ICECE 11), Yichang, 16-18 September 2011, 5126-5129.
15. Feel, H.T.A. and Khafagy, M.H. (2011) OCSS: Ontology Cloud Storage System. First International Symposium on Network Cloud Computing and Applications (NCCA 11), Toulouse, 21-23 November 2011, 9-13.
16. Srinivasan, J., Wei, W., Ma, X. and Yu, T. (2011) EMFS: Email-Based Personal Cloud Storage. 6th International Con- ference on Networking, Architecture and Storage (NAS 11), Dalian, 28-30 July 2011, 248-257.
17. He, Q., Li, Z. and Zhang, X. (2010) Study on Cloud Storage System Based on Distributed Storage Systems. International Conference on Computational and Information Sciences (ICCIS 11), Chengdu, 17-19 December 2010, 1332- 1335.
18. Liu, W. (2012) Research on Cloud Computing Security Problem and Strategy. 2nd International Conference on Consumer Electronics, Communications and Networks (CECNet 12), Yichang, 21-23 April 2012, 1216-1219.

CHAPTER

14

Survey on Public Key Cryptography Scheme for Securing Data in Cloud Computing

J. Athena, V. Sumathy

Department of ECE, Government College of Technology, Coimbatore, India

ABSTRACT

Numerous advancements in the Information Technology (IT) require the proper security policy for the data storage and transfer among the cloud. With the increase in size of the data, the time required to handle the huge-size data is more. An assurance of security in cloud computing suffers various issues. The evolution of cryptographic approaches addresses these limitations and provides the solution to the data preserving. There are two issues in security assurance such as geographical distribution and the multi-tenancy

Citation: Athena, J. and Sumathy, V. (2017), "Survey on Public Key Cryptography Scheme for Securing Data in Cloud Computing". *Circuits and Systems*, **8**, 77-92. doi: 10.4236/cs.2017.83005.

of the cloud server. This paper surveys about the various cryptographic techniques with their key sizes, time required for key/signature generation and verification constraints. The survey discusses the architecture for secure data transmissions among the devices, challenges raised during the transmission and attacks. This paper presents the brief review of major cryptographic techniques such as Rivest, Shamir Adleman (RSA), Dffie Hellman and the Elliptic Curve Cryptography (ECC) associated key sizes. This paper investigates the general impact of digital signature generation techniques on cloud security with the advantages and disadvantages. The results and discussion section existing in this paper investigate the time consumption for key/signature generation and verification with the key size variations effectively. The initialization of random prime numbers and the key computation based on the points on the elliptic curve assures the high-security compared to the existing schemes with the minimum time consumption and sizes in cloud-based applications.

Keywords: Cloud Computing, Cryptography, RSA, Diffie Hellman, Elliptic Curve Cryptography, Digital Signature

INTRODUCTION

Cloud computing enables on-demand services to the users in the pay-as-use basis with the highest level of scalability and flexibility. The cloud services include Software as a Service (SaaS), Platform as a Service (PaaS), and Infrastructure as a Service (IaaS). The cloud usage eliminates the burden of system maintenance, software license purchase, and the cost of hardware components. The benefits of cloud computing improve accessibility, automatic software integration, quick deployment, high scalability, low investment cost and flexibility [1] . On the basis of the services offering by the cloud computing, the clouds are categorized into four types such as private, public, hybrid and community clouds.

- ▪ Public clouds: The provisions of the services through the off-premise third party to the general public and computing resources fall into this category.
- ▪ Private clouds: They enable the large size organizations to achieve the efficiencies with the responsibility constraint of data.
- ▪ Hybrid clouds: Some enterprises utilize the public clouds for general computing and private clouds for customer data protection to assure the security.

- Community clouds: Distinct groups of organizations have the compliance and security considerations and the infrastructures offered by the internal and external third party suppliers.

The major characteristics of the cloud computing are self-service, per-usage method, elastic and customizable. When an organization adapts public cloud services, most of the computing system infrastructures will be under the control of cloud service provider. With the aim of achieving the profit, cloud service provider may not store all the data, which leads to incorrect and incomplete data storage. This data loss will be hidden to retain the reputation of the service providers in the market. The storage of data in the third party remote server may be accessed by the unauthorized users. Even though, the process of data outsourcing reduces the storage and maintenance overhead, the resource pooling in a third party data center leads to several security issues.

The creation and the management of secured cloud space are a more challenging task than the creation of classical IT environment. The misunderstanding responsibilities, issues in confidentiality, lack of standards, interoperability issues and malicious insiders in the cloud computing caused the several issues to preserve the data from the attacks. Security issues have been categorized into data breaches, malicious attack, data loss, and inadequate diligence, sensitive data access, data segregation, etc. [2]. The confidentiality, integrity and availability must be ensured to achieve data security.

The data security has become a complex challenge in cloud computing due to the following reasons:

- The necessity to guard the confidential and sensitive data related to government and business organizations.
- The sharing of cloud infrastructure among various clients.
- Legal and regulatory compliances during data mobility.
- Issues in auditing and reporting.
- Lack of backup and storage standards.
- Key management issues and unauthorized access

In order to overcome these security challenges, there are several solutions available in secure cloud storage server. The confidentiality can be attained by applying the access controls, authentication mechanisms, cryptography schemes etc. The access to control and authentication mechanisms allows the authorized user access, whereas the cryptography techniques allows only the specific user, who possess the keys to access the data. Hence, the cryptography schemes are the best way to provide data security, in which the user cannot access the data without the knowledge of key. Generally, most of the cryptography techniques include three major steps as follows:

- Key generation;
- Encryption;
- Decryption.

Figure 1 shows the data flow and message flow in cloud storage server for secure data transmission. Key generation is the process of producing the keys that are used for encryption and decryption. The encryption is the process of converting the original data into an unreadable form known as cipher text by the keys. The decryption is the process of retrieving back the original message from the cipher text using the appropriate keys. The cryptography schemes are classified into two types such as symmetric or conventional cryptography and asymmetric or public key cryptography. The symmetric cryptography uses same key for both encryption and decryption, whereas the public key cryptography uses different keys. The symmetric cryptography schemes are fast but there is no guarantee for secure key distribution. As they use the same key for encryption and decryption, the third party, who is snooping while key transmission may decrypt the data.

In order to overcome this issue, public key cryptography is introduced with a pair of keys, namely, public key and private key. The key advantage of public key cryptography is that the private keys used for decryption is never shared or transmitted [3] .

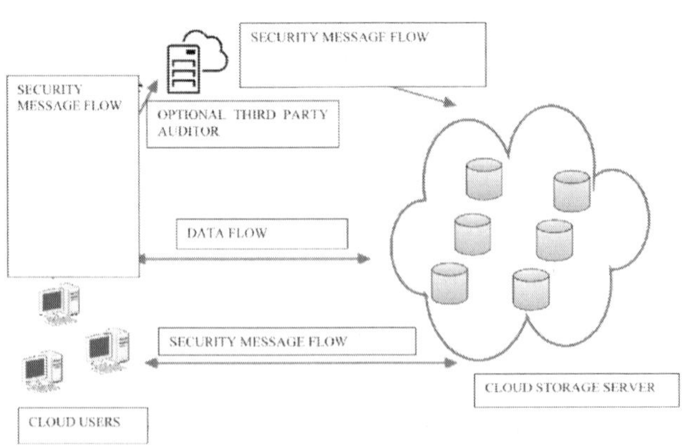

Figure 1. Data transmission in a secure cloud storage server.

The public key will be broadcasted, using which the data can be encrypted. The authorized user who possess the private key can only have the right to decrypt the data.

The remaining sections of this paper are organized as follows: Section II presents the security challenges in cloud computing. Section III provides the list of cloud security attacks. Section IV describes various public key cryptography techniques to overcome the security issues. Section V shows the results and discussion of the cryptography schemes. The survey is concluded in Section VI.

SECURITY CHALLENGES IN CLOUD

Security is an important concern for several organizations that adopts cloud for data storage and maintenance. A minor mistake in any of the client application will pave a way to the hackers to access the entire data in the cloud storage server. If there is vulnerability in the cloud, the unauthorized user may access, corrupt, modify or delete the records in the cloud.

The security challenges arise in the deployment models, service models and in the network [4] .

It is the responsibility of the security manager to define the security framework of an organization based on asset, threat and vulnerability risk assessment matrices. Confidentiality, integrity, and availability are the three main are of data security [5] .

Data confidentiality is significant in a place, where a critical data is stored in a remote server with multi user access. Figure 2 shows various security challenges in cloud computing.

In a multitenant cloud infrastructure, the access privileges must be provided to the users to achieve security.

Hence, the data of an organization cannot be accessed by the users of any other organization. Integrity is an important factor to maintain the reputation of the service provider.

The trust and security can be enhanced by allowing only the authorized person to update the data of an organization.

Data loss and data leakage can be prevented by employing integrity. Thus, authentication and identity management is used to provide authorized access.

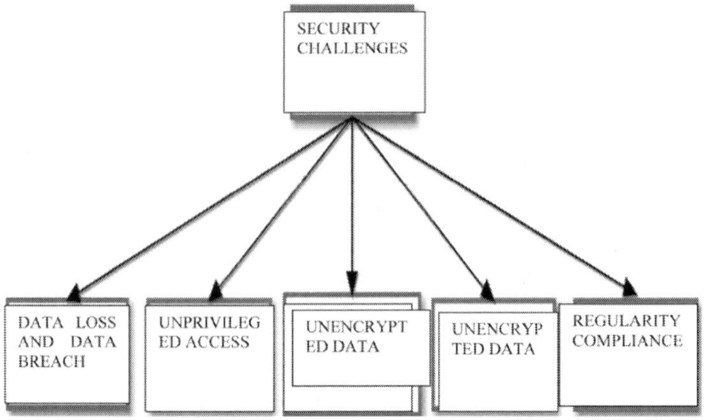

Figure 2. Security challenges in cloud computing.

The service level agreement is signed between the vendor and the provider to eliminate the downtime of the server and to make the data always visible [6] . The major security challenges include data segregation and data leakages. The security challenges in cloud computing are listed below.

Data Breaches and Data Loss

The disclosure of sensitive data to the unauthorized user is termed as data breach. The causes of data breach are lack of authentication, audit, and authorization controls and a few defects in the design of infrastructure and application. It may also take place due to several unfortunate transmissions and insider attacks. When a hacker gets access to the cloud via a single application, then the entire cloud infrastructure will be under attack prone area [7] .

Data loss results in the leakage of confidential and sensitive data. This is due to the modification or deletion of data by the hackers with an intention of delivering altered information or to hide the information from the users. Loss of encryption keys, natural disasters and storage system faults will also lead to data loss.

Regulatory Compliance

The distributed cloud infrastructure stores data in multiple remote servers that are located in different geographical locations. The legal constraints vary from place to place and hence, it is difficult to assign a particular server to be used for data transmission at the borders of a region.

Unencrypted Data

The unencrypted data leads to data confidentiality, data breaches and data loss by exposing the original data. The cloud users depend on the service provider for encryption and the keys can be either managed by the user or the provider. Key management and distribution is a sensitive process, as the message can be read by any one, who gets the key. In order to improve the security, the keys are split into several units and distributed among the users, provider and the third party service that is responsible for encryption [8] .

Unprivileged Access

The access control mechanisms must be incorporated to prevent the unauthorized users from accessing the data. The sensitive data must be secured by providing access only to a very few important persons of an organization. The data are classified based on its sensitivity and need. The users are mapped only to the required data and they are prohibited to access or view the other unnecessary data [9] . Data abstraction and transparency is implemented for privileged access.

Service Hijacking

Service hijacking is the illegal access by unauthorized users to certain services. It leads to software exploitation, fraud, criminal activities and phishing through e- mail. The services must be registered in the service providers to avoid hijacking.

Lack of Authentication and Identity

The lack of authentication allows malicious users in the storage server. Each and every user must be provided with an identity and authentication password to enter the storage space [10] . Without authentication any one can alter the data of an organization. It is one of the severe concerns to data security.

CLOUD SECURITY ATTACKS

Side Channel Attack

Side-channel attack urges the application of cryptographic techniques to prevent the cloud systems from security threat. Therefore, it is necessary to evaluate the resilience of the cryptographic system against the side-channel attacks.

Authentication Attack

Authentication is a weak point in hosted and virtual services and is frequently targeted.

There are many different ways to authenticate users. The mechanisms used to secure the authentication process and the methods used are a frequent target of attackers. Currently, regarding the architecture of SaaS, IaaS, and PaaS, there is only IaaS offering this kind of information protection and data encryption.

Man-In-The-Middle Attack

This attack is carried out when an attacker places himself between two users. Anytime attackers can place themselves in the communication's path, there is the possibility that they can interfere and modify communications.

PUBLIC KEY CRYPTOGRAPHY TECHNIQUES

Cryptography plays a significant role in securing the data by converting it into an unreadable form during storage and transmission.

The asymmetric encryption, which is also known as public key cryptography, applies public and private keys for encryption and decryption respectively.

This adds key strength and hence, key exchange is not a problem in this scheme. Figure 3 shows the various public key cryptography techniques.

Rivest, Shamir, Adleman (RSA)

RSA algorithm is one of the public key cryptography schemes that is used for secure data transmission. The algorithm is named after its inventors Ron Rivest, Adi Shamir, and Leonard Adleman [11] . In RSA, a public-private key pair is generated, where the public key is published to all for encryption and the private key is kept safe for decryption. The three major steps are:

- Key generation;
- Encryption;
- Decryption.

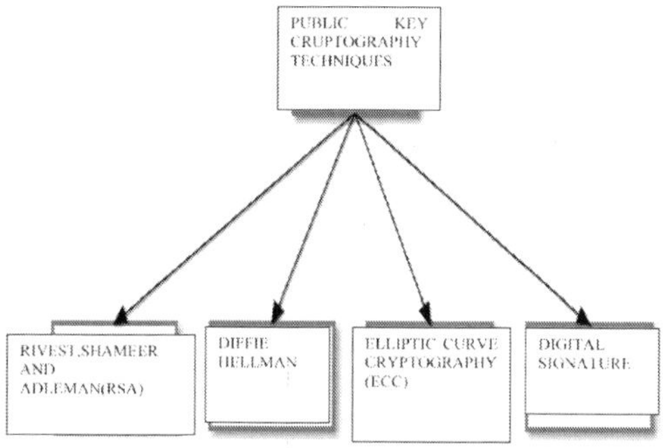

Figure 3. Public key cryptography techniques.

In the key generation phase, each user generates a public key and a private key pair by selecting two large prime in a random order. It uses Euler's theorem, square and multiply algorithm for exponentiation. A repeated squaring is performed on the base number and the exponents are multiplied to compute the result. Figure 4 shows the workflow of key generation process in RSA.

Steps for key generation

Step 1: Two dissimilar large prime numbers are selected in random.

Step 2: The key length of the public and private keys are represented in bits. The modulus of the keys are calculated as $m = a \times b$.

Step 3: The Euler's function is calculated as $\varphi(m) = \varphi(a)\varphi(b) = (a-1)(b-1)$.

Step 4: An integer for public key, namely, $encr$ that lies between 1 and $\varphi(m)(1 < encr < \varphi(m))$ is selected, in such a way that $encr$ is a co-prime of $\varphi(m)$.

Step 5: The value of private key, namely, $decr$ is computed as follows

$decr \times encr = 1(mod(\varphi(m)))$.

Step 6: The public that is used for encryption $(encr, \varphi(m))$ is published.

Step 7: The private key used for decryption $(decr, \varphi(m))$ is kept safe along with the random prime numbers a, b and the Euler's function $\varphi(m)$.

In the encryption step, the sender publishes the public key (m, encr) and keeps the private key. The padding scheme is used to convert the original data D to cipher text

Cipher=Dmodm.Cipher=Dmodm.

In the decryption step, the original data D is obtained as follows:

D=Ciphermodm.D=Ciphermodm.

Attacks in RSA

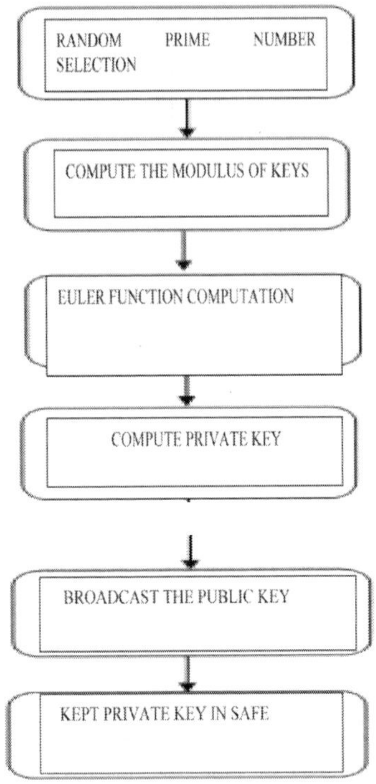

Figure 4. Workflow of RSA.

The RSA algorithm is attacked by brute force key search, mathematical attacks, and timing attacks. The attacks can be resolved by using a constant exponentiation time and by adding random delays.

Some of the three approaches that attack the RSA algorithm are:

Physical Force (Brute Force attack)—it means testing out all the possible private keys.

Arithmetical attacks—the approaches of all equivalent in effect to factoring the product of 2 primes.

Timing incursion (attacks)—these depend on the running time of the decryption algorithm.

Advantages

1. Integrity, authentication, non-repudiation, and secrecy and privacy are the features of RSA algorithm.
2. Private keys are never exposed.

3. Non-repudiation can be achieved using the digital signatures provided by RSA.
4. Key strength is high, as the key size is large.

Disadvantages

1. RSA requires exponential amount of time because of large key sizes.
2. Key generation is complex.
3. No tradeoff between time and security.

Applications

1. Secure Socket Layer (SSL) protocol.
2. Secure Shell (SSH) remote connection.
3. Pretty Good Privacy (PGP) to guarantee security and privacy.

Diffie Hellman Key Exchange

Diffie Hellman key exchange algorithm is used to share a public and private key pair for encryption and decryption in a secure way. This algorithm is name after its inventors Whitfield Diffie and Martin Hellman [12] . Diffie-Hellman is not an encryption algorithm but it is a secure key exchange algorithm, which accomplishes secure exchange by creating a shared secret key. The symmetric key is encrypted using the shared secret key for secure transmission. The public key is certified by the certificate authority to prevent man-in-the-middle attack. Any number of participants can take part in secure exchanges by performing iterations on the agreement protocol and exchanging intermediate data. Here, two users, who are unknown to each other share secret key via an insecure channel. Initially, both of them share a public key for authentication. The third party may access the keys, while transmission, which is commonly known as man in the middle attack [13] . It may alter the key shared between both the sender and the receiver. The workflow of key exchange process is illustrated in Figure 5.

Steps for key exchange

Step 1: Two integers such as a prime number P and a generator G is selected by both the sender and the receiver.

Step 2: Two random numbers a,b that are less than the prime number are selected as private keys.

Step 3: The public keys of the sender and the receiver is computed as follows:

Public key of sender: $G^a mod\ P$;

Public key of receiver: $G^b mod\ P$.

Step 4: These public keys were exchanged between the sender and the receiver via an insecure channel.

Step 5: The private keys are calculated as follows:

Private key of sender: $(G^b mod\ P)^a$;

Private key of receiver: $(G^a mod\ P)^b$.

Step 6: Then, the shared secret key of both the sender and the receiver must be same *i.e.*,

$(G^b mod\ P)^a = (G^a mod\ P)^b$.

Advantages

1. Improves security for the shared secret key.
2. As the key size is small, the computation is fast.

Disadvantages

1. Messages cannot be encrypted using Diffie Hellman algorithm.

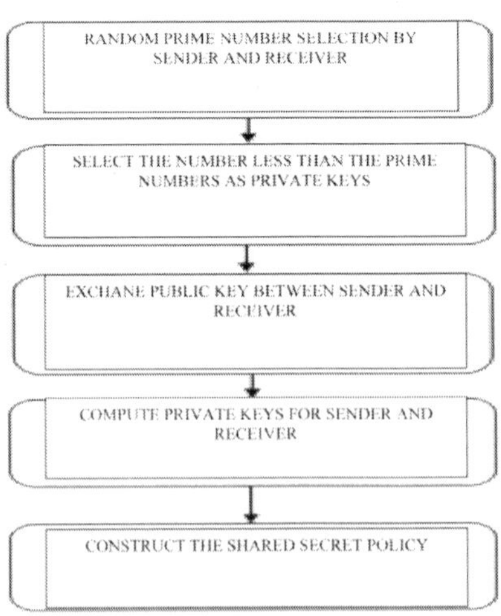

Figure 5. Workflow of key exchange.

2. *Prone to denial of service and man in the middle attacks [14] .*
3. No authentication between the sender and the receiver [14] .
4. Lack of forward secrecy [15] .

Applications

1. Secure Socket Layer (SSL) protocol [16] .
2. Internet Protocol Security (IPSec).
3. Public Key Infrastructure (PKI).
4. Secure Shell (SSH) remote connection [16] .

Elliptic Curve Cryptography (ECC)

Elliptical curve cryptography (ECC) is one of the public key encryption technique that generates best cryptographic keys according to the elliptic curve theory. It creates smaller keys within a short period.

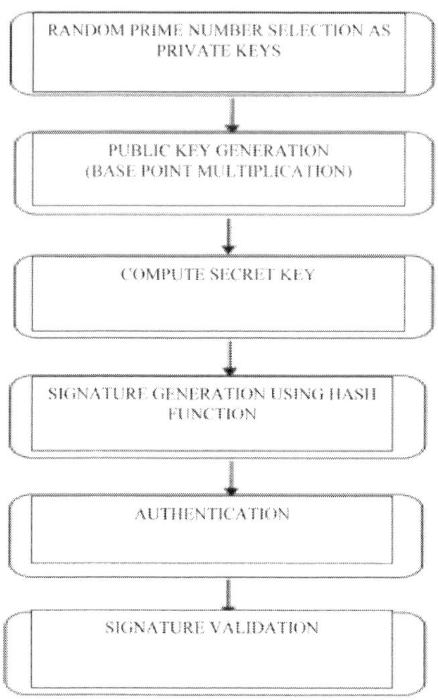

Figure 6. Workflow of ECC.

Rather than using large prime numbers for key generation, ECC uses the properties of elliptic curves to generate keys.

Elliptic curve is a nonsingular cubic curve with two variables in a certain field and an infinite rational point [17] .

Each user generates a public-private key pair, where the public key is applied for encryption and signature verification and the private key is applied for decryption and signature generation.

The high level of security can be achieved in ECC using a 164 bit key, where the traditional techniques need 1024 bit key.

ECC is widely used because of its low computing complexity and better utilization of batter power. Security is attractive feature of elliptic curve cryptography. Figure 6 shows the key processes in ECC.

ECC includes the following major steps [17] :

- Key generation;
- Signature generation;
- Encryption;
- Decryption;
- Signature verification.

Steps for ECC

Step 1: The sender and receiver selects two integers $Pri\ A, Pri\ B$ as private keys.

Step 2: The public keys of both sender and receiver are generated by multiplying the base point B of the elliptic curve with the corresponding private keys.

Public key of sender: $PubA = PriA \times B$;

Public key of receiver: $PubB = PriB \times B$.

Step 3: The security key is generated as follows:

Secret Key of sender: $SK = PriA \times PubB$;

Secret Key of receiver: $SK = PriB \times PubA$.

Step 4: The signature is generated using the hash functions.

Step 5: The signature is sent to the receiver for authentication.

Step 6: At the encryption phase, the message is converted into cipher text using the public keys and a point on the curve.

Step 7: The cipher text is decrypted at the receiver end using the private key.

Step 8: The signature is validated, if the sender's public key is encoded in it.

Advantages

1. Strong security with small keys.
2. Faster performance.
3. Low computational complexity.
4. Increased level of authentication and confidentiality.

Disadvantages

1. Size of the encrypted message is increased.
2. Implementation is difficult.

Applications

1. Secure Socket Layer.
2. Debit/Credit cards.
3. E-mails.

DIGITAL SIGNATURE

The digital signature standard is used to detect unauthorized modifications and to verify the document's identity. The digital signature is represented as binary digits and computed using a set of rules and parameters. The signature is generated by the use of a private key, which is known only to the user [18] . The signature is verified using a public key that is corresponding to the private key. The signature is generated by the user with the help of the private key, which is never shared. A Secure Hash (SSH) function is used in the signature generation process to obtain a condensed version of the data called a message digest. A digital certificate contains the digital signature of the certificate issuing authority so that anyone can verify the originality of the certificate [19] . The digital certificates will expire after specific duration, which results in insecurity.

Advantages

1. Legal compliance.
2. Less processing time.
3. Reduced overhead.
4. Improved security.

Disadvantages

1. Short life span.
2. Complicates sharing in case of incompatibility.

Applications

1. E-mails.

2. Fund transfers.
3. Data interchange.
4. Software distribution.

RESULTS AND DISCUSSION

In general public key encryption, or asymmetric encryption, is about 10,000 times slower than private key encryption. This is because of the use of two different keys for encryption and decryption. Even though, they are smaller they provide high degree of security.

RSA vs. Diffie-Hellman

Diffie-Hellman allows two users A and B, who have never met anywhere, they decide to work together and establish a secret key in order to communicate secretly manner, even in the presence of some intruder. In RSA only the Receiver needs to perform calculations to establish what is called a secret key and a public key. The Receiver doesn't have to necessarily know the Sender of the messages.

RSA vs. ECC

RSA is commonly used cryptography scheme to provide data confidentiality in cloud storage. As the key size increases, the security also increases and storage capacity required to store key in key management server will be large. Security is attractive feature of elliptic curve cryptography. Elliptic curve cryptosystems also are more computationally efficient RSA and Diffie-Hellman. The computation time of ECC is less when compared to RSA and Diffie Hellman, but it is more complex to implement [20] . RSA and Diffie-Hellman algorithms dominate public-key cryptography and have proved its efficiency in real-world applications. ECC promises particularly in smart cards or other restricted environments. The ECC and RSA are compared in terms of key generation time, signature generation and verification time.

Table 1 compares the key sized of RSA, Diffie Hellman and ECC techniques with the symmetric scheme [20] . The key size for symmetric cryptography ranges from 80 to 256 bits, 1024 to 15,360 bits for RSA and Diffie Hellman respectively. But, the key size variations for ECC are 160 to 521 bits. The public, private key generation and the signature generation through the random numbers on elliptic curve reduces the key size considerably. As the symmetric key size increases, the key size of RSA,

Diffie Hellman and ECC also increases. The size of ECC is twice that of symmetric key and the key size of RSA and Diffie Hellman increases in terms of exponents. Table 2 Comparison of key generation time and Table 3 Comparison of signature generation time

Table 2 depicts the comparison of key generation time of RSA and ECC schemes [20] . By varying the key length from 1024 to 15,360 bits, the time required for key generation increases linearly. In RSA, the minimum time required for key generation is 0.16 secs for 1024 bits and the maximum time is 679.06 secs for 15,360 bits. Similarly, the time required for key generation in ECC is 0.08 and 1.4 secs for the key size of 163 and 571 bits respectively. The comparative analysis between the RSA and ECC states that the proposed EC offers significant performance improvement. The key lengths are measured in bits and the key generation time is computed in seconds. The key generation time varies based on the key length. As the key length increases, the key generation time also increases. Table 3 shows the time requires to generate the signature in RSA and ECC techniques [20] . The signature is generated for user authentication and it is measured in terms of seconds. The time required for signature generation depends on the key size.

Table 1. Key size comparison.

Symmetric key size (bits)	RSA and Diffie Hellman key size (bits)	Elliptic Curve Cryptography key size (bits)
80	1024	160
112	2048	224
123	3072	256
192	7680	384
256	15,360	521

Table 2. Key generation time analysis.

Key length (bits)		Key generation time (s)	
RSA	ECC	RSA	ECC
1024	163	0.16	0.08
2240	233	7.47	0.18
3072	283	9.8	0.27
7680	409	133.9	0.64

15,360	571	679.06	1.4

Table 3. Signature generation time analysis.

Key length (bits)		Signature generation time (s)	
RSA	ECC	RSA	ECC
1024	163	0.01	0.15
2240	233	0.15	0.34
3072	283	0.21	0.59
7680	409	1.53	1.18
15,360	571	9.2	3.07

By varying the key length from 1024 to 15,360 bits, the time required for signature generation increases linearly. In RSA, the minimum time required for signature generation is 0.01 secs for 1024 bits and the maximum time is 9.2 secs for 15,360 bits. Similarly, the time required for signature generation in ECC is 0.15 and 3.07 secs with respect to key length variations. The comparative analysis between the RSA and ECC states that the proposed EC offers significant performance improvement.

Table 4 presents the comparison of signature verification time of RSA and ECC schemes [20] . By varying the key length from 1024 to 15,360 bits, the time required for signature verification increases linearly. In RSA, the minimum time required for signature verification is 0.01 secs for 1024 bits and the maximum time is 0.01 secs for 15360 bits. Similarly, the time required for signature generation in ECC is 0.23 and 4.53 secs with respect to the key length variations. The signature is verified at the decryption stage and it also depends on the key length. As the number of bits in the key size increases, the time required for signature verification also increases.

Table 4. Signature verification time analysis

Key length (bits)		Signature verification time (s)	
RSA	ECC	RSA	ECC
1024	163	0.01	0.23
2240	233	0.01	0.51
3072	283	0.01	0.86
7680	409	0.01	1.80
15,360	571	0.03	4.53

CONCLUSION

This paper addressed the limitations in the security assurance and the data privacy limitations with increase in size of the data on cloud. The evolution of cryptographic approaches addressed these limitations and provided the solution to the preserving process. Due to the multi-tenancy property of the cloud, server and the geographical factors limited the security of the cloud data access and storage. This paper surveyed about the various cryptographic techniques with their key sizes, time required for key/signature generation and verification constraints. The survey discussed the architecture for secure data transmissions among the devices, challenges raised during the transmission and attacks. This paper presents the brief review of major cryptographic techniques such as RSA, Dffie Hellman and the ECC associated key sizes. This paper investigated the general impact of digital signature generation techniques on cloud security with the advantages and disadvantages. The results and discussion section existing in this paper investigated the time consumption for key/signature generation and verification with the key size variations effectively. Finally, the results of these approaches were compared in terms of key size, key generation time, signature generation time and signature verification time. The initialization of random prime numbers and the key computation based on the points on the elliptic curve assured the high-security compared to the existing schemes with the minimum time consumption and sizes in cloud-based applications.

REFERENCES

1. Vuyyuru, M., Annapurna, P., Babu, K.G. and Ratnam, A. (2012) An Overview of Cloud Computing Technology. International Journal of Soft Computing and Engineering, 5, 2231-2307.
2. Asma, A., Chaurasia, M.A. and Mokhtar, H. (2012) Cloud Computing Security Issues. International Journal of Application or Innovation in Engineering & Management, 1, 141-147.
3. Agrawal, M. and Mishra, P. (2012) A Comparative Survey on Symmetric Key Encryption Techniques. International Journal on Computer Science and Engineering, 4, 877.
4. Kaur, M. and Kaur, K. (2016) A Comparative Review on Data Security Challenges in Cloud Computing. International Research Journal of Engineering and Technology, 3, 334-339.
5. Chen, D. and Zhao, H. (2012) Data Security and Privacy Protection Issues in Cloud Computing. 2012 International Conference on Computer Science and Electronics Engineering, Hangzhou, 23-25 March 2012, 647-651. https://doi.org/10.1109/ICCSEE.2012.193
6. Rao, R.V. and Selvamani, K. (2015) Data Security Challenges and Its Solutions in Cloud Computing. Procedia Computer Science, 48, 204-209. https://doi.org/10.1016/j.procs.2015.04.171
7. Sookhak, M., Gani, A., Talebian, H., Akhunzada, A., Khan, S.U., Buyya, R., et al. (2015) Remote Data Auditing in Cloud Computing Environments: A Survey, Taxonomy, and Open Issues. ACM Computing Surveys, 47, 65. https://doi.org/10.1145/2764465
8. Bhore, R.S. and Sheikh, R. (2015) Technical Review on Security Issues & Cryptographic Algorithm in Cloud Computing.
9. Ren, K., Wang, C. and Wang, Q. (2012) Security Challenges for the Public Cloud. IEEE Internet Computing, 16, 69-73. https://doi.org/10.1109/MIC.2012.14
10. Wu, L., Zhou, S., Zhou, Z., Hong, Z. and Huang, K. (2015) A Reputation-Based Identity Management Model for Cloud Computing. Mathematical Problems in Engineering, 2, 1-15. https://doi.org/10.1155/2015/238245
11. Mahajan, S. and Singh, M. (2014) Analysis of RSA Algorithm Using GPU Programming. arXiv:1407.1465
12. cs.CR.

13. Gola, K.K., Rathore, R., Sharma, V. and Kandpal, M. (2015) Secure Key Exchange in Diffie-Hellman Key Exchange Algorithm.
14. Chaturvedi, A., Srivastava, N. and Shukla, V. (2015) A Secure Wireless Communication Protocol Using Diffie-Hellman Key Exchange. International Journal of Computer Applications, 126, 126-132.
15. Boni, S., Bhatt, J. and Bhat, S. (2015) Improving the Diffie-Hellman Key Exchange Algorithm by Proposing the Multiplicative Key Exchange Algorithm. International Journal of Computer Applications, 130, 7-10.
16. Adrian, D., Bhargavan, K., Durumeric, Z., Gaudry, P., Green, M., Halderman, J.A., et al. (2015) Imperfect Forward Secrecy: How Diffie-Hellman Fails in Practice. Proceedings of the 22nd ACM SIGSAC Conference on Computer and Communications Security, Denver, 12-16 October 2015, 5-17. https://doi.org/10.1145/2810103.2813707
17. Garg, V. and Ri, S.R. (2012) Improved Diffie-Hellman Algorithm for Network Security Enhancement. International Journal of Computer Technology and Applications, 3, 1327-1331.
18. Setiadi, I., Kistijantoro, A.I. and Miyaji, A. (2015) Elliptic Curve Cryptography: Algorithms and Implementation Analysis over Coordinate Systems. 2015 2nd International Conference on Advanced Informatics: Concepts, Theory and Applications, Chonburi, 19-22 August 2015, 1-6. https://doi.org/10.1109/icaicta.2015.7335349
19. Pornin, T. (2013) Deterministic Usage of the Digital Signature Algorithm (DSA) and Elliptic Curve Digital Signature Algorithm (ECDSA).
20. Poulakis, D. and Rolland, R. (2015) A Digital Signature Scheme Based on Two Hard Problems. Springer International Publishing, New York, 441-450. https://doi.org/10.1007/978-3-319-18275-9_19
21. Sinha, R., Srivastava, H.K. and Gupta, S. (2013) Performance Based Comparison Study of RSA and Elliptic Curve Cryptography. International Journal of Scientific & Engineering Research, 4, 720-725.

SECTION 4
CASE STUDIES

CHAPTER

15

Cloud Security: Services, Risks, and a Case Study on Amazon Cloud Services

Patrick Mosca[1], Yanping Zhang[1], Zhifeng Xiao[2], Yun Wang[3]

[1]Department of Computer Science, Gonzaga University, Spokane, USA

[2]Department of Computer Science & Software Engineering, Penn State Erie, Erie, USA

[3]Department of Computer Science and Information Systems, Bradley University, Peoria, USA

ABSTRACT

Recent advances have witnessed the success and popularity of cloud computing, which represents a new business model and computing paradigm. The feature of on-demand provisioning of computational, storage,

Citation: Mosca, P. , Zhang, Y. , Xiao, Z. and Wang, Y. (2014), "Cloud Security: Services, Risks, and a Case Study on Amazon Cloud Services". *International Journal of Communications, Network and System Sciences*, **7**, 529-535. doi: 10.4236/ijcns.2014.712053.

and bandwidth resources has driven modern businesses into cloud services. The cloud is considered cutting edge technology and it is solely relied on by many large technology, business, and media companies such as Netflix or Salesforce.com. However, in addition to the benefit at hand, security issues have been a long-term concern for cloud computing and are the main barriers of the widespread use of cloud computing. In this paper, we briefly describe some basic security concerns that are of particular interest to cloud technology. We investigate some of the basic cloud concepts and discuss cloud security issues. Amazon Web Services is used as a case study for discussing common cloud terminology. Data security, as well as some cloud specific attacks is introduced. The current state and the future progression of cloud computing is discussed.

Keywords: Could computing, security, Amazon, cloud storage

INTRODUCTION

Recent advances have witnessed the success and popularity of cloud computing, which represents a new business model and computing paradigm [1] . The feature of on-demand provisioning of computational, storage, and bandwidth resources has driven modern businesses into cloud services [2] . The cloud is considered cutting edge technology and it is solely relied on by many large technology, business, and media companies such as Netflix or Salesforce.com. However, in addition to the benefit at hand, security issues have been a long-term concern and are the main barriers of the widespread use of cloud computing [1] . There are three main challenges [1] for building a secure and trustworthy cloud:

- Outsourcing reduces both capital expenditure and operational expenditure for cloud customers [1] . However, outsourcing also indicates that cloud customers no longer retain the physical control on hardware, software, and data. To address this challenge, a trustworthy cloud is expected, meaning that cloud customers are enabled to verify the data and computation in terms of confidentiality, integrity, and other security services [1] .
- Multi-tenancy means that a cloud is shared by multiple customers [1] . Virtualization is heavily used by cloud vendors to optimize resource allocation and management [1] . A common but risky situation is that data belonging to different customers may be stored in the same physical machine. Adversaries can exploit this vulnerability to launch various attacks such as data/computation breach, flooding attack, etc. [1] .

- Massive data and intensive computation are two other features of cloud computing. Therefore, traditional security mechanisms may not suffice the new security requirements due to unbearable computation or communication overhead [1] .

This paper investigates various aspects on cloud security [2] -[4] , including data security [5] , cloud risks [8] and API concerns [9] [10] , cloud services and account hijacking [2] -[14] . The goal of this paper is twofold: first, we focus on the valuable and unique security aspects of the cloud that are different from security issues that widely exist in other computing platforms, since there are certain risks and vulnerabilities only presenting themselves on the cloud environment; second, our intention is to provide an overview of cloud security from the practitioners' point of view. Therefore, we start from Amazon's cloud service [12] , and then proceed to discuss the security concerns and the applicable criteria that follow (figure 1).The rest of this paper is organized as follows: Section 2 presents the background knowledge of Amazon's cloud storage; Section 3 discusses the aspect of data security in cloud; Section 4 investigates other cloud risks and API concerns; Section 5 reviews cloud services and the risk of account hijacking; Section 6 sheds some light on the future of cloud security; Section 7 concludes the paper.

AMAZON'S CLOUD STORAGE

In this section, we will discuss basic technical terms and concepts associated with Amazon's cloud platform. There are different types of storage on Amazon's cloud: AMI (Amazon Machine Image) [15] , EBS (Elastic Block Store) [16] , snapshots [17] , and volumes [16] -[19] .

- A volume consists of stored data and possibly empty space. Also, a volume can exist virtually or can consume a full physical hard drive [18] .

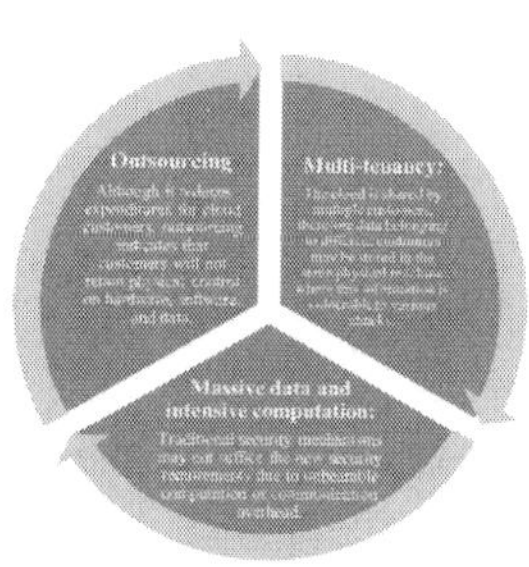

Figure 1. Three main challenges in cloud secruity [1] .

- A snapshot is simply a backup or copy of an instance's volume data. A snapshot can be used to restore the data on an instance, similar to restoring from a backup. A snapshot is typically not a bootable form of storage [17] .
- EBS is a new form of data storage. An EBS is virtual data storage that acts identically to a volume, but the data can be spread across many physical hard drives and can be moved quickly and easily [16] . The motivation behind EBS is to increase storage efficiency in the cloud. Cloud providers can then sell leftover storage to more customers. Additionally, an EBS can consist of multiple volumes, similar to partitions on a drive [16] .
- An AMI is an advanced image of a virtual machine that can be used to create one or more instances of that AMI [15] . These images are similar to bootable snapshots that carry additional information about the virtual machine. An AMI is loaded onto an EBS when an instance is created [15] . For example, when a user obtains an instance and sets it up to host his or her website, all he or she needs to do is save the instance as an AMI, copy it to clouds across the world, and then produce duplicate instances of that AMI. All of his or her instances are live, working clones of the original image that are spread throughout regions.

DATA SECURITY

Cloud customers may store sensitive information in cloud instances. From a security perspective, cloud companies need to ensure the confidentiality of the service [2]. For example, this data could be the backend database for a financial service. A client of any cloud service is supposed to know the risks associated with data security, e.g., data loss and data theft [8]. When storing sensitive information, encryption is always a powerful scheme. Naturally, it would make sense to encrypt sensitive information such as credit card numbers that are stored in the cloud. A potential weakness to encryption in the cloud is the security of the keys. In the hacker world, it is commonly known that physical access to a machine always results in game over. This is because an attacker has control over the machine [2] [5] . Simple passwords on the operating system will not prevent an attacker from stealing data. A break-in is unavoidable unless the full disk is encrypted [8] . Full disk encryption means that the entire volume is encrypted, including the operating system [20] . While full disk encryption is possible in the cloud-computing world, many clients do not encrypt their data for performance and financial reasons. Disk encryption adds additional overhead to the total data stored. Even though data rates vary from region to region, when clients pay by the terabyte, less data is best (see Table 1) [3] . Additionally, many large data stores require quick access. For example, a video streaming service needs to read data quickly [3] . Disk encryption will slow this process down significantly and increase business costs. To this end, many cloud customers do not encrypt their volumes.

When cloud customers do not encrypt their volumes, a security risk is presented. A rogue employee of the provider has the power to snoop around without the customer's knowledge. Since the employee has physical access to the costumer's cloud instance, there is nothing to stop the employee from grabbing vital information and any other private keys [2] [8] . This employee can do this simply by cloning the victim's virtual machine, and then running the clone on a second offline hypervisor [5] . The employee can monitor the behavior of the virtual machine and take their time looking for valuable data. The rogue employee can then proceed to steal the data or use the keys to break into more cloud instances. When storing data in the cloud, trust is a very important part of data privacy. "The threat of a malicious insider is well-known to most organizations. This threat is amplified for consumers of cloud services by the convergence of IT services and customers under a single management domain, combined with a general lack of transparency into provider process and procedure" [2] . Therefore, a trustworthy cloud is an essential step toward the success of cloud computing.

A key concern when encrypting data is determining whether or not the encryption software is open source.

Table 1. Amazon storage pricing [3].

	Standard storage	Glacier storage
First 1 TB/month	$0.105 per GB	$0.011 per GB
Next 49 TB/month	$0.090 per GB	$0.011 per GB
Next 450 TB/month	$0.075 per GB	$0.011 per GB
Next 500 TB/month	$0.070 per GB	$0.011 per GB
Next 4000 TB/month	$0.065 per GB	$0.011 per GB
Next 5000 TB/month	$0.060 per GB	$0.011 per GB

Opening encryption software is key to ensuring that no back doors or additional keys are created [1] . This has become a major problem for many services such as text messaging, videoconferencing, and email. For example, Apple has a service called, "iMessage" that handles text messages in the cloud. All messages are encrypted end-to-end, ensuring that no middleman can read your conversations [4] . What Apple does not tell you is that they are legally required to keep a copy of the key. Again customers are putting trust in the provider, Apple.

CLOUD RISKS AND API CONCERNS

General Server Risks

Of all the risks being reported by the news and blogs on the Internet, many of them are not risks inherent to cloud services, meaning they would apply to all servers. Although, the cloud does increase the risk of some of them (figure 2):

- Denial of Service (DoS) [5] being of the latter is obviously always an issue for servers. The added risk to using the cloud is that attacks on other users of the cloud would affect your portion. If an attack on the cloud unrelated to you brought it down it would also bring your server down or at least slow it down [5] . So while your server may not be the target of attacks, consideration needs to be added which include the notion that you may be working on the same hardware with anyone.
- Data breaches have greater potential of disaster on the cloud. A single flaw in a cloud service could cause one data breach to extend to a breach of the entire system [2] . Methods more simple than side channeling could extract keys or gather unencrypted data. While some individuals think that it is a considerable risk of cloud computing, it is in fact more realistically less of a risk than it would be to create one's own server and service it [8] . In the latter case there are many precautions to be taken, which have already been implemented by cloud services.
- Data loss is an issue not unique to the cloud. Power loss is a potential scenario everywhere on Earth and sometimes unavoidable [8] . Articles have defamed cloud services for losing data when in reality those servers probably have better surge and outage protection than you could afford [14] .
- The risk of giving other access to your server's internals and secrets is once again almost unavoidable [2] [5] . Unless you were to buy, setup,

and implement your own server in your home you will probably have to trust someone else to help you, thereby risking the data's integrity. It would be unwise to attempt to secure grand amounts of money on the cloud for this reason; even on your own server the temptation would exist for the valuables to be stolen [2] . Perhaps an employee would risk their job and reputation for a chance at this money or perhaps the cloud service has taken precautions against employees gaining too much valuable information. This much is unclear and unreported by cloud service businesses. Nonetheless if looking toward using a cloud one should remember that risks surround every server and the most important question is: would you do the extra work for the extra security?

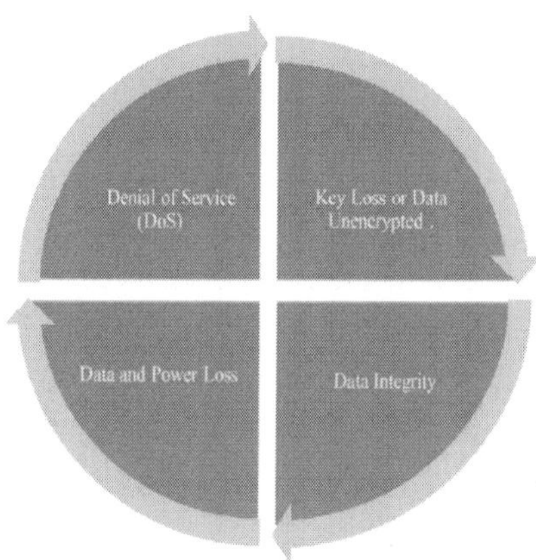

Figure 2. Four general server risks in the cloud [5] [8] .

API Keys

Application Programming Interface (API) Keys [19] on the cloud were first used solely as the identifier for client programs running on a cloud. This allowed for the management of client programs and users to be monitored so as to backtrack events and log usage. While initially this had no security issues involved, later progress on cloud infrastructure has expanded the use of these keys [2] . In some cases it has been reported that these keys are used for authorization. Thus having this key gives one the power to alter delete or transfer an account's data or to use the servers for any other purpose, which would then be traced back and billed to the account holder [2] . After these keys became security risks the major problem was that they were not treated like them. Developers would email them around and store them in their hard drives, where snooping and sniffing could find them.

Years ago Google and Yahoo were making this mistake, but it was not long until the risks were found. They have since bulked their authorization security using Security Assertion Markup Language [21] , and hashed- based authentication codes [22] . Yet the issue remains a threat as developers fail to follow best practices and continue to use API Keys for security purposes [2] . The older, more experienced businesses like Yahoo, Google, and Amazon have all either fallen into this trap before or are aware of the faults present. These companies can be trusted to build better software and control data flow than startups. If API Keys are going to secure information, they need to be handled with greater care.

APIs

Application Programming Interfaces or APIs, give what is almost a roadmap into how an application works [9] [10] . They are usually treated securely but not often enough. The University of Texas at Austin and Stanford University examined several commonly used web services [10] . Payment services at several of them were found to have vulnerabilities in the Secure Sockets Layer (SSL) protocol when accessed through APIs not meant for a browser [3] . Taking advantage of this flaw led to getting access to a user's files. Applications like Chase Mobile Banking and Instagram failed to implement SSL with complete security [10] .

SERVICE AND ACCOUNT HIJACKING

At this point in its development, the cloud is seriously at risk for service and account hijacking [2] . This entails the unauthorized access to and use of the accounts and services of clients who utilize the cloud. This hijacking can happen any number of ways—since the cloud is simply a network run on many different servers, it is vulnerable to all the same attacks as both networks and servers [2] .

Once an attacker has hijacked a service or account, he or she may be able to eavesdrop on the activities of the authorized users, impersonate authorized users, tamper with the network data, or utilize the service or account to propagate malware, e.g. by redirecting clients to malicious websites—all the threats typical for non-cloud networks and servers [2] . Unique to the cloud, however, the attacker may use the hijacked service or account as a base of operations to perform further attacks on other machines in the cloud [2] [5] .

Recent Examples

In recent years, one of the companies on the vanguard of cloud technology—Amazon.com, Inc.—fell prey to such an attack. In 2010 hijackers performed a cross-site scripting (XSS) attack on some site to gain its credentials, and were successful [23] . The attackers then infiltrated the Amazon Relational Database Service (RDS) [7] such that, even if they lost their original access, they would still have a backend into the Amazon system. From that point on, they could capture the login information of anyone who clicked the login button on the Amazon homepage.

The attackers used their servers to infect new machines with the Zeus Trojan horse [23] and control machines already infected with it (Zeus is a piece of malware designed for Windows most often used for stealing bank information through form-grabbing and password-logging via a man-in-the-browser attack [24] [25]). Computers infected with the malware began to report to Amazon's EC2 for updates and instructions [23] .

One of the most interesting facts about this case was that it was not, strictly speaking, Amazon's fault. The attackers gained access through some other, more vulnerable domain [23] . This reveals one truth about the cloud: on it, even one vulnerable system may lead to the compromising of the whole network. Furthermore, Amazon was only one of several sites to suffer this type of attack in the period of just a few months, and it was not in bad company: Twitter, Google's app engine, and Facebook all experienced similar threats [23] .

Possible Defenses

To prevent this type of breach, the Cloud Security Alliance (CSA) admonishes organizations to disallow users and services from sharing account credentials between themselves, and in addition to employ multi-factor authentication requirements when feasible [2] . However, both these changes may make systems more difficult to use, more expensive, and slower. Multi-factor authentication [26] is authentication demanding at least two of the following: knowledge, or something one knows; possession, or something one has; and inference, or something one is. Thus, multi-factor authentication places much more of a burden on users and services than single-factor authentication. And if users and services are disallowed from directly sharing credentials, cloud service providers may have to construct secure channels (an expensive undertaking) or hire a third party for communication between users and services (likewise expensive) [26] .

THE FUTURE OF CLOUD SECURITY

PRISM Scandal

In June 2013 Edward Snowden revealed that the National Security Agency (NSA) has been collecting enormous amounts of communication and search data from internet companies such as Microsoft, Yahoo, Google, and many more, including data about the activities of American citizens [27] . Snowden also explained that even low-level NSA employees have the ability to access this data without warrants. Such surveillance has taken place since January 2007. It may not be immediately clear why this information is particularly relevant to the cloud. The government can force cloud service providers to install backdoors in their hypervisors, but it can do the same for operating systems and even individual machines [11] . However, targeting the machine of one individual is much less likely, since at that point the government has singled out that user specifically. Instead, the cloud provides the NSA with a brimming ocean of network activity, in which it can cast its net and hope to catch something of use—much more efficient than targeting individual machines. As one writer for Porticor said: "Scanning all the data from a cloud provider is relatively easy, because massive amounts of data from multiple owners is all available" [11] . Porticor recommends that users encrypt their own data to combat such invasions of privacy, but it is doubtful that such a solution will ever prove widely acceptable, seeing as it places undue responsibility on users and requires a degree of expertise. The example of PRISM [27] touches on many issues within the future of cloud security: maintenance of privacy, government policy, and data theft (since attackers may capture user data using NSA techniques, or even the NSA channels themselves). These issues are not often considered by users of cloud services, and are not being discussed on a large scale.

A Better Cloud

There are organizations working towards a more secure cloud, such as the CSA [2] . Another is Silver Sky, an expert provider of cloud security and provider of "the industry's only advanced Security-as-a-Service platform from the cloud" [13] [28] . The CTO of Silver Sky, Andrew Jaquith, explains that many CIOs are moving their services to the cloud in order to save money, but that security remains a key concern and these moves may be insecure or at least hasty. But on the other hand, he also explains that many cloud service providers are becoming clearer, more transparent, and more assured than ever before that they could protect customer data [13] .

Thus, the move to the cloud, while it may in some ways be insecure, does not herald anyone's doom. And, with its ever-increasing popularity, even hesitant companies may not soon have a choice.

CONCLUSION

Patrick Mosca, Yanping Zhang, Zhifeng Xiao, Yun Wang (12,92)">12] as a case study, we are able to implore some of the basic terms and concepts of cloud computing. We then proceed to discuss data security, API concerns, account hijacking, and other security concerns. These general concerns are shown to be of particular interest to cloud security. The main differences between traditional services and cloud services are compared from a security perspective. Service and account hijacking is covered, as well as possible defenses. We investigate differences between security issues in cloud services and in traditional services. From the practitioners' view, we briefly overview the security in cloud. The study in this paper provides a guideline of research on cloud services and security issues. Finally, we give some ideas on how to build a more secure cloud. Our future work will focus on the security concerns in cloud services. It will include the privacy protection of data information stored in cloud, data integrity with multiple backups for services purpose, etc.

REFERENCES

1. Xiao, Z. and Xiao, Y. (2013) Security and Privacy in Cloud Computing. IEEE Communications Surveys & Tutorials, 15, 843-859.
2. Cloud Security Alliance (2010) Top Threat to Cloud Computing. https://cloudsecurityalliance.org/topthreats/csathreats.v1.0.pdf
3. Amazon: Amazon Glacier. http://aws.amazon.com/glacier/
4. Quarks Lab (2013) iMessage Privacy. http://blog.quarkslab.com/imessage-privacy.html
5. Mutch, J. (2010) How to Steal Data from the Cloud. http://www.cloudbook.net/resources/stories/how-to-steal-data-from-the-cloud
6. Yorozu, Y., Hirano, M., Oka, K. and Tagawa, Y. (1982) Electron Spectroscopy Studies on Magncto-Optical Media and Plastic Substrate Interface. IEEE Translation Journal on Magnetics in Japan, 2, 740-741.
7. Amazon: Service Level Agreement. http://aws.amazon.com/ec2-sla/
8. Kirchgaessner, S. (2013) Cloud Storage Carries Potent Security Risk. http://www.ft.com/cms/s/0/4729ed7c-3722-11e3-9603-00144feab7de.html
9. Lemos, R. (2012) Insecure API Implementations Threaten Cloud. http://www.darkreading.com/cloud/insecure-api-implementations-threaten-cl/232900809
10. Lemos, R. (2013) Vulnerable APIs Continue to Pose Threat to Cloud. http://www.darkreading.com/services/vulnerable-apis-continue-to-pose-threat/240146453
11. Porticor Cloud Security (2013) Did Snowden Compromise the Future of Cloud Security? http://www.porticor.com/2013/07/cloud-security-snowden/
12. Amazon: Amazon Web Services. http://aws.amazon.com
13. SilverSky (2013) The Future of Cloud Computing and the Latest Security Threats. https://www.silversky.com/blog/the-future-of-cloud-computing-and-the-latest-security-threats
14. Columbia University (2012) Fog Computing: Mitigating Insider Data Theft Attacks in the Cloud. http://www.cs.columbia.edu/~angelos/Papers/2012/Fog_Computing_Position_Paper_WRIT_2012.pdf
15. Amazon: Amazon Machine Image (AMI). http://docs.aws.amazon.com/AWSEC2/latest/UserGuide/AMIs.html
16. Amazon: Amazon EBS. http://aws.amazon.com/ebs/

17. Amazon: Amazon EBS Product Details. http://aws.amazon.com/ebs/details/#snapshots
18. Amazon: Amazon EC2 Instance Store. http://docs.aws.amazon.com/AWSEC2/latest/UserGuide/InstanceStorage.html
19. MailChimp (2014) About API Keys. http://kb.mailchimp.com/accounts/management/about-api-keys
20. Janssen, C. Full-Disk Encryption (FDE). http://www.techopedia.com/definition/13623/full-disk-encryption-fde
21. Cover, R. (2010) Security Assertion Markup Language (SAML). http://xml.coverpages.org/saml.html
22. United Sates Department of Veterans Affairs (2014) Keyed-Hash Message Authentication Code (HMAC). http://www.va.gov/trm/StandardPage.asp?tid=5296
23. Goodin, D. (2009) Zeus Bot Found Using Amazon's EC2 as C&C Server. http://www.theregister.co.uk/2009/12/09/amazon_ec2_bot_control_channel/
24. Nahorney, B. and Nicolas, F. (2010) Trojan.Zbot. http://www.symantec.com/security_response/writeup.jsp?docid=2010-011016-3514-99
25. Acunetix: Cross Site Scripting Attack. https://www.acunetix.com/websitesecurity/cross-site-scripting/
26. Amazon: Multi-Factor Authentication. http://aws.amazon.com/iam/details/mfa/
27. The Guardian: The NSA Files. http://www.theguardian.com/world/the-nsa-files
28. SilverSky (2013) About Us. https://www.silversky.com/about-us

CHAPTER

16

A Quick Survey on Cloud Computing and Associated Security, Mobility and IoT Issues

Michael Perez, Sanjeev Kumar

Department of Electrical and Computer Engineering, University of Texas-RGV, Edinburg, TX, USA

ABSTRACT

This survey paper provides a general overview on Cloud Computing. The topics that are discussed include characteristics, deployment and service models as well drawbacks. Major aspects of Cloud Computing are explained to give the reader a clearer understanding on the complexity of the platform. Following this, several security issues and countermeasures are also discussed to show the major issues and obstacles that Cloud Computing

Citation: Perez, M. and Kumar, S. (2017), "A Quick Survey on Cloud Computing and Associated Security, Mobility and IoT Issues". *Journal of Computer and Communications*, **5**, 80-95. doi: 10.4236/jcc.2017.512009.

faces as it is being implemented further. The major part of countermeasures focuses on Intrusion Detection Systems. Moving towards Mobile Cloud Computing and Internet of Things, this survey paper gives a general explanation on the applications and potential that comes with the integration of Cloud Computing with any device that has Internet connectivity as well as the challenges that are before it.

Keywords: Cloud Computing, Cloud Service Models, Platform, Security, Mobility, Internet of Things (IoT)

INTRODUCTION

Cloud computing is a model that is completely based on the Internet and remote servers to utilize large amounts of data, software, and applications. It is a promising new platform for services to be provided on the Internet. These include storage, applications, and hardware services that clients can utilize as an on-de- mand basis. The listed services are provided without the clients having to own the particular service or application. As for hardware services, clients do not have to have them installed locally. They are usually paid for by clients "per use" basis, which results in overall cost reductions. Along with reduced costs, major companies such as Google and Amazon utilize the features and benefits of cloud computing such as low investment cost, easy to manage, and flexibility to provide their services [1] . The purpose of this survey paper is to give the reader a much clearer understanding of the fundamentals of cloud computing ranging from a general overview of cloud computing to the security issues and vulnerabilities that are involved with the platform.

The topics presented in this paper can be divided into four major categories. This includes a general Cloud Computing overview, Cloud Computing security, Mobile Cloud Computing, and Internet of Things. For the cloud computing overview, the reader will find detailed explanations for each individual aspect of cloud computing to get a clearer understanding on the platform ranging from its architecture to each service model. The cloud computing security section will provide an overview of a variety of different security threats and vulnerabilities that cloud computing faces. Mobile Cloud Computing and Internet of Things both act as extensions to the general overview of Cloud Computing with subtopics including Cloud Computing limitations, new applications, and the future outlook, as Cloud Computing is further integrated with mobile devices.

CLOUD COMPUTING GENERAL OVERVIEW

There are various levels of Cloud computing that need to be taken into consideration when trying to understand the platform. Like most forms of technology it has its own set of benefits and drawbacks, which will be discussed shortly, but also has defining characteristics that set it apart from other forms of technology. Other levels of cloud computing include the various service and deployment models. Each of these models allows for versatility in order to satisfy a specific set of needs for different customer bases. On a higher level the cloud architecture can be used to describe each component of cloud computing ranging from the physical servers and networks, the middleware, and even to individual application function that are more commonly associated by clients for cloud computing. Figure 1 shows a general overview of each architectural layer of cloud computing.

Cloud Computing Architecture

It is suggested that cloud computing can be divided into three levels with each layer representing a key part of cloud computing. The application layer contains the data and various applications used by clients such as web interfaces, programming interfaces for application development, and the main engines for cloud applications known as the application core. The virtualization layer backs up applications by providing them with the necessary resources and demands. Database access and server functionality is found at this layer as well as connectivity components such as Internet Protocol and Domain Name System (DNS). Here also, the virtualization of the physical infrastructure is provided where anything related to virtual machines is defined and controlled from the virtual components.

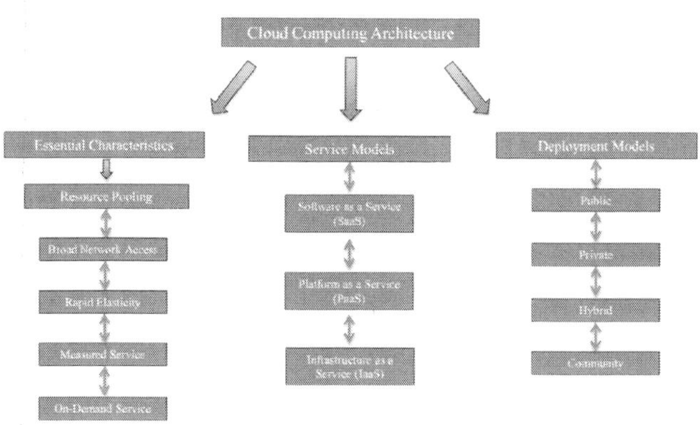

Figure 1. Cloud computing architecture and general overview.

The physical layer is the hardware and resources that the two layers above utilize to perform their required tasks. Hardware includes individual servers, switchers, and routers. The facilities that house the hardware is also a part of this layer along with the power systems related to maintaining proper operation of the physical components in house. This includes heating, ventilation, air conditioning, and emergency power [2] .

Cloud Computing Benefits

The adoption of cloud computing has allowed for many companies to experience several benefits from it's implementation. Reduction of costs from different payment schemes such as a onetime payment or pay-as-you-use instead of an extensive purchase of a large number of computers and related hardware has been a major benefit. Also the combination of needs from a customer base reduces the overall cost and with the higher computer utilization from cloud computing services, this makes it an enticing option for major companies. Another benefit offered is the reduced deployment times. With cloud computing, whole systems can become fully functional in a fraction of the time traditional methods would have. Examples include virtual web servers that can be brought online in the cloud and the launching of products or services [1] [3]. Different aspects of services also benefit from cloud computing including introducing new services, scalability, and easy access. The cloud allows information to be easily accessible anywhere with proper access. For scalability, the cloud can scale services and provide new ones easily with the demands of customers. Along with this, backup and recovery is another key benefit of cloud computing, which allows easier storage than physical media [1] .

Cloud Computing Drawbacks

Like all other forms of technology with all the benefits that cloud computing offers there are some drawbacks. Security issues are the main drawback to cloud computing as sensitive data is usually handed over to third party cloud servers, which could lead to trust issues within organizations of who they work with. The amount of data used in cloud computing also makes it vulnerable to attacks, which requires constant monitoring. Also technical issues such as server downtimes and even data losses can hinder job completions from organizations. Application inflexibility can also be considered a drawback to cloud computing because of the lack of support for different formats [1].

Cloud Computing Characteristics

With Cloud Computing being so complex there are several basic characteristics that define the technology that is universally understood as the foundation for the platform. These characteristics allow the services of Cloud Computing to be provided which include elasticity, on demand self-service, multi-tenancy, and shared resource pooling to name a few [1] [3] [4] .

Elasticity allows cloud computing to scale either up or down quickly in order to make a user think that there are unlimited resources available at all times. Multi-tenancy allows the same infrastructure to be shared by different businesses. Each one would have its own responsibilities of its own respective layer while sharing the same infrastructure provider and same data center. Shared resource pooling allows the provider to combine computing resources to serve different customers, and assign and reassign physical and virtual resources as customer demand changes. This allows more flexibility to the infrastructure providers for resource management and costs. Broad network access is another key characteristic of cloud computing. Since the platform is Internet based, the only thing required for any Internet ready device to access cloud mechanisms, services, and resources is an Internet connection [1] [3] [4] .

Cloud Computing Deployment Models

The type of model cloud computing can be classified as depends on location and organization. Public clouds are considered the standard cloud model. Multiple users access the cloud resources and services on the same public infrastructure. Each user is charged by the amount of time accessing the resources that they need. Drawbacks to this model include the fact that it is prone to attacks and have various security issues that will be discussed in later sections.

Private clouds contain an individual in a protected cloud environment which only the single user can utilize the cloud services. On an organizational level, the cloud is only assessable within the same company and it is also managed internally. Benefits include security and easy maintenance however; the privatization of this cloud can result in high costs. A community cloud is implemented as an access between several organizations and belongs to the same community. Privacy requirements, policies, and security concerns are all shared. Infrastructure locations can vary such as the same company hosted by a third-party. Hybrid clouds combined private and public clouds or multiple clouds of the same type under a standard protocol. Companies can utilize aspects of which types of clouds are present in the hybrid cloud to allocate where to perform certain tasks that can improve productivity [1] [5] .

Cloud Computing Service Models

There are three service models used to describe cloud services. These include Software as a Service, Platform as a Service, and Infrastructure as a Service. Software as a Service (SaaS) allows clients to access cloud applications without having to install the application on their own computer. The service provider maintains the cloud-computing infrastructure, and control from a user's standpoint is only at the application settings [6] . The advantages of this model include reduction of software licensing costs, security, and it allows multiple clients to use the same application at the same time [7] . Platform as a Service (PaaS) is somewhat opposite of the previous model where now clients can create and deploy their own applications to the cloud. These applications are developed by programming and configuration tools and are mainly used by developers, testers or administrators [6] . This platform allows individuals to develop applications without the need to have the proper environment installed locally. Control over the application's configuration is in the client's hands while the actual cloud infrastructure is not since they are renting the virtual servers for development and testing. Advantages of Platform as a Service include increased flexibility for developers allowing them to create new platforms on demand to meet newer requirements along with security benefits of the service for data, which include backup and recovery [7] . Infrastructure as a Service (IaaS) the client now has access to the actual infrastructure of the cloud service provider. They can use the virtual hardware to use development tools to build applications on the given infrastructure. Clients include higher level IT personnel including system administrators and developers [6]. Advantages of Infrastructure as a Service include fluctuation of the infrastructure on demand and reduction of costs from hardware and human resources as well as from the ability to have many users use single hardware [7].

CLOUD COMPUTING SECURITY

Each level of Cloud Computing can have the potential for security risks that need to be taken into consideration. The number one concern with the amount of data being processed and stored in clouds is data security and privacy. In most cases users and clients do not know this information, as this aspect of Cloud Computing is essential but out of their hands. This concern of Cloud Computing will be discussed in further detail. Looking at various security threat examples and countermeasures pertaining to topic discussed previously such as Cloud Computing service models and characteristics can give a good overview on the obstacles that Cloud Computing faces as it is further implemented and more widely used.

Cloud Computing CIA Triad

The CIA Triad model stands for Confidentiality, Integrity and Availability for securing systems and plays a key role in maintaining proper security for cloud computing. With the amount of data being exchanged on the platform each part of the triad must be kept in check. Confidentiality prevents the access of data by unauthorized party and in essence main role is to keep data private. There are several parts of cloud computing that are related to this part of the CIA Triad. Encryption, covert channel, and traffic analysis are just a few examples of what is associated with confidentiality in cloud computing. Integrity maintains consistent and unaltered information being used on the cloud. This means that there is no unauthorized modification of data present. Availability in cloud computing means that the resources and data are reliable and can be accessed at any time as user needs [8] [9] .

CIA Triad General Security Threat Examples

General security threats also apply to cloud computing such as eavesdropping, fraud, theft, and external attacks. Each of these affect the CIA Triad for cloud computing. Eavesdropping allows the unauthorized gathering of information, fraud can be either data manipulation or falsification, and external attacks can result in lack of availability for cloud computing services. There are several techniques used to compromise the CIA Triad for cloud computing. Reconnaissance can involve various methods of collection methods and social engineering to gather information to be granted unauthorized cloud access. These can include physical break-ins to get to specific machines to access information, dumpster diving to retrieve discarded information which can sometimes still be valid, and social engineering to manipulate individuals into giving out secret information such as passwords. Denial of Service is the main culprit for affecting the availability of cloud computing in the CIA Triad. Resources such as CPU, Network, and Memory are the main targets to bring down access to cloud related services. General methods implemented can be buffer overflows and packet flooding. Other general methods used to violate the CIA Triad include account cracking and malicious software. Account cracking from brute force password attacks can lead to unauthorized access to accounts and thus can result in data manipulation and data being stolen. Malicious software such as viruses, spyware, and worms can all in their own way affect each part of the CIA Triad [9] .

Cloud Computing Threats and Countermeasures

With the amount of sensitive applications and data taking part in cloud computing there are various aspects of the technology where specific security issues can take place. Security threats in the cloud computing environment have their own exploits for taking advantage of different vulnerabilities. In virtualization, with the amount of operating systems running on single hardware, it is possible to loose track of all the machines present. This can result in a new machine running malicious code to either gain control of the entire system or bring the system down. Rootkits can be installed to infect machines to hide key components from being identified by different security tools and programs. Countermeasures for this type of attack revolve around authenticity checks for messages from the client machines. A comparison of an original image file to upcoming service request via hash values is one specific method.

The software interfaces that clients use for cloud computing also have their own set of risks. The control over several virtual machines and systems in combination with potential insecure interfaces and application program interfaces can lead to unauthorized access, reusable passwords, and limited logging to name a few. Countermeasures can include strong authentication methods and encrypted transmissions. The storage of data by third party data center can result in data breaches that leak information and cause data corruption. In particular, by renting a server from other service providers for reduction of costs and flexibility, cloud providers run the risk for malicious insiders to steal the valuable data on the service provider servers. There are multiple security threats that can result in data breaches such as identify theft, malware, SQL injection, and phishing. Data breach aftermaths can result in cloud service providers to close because of the financial and legal issues that arise with customer data loss and corruption. Countermeasures include filter techniques for user inputs, active content filtering for SQL attacks, and web application vulnerability detection.

Related to the data breach risks stated previously, since data in cloud computing can be stored anywhere in the world this can lead to access problems for clients. This makes any type of localized attacks at the storage areas completely out of the customer's control. For a customer and provider, knowing who is managing their data and what are their privileges is part of the preventative maintenance process for making sure their data is secure. With storage locations being unknown, identity management and authentication is key. Brute force attacks can decrypt passwords and lead to unauthorized access. On a related note, with storage facilities being all over the world there are privacy concerns that are associated in the cloud-computing environment. Different countries may have different privacy regulations with their own restrictions and guidelines on data security. This can lead to data being prone to man-in-the-middle attacks and other eavesdropping techniques. The countermeasures to protect data because of data location and the privacy issues include high-level password authentications and data access policies, sniffing detection platforms, and separating endpoint and server security processes [10] .

Security Threats to Cloud Computing Characteristics

Looking at the characteristics of cloud computing that were discussed in a previous section, here we can find and describe security risks to the cloud service environment. The elasticity nature of cloud computing makes security breaches possible even though safety measures are in place such as data encryption. For multi-tenancy, the service placement engine, which overlooks the lists of available resources for the cloud resource pool, must have several security requirements. These are needed to avoid the placement of multiple cloud services on the same hardware resource, which can create data vulnerabilities. With shared resource pooling comes a certain distribution and multi-user environment. Here risks are always present because of the lack of control users have in this type of environment. Referring back to the previous section on specific CIA threats with the issues of control over data and applications, since customers have to trust the service provider with sensitive data without knowing exactly where the services or applications are located in general, the data itself is vulnerable in each area of the CIA triad. Adding on to characteristics, there is also a lack of standard at each cloud tier. High flexibility in a cloud computing environment can make users become dependent on only one service provider which can make them even more vulnerable from the lack of diversity [11] .

Security Threats to Cloud Computing Service Models

Each service model has its own set of unique vulnerabilities based on its structure. This comes from the differences in what is managed by users and the cloud service providers for each service model. Software-as-a-Service (SaaS) specific vulnerabilities include identity management, lack of standards, service secrecy, anywhere access, and general infrastructure security. For identity management the use of third parties creates differences in how they approach restricting system access to authorized users increases vulnerabilities. Also with lack of standards and service secrecy, the fact that the information on where data is stored and the lack of disclosers on how it is secured creates vulnerabilities for users. With this lack of information the service providers do not guarantee the safety of data other than just general formalities saying that thc data is secured. With this service model, since access can occur anywhere, individual users and endpoints cannot be guaranteed to be secure. This can create openings for threats to this cloud service model. Now as stated before, there will be issues with data security when running an application on the cloud as the infrastructure security is totally dependent on the service provider.

Platform-as-a-Service model vulnerabilities include attacks that affect availability, API security, platform applications upgrades, and general development security. This service model is susceptible to Denial of Service (DDoS) attacks. With no standards for API security this makes authentication issues arise which can lead to the cloud to be exposed to attacks from other users. The upgrading of platform components and patch updates together can stop possible service downtime because of this. Overall changes though can lead to compromised data and applications. With this service model providing the development environment tools to customers, the customers do not have a guarantee that they are secure.

Infrastructure-as-a-Service (IaaS) model vulnerabilities include enforcement of Service Level Agreement, virtualization, and security of virtual machines. The enforcement of service level agreements has to be done by both the cloud service provider and customers when necessary. The lack of enforcement and monitoring of quality of services can create security issues. For virtualization, changes to virtual machines in general can create security threats and the lack of a controlling system to monitor virtual machines and the communications that take place also creates a high-risk environment. The security of virtual machines in particular the communication and mobility must be secure to prevent cloud servers from being susceptible to

DDoS related attacks. Overall, for the three service models they each share vulnerabilities that relate to the CIA triad such as each one can be susceptible to DDoS attacks, which affect availability, or the assurance of information, which affects confidentiality, and maintaining data integrity in general [11] .

Intrusion Detection Systems

The previously mentioned cloud computing threats can be categorized into two areas, they are insider attacks which include cloud users doing unauthorized tasks, and outsider attacks such as DDoS. Preventing these attacks is a challenge for Intrusion Detection Systems (IDS) [12] . "The definition for Intrusion Detection Systems is the process of monitoring events occurring in a computer system or network and analyzing them to look for intrusions" [12] . The system itself can be both hardware and software. However there are some limitations to existing IDS that make it a challenge to work within the cloud-computing environment. They do not have autonomic self-adaptation, lack scalability, and are not deterministic. Thus new cloud based IDS are needed [12] .

Looking at the detection techniques used by IDS they are categorized by signature based, anomaly based, and hybrid based detection. Signature based detection compares current information on a network to a pre-established database of signatures that is used to determine if current information corresponds to an attack. Pattern recognition techniques are used by this method in the decision making process of whether or not current traffic matches to a known signature. Benefits to this type of detection method is that it has high accuracy and is flexible as new signatures can be added to the database to keep the system up to date. One major drawback though is the fact that it relies on a current database. If an unknown new attack would occur, the system would have no way of recognizing it. Anomaly-based detection actively tries to find suspicious activity on a network or system. Preload profiles are used with current user activities to detect any possible intrusions. Profiles are created within a given timeframe known as a training period, which the regular activities of users and overall network usage are considered. This gives the IDS time to identify habits within a network over a certain period of time such as CPU usage, file access times, and incorrect logins. The benefit that this type of detection has over signature-based is that it can detect unknown attacks by comparing current network and system activities to the profiles that it has created to determine that an attack is taking place. Hybrid detection is the combination of signature-based and anomaly-based detection using both methods as one IDS [12] .

Cloud Computing Intrusion Detection Systems

The types of cloud-computing IDS are Network based, Host based, distributed, and Hypervisor-based. Network based IDS can use both signature and anomaly based techniques to identify potential malicious activities. After it scans the traffic for a network, it uses the IP and transport layer headers of each packet in its detection. This type of system however, cannot analyze encrypted traffic and intrusions in a virtual network by a virtual machine monitor which creates and runs virtual machines.

Host based IDS instead of collecting information from the entire network it collects and analyzes information from a specific host machine to detect any possible intrusions. Information that is used includes network events, system calls, and file usage to name few. Any modification in the host kernel, host file system, or overall behavior of the program that seems to be unusual is reported as an attack. In cloud computing, Host based IDS can be deployed on the hypervisor (creates and runs virtual machines) or host. Here it can use system logs, user logins, and policies to detect any potential threat within the cloud. Benefits over Network based IDS include the ability to now analyze encrypted traffic, but this type of detection system is vulnerable to DDoS attacks.

Distributed IDS combines many Network based and Host based IDS, which are deployed on a large network. Each individual IDS communicate with a centralized server.Hypervisor-based IDS is used for virtual machines as it is set up at the hypervisor layer. This system monitors communication at different levels such as communication between virtual machine and hypervisor to detect any type of anomalies [12] .

MOBILE CLOUD COMPUTING

Mobile Cloud Computing has been made prominent with the dramatic rise of mobile devices being connected to the Internet. Mobile Cloud Computing is defined as a system in which both the data processing and data storage are performed outside the mobile environment [13] . With applications needing constant access to the Internet the services provided by Mobile Cloud Computing can offer convenience and ease of use. Applications now have a larger scope with computations and data storage being used in the cloud instead of being all directly on the mobile device [13] . Looking first at the architecture of Mobile Cloud Computing can allow for a better understanding of the platform and the differences between itself and regular Cloud Computing.

Mobile Cloud Computing Architecture

Mobile cloud computing services have some differences than the cloud services as regular cloud computing with Software as a Service (SaaS), Platform as a Service (PaaS), and Infrastructure as a Service (IaaS). This is due to these classifications being based on virtualization [14] . With the increasing number of mobile clients in cloud computing using mobile applications that are linked to servers operating in the cloud, breaking down mobile cloud computing architecture into its components can help with understanding how mobile devices and clients work with cloud computing. These components are mobile clients, middleware, and cloud services. Each mobile client connects to the cloud, which is managed by service providers' thorough middleware. The middleware component pushes updates to services via hypertext transfer protocol [15] .

For mobile cloud service models, they are classified based on the roles of computational entities within a service framework. Specific models are titled Mobile as a Service Consumer (MaaSC), Mobile as a Service Provider (MaaSP), and Mobile as a Service Broker (MaaSB). The most popular model for mobile cloud computing is MaaSC. Mobile devices using this model can achieve higher performance and have a broader range of application capabilities by outsourcing computation and storage to the cloud. MaaSP is the opposite of MaaSC where now each client has the capability of the service provider. Services provided here are based on sensing and processing capabilities of the connecting mobile devices with application data ranging from GPS, camera, and other device related data. Other local devices receive this data in order to improve performance and accuracy of various applications. MaaSB is used when mobile devices are limited in their capabilities. This model allows an extension to sensor networks where a mobile device can be used as a gateway to provide network services via Bluetooth, WiFi, and cell phone provider network in order to communicate and send data to cloud resources. Mobile devices can also act as a security layer to sensor networks under this service model [14] . Figure 2 shows an overview of each mobile cloud service model.

Mobile Cloud Challenges

Similar to regular Cloud Computing, the challenges with Mobile Cloud Computing revolve around security and resources especially with the mobile devices themselves. Each mobile device can have limited battery and computational power in comparison to desktop and laptop computers, which is a major factor to take into consideration when using applications on the cloud. Also with varying signals and network problems that mobile device carriers can have may lead to inefficient operation. This can lead to the lack of Internet connectivity which means cloud operations will not be fully functional. For security, the risks are similar to traditional devices that connect to the Internet as mobile devices are at risk for malicious attacks as well as the general cloud security [13] , which was discussed earlier in the paper.

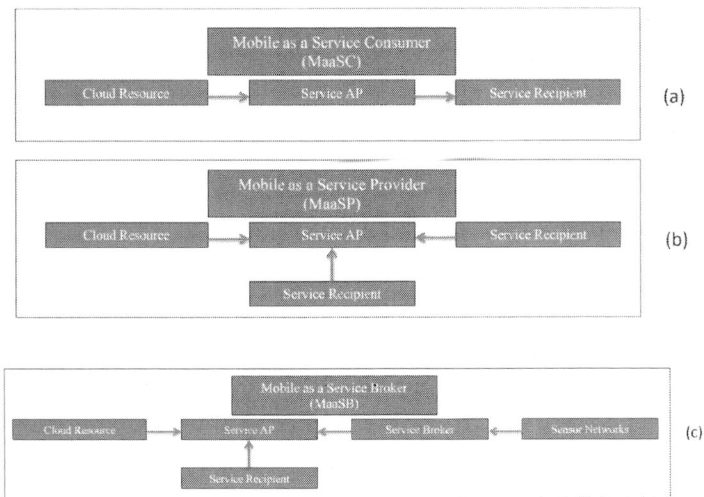

Figure 2. Mobile cloud computing service models: (a) Mobile as a service consumer model; (b) Mobile as a service provider; (c) Mobile as a service broker.

Mobile Cloud Applications

Current applications that are being used as a result of the increased popularity of mobile devices are email, banking, healthcare, and gaming to name a few. Email acts as the main application of the Mobile Cloud as emails are stored on a remote server and are accessed and updated regularly by mobile devices. Banking and commerce in general, is utilizing the Mobile Cloud for performing different transactions such as Mobile Banking and shopping. For healthcare the Mobile Cloud is used to provide better overall service and treatment for patients such as ease of access of patient health records. On the entertainment side, Mobile Gaming has taken advantage of using the Mobile Cloud for computing resources to allow users to play advanced type of games on their mobile devices [13] .

The list of mobile cloud applications described in [14] includes computation, storage, security and privacy, and context awareness. One obstacle faced by mobile cloud computation is that dividing tasks between a local mobile device and the cloud can be inefficient leading to high energy consumption, CPU usage, and network delays. Various services mitigate these inefficiencies by offering runtime environments to make mobile applications run seamlessly between local devices and the cloud servers. Other services use code to maximize energy consumption as well as offloading tasks to the cloud is made efficient by having this process to be automatic. For mobile cloud storage, automatic synchronization is a preferred feature to send data to storage services. Examples of storage services include Dropbox and Google Drive. Each mobile device has a limited amount of storage capacity and sensitive data used in automatic synchronization such as history, contacts, and preferences has to be kept in a secure and reliable space [14] .

INTERNET OF THINGS (IOT)

With the concept of Internet of Things (IoT) now a reality, the amount of devices connected to the Internet has grown exponentially. The combination of cloud computing, sensors, and actuators creates a network never seen before. These smart devices can range from practically anything including wearables, security solutions, healthcare, smart electric meters, smart appliances, and power grids to name a few [16] . The incorporation of these devices with cloud computing has increased performance potential and they also have many challenges.

Internet of Things and Cloud Computing

Cloud IoT is the name given for the combination of Internet of Things and Cloud Computing. Cloud Computing has most of the issues that Internet of Things has solved with nearly unlimited capabilities in processing power and storage. Now Internet of Things can also benefit Cloud Computing by extending its scope and bring new types of services. Looking at specifics, Internet of Things produces a large amount of data from the information it gathers and Cloud Computing is the most cost effective and convenient way to handle the amount of data produced by Internet of Things. For processing power, each Internet of Things device has limited processing power and resources. Usually data is transferred to more powerful capable devices for processing. Cloud Computing can offset this drawback of Internet of Things and create higher levels of complexity with these devices. Looking at connectivity, each device that is part of Internet of Things has to be IP-enabled and the costs for support can be rather high. Cloud Computing offers a much more cost-effective solution and these devices can be managed and monitored in real-time from applications on the cloud. Overall the addition of Cloud Computing to Internet of Things can solve the issues of scalability, reliability, and security [17] .

Cloud IoT Applications

The area of healthcare can benefit greatly from Cloud IoT as it creates a solution to managing healthcare sensor data efficiently. Mobile devices that are tailored for healthcare can be made more secure and available as with regular Internet of Things devices they generate a large amount of data that has to be managed and processed. With the introduction of Cloud Computing, these devices can allow for innovation in this industry, and create cost effective, efficient, and high quality services [17] .

Smart Home applications can range from managing energy consumption, lighting, and air conditioning. Each relies on a sensor network, which can produce a large amount of data. The rise of home automation and Internet-enabled devices in a household create an opportunity for an integration of a cloud to manage these devices. The cloud must provide internal network connections, intelligent remote control, and automation. Another home related application is video surveillance. Using the cloud can mitigate any potential storage constraints that may arise with the amount of data gathered in surveillance. Cloud based solutions can be used to store and mange content from surveillance feeds and deliver it to authorized user devices via the Internet [17] .

Smart Energy can utilize Cloud IoT to provide intelligent management of energy systems such as energy distribution and energy consumption. For distribution, electricity can be better managed by providing services after analyzing data collected from nodes that have sensing, processing power, and network capabilities. Each node along with the cloud can distribute tasks and the decision-making can be made on the cloud [17] .

The automotive industry also can have many benefits with the integration of Cloud Computing and Internet of Things with transportation technologies. These IoT-based vehicular data clouds benefits can include increased road safety, reduced traffic, and vehicle maintenance [17] . "Vehicular Clouds are designed to expand the conventional Clouds in order to increase on-demand the whole Cloud computing, processing, and storage capabilities, by using under- utilized facilities of vehicles" [17] . Issues with vehicular clouds include scalability due to the amount of vehicles and number changes. Along with this the various speeds and locations where vehicles travel can cause interruption in communications, which reduce performance, reliability, and quality of service. Security is also an issue due to the lack of an established infrastructure preventing any effective authentication [17] .

CONCLUSION

In summary, this survey paper provides a general overview of Cloud Computing and various subtopics related to the technology behind it including mobile, security and IoT. The scope and potential for Cloud Computing can be endless but it has several drawbacks and security risks that need to be addressed in order for it to become more reliable and more accepted. As a new Information Technology model and platform for the consumptions and delivery of services on the Internet, there are many benefits from both a business and personal standpoint. These applications can utilize Cloud Computing to provide better and more efficient services as discussed in the previous sections. Full utilization of Cloud Computing has yet to be realized but as the technology and architecture become more adopted along with possible standardizations that are needed, many devices and applications can have a much larger scope and greater performance potential from Cloud Computing.

ACKNOWLEDGEMENTS

This work was supported in part by the US National Science Foundation, under Grant# 0421585 and Houston Endowment Chair in Science, Math and Technology Fellowship

REFERENCES

1. Kamboj, S. and Ghumman, N.S. (2016) A Survey on Cloud Computing and Its Types. 2016 3rd International Conference on Computing for Sustainable Global Development (INDIACom), New Delhi, 2971-2974.
2. Colman-Meixner, C., Develder, C., Tornatore, M. and Mukherjee, B. (2016) A Survey on Resiliency Techniques in Cloud Computing Infrastructures and Applications. IEEE Communications Surveys & Tutorials, 18, 2244-2281. https://doi.org/10.1109/COMST.2016.2531104
3. Arinze, B. and Anandarajan, M. (2013) Adapting Cloud Computing Service Models to Subscriber Requirements. 2013 16th International Symposium on Wireless Personal Multimedia Communications (WPMC), Atlantic City, 1-5.
4. Savu, L. (2011) Cloud Computing: Deployment Models, Delivery Models, Risks and Research Challenges. 2011 International Conference on Computer and Management (CAMAN), Wuhan, 1-4. https://doi.org/10.1109/CAMAN.2011.5778816
5. Mirobi, G.J. and Arockiam, L. (2015) Service Level Agreement in Cloud Computing: An Overview. 2015 International Conference on Control, Instrumentation, Communication and Computational Technologies (ICCICCT), Kumaracoil, 753-758. https://doi.org/10.1109/ICCICCT.2015.7475380
6. Polash, F., Abuhussein, A. and Shiva, S. (2014) A Survey of Cloud Computing Taxonomies: Rationale and Overview. The 9th International Conference for Internet Technology and Secured Transactions (ICITST-2014), London, 459-465. https://doi.org/10.1109/ICITST.2014.7038856
7. Bokhari, M.U., Shallal, Q.M. and Tamandani, Y.K. (2016) Cloud Computing Service Models: A Comparative Study. 2016 3rd International Conference on Computing for Sustainable Global Development (INDIACom), New Delhi, 890-895.
8. Kanday, R. (2012) A Survey on Cloud Computing Security. 2012 International Conference on Computing Sciences, Phagwara, 302-311. https://doi.org/10.1109/ICCS.2012.6
9. Patil Madhubala, R. (2015) Survey on Security Concerns in Cloud Computing. 2015 International Conference on Green Computing

and Internet of Things (ICGCIoT), Noida, 1458-1462. https://doi.org/10.1109/ICGCIoT.2015.7380697

10. Jouini, M. and Rabai, L.B.A. (2014) Surveying and Analyzing Security Problems in Cloud Computing Environments. 2014 Tenth International Conference on Computational Intelligence and Security, Kunming, 689-693. https://doi.org/10.1109/CIS.2014.169
11. Girma, A., Garuba, M. and Li, J. (2015) Analysis of Security Vulnerabilities of Cloud Computing Environment Service Models and Its Main Characteristics. 12th International Conference on Information Technology New Generations, Las Vegas, 206-211. https://doi.org/10.1109/ITNG.2015.39
12. Chiba, Z., Abghour, N., Moussaid, K., El Omri, A. and Rida, M. (2016) A Survey of Intrusion Detection Systems for Cloud Computing Environment. International Conference on Engineering & MIS, Agadir, 1-13. https://doi.org/10.1109/ICEMIS.2016.7745295.
13. Mallya, K.R. and Dhas, C.S.G. (2016) Secure Learning in the Mobile Cloud. IEEE International Conference on Advances in Computer Applications, Coimbatore, 125-130. https://doi.org/10.1109/ICACA.2016.7887936
14. Huang, D., Xing, T. and Wu, H. (2013) Mobile Cloud Computing Service Models: A User-Centric Approach. IEEE Network, 27, 6-11. https://doi.org/10.1109/MNET.2013.6616109
15. Tuli, A., Hasteer, N., Sharma, M. and Bansal, A. (2013) Exploring Challenges in Mobile Cloud Computing: An Overview. Confluence 2013: The Next Generation Information Technology Summit, Noida, 496-501. https://doi.org/10.1049/cp.2013.2364
16. Saha, H.N., Mandal, A. and Sinha, A. (2017) Recent Trends in the Internet of Things. 7th Annual Computing and Communication Workshop and Conference, Las Vegas, 1-4. https://doi.org/10.1109/CCWC.2017.7868439
17. Botta, A., de Donato, W., Persico, V. and Pescapé, A. (2014) On the Integration of Cloud Computing and Internet of Things. International Conference on Future Internet of Things and Cloud, Barcelona, 23-30. https://doi.org/10.1109/FiCloud.2014.14

CHAPTER

17

Block Level Data Integrity Assurance Using Matrix Dialing Method towards High Performance Data Security on Cloud Storage

P. Premkumar[1], **D. Shanthi**[2]

[1]Department of Computer Science and Engineering, K.L.N. College of Engineering, Pottapalayam, India

[2]Department of Computer Science and Engineering, PSNA College of Engineering & Technology, Dindigul, India

ABSTRACT

Data outsourcing through cloud storage enables the users to share on-demand resources with cost effective IT services but several security issues arise like confidentiality, integrity and authentication. Each of them plays an important role in the successful achievement of the other. In cloud

Citation: Premkumar, P. and Shanthi, D. (2016), "Block Level Data Integrity Assurance Using Matrix Dialing Method towards High Performance Data Security on Cloud Storage". *Circuits and Systems*, 7, 3626-3644. doi: 10.4236/cs.2016.711307.

computing data integrity assurance is one of the major challenges because the user has no control over the security mechanism to protect the data. Data integrity insures that data received are the same as data stored. It is a result of data security but data integrity refers to validity and accuracy of data rather than protect the data. Data security refers to protection of data against unauthorized access, modification or corruption and it is necessary to ensure data integrity. This paper proposed a new approach using Matrix Dialing Method in block level to enhance the performance of both data integrity and data security without using Third Party Auditor (TPA). In this approach, the data are partitioned into number of blocks and each block converted into a square matrix. Determinant factor of each matrix is generated dynamically to ensure data integrity. This model also implements a combination of AES algorithm and SHA-1 algorithm for digital signature generation. Data coloring on digital signature is applied to ensure data security with better performance. The performance analysis using cloud simulator shows that the proposed scheme is highly efficient and secure as it overcomes the limitations of previous approaches of data security using encryption and decryption algorithms and data integrity assurance using TPA due to server computation time and accuracy.

Keywords: Cloud Computing, Data Integrity, Data Security, SHA-1, Digital Signature, AES, Encryption and Decryption

INTRODUCTION

Cloud computing is a modern computing paradigm in which scalable resources are shared dynamically as various services over the internet [1] . Cloud storage services enable the user to enjoy with high capacity and quality storage with less overhead but it has many potential threats like data integrity, data availability, data privacy and so on. The two issues mainly occur while outsourcing the data using cloud storage is data integrity and data security due to unfaithful cloud service provider [2] . Data integrity is the form of protection of data against loss and damage caused by hardware, software and network failure [3] [4] . Normally data inaccuracy can occur either accidently through programming errors or maliciously through breaches or hacks. It is one of the important aspects among the other cloud storage issues because data integrity ensured that data are of quality, correctness, consistency, accuracy, security, confidentiality, reliability, and accessibility but assurance of data integrity in the cloud is a major challenge that is faced by today's cloud users [5] . It refers to assurance by the user that the data are not modified or corrupted by the service provider or other users. The performance of data integrity is measured by using the parameters like computation time, encryption time and decryption time, memory utilization and output size. While outsourcing their data using cloud storage does not maintain a local copy. Hence, cryptographic measures cannot be used directly to monitor the integrity of data and also downloading the data for monitoring integrity is not a viable solution. Therefore, an external Third Party Auditor (TPA) is required [6] . The TPA is an independent authority that has capabilities to monitor the integrity of outsourced data by the client and also inform on data corruption or loss, if any. But it requires separate memory and also takes more time for verification of data to ensure integrity of data; hence the overall performance is degraded. Nowadays, software professionals employ number of practices to ensure data integrity which includes data encryption, data backup, access controls, input validation, data checking, error detection and correction while transmitting and storing the data. The performance of data violation checking methods is affected due to communication overhead, memory overhead, key size, encryption time, decryption time, and computation time. The scope of the data integrity assurance mechanism can be classified into two levels: first is to prevent data corruption and second is to detect and correct data violation. This paper only focuses on detection of data violation. The algorithms and methods to ensure data integrity are discussed in [7] . In paper [8] , certain degree of integrity assurance is provided by RAID technique but it operates only on binary data, takes more computation time and also the value of determinant factor is three bits long and hence needs large memory for storage. In paper [9] , to evaluate the performance of the encryption algorithm for text files, it uses AES, DES [10] [11] and RSA algorithm and the parameters such as computation time, memory usage, and output bytes are considered. The time taken to convert the plain text into cipher text is known as encryption time. The decryption time is the time that a decryption algorithm takes to reproduce a plaintext from a cipher text. Comparing these three algorithms, RSA takes more time for computation [12] . The memory usage of each algorithm is byte level. RSA requires more memory than AES and DES. In paper [13] , various algorithms such as AES, 3DES, Blowfish and DES are discussed. Throughput is equal to total encrypted plaintext in bytes divided by the encryption time. Higher the throughput, higher will be the performance [14] . Asymmetric encryption techniques are slower than symmetric techniques, because they require more computational processing power. Also, Blowfish algorithm gives better performance than all other algorithms in terms of throughput [15] [16] . In paper [17] and paper [18] , the performance evaluation of AES and Blowfish algorithms is discussed [19] . The parameters such as time consumption of packet size for 64 bit encodings and hexadecimal encodings, performance for encryption of text files and the throughput are considered. The result shows that Blowfish has better performance than AES in almost all the test cases. The paper is organized as follows: Section 1 describes introduction and related work. The proposed methodology is discussed in Section 2. Section 3 describes comparison of results and analysis. Section 4 concludes the paper.

PROPOSED METHODOLOGY

The proposed technique is based on the Determinant Factor (DF) approach to enhance both data integrity and security which involves the following steps:

Before transmitting the series of data, it is divided into N-matrices, where N is given by:

$$N = \frac{\text{total number of data}}{(d * d)}$$

where (d × d) is the number of elements per matrix. The determinant factor of each matrix is computed and appended with the data. At retrieving stage, it is compared with the determinant factor of the sender's data for data integrity assurance. But it is observed that there is one defect with this method. The DF is zero if any one of the rows is proportional to another row; the same is true for columns. Also, the DF does not change if some of the rows or some of the columns are interchanged. In addition, the DF is zero if any single row or column has zero values only. In order to alleviate this problem, a new technique is performed as given below: For each element of the matrix is reconstructed using matrix dialing method to formalize the original data matrix into a new matrix [20] . The determinants of both original and Dialing rotational matrices computed and appended with each matrix. For example, DF value for the following matrix is zero. After applying this new technique, DF value of the resultant matrix is not zero.

$$\begin{pmatrix} e1 & e2 & e3 \\ e4 & e5 & e6 \\ e7 & e8 & e9 \end{pmatrix} = \begin{pmatrix} e4 & e1 & e2 \\ e7 & e5 & e3 \\ e8 & e9 & e6 \end{pmatrix}$$

Then encrypted digital signature for each determinant factor is generated using the combination of SHA-1 and AES algorithms. Finally, data coloring is applied on each digital signature before transmission or storing the data on cloud to enhance data security. At the receiver side, both determinants are recomputed again and also degenerate the Message Digest then compared with the sender's values. If there is a match, it ensures that there is no modification in the given data during the transmission otherwise particular block of data is to be violated. The results of the proposed system shows that block based matrix dialing method outperforms than other data integrity checking methods and also provides data privacy for securing the data from unauthorized users. Figure 1 shows the architecture of the proposed system.

Steps involved in Block based determinant approach is given below:

Sender's End

1) Data is taken as a string format. Each string is converted as bytes and the number of bytes that constitute a block is decided. Next bytes will be added and divided into number of blocks.
2) Convert each block of data into square matrix.
3) Find Determinant Factor (DF) for each matrix.
4) Construct a new matrix using Block Based Matrix Dialing Rotational method to ensure DF is not Zero.
5) Find DF for the matrix constructed in Step 4.
6) Generate Hash value is known as Message Digest using SHA-1for each DF calculated in Step 5.
7) Encrypt this Hash value using AES algorithm to generate Digital Signature.
8) Apply data coloring on each digital signature generated in the Step 7.

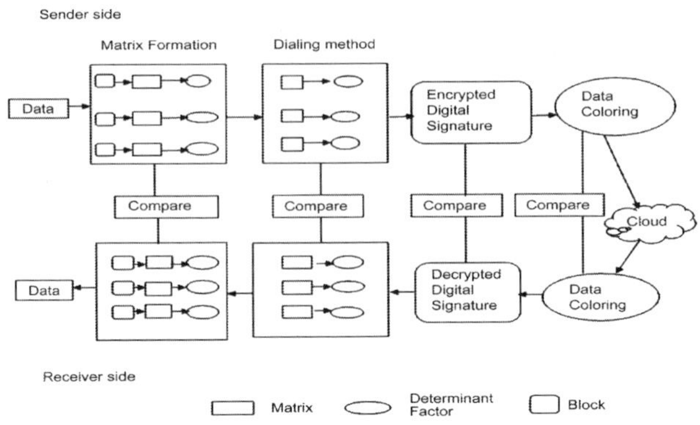

Figure 1. Architecture of the proposed system.

9) Store the colored data into cloud storage.

Receiver's End

1) Regenerate the colors from the colored data.
2) Decrypt the Message Digest.
3) Reconstruct the new matrix.
4) Calculate DF for the matrix constructed in Step 3.
5) Reconstruct the new matrix and calculate DF.
6) Compare the results obtained in steps 1, 2, 4, 5 respectively of Receiver's End with 8, 6, 5 and 3 of Sender's End.
7) If the results are same in all the steps mentioned in Step 6, then this ensures data integrity otherwise integrity of data is not attained i.e., a particular block of data has been violated i.e. modified the given data by unauthorized users.

Steps 6, 7 of sender side and also Step 2 of receiver side is explained in detailed as given below:

Signed and Encryption

1) Sender sends a message as DF
2) Calculate Digest

Digest = $[\text{Message}]_{hash}$.

3) Sign the Digest

Message + $[\text{Digest}]k_{pri} + k_{pub}$.

4) Encrypt with Symmetric key

[Message + [Digest]k_{pri} + k_{pub} + k_{sym}.

5) Send signed and encrypted message to Recipient.

Here Steps 1), 2) and 3) are for Signature generation and Step 4) for encryption (AES algorithm).

Decrypt and Verifying message

1) [Message + [Digest]k_{pri} + $k_{pub]}$ + [k_{sym}].
2) Decrypt K_{sym} with receivers private key [Message + [Digest]k_{pri} + $k_{pub]}$ + k_{sym}.
3) Decrypt Digest using Public key and also evaluate the Digest

Digest = $[Message]_{Hash}$.

4) Compare these two Digests.

If two digests viz., actual and expected digests are equal then the signature is verified. Here Steps 1, 2 and 3 are for Decryption and Step 4 for Verification.

The following steps are involved to generate encrypted digital signature; it described by Figure 2.

Step 1. The document will be crunched into fixed few lines by using SHA-1 algorithm to generate Message digest.

Step 2. At Sender side encrypt the message digest using its public key to generate digital signature.

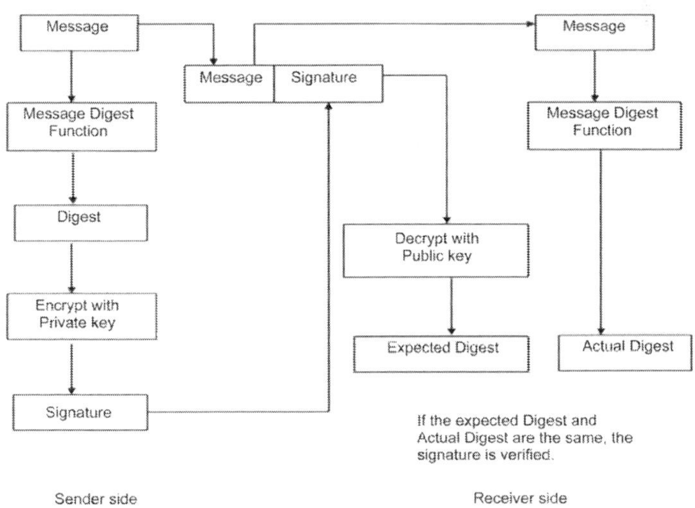

Figure 2. Block diagram for generation of digital signature.

Step 3. At Receiver side decrypt the message using their own private key.

Step 4. Regenerate the Message Digest.

Step 5. Finally the Signature is verified using Sender's public key.

Message digest function also called as hash function used to generate digital signature of the data which is known as message digest. SHA-1 algorithm is used to implement integrity of the message which produce message digest of size 128 bits. These are mathematical functions that process information to produce different message digest for each unique message. It processes the message and generates 128 bits message digest. The AES algorithm consists of the following steps and also it described by Figure 3.

Step 1: Add Padding to the end of the genuine message length is 64 bits and multiple of 512.

Step 2: Appending length. In this step the excluding length is calculated.

Step 3: Divide the input into 512-bit blocks. In this step the input is divided into 512 bit blocks.

Step 4: Initialize chaining variables. In this step chaining variables are initialized. In the proposed method 5 chaining variables are initialized each of size 32 bits giving a total of 160 bits.

Step 5: Process Blocksie., Copy the chaining variables, Divide the 512 into 16 sub blocks, Process 4 rounds of 20 steps each.

Step 6: Output Generation.

Further this algorithm is divided into 5 steps: Key Generation, Digital Signing, Encryption, Decryption and Signature Verification are discussed as below:

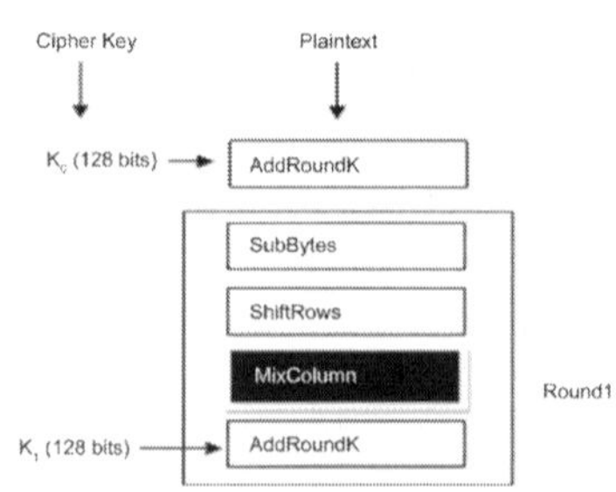

Figure 3. Block diagram for AES algorithm process.

Step 1: Key Generation

Different combinations of key size such as 128, 192 or 256 bits are used. To perform the AES algorithm, round keys must be generated from the user provided key. The Key Schedule of this algorithm provides 33 128-bit keys to be mixed with the text blocks during the Round function of the algorithm. First create 8 32-bit pre keys using the key provided by the user. The user's key is split every 32 bits to do this and then generate 132 intermediate keys using the following reoccurrence: for i from 0 to 131. The 33 round keys are generated from these intermediate keys by running through the S-Boxes and combining them into 128-bit blocks.

Step 2: Digital Signing

Generate message digest of the document to be send by using SHA-1 algorithm.

The digest is represented as an integer m.

Digital signature S is generated using the private key (n, d).

S = md mod n.

Sender sends this signature S to the recipient.

Step 3: Encryption

Sender represents the plain text message as a positive integer m.

It converts the message into encrypted form using the receiver's public key (e, n).

C = me mod n

Sender sends this encrypted message to the recipient. Here, n is the modulus and e is the encryption exponent.

Step 4: Decryption

Recipient does the following operation:

Using his private key (n, d), it converts the cipher text to plain text "m".

M = Cd mod n

where d is the secret exponent or decryption exponent.

Step 5: Signature Verification

Receiver does the followings to verify the signature:

An integer V is generated using the sender's public key (n, e) and signature S.

V = Se mod n

It extracts the message digest M1, from the integer V using the same SHA-1 algorithm. It computes the message digest M2 from the signature S. If both the message digests are identical i.e. M1 = M2, then signature is valid.

The block diagram for generating color coding is shown in Figure 4.

Each user is specified by a color that helps to protect and also avoids the manipulation of original data. Figure 4 shows the details involved in the data coloring process, which aims to associate a colored data with its own, whose user identification is also colored with the same expected value (Ex), entropy (En) and hyperentropy (He) identification characteristics. The cloud drops are added into the input and remove color to restore the original. The process uses three data characteristics to generate the color: the expected value (Ex) depends on the data content known only to the data owner. Whereas entropy (En) and hyperentropy (He) add randomness or uncertainty which are independent of the data content and these three functions generate a collection of cloud drops to form a unique color that the providers or other cloud users cannot detect. This technique can also be applied to protect documents and images in the cloud. In cloud model, the overall property of colored drops can be represented by three numerical characters. On one hand, construct forward cloud generator to produce a lot of drops as illustrated in Algorithm 1. On the other hand, construct reverse cloud generator

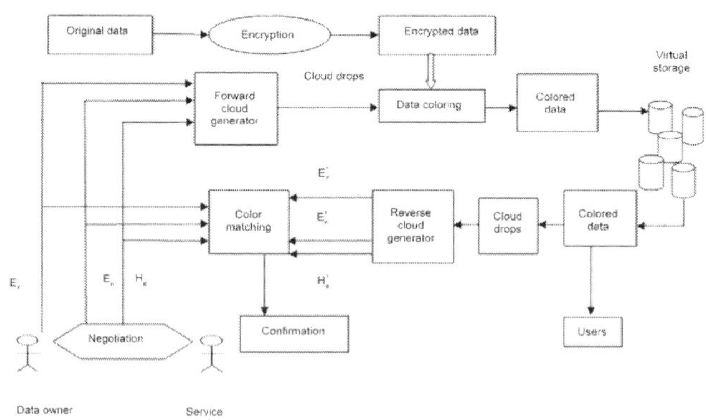

Figure 4. Block diagram for color coding generation.

to cope with the colored drops and revert Ex, En, and He, as illustrated in Algorithm 2.

Algorithm 1: Forward cloud generator

Step 1: Generate a normally distributed random number

$$En_i' = NORM\left(En, He^2\right).$$

Step 2: Generate a normally distributed random number $x_i = NORM\left(Ex, En_i'^2\right)$.

Step 3: $\mu_i = \exp\left[-\frac{(x_i - Ex)^2}{2(En_i')^2}\right]$.

Step 4: x_i with certainty degree of μ_i is a cloud drop in the domain.

Step 5: Repeat Steps 1 to 4, and generate drops.

Algorithm 2: Reverse cloud generator

Step 1: Calculate mean $\overline{X} = \frac{1}{n}\sum_{i=1}^{n} x_i$ and variance $S^2 = \frac{1}{n-1}\sum_{i=1}^{n}\left(x_i - \overline{X}\right)^2$.

Step 2: $Ex' = \overline{X}$.

Step 3: $En' = \sqrt{\frac{\pi}{2}} \times \frac{1}{n}\sum_{i=1}^{n}\left|x_i - Ex\right|$.

Step 4: $He' = \sqrt{S^2 - En'^2}$.

Ex is provided by data owner; En and He are produced by negotiation of data owner and service provider. Each cloud user is provided with a value called expected value which is known only to the user. The negotiated values with the CSPs are Entropy which is unique for all users in the particular group sharing the data in the cloud. Hyperentropy is the value which is common to all the group users of the data. Then, a lot of cloud drops will be formed by forward cloud generator (see Algorithm 1) and are used to color the user data. When the data are used, the cloud drops are extracted from colored data Ex0, En0, and He0 will be produced by reverse cloud generator (see Algorithm 2). Final color matching which indicates data is not modified by others. Data owner and storage service provider negotiate together to select En and He, just like the key. Ex, En, and He are three mathematical characters. En and He can be used to transform a certain print to uncertain print drops. Figure 4 shows different paint drops according to different En. Also compute the entropy of each cloud drop (En0) and compare the difference between En and En0. To provide the continuous authentication within the group, an automated validation of data can be made at regular intervals of time. The experiment result is illustrated in the concerned tables, and the curve of case is shown in concerned Figures. The performance of the proposed system is evaluated based on the parameters viz., Execution Time, Encryption Time and Decryption Time, Memory utilization, Key size and Digital signature creation time regards with different data size. The performance results have been summarized in various tables regarding with various parameters and also conclusion has been presented. Based on the experimental results, it concluded that AES is the best performing algorithm among the various algorithms chosen for implementation with respect to encryption time and decryption time. Figure 5 describes Encryption time for various block size of data given in Table 1. It can be seen that as the block size increases the encryption time also increases gradually.

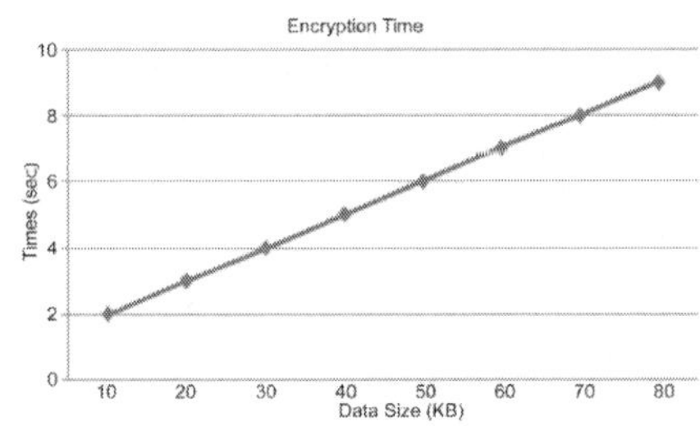

Figure 5. Encryption time.

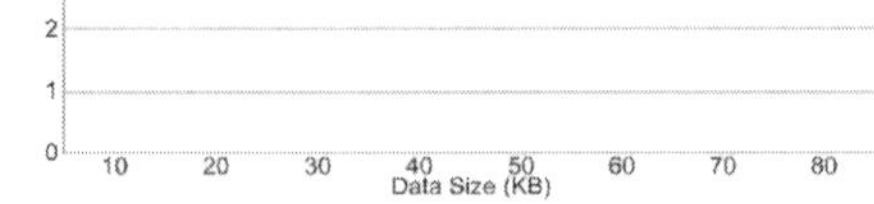

Figure 6. Decryption time.

Table 1. Encryption time.

Data size (KB)	Time (Sec)
10	2
25	3
30	4
40	5

50	6
60	7
70	8
80	9

Figure 6 describes Decryption time for various block size of data given in the Table 2. It can be seen from the figure that decryption time is linearly proportional to the block size. Figure 7 describes time taken for digital signature generation regards with various block size of data given in Table 3. It can be seen from the figure that the digital signature generation time is linearly proportional to the block size. Figure 8 describes time taken for executing various block size of data given in Table 4. It can be seen from the figure that the Average Finishing time is constant proportional to the block size. Figure 9 describes Resource Utilization in terms of CPU and Memory for various Data Sizes as mentioned in Table 5. Figure 10 describes Accuracy checking in terms of number of defects detected for various Data Sizes as mentioned in Table 6. Figure 11 describes Throughput in terms of Encrypted data and Time as mentioned in Table 7. Figures 12-15 gives the comparison between Two fish, Serpent algorithm with AES algorithm in terms of Encryption time and Decryption time and Execution Time, output size for each block of data given in Tables 8-11 respectively. Based on the results AES algorithm provides better performance in terms of encryption time and decryption time and execution time.

Table 2. Decryption time.

Data size (KB)	Time (Sec)
10	3
20	4
30	4.5
40	5
50	5.5
60	6
70	6.5
80	7

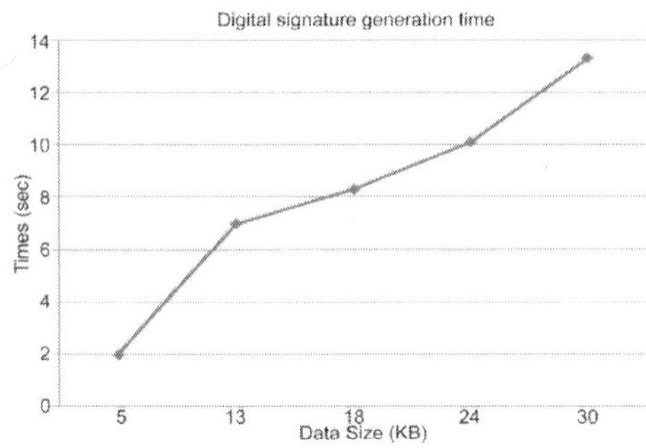

Figure 7. Generation of digital signature.

Table 3. Digital signature creation time.

Data size (KB)	Time (Sec)
5	2
13	7
18	8.3
24	10.1
30	13.3

Table 4. Execution time.

Data size (KB)	Start time (Sec)	Finish time (Sec)	Execution time (Sec) = (finish time − start time)
5	5	7	2
10	5	7	2
15	10	13	3
20	15	18	3
25	20	23	3
30	20	23	3
35	24	27	3
40	25	28	3
45	30	33	3
50	30	34	4

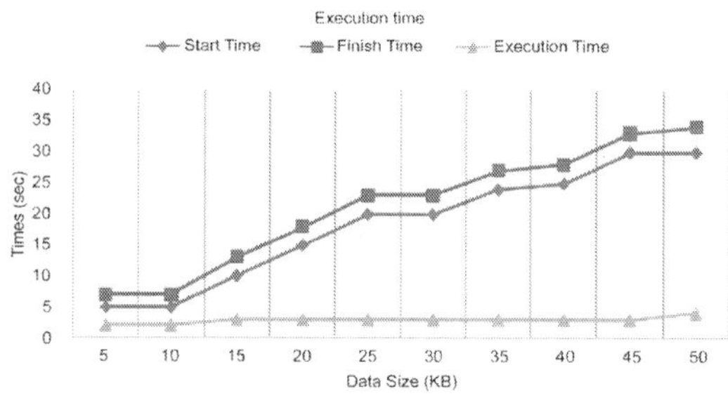

Figure 8. Execution time.

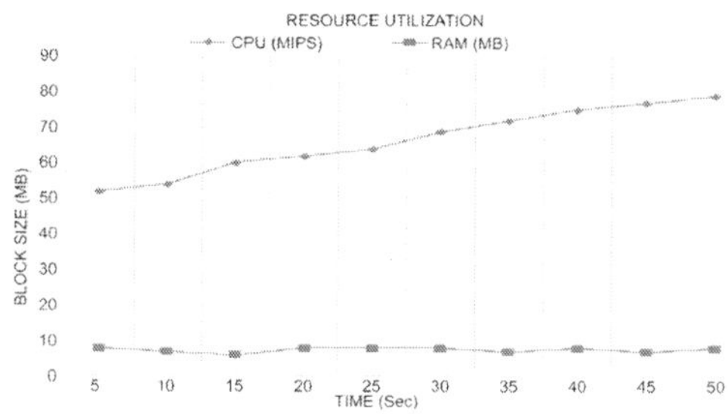

Figure 9. Memory utilization.

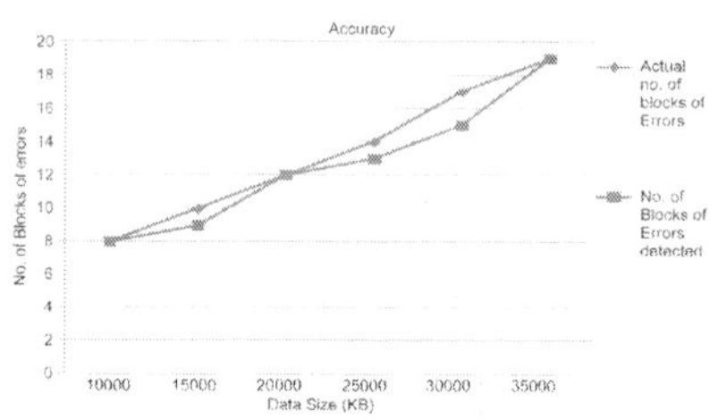

Figure 10. Detection of errors with various block size.

Table 5. Memory utilization.

Data size (MB)	Time (Sec)	CPU (MIPS)	RAM (MB)
10	5	52	8
20	10	54	7
30	15	60	6
40	20	62	8
50	25	64	8
60	30	69	8
70	35	72	7

80	40	75	8
90	45	77	7
100	50	79	8

Table 6. Accuracy checking.

Data size (bytes)	Actual No. of blocks of errors	No. of blocks of errors detected by the proposed method	Accuracy of proposed method (%)
10000	08	08	100
15000	10	09	99.91
20000	12	12	100
22000	14	13	99.91
30000	17	15	99.66
33000	19	19	100

Table 7. Throughput.

Data size (KB)	Time (Sec)	Encrypted size (KB)	Throughput
10	2	7.5	3.75
20	3	15	5
30	4	22.5	5.62
40	5	30	6
50	6	37.5	6.25
60	7	45	6.42
70	8	52.5	6.56
80	9	60	6.66

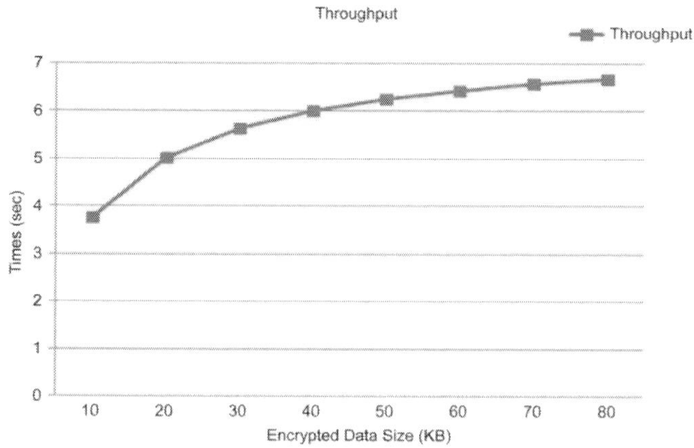

Figure 11. Encrypted data size vs time.

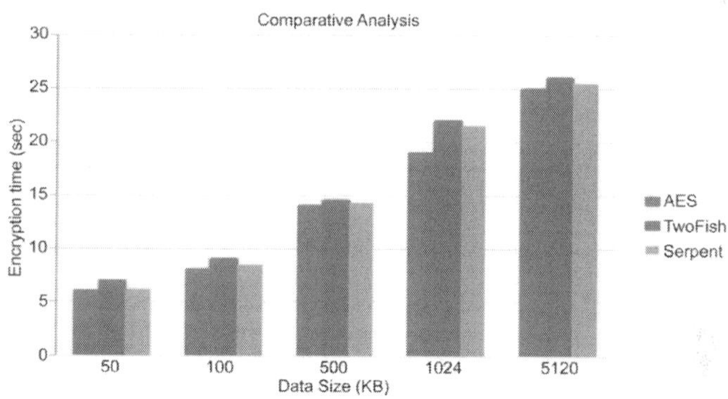

Figure 12. Encryption time.

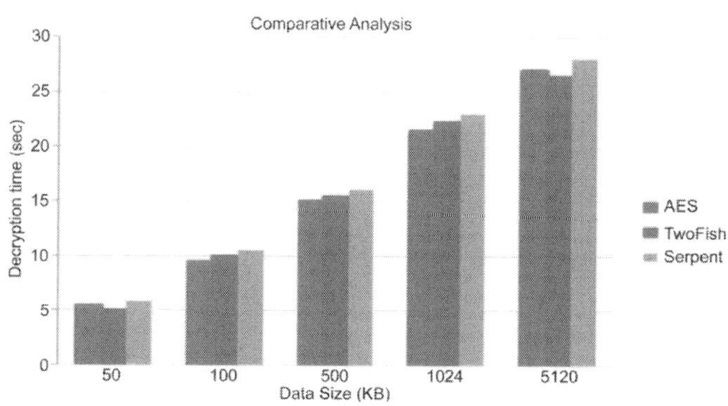

Figure 13. Decryption time.

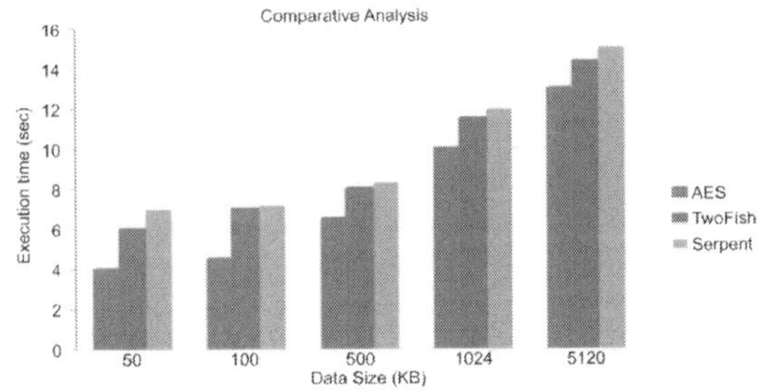

Figure 14. Execution time.

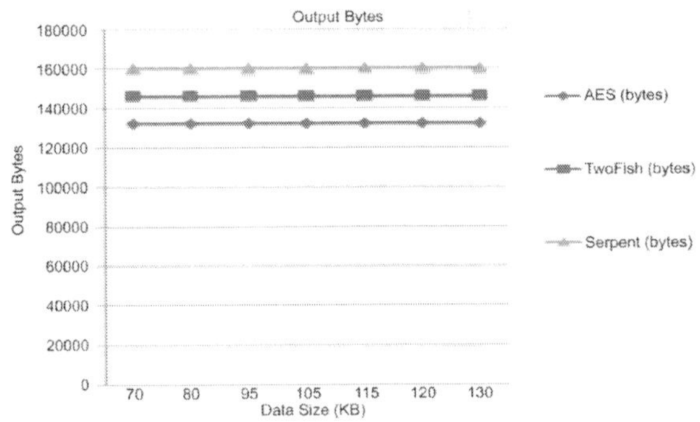

Figure 15. Output size.

Table 8. Encryption time.

Data size (KB)	AES (Sec)	Two Fish (Sec)	Serpent (Sec)
50	5.5	5	5.9
100	9.5	10	10.5
500	15	15.4	16
1024	21.5	22.3	23
5120	27	26.5	28

Table 9. Decryption time.

Data size (KB)	AES (Sec)	Two Fish (Sec)	Serpent (Sec)
50	6	7	6.2
100	8	9	8.5

500	14	14.5	14.3
1024	19	22	21.5
5120	25	26	25.5

Table 10. Execution time.

Data size (KB)	AES (Sec)	Two Fish (Sec)	Serpent (Sec)
50	4	6	7
100	4.5	7	7.2
500	6.5	8	8.3
1024	10	11.5	11.9
5120	13	14.3	15

Table 11. Ouput size.

Data size (KB)	AES (output bytes)	Two Fish (output bytes)	Serpent (output bytes)
70	132,082	146,022	160,030
80	132,082	146,022	160,030
95	132,082	146,022	160,030
105	132,082	146,022	160,030
115	132,082	146,022	160,030
120	132,082	146,022	160,030
130	132,082	146,022	160,030

The two main characteristics of a good encryption algorithm are: Security and Speed. In this paper, analyze security V/s performance of three algorithms Two Fish, Serpent and AES based on the experimental results using cloud simulator.

COMPARISON OF RESULTS AND ANALYSIS

The performance are evaluated based on the parameters viz., Execution Time, Incryp- tion Time, Decryption Time and Output Bytes. The encryption time is also used to calculate the throughput of an encryption scheme, calculated as the total plaintext in byes encrypted divided by the encryption time.

Comparison, analysis of the results of various algorithms are performed. The Experimental result for Encryption, Decryption and Execution algorithm AES, Two fish and Serpent are shown in Tables 8-10 which shows the comparison of three algorithm AES, Two fish and Serpent using same text file for five experiment, output byte for AES, Two fish and Serpent is same for different sizes of files. By analyzing Table 11, noticed the AES has very smaller output byte compare to Two fish and Serpent algorithm. Time taken for encryption, decryption and execution by Two fish and Serpent algorithm is much higher compare to the time taken by AES algorithm. By analyzing Figures 12-14, one which shows time Taken for encryption on various size of text file by three algorithms i:e AES, Two fish and Serpent, noticed that Serpent algorithm takes much longer time compare to time taken by AES and Two fish algorithm.AES algorithm consumes least time for encryption. Two fish and Serpent algorithm shows very minor difference in time taken for encryption and decryption. Figure 15 shows the size of output byte for each algorithm used in experiment. The result shows same size of output byte for different size of text file in case of all three algorithms and noticed that Serpent algorithm output bytes are highest for all sizes of text file.

CONCLUSION

This paper presents a new technique for enhancing data security through improving data integrity violation checking over the cloud storage without using TPA. In the proposed technique, the data are divided into blocks, where each block is arranged into square matrix. An element in this matrix is arranged into a new form using Matrix Dialing method which leads to memory saving through bits reduction and also to enhance accuracy of data. Also digital signature is applied on each determinant factor to enhance data integrity assurance. This model also uses data coloring on encrypted digital signature to enhance the data security which helps the user to verify and examine the data from unauthorized people who manipulate the data in the cloud storage. In this method accuracy is maintained at satisfied level by rearranging the data two times via original matrix and its corresponding Dialing method Rotational matrix. Though it requires more computation time it provides good level of accuracy and security of data. Thus, here it tries to provide a new insight to improve the cloud storage security through detection of data integrity violations in block level during storing or transmission. Encryption algorithm plays an important role in data security where encryption time, memory usages and output byte are the major issue of concern. The selected encryption AES, Two Fish and Serpent algorithms are used for performance evaluation. Based on the text files used and the experimental result it was concluded that AES algorithm consumes least encryption time and least memory usage. Serpent algorithm consumes longest encryption time and memory usage is also very high but output byte is least. The simulation results show that the new method gives better results compared to the Two Fish and Serpent algorithms and has resolved all of their deficiencies that go along with data integrity assurance methods towards data security. The performance measures viz., better encryption/decryption time and also computation time, memory utilization, and quicker detection of violation are considered. In future work this proposed model can be implemented for conducting more experiments using various algorithms and methods in cloud computing on other types of data like image, sound and multimedia data and test the performance of the proposed approach. The focus will improve encryption time and less memory usage.

REFERENCES

1. Chavan, A. (2014) Cloud Computing. Asian Journal of Management Sciences, 2, 1-6.
2. Diffie, W. and Hellman, M.E. (1976) New Directions in Cryptography. IEEE Transactions on Information Theory, 22, 644-654. http://dx.doi.org/10.1109/TIT.1976.1055638
3. Kahate, A. (2008) Cryptography and Network Security. Tata McGraw-Hill Publishing Company, New Delhi.
4. Shantala, C.P. and Kumar, A. (2014) Integrity Check Mechanism in Cloud Using SHA-512 Algorithm. International Journal of Engineering and Computer Science, 3, 6033-6037.
5. Wang, C., Wang, Q. and Ren, K. (2009) Ensuring Data Storage Security in Cloud Computing. 17th International Workshop on Quality of Service (IWQoS), IEEE Conference Publication.
6. Govinda, K., Gurunathprasad, V. and Sathishkumar, H. (2012) Third Party Auditing for Secure Data Storage in Cloud through Digital Signature Using RSA. International Journal of Advanced Scientific and Technical Research, 4.
7. Bhagat, A. and Sahu, R.K. (2013) Cloud Data Security While Using Third Party Auditor. International Journal of Computer Applications, 70.
8. Ghaeb, J.A., Smadi, M.A. and Chebil, J. (2010) A High Performance Data Integrity Assurance Based on the Determinant Technique. Elsevier, April.
9. Zhang, T.N.T. (2009) A Study of DES and Blowfish Encryption Algorithm. Tencon IEEE Conference.
10. (2015) DES Algorithm. http://orlingrabbe.com/des.htm
11. Coppersmith, D. (1994) The Data Encryption Standard (DES) and Its Strength against Attacks. IBM Journal of Research and Development, 38, 243-250. http://dx.doi.org/10.1147/rd.383.0243
12. Seth, S.M. and Mishra, R. (2011) Comparitive Analysis of Encryption Algorithms for Data Communication. IJCST, 2, 292-294.
13. Stallings, W. (2006) Cryptography and Network Security. 4th Edition, Pearson Prentice Hall.
14. Singh, G., Singla, A.K. and Sandha, K.S. (2011) Throughput Analysis of Various Encryption Algorithms. IJCST, 2, 527-529.

15. (2012) Performance Analysis of AES and BLOWFISH Algorithms. National Conference on Computer Communication & Informatics, School of Computer Science, RVS College of Arts and Science, 7 March 2012.
16. Schneier, B. (1994) Description of a New Variable-Length Key, 64-Bit Block Cipher (Blowfish) Fast Software Encryption. Cambridge Security Workshop Proceedings, SpringerVerlag, December 1993, 191-204. http://dx.doi.org/10.1007/3-540-58108-1_24
17. (2015) Blowfish Algorithm. http://pocketbrief.net/related/BlowfishfEncryption.pdf
18. (2015) Blowfish Algorithm. http://www.schneier.com/blowfish.html
19. Schneier, B. (2008) The Blowfish Encryption Algorithm.
20. Camara, L., Li, J., Li, R. and Kagorora, F. (2014) Block-Based Scheme for Database Integrity Verification. International Journal of Security and Its Applications, 8, 25-40. http://dx.doi.org/10.14257/ijsia.2014.8.6.03.

CHAPTER

18

Current Status of the Use of Cloud Computing in SMEs in the City of Latacunga, Ecuador

Gabriela Cajamarca-Palomo[1], Mauricio Quisimalin-Santamaría[1], Patricio Medina-Chicaiza[2]

[1]Facultad de Ciencias Administrativas, Universidad Técnica de Ambato, Ambato, Ecuador.

[2]Facultad de Ciencias Administrativas, Universidad Técnica de Ambato, Pontificia Universidad Católica del Ecuador, Ambato, Ecuador.

ABSTRACT

This document is the result of a descriptive research on and analysis of hierarchical conglomerates. Its purpose is to investigate the current state of Cloud Computing (CC) use in small and medium enterprises (SMEs) in the

Citation: Cajamarca-Palomo, G. , Quisimalin-Santamaría, M. and Medina-Chicaiza, P. (2019), "Current Status of the Use of Cloud Computing in SMEs in the City of Latacunga, Ecuador". *Open Journal of Business and Management*, **7**, 633-649. doi: 10.4236/ojbm.2019.72043.

city of Latacunga, Ecuador. The construction of the instrument was based on the planning, application, analysis and validation of a questionnaire using Kuder Richarson 20 (KR20), which resulted in 0.81. The SPSS and Nvivo software were used with the participation of 43 SMEs from productive sectors, such as agriculture, manufacturing, commerce and service. The questionnaire was made up of 17 questions, grouped in two parts for the Department of Information Technology (IT) and administrative personnel. The results show that 65.1% know about CC, however, a low applicability is evident. A set of more relevant questions determines the decision making of the use of Cloud Computing in SMEs.

Keywords: Cloud Computing, Small Business, Security, Information Technology, Infrastructure as a Service, Platform as a Service, Software as a Service

INTRODUCTION

Small and medium enterprises (SMEs) have an important economic role in different countries. Some authors [1] [2] [3] mention that SMEs represent 79% of businesses worldwide, 95% in Latin America, and 99% in Ecuador. SMEs in Ecuador are established as the main source of direct and indirect work, and their participation in the development of the country is transcendental. According to data from the National Institute of Statistics and Census[1] (INEC), 8447 companies were registered in Ecuador, divided into 19 productive activities, of which 90.5% are SMEs. This information is compiled by the Board of Directors of Companies from records generated by the Internal Revenue Service[2] (SRI) and the Social Security Institute[3] (IEES) from a sectoral and territorial perspective. According to [4] , SMEs are defined by sales volume, social capital, number of employees, and their level of production; which are received in Ecuador and are regulated by the law of company and tax regime.

SMEs play an important role in the country's economy, because apart from contributing to the creation of jobs, they also promote the economic recovery of certain regions and foster technological progress. Their capacity depends fundamentally on the ability of the manager/owner to invest in intangible products, technological products and their capacity for flexible innovation.

Authors [5] [6] [7] agree that one of the most important technological developments of recent years is Cloud Computing. The potential benefits of these technologies include the benefits of an operational nature to implement the automation of routine procedures through a broad network that acts on demand through a group of virtualized resources and configured among themselves and the quick provisioning of information to any part of the world.

In this sense, other authors [8] [9] add that Cloud Computing works through the Internet, through a subscription for payment for service use. It manages three relevant models among its services, which are: IaaS (Infrastructure as a service), which is considered as the traditional hosting service in a data center, PaaS (Platform as a service), which includes Infrastructure as a service plus additional ones, and SaaS (Software as a service), where applications are given by a provider. In relation to the above, Cloud Computing offers different functionalities, ready to meet the business need, which can be used in administrative processes that the company has, such as accounting, billing, human talent, among others.

From this approach, according to authors [8] [10] [11] , the importance of the use of CC in public and private companies is shown, because the incessant technical innovation allows companies to have data storage, backup copies, access to information from different computers, among others. With this, decision making is carried out in a timely manner, when information is required unexpectedly. In this sense, according to [12] in its article entitled Incipient "Adoption of Cloud"[4], it is detailed that from 100% of Ecuadorian companies, only 17% make use of this service among large companies and SMEs, which is considerably below compared to neighboring countries such as Colombia, Peru and Chile, with 58%. It is assumed that a large part of SMEs are unaware of the benefits offered by the implementation of this service, as well as of cases of application in the Ecuadorian environment.

Likewise, the factors related to the use of Cloud Computing in Ecuador have been approached from different authors' perspectives [13] [14] [15] where methodologies and results of the use of ICT in the business area are generally evident. However no study provides information on its application, as well as the use of Cloud Computing in the productive sectors such as: agriculture, manufacturing, service and commerce in the study city, which allows businessmen to make decisions for the implementation of Cloud Computing. With the aforementioned background, the objective of this study is to present the current state of the use of Cloud Computing in SMEs in the city of Latacunga-Ecuador.

In addition to this, the contributions of this study are mainly based on the adaptability of the cloud computing service to the different requirements and needs of the companies; they also involve economic aspects, because they allow a reduction in their costs, when using this service. Therefore, managers or owners of companies have access to personalized information for each one, which can share it internally and access it from any connection point.

The article is organized as follows, as the first point is the definition of SMEs with an international context, showing their classification and their sectors in Ecuador, as well as the use of ICT and the current state of CC in the country. As a second point, the methodology applied for this research is detailed, as well as the instruments for data collection and validation. From this, the results are manifested and finally, the conclusions of the investigation.

THEORETICAL FRAMEWORK

Small and Medium Enterprises (SMEs)

The definition of SMEs arises at the end of the seventies as a result of the economic failure of 500 large companies in the United States [16] . In addition, SMEs are productive or service entities which are formally constituted and managed independently [13] [14] [15] [17] [18] . It is important to clarify that there are different definitions and classifications of SMEs according to each country [1] [19] [20] . To this, the proposal of [21] is assumed, who mention that SMEs are considered among other factors, according to the number of workers and the amount of income they produce.

Table 1. Criteria for the classification of SMEs.

Classification	Number of employees	Annual sales (USD)	Total assets (USD)
Micro	1 to 9	≤100,000	≤100,000
Small	10 to 49	100,001 to 1,000,000	100,001 to 750,000
Medium	50 to 99	1,000,001 to 5,000,000	750,001 to 4,000,000
Big	200 or more	More than 5,000,000	More to 4,000,000

***Source**: Andean Community of the United Nations [23] .*

In the same sense, Table 1 shows the classification by size of SMEs in accordance with the plan presented by the Andean Community of the United Nations (CAN[5]), adopted in this investigation. According to [22] , in Ecuador economic growth has been on the rise, thanks to the fact that SMEs contribute to the improvement of the quality of life of Ecuadorians through the generation of employment and family support, motivating governments to show interest in the implementation of policies that promote the creation and sustenance of these companies.

It is important to point out that in Ecuador, in addition, the file called the International Standard Industrial Classification (CIUU[6]), established by the United Nations, which catalogs the activities in a series of categories and subcategories, is used for the classification of SMEs in sectors.

Table 2 shows the sectors that operate in the country where the agricultural, cattle raising, forestry and fishing sectors reflect a percentage of 40%; followed by trade with 9% and public administration and defense with 7%, considering that they are also managed by their own policies. It is important to mention that this achievement is also due to the support of private financial entities such as banks, cooperatives, mutualists, financial companies and credit cards which, through satisfactory financing, promote the development of SMEs.

Table 2. Distribution of SMEs in Ecuador by sector.

Economic sectors	Number of SMEs
Agriculture, cattle raising, forestry and fishing	26,282
Mining and quarrying	4075
Manufacturing industries	2381
Electricity, gas, steam and air conditioning supply	1055
Water distribution; sewerage, waste and sanitation	672
Building	1730
Trade, automotive repair and motorcycles	5940
Transportation and storage	2010
Accommodation and meal service activities	3010
Information and communication	1342
Financial and insurance activities	277
Real estate activities	1304
Professional, scientific and technical activities	4596

Administrative and support services activities	334
Public administration and defense, social security	5729
Teaching	75
Activities for human health care and social assistance	117
Arts, training and recreation	3791

Source: *adapted from [24] , from INEC (2015).*

Information and Communication Technologies (ICT) in Companies in Ecuador

The use of technologies in companies brings competitive strategies to national and international levels, along with the economic growth and profitability of the country. This, in turn, induces interest to build new explanatory theories from a perspective of competitive advantage in terms of the extent of use of ICT in the key activities of the company at the time of storage, processing and acquisition of information [25] [26] [27] . Therefore, the need to integrate ICT to the business model is prevailing for competition on equal terms.

Given this situation, [28] MINTEL[7], indicates that a project has been implemented in Ecuador to train micro enterprises in basic uses of business ICT through a National Infocenter Network[8] with the objective of increasing the use of specific ICTs in SMEs according to their sector, industry and economic activity. This project is framed in Guideline 11.3 of the National Plan for Good Living[9] 2013-2017 approved by the National Planning Council[10] [29] in order to strengthen ICT use capabilities in SMEs. This is why such an impulse is offered in the country for the use of this technology.

Regarding technological investment for universities, on the one hand, it is an instantaneous moment to adopt the SMEs of the 11%, while large companies evidence a decrease in investment. This variance could be due to the fact that SMEs participate actively and even dominantly in the country (Figure 1).

Figure 2 shows that the manufacturing sector has the greatest investment in ICT use, reaching 48.8%. Also, commerce has had a considerable growth along with services; mining presents very low values, which makes their little investment in ICT evident. These results reflect that investment in ICT varies in relation to the activity to which SMEs are dedicated. It should be noted that the research study does not show whether the investment was in hardware or software.

Regarding the use of provincial ICT according to INEC data, the provinces that are most linked to the use of technology are Galapagos with 68.4% and the province under study, Cotopaxi, where its use reaches 50.4%, thus showing that growth and adaptation to this resource is rapid, with a slight difference of 18%.

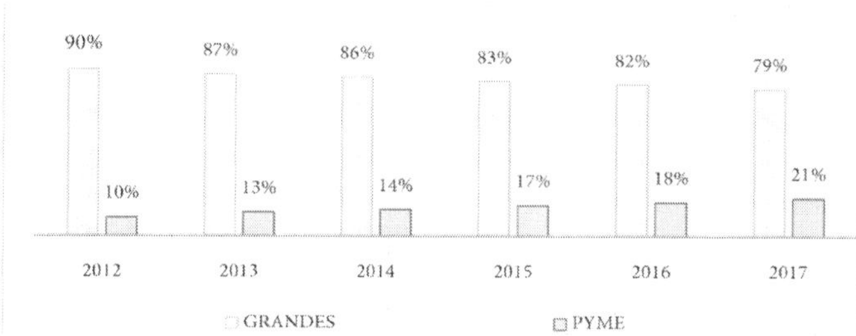

Figure 1. Investment in ICT according to the size of the company.

Source: *adapted from [28]* .

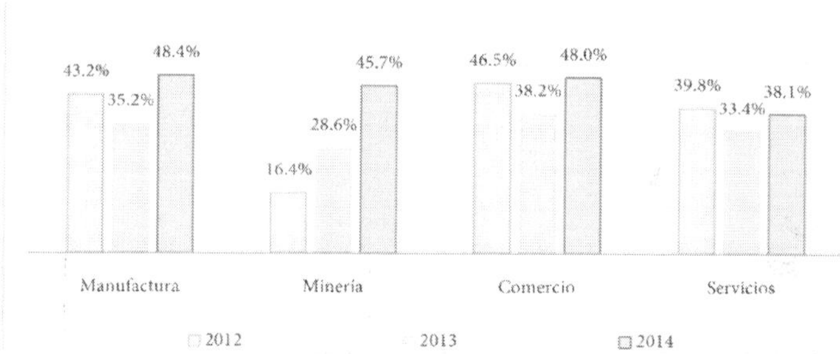

Figure 2. Investment in ICT by sector USD.

Source: *adapted from [30]* .

Cloud Computing

Some authors [31] [32] [33] indicate that Cloud Computing has been contextualized in different ways. They also establish that the most common definition is adopted by the National Institute of Standards and Technology (NIST[11]), which refers to Cloud Computing as computer groups, features and models. References [34] [35] [36] state that Cloud Computing integrates the stability, scalability and delivery of a service. In addition, [37] [38] point out that it is a business application on a website, through which organizations today have opted to manage their information. Therefore, Cloud Computing allows users to access data resources from any geographical location through the Internet.

Cloud Computing offers three main models [39]: Software as a Service (SaaS), where customers can access applications that are hosted by the service provider [40] ; platform as a service (PaaS), which is more oriented towards software developers in working groups for programmers [41] ; and infrastructure as a service (IaaS), where users make use of virtual servers with characteristics that they choose [42] . In this sense, it should be noted that each of them, although belonging to the same service, manages its own benefits and costs.

The general idea of Cloud Computing lies in its online expansion to share, process and synchronize data from a perspective of advantages in terms of installation, configuration, updating, maintenance, costs and others. However, [43] [44] [45] describe that, despite the advantages in the use of CC, its adoption is not so fast and widespread due to difficulties such as: security and privacy, interception or manipulation of data by third parties, loss of information, direct dependence on a provider, connectivity to the network, among others. This is why it is necessary to give information about CC use so as not to generalize fortuitous cases of management.

While the advantages and disadvantages of the use of CC differ, the notion of service brings significant impacts to the economy because of the rapid development and the changing and competitive environments in which companies operate [46] [47] . Therefore, it is necessary to have a fast coupling and adjustment to the commercial models that come up. In addition, the authors [48] [49] [50] state that the level of maturity varies based on the model presented, such is the case of SaaS, which is in the stage of growth, while models such as IaaS and PaaS are at a level of initial maturity in terms of use in SMEs.

Reference [51] indicate that companies must be aware of the digital transformation to which they are exposed and also be prepared to adapt to it. It is evident then that Ecuador cannot be the exception, that is why [52] publishes the White Paper on Digital Territories in Ecuador[12], where information about the adoption of cloud computing technologies is revealed. In this document, the information coincides with the magazine Computer World in terms used to refer to the adoption of Cloud Computing in Ecuador as incipient, since 42% of SMEs surveyed, only 25% use Cloud Computing and 22% do not. This is due to the fact that the organizations express their perception of security risk, but that in turn the reduction of infrastructure costs is their main motivation for the acquisition of this service.

In addition, Ecuador highlights the need to implement five axes to strengthen the Information and Knowledge Society, which highlights the importance of one of its axes linked to the digital economy and emerging technologies in order to improve the productivity and competitiveness of the productive sectors of the country and the analytical services of handling large volumes of data, such as Cloud Computing. This highlights the importance of having studies on these elements.

METHODOLOGY

In this study, regulatory sites of the Ecuadorian business regulations and documents in Spanish and English were reviewed from online journals of Scopus, Science Direct, Web of Science and ProQuest published in the last 10 years, the studies were identified with key words, among which stand out: IT in the company, cloud computing, cloud computing services and Cloud Computing in SMEs, where 498 results were found in relation to the subject. The criteria of selectivity was based on: advantages and disadvantages of Cloud Computing, ICT applications in Ecuador and Cloud Computing use survey models, which contributed to the study topic.

Similarly, the recommendations for the construction of the theoretical, statistical and explanatory framework of the object of study were accepted [53] [54] . The investigation started from the analysis of empirical studies in a systematic way of the selected sources [6] [55] [56] .

For the qualitative study, an exploratory analysis was carried out using hierarchical conglomerates, which according to [57] [58] [59] consists of determining the dimensions established in groups, which allowed to identify how these variables influence the use of Cloud Computing of SMEs in the city of Latacunga-Ecuador, through intergroup links and chi-square measurement counts. In addition to better understanding, a dendrogram is established that clearly reflects the groups conformed by the nominal variables established in the questionnaire questions.

On the other hand, the exploration was carried out through a questionnaire, divided into two parts. The participation profiles to answer the items in the first part were addressed to staff with administrative positions and access to a computer, without requirement of deep knowledge of Cloud Computing. In the second instance, the survey was explicitly directed to the IT department. Likewise, the technique of the personal pilot interview was used with a questionnaire of five questions that lasted an average of 15 minutes per person. This served as input for the design of a questionnaire of 17 questions and application of the questionnaire.

The information was collected through Google Drive, with an online survey sent by email to the companies under study, in which information relevant to this research was collected. The questions were of dichotomous type that allowed to obtain precise information, in order to justify the answers, through a statistical analysis, Kuder Richarson20 (KR20) was used, for the validation of the instrument.

Formula:

$$KR20 = \left(\frac{n}{n-1}\right)\left(\frac{Vt - \sum pq}{Vt}\right)$$

where:

KR20 = Reliability Coefficient (Kuder Richarson)

n = number of items that the instrument contains

Vt = Total variance of the test

p = positive probability

q = Negative probability (1 − p)

After applying the formula a level of reliability according to data was obtained:

KR20 = 0.81

The population under study of this research are the SMEs of the agricultural (A), manufacturing (C), commerce (G) and services (N) sectors of the city of Latacunga, since they are companies of greater number within the province, that use or are benefited by the Cloud Computing technology service in its different strategies.

The report was initially developed with a population of 76 SMEs, however, only 43 SMEs from the city under study were involved, due to the fact that not all SMEs were still active, some maintain certain data disclosure restriction policies, among other reasons. These SMEs contained a range of existence in the market, going from 5 years to 21 years.

RESULTS

The NVivo software was applied for the findings, which allowed analyzing qualitative data in relation to most used clouds in SMEs. As for the qualitative analysis, data was processed in the SPSS software (Statistical Package for the Social Sciences), for the obtaining of descriptive results and the realization of hierarchical conglomerates.

Main results

Table 3 shows the sectors of the SMEs under study versus the range of years to which they belong expressed in percentages.

As shown in the table above, most of the companies corresponding to 32.6% are in a range of between 6 and 10 years in the market, most of them dedicated to commercial activities. It is also observed that 27.9% are have 5 years and that most of them carry out agricultural activities.

The main Internet uses of the 43 companies surveyed show that: a) 81.4% use the Internet for activities such as social networks; while b) 65.1% use it for communication through e-mail, since the respondents stated that it is an effective means of communication inside and outside the company, in addition to being an economic and ecological mean, which saves resources; and c) 44% respond to the payment of basic services.

In addition, in terms of the departments that make the most use of computer programs for the execution of their tasks there are management, accounting, information technologies and human talent, which have more access to the tool for the execution of their tasks with 97.7%, 81.4%, 65.1% and 53.5% respectively. Departments such as purchasing, marketing, finance, risk management and others, do not operate through this resource. In relation to security, the results show that 69.8% claim to use user ID and password to access their computer; 65.1% say they make backup copies of their digital documents in flash memory and compact discs; and 51.2% of SMEs maintain security policies; while an average of 38.1% affirm that they do not use any of these three means of security. These results reflect the use of ICT within SMEs; but not the benefits of including Cloud Computing.

With respect to ICT staff training, 23.3% state that they receive training at least twice a year, however, a high percentage, 76.7%, indicate that they have no training in this regard, which is obvious lack of foray into specific issues such as services and use of Cloud Computing. On the other hand,

60.5% of the companies said they had personnel exclusively in charge of computer systems management; however, results show that 39.5% do not have exclusive personnel for said department.

Table 3. Sector versus years of existence in the SME market.

Year range in which the company is found	Agriculture, cattle raising and fishing	Manufacturing	Commerce	Services	Total
Up to 5 (years)	9.3%	7.0%	7.0%	4.7%	27.9%
Between 6 and 10 (years)	9.3%	7.0%	16.3%	0,0%	32.6%
Between 11 and 15 (years)	2.3%	0,0%	14.0%	0,0%	16.3%
Between 16 and 20 (years)	0,0%	2.3%	2.3%	0,0%	4.7%
From 21 (years)	7.0%	7.0%	2.3%	2.3%	18.6%
Total	27.9%	23.3%	41.9%	7.0%	100.0%

Source: *own elaboration.*

Regarding the application of Cloud Computing services in SMEs in the city of Latacunga, it were found that young companies of 5 years and those that range between 6 and 10 years choose to venture into the use of Cloud Computing with 32.1%, while by sectors, it was detected that commerce makes more use of Cloud Computing with a percentage of 42.9%. On the other hand, the remaining companies that do not contract the service say that it is because they have little or no knowledge about it, the cost of implementation, insecurity and dependence on a provider.

On the other hand, 65.1% of SMEs admit having heard the concept of Cloud Computing; however, 28.5% make use of Cloud Computing, 12.6% is assigned to IaaS as a more affordable model, 15.9% to PaaS and 0% to SaaS, the latter because although it seems to be more advantageous in use for companies, its limitation is the high economic implications of using the service.

In Figure 3, the frequency of use of cloud computing services is analyzed, where the repetition of the terms found is first associated with the size of the words and second with their location, the larger the term, and is located in the center, the greater its use. In this regard, the cloud services for SMEs in Latacunga stand out: office 365, abanq, sky drive, generated from an open question about CC.

Therefore, the relevant indexes were evaluated in terms of the advantages of the use of Cloud Computing, where: 86.1% thought they were saving infrastructure and personnel costs; 72.1% in portability when accessing information from anywhere in the world; 69.8% to the full availability of the service in relation to access without schedules and from any device and 67.4% to automatic storage of information.

Figure 3. Frequency of use of cloud services.

Source: own elaboration

On the other hand, in the disadvantages section, confidentiality of information and security is one of the most relevant concerns with 76.7%; the dependency of a provider with 72.1%; as well as bandwidth problems with 68.9% due to the fact that, sometimes, this is suspended for some reason that causes delays in business activities.

In addition, the average investment made by companies in hiring the Cloud service was identified, where 27.9% indicate maintaining an investment percentage of more than 9001 dollars per year, followed by a percentage no greater than 14.0% in values of between 6001 and 9000 dollars, although the data that stands out the most is 48.8% of the respondents who prefer not to answer due to confidentiality issues.

Finally, to determine the level of maturity, an item was developed in a measurement scale of 5 points (not at all, not very, usually, almost and very mature), in which 39.5% answered that Cloud's level of maturity Computing is not mature, 32.6% that is in a range of usually mature, 20.9% said that it was not very mature and only 7.1% said that it could be said that it is almost mature. This suggests that Cloud's average maturity is approximately 25%, which indicates that there has not yet been a Cloud acceptance level and therefore its adoption is very low.

Hierarchical clusters

The results of the exploratory analysis by classification of hierarchical clusters are shown in the following table of clusters of belonging:

Table 4. Clusters of belonging.

Variable	4 clusters	3 clusters	2 clusters
It has a main computer (exclusive server)	1	1	1
Does your company use free software?	2	2	1
User and password security	1	1	1
Backup copies	1	1	1
Security policies	3	3	2
On a regular basis, their workers receive ICT management training	2	2	1
The company has staff dedicated exclusively to the area of Information Systems, also known as the Department of Information Technology (IT)	1	1	1
Do you know the concept of Cloud Computing?	1	1	1
SaaS (Software as a service)	2	2	1
IaaS (Infrastructure as a service)	4	2	1
PaaS (Platform as a service)	1	1	1
The company hires a cloud service Cloud Computing	1	1	1

Source: *own elaboration.*

The calculation made to form 2 to 4 groups (shown in Table 4) exposes the variables that belong to each cluster or dimension, that is, the questions that most relate to each other have been grouped.

The groups allow to analyze the behavior of the different variables, which influence the decision of SMEs to use or not the Cloud Computing application are presented:

Cluster 1

- It has a main computer (exclusive server)
- User and password security
- Backups

- The company has personnel dedicated exclusively to the area of Information Systems, also known as the Department of Information Technology (IT)
- Do you know the concept of Cloud Computing?
- PaaS (Platform as a service)
- The company hires a cloud service Cloud Computing

Cluster 2

- Does your company use free or free software?
- On a regular basis, their workers receive ICT management training
- SaaS (Software as a service)

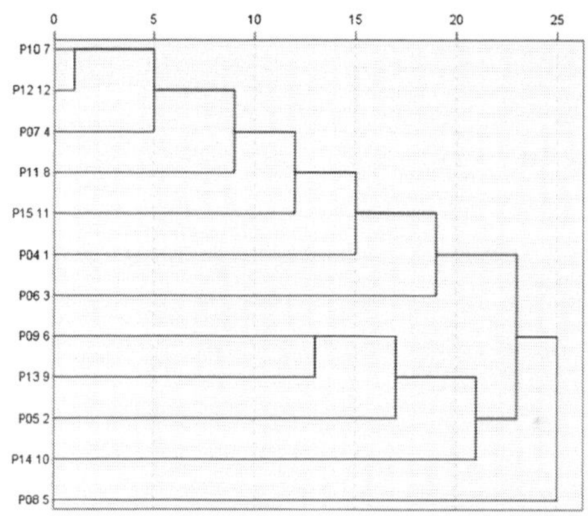

Figure 4. Combination of clusters of re-scaled distances.

Source: *own elaboration.*

The dendrogram, (Figure 4) is a graphic summary of the cluster solution, where the variables (items) are found along the left vertical axis. The horizontal axis shows the distance between the groups when they were joined (from 0 to 25). The analysis of the classification tree to determine the number of groups, from right to left, with a gap that goes from 20 to 25 suggests two clusters: (7, 12, 4, 8, 11, 1,3) (3, 6, 9, 2, 10, 5). Therefore, this figure shows how conglomerates are formed, which are groups of questions of greater similarity, for determining the use of CC in SMEs. In this way, two relevant groups are identified that analyze technological aspects, human talent in the area of ICT, security and their availability of resources, which influence the decision to adopt CC.

CONCLUSIONS

Once the main results have been presented relative to the analysis variables that define the usability of Cloud Computing in SMEs of the city of Latacunga, and by way of conclusion, it is determined that:According to the bibliography found, SMEs play an important social role, both as a generator of employment and as a significant sector in national and international economies. In this context, the development of emerging technologies means that companies choose to acquire new technological services as a competitive advantage over their peers, which allows SMEs to reach a market segment in digital environments.

In this framework, the investigation of the current state of use of Cloud Computing in the SMEs of the city under study allowed to identify the factors that would promote or affect the hiring of this type of service. Among the disadvantages that stand out is security of the information. On the other hand, its main advantages are: cost savings in servers and permanent advice. The result of the diagnosis made is that young companies in the market choose this resource being the PaaS model the most used because they develop their own computerized systems, 65.1% admit having heard about the subject, 28.5% adopt this service in office automation applications, document repositories and in minimum amount contract SaaS, especially in the billing area. Companies that exceed 10 years remain indifferent to adopting this service.

NOTES

[1]Nacional de Estadísticas y Censos.

[2]Servicio de Rentas Internas.

[3]Seguridad Social.

[4]Incipiente adopción de Cloud.

[5]Comunidad Andina de las Naciones Unidas.

[6]Clasificación Industrial Internacional Uniforme.

[7]Ministerio de Telecomunicaciones y de la Sociedad de Información.

[8]Red Nacional de Infocentros.

[9]Plan Nacional del Buen Vivir.

[10]Consejo Nacional de Planificación.

[11]Nacional de Estándares y Tecnología.

[12]Libro Blanco de Territorios Digitales en Ecuador.

REFERENCES

1. Solano-Gallegos, S. (2018) The Importance of Small and Medium Enterprises in the City of Cuenca-Ecuador and Their Contribution to the Creation of Employment. Academy of Accounting and Financial Studies Journal, 22, 1-17.
2. Coutinho, M.C. (2009) Ethics and Corporate Social Responsibility in Latin American Small and Medium Sized Enterprises: Challenging Development. African Journal of Business Ethics, 4, 37-47.
3. Wisuttisak, P. (2017) Law for SMEs Promotion and Protection in Vietnam and Thailand. Review of Integrative Business and Economics Research, 6, 60-67.
4. Odlin, D. (2019) Domestic Competitor Influence on Internationalizing SMEs as an Industry Evolves. Journal of World Business, 54, 119-136.
5. Assis, M.R.M. and Bittencourt, L.F. (2016) A Survey on Cloud Federation Architectures: Identifying Functional and Non-Functional Properties. Journal of Network and Computer Applications, 72, 51-71. https://doi.org/10.1016/j.jnca.2016.06.014
6. Ramachandra, G., Iftikhar, M. and Khan, F.A. (2017) A Comprehensive Survey on Security in Cloud Computing. Procedia Computer Science, 110, 465-472. https://doi.org/10.1016/j.procs.2017.06.124
7. Ravi, K., Khandelwal, Y., Krishna, B.S. and Ravi, V. (2018) Analytics in/for Cloud—An Interdependence: A Review. Journal of Network and Computer Applications, 102, 17-37. https://doi.org/10.1016/j.jnca.2017.11.006
8. Vafamehr, A. and Khodayar, M.E. (2018) Energy-Aware Cloud Computing. Electricity Journal, 31, 40-49. https://doi.org/10.1016/j.tej.2018.01.009
9. Ratten, V. (2015) Continuance Use Intention of Cloud Computing : Innovativeness and Creativity Perspectives. Journal of Business Research, 69, 1737-1740.
10. Bernal-Barcia, E.C. (2017) An Approach of the New Technology in the Different Sectors of Society. 3, 3-12.
11. Trun, P. (2019) Infrastructures for High-Performance Computing: Cloud Computing. Encyclopedia of Bioinformatics and Computational Biology, 1, 236-239.
12. Suárez, D. (2017) Flexibilidad Escalabilidad Almacenamiento. 26-43.

13. Slusarczyk Antosz, M. (2015) Diagnosis of the ICT Aplication in the SMEs of Riobamba-Ecuador. 4, 145-168.
14. Martínez-García, D., Medina-Chicaiza, P., Silva-Ordoñez, F., Mejía-Vayas, V. and Beltrán-Mesías, C. (2018) Diagnóstico del uso de la tecnología Cloud Computing en la administración de las empresas de servicios de la ciudad de Ambato. 1-21.
15. López-Sevilla, G., Medina-Chicaiza, P., Freire-Aillón, T. and Fiallos-López, W. (2018) Characterization of Technologies "SAAS" as a Tool in Optimizing It Resources. Pulse, 2, 146-153.
16. Hosseini, M. and Nord, T. (2018) A Combined Focused Industry and Company Size Investigation of the Internationalization-Performance Relationship: The Case of Small and Medium-Sized Enterprises (SMEs) within the Swedish Wood Manufacturing Industry. Forest Policy and Economics, 97, 110-121.
17. Bagheri, M., Mitchelmore, S. and Bamiatzi, V. (2019) Internationalization Orientation in SMEs: The Mediating Role of Technological Innovation. Journal of International Management, 25, 121-139. https://doi.org/10.1016/j.intman.2018.08.002
18. Chi, T. (2015) Business Contingency, Strategy Formation, and Firm Performance: An Empirical Study of Chinese Apparel SMEs. Administrative Sciences, 5, 27-45.
19. Muñoz, M., Gasca, G. and Valtierra, C. (2014) Caracterizando las Necesidades de las Pymes para Implementar Mejoras de Procesos Software: Una Comparativa entre la Teoría y la Realidad. RISTI, 1-15.
20. Tovar, C. (2017) Investigación sobre la aplicación de business research on business intelligence application in the argentine SMEs Management. Palermo Business Review, No. 15, 79-98.
21. Sánchez-Val, M.M. and Llorens, M.C.R. (2016) La incidencia de los entornos regionales sobre las restricciones financieras en pequeñas y medianas empresas. Trimestre Economico, 83, 37-60. https://doi.org/10.20430/ete.v83i329.191
22. J Garcia-Noboa, J.P., Castillo-Torres, L.B. and Torres-Miranda, J.E. (2017) Retos y Perspectivas del Desarrollo Económico en el Ecuador y América Latina. Centro de Investigación y Desarrollo Ecuador, 1, 51-66.
23. CAN. (2009) Año XXVI-Número 1743 Lima, 24 de agosto de 2009 Secretaría General de la Comunidad Andina Resolución 1259

Disposición Técnica para la Transmisión de Datos de Estadísticas Coyunturales de la Industria Manufacturera de los Países Miembros de la Comunidad. 1-116.

24. Campuzano Rodriguez, M.A., Ziadet Bermùdez, E.I. and Echeverria Vasque, H.G. (2016) Gestión del Talento Humano en las PYMES. Revista Publicando, 3, 438-448. https://revistapublicando.org/revista/index.php/crv/article/view/272/pdf-145
25. Daneshgar, F., Low, G.C. and Worasinchai, L. (2013) An Investigation of "Build vs. Buy" Decision for Software Acquisition by Small to Medium Enterprises. Information and Software Technology, 55, 1741-1750.
26. Guercio, M.B., Martinez, L.B. and Vigier, H. (2017) Las limitaciones al financiamiento bancario de las Pymes de alta tecnología. Estudios Gerenciales, 33, 3-12. https://doi.org/10.1016/j.estger.2017.02.001
27. Platero-Jaime, M., Benito-Hernández, S. and Rodríguez-Duarte, A. (2017) The Moderator Effect of Training in the Adoption of ICT in Microenterprises. Cuadernos de Gestion, 17, 87-108. https://doi.org/10.5295/cdg.150539mp
28. Ministerio de Telecomunicaciones y de la Sociedad de Información (2016) Plan Nacional de Telecomunicaciones y Tecnologías de Información del Ecuador. Journal of Experimental Psychology: General, 1-66.
29. Consejo Nacional de Planificacón (2013) Plan Nacional del Buen Vivir (Global Network). 1-133.
30. INEC (2015) Empresas y TIC (Tecnologías de la Información y la Comunicación). Inec, 54.
31. Herrera, A. and Janczewski, L. (2014) Issues in the Study of Organisational Resilience in Cloud Computing Environments. Procedia Technology, 16, 32-41. https://doi.org/10.1016/j.protcy.2014.10.065
32. Oliveira, T., Thomas, M. and Espadanal, M. (2014) Assessing the Determinants of Cloud Computing Adoption: An Analysis of the Manufacturing and Services Sectors. Information and Management, 51, 497-510. https://doi.org/10.1016/j.im.2014.03.006
33. Priyadarshinee, P., Raut, R.D., Kumar, M. and Kamble, S.S. (2017) A Cloud Computing Adoption in Indian SMEs: Scale Development and Validation Approach. The Journal of High Technology Management Research, 28, 221-245.

34. Al-samarraie, H. and Saeed, N. (2018) A Systematic Review of Cloud Computing Tools for Collaborative Learning : Opportunities and Challenges to the BlendedLearning Environment. Computers and Education, 124, 77-91. https://doi.org/10.1016/j.compedu.2018.05.016
35. Cayirci, E. and de Oliveira, A.S. (2018) Modelling Trust and Risk for Cloud Services. Journal of Cloud Computing, 7, Article No. 114. https://doi.org/10.1186/s13677-018-0114-7
36. Indu, I., Anand, P.M.R. and Bhaskar, V. (2018) Identity and Access Management in Cloud Environment: Mechanisms and Challenges. Engineering Science and Technology, 21, 574-588. https://doi.org/10.1016/j.jestch.2018.05.010
37. Ali, M., Khan, S.U. and Vasilakos, A.V. (2015) Security in Cloud Computing: Opportunities and Challenges. Information Sciences, 305, 357-383. https://doi.org/10.1016/j.ins.2015.01.025
38. Souri, A., Navimipour, N.J. and Rahmani, A.M. (2018) Formal Verification Approaches and Standards in the Cloud Computing: A Comprehensive and Systematic Review. Computer Standards and Interfaces, 58, 1-22.
39. Rocha, L., Gomez, A., Araújo, N., Otero, C. and Rodrigues, D. (2016) Cloud Management Tools for Sustainable SMEs. Procedia CIRP, 40, 220-224. https://doi.org/10.1016/j.procir.2016.01.106
40. Aslam, S., ul Islam, S., Khan, A., Ahmed, M., Akhundzada, A. and Khan, M.K. (2017) Information Collection Centric Techniques for Cloud Resource Management: Taxonomy, Analysis and Challenges. Journal of Network and Computer Applications, 100, 80-94. https://doi.org/10.1016/j.jnca.2017.10.021
41. Abdel-Basset, M., Mohamed, M. and Chang, V. (2018) NMCDA: A Framework for Evaluating Cloud Computing Services. Future Generation Computer Systems, 86, 12-29. https://doi.org/10.1016/j.future.2018.03.014
42. Aznoli,F.andNavimipour,N.J.(2017)CloudServicesRecommendation: Reviewing the Recent Advances and Suggesting the Future Research Directions. Journal of Network and Computer Applications, 77, 73-86. https://doi.org/10.1016/j.jnca.2016.10.009
43. Bogataj Habjan, K. and Pucihar, A. (2017) The Importance of Business Model Factors for Cloud Computing Adoption: Role of Previous Experiences. Organizacija, 50, 255-272. https://doi.org/10.1515/orga-

2017-0013

44. Noor, T.H., Zeadally, S., Alfazi, A. and Sheng, Q.Z. (2018) Mobile Cloud Computing: Challenges and Future Research Directions. Journal of Network and Computer Applications, 115, 70-85. https://doi.org/10.1016/j.jnca.2018.04.018
45. Tan, C.B., Hijazi, M.H.A., Lim, Y. and Gani, A. (2018) A Survey on Proof of Retrievability for Cloud Data Integrity and Availability: Cloud Storage State-of-the-Art, Issues, Solutions and Future Trends. Journal of Network and Computer Applications, 110, 75-86.
46. Jafarnejad Ghomi, E., Masoud Rahmani, A. and Nasih Qader, N. (2017) Load-Balancing Algorithms in Cloud Computing: A Survey. Journal of Network and Computer Applications, 88, 50-71. https://doi.org/10.1016/j.jnca.2017.04.007
47. Vasiljeva, T., Shaikhulina, S. and Kreslins, K. (2017) Cloud Computing: Business Perspectives, Benefits and Challenges for Small and Medium Enterprises (Case of Latvia). Procedia Engineering, 178, 443-451. https://doi.org/10.1016/j.proeng.2017.01.087
48. Galdino-Evangelista, W. and Souza-Neto, J. (2016) Modelo de avaliação da capacidade das organizações da administração pública federal para a adoção de software as a service (SaaS) público. Revista Do Serviço Público, 67, 173-202.
49. Iglesias, A. (2017) El "cloud" en españa se hace mayor de edad.
50. Lazo Villela, S. (2012) Factores relevantes que inciden en la adopción de la Computación en Nube en las Universidades de Puerto Rico, 129.
51. Henao-Diaz, L.F., Pacheco-Fernández, N.M., Argüello-Bernal, S., Moreno-Arocha, M.M. and Stevenson, P.R. (2012) Patrones De Diversidad De Epífitas En Bosques De Tierras Bajas Y Subandinos. Colombia Forestal, 15, 161-172. http://revistas.udistrital.edu.co/ojs/index.php/colfor/article/view/3758/5617 https://doi.org/10.14483/udistrital.jour.colomb.for.2012.2.a02
52. MINTEL (2018) Libro blanco de la Sociedad dc la Información y del Conocimiento. Telecomunicaciones. Gob. Ec, 1, 1-155.
53. Kestin, I. (2018) Statistics in Clinical Trials and Audit. Anaesthesia and Intensive Care Medicine, 19, 144-148. https://doi.org/10.1016/j.mpaic.2017.12.004
54. Leppink, J. (2017) Helping Medical Students in their Study of Statistics: A Flexible Approach. Journal of Taibah University Medical Sciences,

12, 1-7. https://doi.org/10.1016/j.jtumed.2016.08.007

55. Budgen, D., Brereton, P., Williams, N. and Drummond, S. (2018) The Contribution that Empirical Studies Performed in Industry Make to the Findings of Systematic Reviews: A Tertiary Study. Information and Software Technology, 94, 234-244. https://doi.org/10.1016/j.infsof.2017.10.012
56. Fernández-Sáez, A.M., Genero, M. and Chaudron, M.R.V. (2013) Empirical Studies Concerning the Maintenance of UML Diagrams and Their Use in the Maintenance of Code: A Systematic Mapping Study. Information and Software Technology, 55, 1119-1142. https://doi.org/10.1016/j.infsof.2012.12.006
57. Boongoen, T. and Iam-on, N. (2018) Cluster Ensembles : A Survey of Approaches with Recent Extensions and Applications. Computer Science Review, 28, 1-25. https://doi.org/10.1016/j.cosrev.2018.01.003
58. Peña, M. (2018) Robust Clustering Methodology for Multi-Frequency Acoustic Data: A Review of Standardization, Initialization and Cluster Geometry. Fisheries Research, 200, 49-60.
59. Sardar, T.H. and Ansari, Z. (2018) Partition Based Clustering of Large Datasets Using MapReduce Framework: An Analysis of Recent Themes and Directions. Future Computing and Informatics Journal, 3, 247-261. https://doi.org/10.1016/j.fcij.2018.06.002.

INDEX

C

D

G

H

I

L

W